A HISTORY
OF PROPHECY
IN ISRAEL

A HISTORY
OF PROPHECY
IN ISRAEL

Joseph Blenkinsopp

THE WESTMINSTER PRESS
Philadelphia

Book Design by Alice Derr

First edition

Published by The Westminster Press®
Philadelphia, Pennsylvania

PRINTED IN THE UNITED STATES OF AMERICA
9 8 7 6 5 4 3 2 1

Library of Congress Cataloging in Publication Data

Blenkinsopp, Joseph, 1927–
  A history of prophecy in Israel.

  Includes bibliographical references and index.
  1. Prophets. 2. Bible. O.T.—Prophecies—History.
I. Title.
BS1198.B53   1983   224'.06   83-10178
ISBN 0-664-24479-3 (pbk.)

In memory of my father
Joseph William Blenkinsopp
1897—1931

CONTENTS

ABBREVIATIONS

AcOr	*Acta Orientalia*
AfO	*Archiv für Orientforschung*
AJSL	*American Journal of Semitic Languages and Literatures*, Chicago
ALUOS	*Annual of the Leeds University Oriental Society*
ANET	*Ancient Near Eastern Texts Relating to the Old Testament*, J. B. Pritchard, ed. (Princeton: Princeton University Press, 1950, 1955², 1969³)
ASTI	*Annual of the Swedish Theological Institute*, Jerusalem/Leiden
BA	*The Biblical Archaeologist*, Cambridge, Mass.
BDB	F. Brown, S. R. Driver, and C. A. Briggs, eds., *A Hebrew and English Lexicon of the Old Testament* (Oxford University Press, 1906; rev. ed. 1957)
Bib	*Biblica*, Rome
BibOr	*Bibliotheca Orientalis*, Leiden
BJRL	*Bulletin of the John Rylands Library*, Manchester
BWANT	Beiträge zur Wissenschaft vom Alten und Neuen Testament (Stuttgart: W. Kohlhammer)
BZ	*Biblische Zeitschrift*, Paderborn
BZAW	Beiheft zur *Zeitschrift für die alttestamentliche Wissenschaft*, Berlin
CAH	*The Cambridge Ancient History*
CBQ	*The Catholic Biblical Quarterly*, Washington
ETL	*Ephemerides Theologicae Lovanienses*, Louvain
EvQ	*Evangelical Quarterly*
EvTh	*Evangelische Theologie*, Munich
ExpT	*The Expository Times*, Edinburgh
HeyJ	*Heythrop Journal*

HTR	*Harvard Theological Review*, Cambridge, Mass.
HUCA	*The Hebrew Union College Annual*, Cincinnati
IB	*The Interpreter's Bible*, G. A. Buttrick, ed. (Nashville: Abingdon Press, 1951-57)
IDB	*The Interpreter's Dictionary of the Bible*, G. A. Buttrick, ed. (Nashville: Abingdon Press, 1962)
IDBS	*The Interpreter's Dictionary of the Bible, Supplementary Volume*, K. Crim, ed. (Nashville: Abingdon Press, 1976)
IEJ	*Israel Exploration Journal*, Jerusalem
Int	*Interpretation*, Richmond, Va.
JAAR	*Journal of the American Academy of Religion*
JBL	*Journal of Biblical Literature*
JJS	*Journal of Jewish Studies*, London
JNES	*Journal of Near Eastern Studies*, Chicago
JNSL	*Journal of Northwest Semitic Languages*
JQR	*Jewish Quarterly Review*, Philadelphia
JRE	*Journal of Religious Ethics*
JSOT	*Journal for the Study of the Old Testament*
JSS	*Journal of Semitic Studies*, Manchester
JTS	*Journal of Theological Studies*, Oxford
LXX	Septuagint
MT	Masoretic text
NEB	New English Bible (1970)
NTT	*Nieuw theologisch Tijdschrift*, Haarlem
OA	*Oriens Antiquus*, Rome
OTS	*Oudtestamentische Studiën*, Leiden
PJB	*Palästina Jahrbuch*, Berlin
RA	*Revue d'assyriologie et d'archéologie orientale*, Paris
RB	*Revue Biblique*, Paris
RHPR	*Revue d'histoire et de philosophie religieuses*, Strasbourg
RSR	*Recherches de science religieuse*, Paris
RTP	*Revue de théologie et de philosophie*, Lausanne
SBL	Society of Biblical Literature
SDB	*Supplément au Dictionnaire de la Bible*, L. Pirot, A. Robert, H. Cazelles, eds. (Paris, 1928-)
SEÅ	*Svensk Exegetisk Årsbok*, Lund
SJT	*Scottish Journal of Theology*
StTh	*Studia Theologica*, Lund
SVT	Supplements to *Vetus Testamentum*, Leiden
TDNT	*Theological Dictionary of the New Testament*, G. Kittel and G. Friedrich, eds. (Grand Rapids: Wm. B. Eerdmans Publishing Co., 1964-76)

TDOT	*Theological Dictionary of the Old Testament*, G. J. Botterweck and H. Ringgren, eds. (Grand Rapids: 1977-)
TGUOS	*Transactions of the Glasgow University Oriental Society*, Glasgow
TLZ	*Theologische Literaturzeitung*, Leipzig
TR	*Theologische Rundschau*, Tübingen
TZ	*Theologische Zeitschrift*, Basel
UF	*Ugaritforschungen*, Münster
VT	*Vetus Testamentum*, Leiden
VTS	Supplement to *Vetus Testamentum*
WO	*Die Welt des Orients*, Göttingen
ZAW	*Zeitschrift für die alttestamentliche Wissenschaft*, Berlin
ZDMG	*Zeitschrift der Deutschen Morgenländischen Gesellschaft*, Leipzig
ZDPV	*Zeitschrift des Deutschen Palästinavereins*, Wiesbaden
ZTK	*Zeitschrift für Theologie und Kirche*, Tübingen

INTRODUCTION

Over the past two thousand years the interpretation of prophetic texts has described an extremely broad arc. One has only to compare millenarian and apocalyptic interpretations with the rabbinic view—which aimed at blunting the disruptive and destabilizing effect of prophecy—to see how different situations, with their own demands and constraints, can produce fundamentally different readings. Modern critical scholarship, the course of which over the last century and a half is outlined briefly in Chapter I, broke decisively with traditional positions in Christianity and Judaism. In spite of significant advances, however, it is still some way from attaining a consensus on such crucial issues as the institutional and social connections and locations of the different kinds of prophecy, the relation between prophetic experience and tradition, and the editorial history of prophetic books. Let us add that it is only recently that the study of prophecy has begun to free itself from theories of development inspired by rigid philosophical and denominational presuppositions, the kind that dominated much of the writing on prophecy in the nineteenth and early twentieth centuries.

The only way to avoid the worst excesses arising from presuppositions of a theological or philosophical character is to keep on returning to the historical phenomenon of prophecy in Israel, which implies the attempt to make sense of its development throughout a long history, parts of which are very poorly documented. It would be much easier, and certainly much safer for one's reputation, to eschew the attempt and continue with the close-up work on specific texts and problems whose results are much easier to assess. From time to time, however, anyone engaged in this work must feel the need to stand back and take stock or, to use a perhaps more appropriate metaphor, to regain perspective on the phenomenon of prophecy as a whole. The simplest justification for adding to the bibliographical mountain on prophecy would be to say that the present work is intended as a provisional stock-taking. Moreover, while one can find many thematic and theological studies of prophecy, there are few critical histories, and those that are available rarely attempt to cover the entire span of the biblical period. In most cases attention is concentrated almost exclusively on the period of "classical" prophecy, the two centuries from Amos to the Second Isaiah of the Babylonian exile. Yet the earliest of these "classical" prophets, Amos and Hosea, could refer back to a prophetic tradition extending over three centuries that had already reached a mature stage of consolidation. To ignore or pass rapidly over these developments puts us at risk of misunderstanding some crucial aspects of prophetic activity during the much better known period of Assyrian and Babylonian hegemony.

Even more harmful, however, is the tendency for historical surveys of prophecy to either peter out or reach a grand finale with the Babylonian exile in the sixth century B.C.E. The effect, if not the intent, is to perpetuate the idea, widespread in the last century, that later developments, with their quite different forms of religious expression, represent a falling away from the high plateau of prophetic religion, a surrender to institutional paralysis. It also absolves us of the task of examining the highly interesting transformations that prophecy underwent during the time of the Second Temple, an epoch that witnessed not only the rise and consolidation of Judaism in the homeland and the Diaspora but the emergence of Christianity with its own forms of prophetic activity.

I have therefore aimed at a historical overview that treats with skepticism distinctions between "primitive" and "classical" prophecy and assertions about the "drying up" of prophetic inspiration after the collapse of the Judean state. It would have been appropriate, and was in fact originally intended, to take the survey down to the end of the Second Temple. Considerations of space, as well as common sense (given the formidable problems involved), dictated otherwise, and that part of the task is left to others.

If a history of prophecy is not to be merely a series of sketches of individual prophetic figures, the lines of continuity throughout the history must be identified and followed up. No one supposes that all the verbal and thematic parallels between different prophetic collections can be explained with reference to the process by which the sayings were transmitted. While our task would have been made easier if prophets had explicitly acknowledged those predecessors on whose sayings they drew, there can be no doubt that it is quite legitimate to speak of a prophetic tradition. Jeremiah's complaint that his prophetic contemporaries were stealing sayings from one another (Jer. 23:30) may be taken to point in that direction, and we have just seen that Amos and Hosea align themselves with an established tradition of prophetic protest. A careful reading of Hosea suggests that he was familiar with the public activity of Amos; Isaiah appears at one stage of his career to be applying the message of Amos to Judah; Jeremiah's debt to Hosea, especially in the early stage of his career, is easily verifiable; Ezekiel borrows from his older contemporary Jeremiah, and so on. A further question arises as this cumulative process of appropriation, assimilation, and adaptation undergoes transformation into a rather different kind of activity, namely, an increasingly formalized exegesis of earlier prophetic sayings in collections dating from the Second Temple. This inner-biblical exegesis provides a valuable indication of changes in the understanding of prophecy itself and leads us to the point where prophetic books, having achieved canonical status, generate their own distinct commentaries.

While affirming the existence of a prophetic tradition, we would have to be prepared to discover that this tradition follows different lines in keeping with different types of prophetic individual and function. In this matter we have to bear in mind that we have at our disposal only a few sources selected according to very specific criteria. One consequence is that those whom we refer to as *the* prophets formed only a small and in several respects anomalous minority of prophets in Israel at any given time. If by "the religion of Israel" we mean to refer to the convictions and activities of the mass of the population, we would have to conclude that the prophets whose sayings have survived were more often than not at odds with it; or, in other words, that more often than not they played a destabilizing rather than a validating role in the religious life of their contemporaries. There were also, however, prophets who remained more closely tied to the established institutions, especially the cult, and it is possible that their sayings, like those of similar figures elsewhere in the Near East, were preserved and transmitted by these institutions. These would then form a distinct class, though we shall see that the task of deciding who belongs to it is by no means simple.

Another approach to multiple prophetic traditions is along geographical lines of demarcation. Considerable attention has been given in recent English-language scholarship (especially by A. W. Jenks and R. R. Wilson) to Ephraimite prophecy as a special type preserving highly distinctive characteristics over several centuries. According to this view the line runs from the Elohist strand in the Pentateuch, through prophetic and Levitical groups which opposed the monarchy in the Northern Kingdom, then to Hosea, Jeremiah, and the Deuteronomic program as embodying elements of what might be called an Ephraimite prophetic theology. Over against this tradition is that of Judean prophecy, first attested during the reign of David in the persons of Gad and Nathan, then taken up by Amos, Isaiah, and the other preexilic, exilic, and postexilic figures in Latter Prophets with the exception of Hosea and Jeremiah. The Ephraimite tradition, it is claimed, has its own characteristic speech forms, its own way of describing the process of prophetic mediation, and gives pride of place to Moses as prototypical prophetic mediator.

While it is entirely plausible that prophecy among the clans of the central highlands of the country would reflect cultural and religious conditions obtaining there, and would therefore differ in significant respects from prophecy in Jerusalem, the distinctiveness has, I believe, been greatly overstated. Even if we grant that the elusive Elohist (E) constitutes a genuinely independent source, its "northern" provenance is simply assumed rather than demonstrated. It is worthy of note, for example, that the three narratives which Jenks presents as major evidence for an independent E strand (Gen. 20:1-17; 21:8-21, 22-34) are all set in the Negeb, and the Reuben-Midianite strand in the Joseph story, also deemed to be from the Elohist, points in the same general direction. The hypothesis of a prophetic-Levitical axis among the Joseph tribes is also unsupported by evidence and clouded by anachronistic assumptions deriving from Chronicles. There are certainly links between Hosea and Deuteronomy, but again it is often overlooked that the social and humanitarian program of Deuteronomy owes nothing to Hosea and, as will be argued in due course, a great deal to Judean prophecy. This is not to deny the existence of an Ephraimite prophetic tradition, but its distinctiveness and influence should not be overstated.

At appropriate points in the historical overview it will be suggested that the distinction between Jerusalemite and Judean or, if you will, metropolitan and provincial, may indicate significantly different prophetic traditions. The most angry, radical, and detailed criticism of contemporary society, and especially the state bureaucracy, is to be found in Amos and Micah, both from the Judean countryside. It will also be argued that Micah and his "school" represent the ethos and interests of the class known as "the people of the land," and that their teaching notably influenced the social program set out in the Deuteronomic lawbook. Enough has been said for the time being, at any rate, to make the point that prophecy developed in different directions and with different emphases, drawing on religious traditions that were often radically reinterpreted in the process.

Protest on behalf of the poor and disadvantaged, the victims of an exploitative social and political order, is one of the most powerful strands in the tradition of prophetic preaching. Beginning with Amos, it is taken up in different ways by Isaiah and Micah, developed further by the disciples or editors of the latter and also, to a lesser extent, by Zephaniah during the last century of Judean independence. It is not nearly so prominent in Hosea and Jeremiah, whose concerns focus more on syncretic cults and the political machinations of king and court. Linked with this is the fundamental prophetic concern for community. In this respect the difference between optimistic and critical prophecy is that the latter, unlike the former, refuses to confer absolute validity on the contemporary institutional form assumed by the community that calls itself Israel. When the critical prophet speaks of "the remnant," he implies that there will indeed be a future for that community even though its present institutional embodiment, i.e., the state, will be swept away in the destructive flow of historical events. According to this predominantly Judean prophetic tradition the fundamental reason is the disregard for justice and righteousness (Amos 5:7, 24; 6:12; Isa. 5:7; etc.). These twinned concepts *(mišpāṭ, ṣᵉdāqāh)* connote the maintenance of right order, of societal structures and judicial procedures that respect the rights of all classes. A society that does not respect that order, even one in which the practice of religion flourishes (cf. Amos 5:21-24; Isa. 1:12-17), does not deserve to survive.

While we know nothing about a group of disciples that gathered around Amos, the victims of injustice on whose behalf he spoke out would presumably have been the most receptive to his message. That they are also described as "righteous" (Amos 2:6; 5:12; cf. Isa. 5:23) may perhaps be taken as a move toward the idea that the nucleus of the new or renewed community is to be found among those who adhere to the prophet's teaching and strive to embody the alternative vision in their lives. The question then arises, and is still of crucial importance, whether that vision can find embodiment at the center of society, even of the ecclesiastical community, or only at the periphery. Our study suggests that there is no clear-cut answer to this question. On the one hand, prophetic protest against injustice and exploitation was given "official" sanction and expression in Deuteronomy and continued thereafter as a powerful force for social renewal in mainline Judaism and Christianity. On the other hand, however, we have to reckon as early as the exilic period with the formation of prophetic groups around a charismatic figure or his teaching that betray some of the characteristics of the sects of a later day. For this reason I have taken the passages referring to the Servant of Yahweh in Second Isaiah and to the servants of Yahweh in Third Isaiah as marking a crucial point in the history of the prophetic movement.

A theological assessment of prophecy does not require us to follow the lead of those nineteenth-century pioneers who contrasted other forms of religious life unfavorably with it. Prophecy is only one of several such forms, and it seems that its fate is to be always necessary but never by itself sufficient. Concluding the survey with Jonah, which contains a profound theological critique of prophecy, is meant to suggest precisely this, and to recall the unsolved and perhaps insoluble problems endemic to prophecy noted at different points throughout the history. On the other hand, no writings in the Scriptures more than these confront us so directly with the reality of God or force us so inescapably to question the mundane and even the religious perceptions that tend to control our lives.

To end on a practical note, it may be necessary to warn some readers that in the critical study of prophecy there are very few "assured results of modern scholarship." It follows, therefore, that few of the solutions to outstanding problems or interpretations of texts offered in this book will pass unchallenged. While obvious limitations of space have not permitted me to present all alternatives worthy of serious attention, I have at least acknowledged their existence while presenting my own views as clearly as possible. The bibliographies are intended to help the reader put these conclusions into the context of contemporary scholarly discussion where they belong. Here, too, choices have had to be made, and it seemed to make sense to give preference, where possible, to recent studies available in English. If, with their help, the reader will be in a position to draw his or her own conclusions, even if they differ from the ones proposed in the book, my purpose in writing it will have been achieved.

I
PROLEGOMENA: DEFINING THE OBJECT OF STUDY

1. THE PROPHETS IN THE CANON

J. **Blenkinsopp,** *Prophecy and Canon,* Notre Dame: University of Notre Dame Press, 1977; H. **von Campenhausen,** *The Formation of the Christian Bible,* Philadelphia: Fortress Press, 1972; B. S. **Childs,** *Introduction to the Old Testament as Scripture,* Philadelphia: Fortress Press, 1979; R. E. **Clements,** *Prophecy and Covenant,* Naperville, Ill.: Alec R. Allenson, 1965; G. W. **Coats** and B. O. **Long** (eds.), *Canon and Authority,* Philadelphia: Fortress Press, 1977; O. **Eissfeldt,** *The Old Testament: An Introduction,* New York: Harper & Row, 1965, 562-571; G. **Fohrer,** *Introduction to the Old Testament,* Nashville: Abingdon Press, 1968, 480-488; D. N. **Freedman,** "The Law and the Prophets," *SVT* 9, 1963, 250-265; "Son of Man, Can These Bones Live?" *Int.* 29, 1975, 171-186; A. H. J. **Gunneweg,** *Understanding the Old Testament,* Philadelphia: Westminster Press, 1978; S. Z. **Leiman** (ed.), *The Canon and Masorah of the Hebrew Bible,* New York: KTAV Publishing House, 1974; *The Canonization of Hebrew Scripture,* Hamden, Conn.: Archon Books, 1976; R. H. **Pfeiffer,** *Introduction to the Old Testament,* New York: Harper & Brothers, 1948[2], 50-70; "Canon of the Old Testament," *IDB* I, 1962, 498-520; G. **von Rad,** *Old Testament Theology* II, New York: Harper & Row, 1965, 3-5, 388-409; J. A. **Sanders,** *Torah and Canon,* Philadelphia: Fortress Press, 1972; A. C. **Sundberg, Jr.,** *The Old Testament of the Christian Church,* Cambridge, Mass.: Harvard University Press, 1964; J. **Wellhausen,** *Prolegomena to the History of Ancient Israel,* New York: Meridian Books, 1957; W. **Zimmerli,** *The Law and the Prophets,* Oxford: Basil Blackwell, 1965.

When we speak of prophecy we are generally thinking of the fifteen books attributed to prophetic authors in the midsection of the Hebrew Bible. Yet these books by no means exhaust the phenomenon of prophecy in Israel. According to a rabbinic dictum (*b. Meg.* 14a) there were forty-eight prophets and seven prophetesses in Israel, a conclusion no doubt based on a head count over the entire Hebrew

Bible. None of the books accepted as canonical is ascribed to a prophet who lived before the eighth century B.C.E., yet the earliest of these canonical prophets, Amos and Hosea, not only knew of prophetic predecessors but stood quite consciously within a prophetic tradition (Amos 2:11-12; Hos. 6:5; 9:7-8; 12:10, 13). By the eighth century, in fact, Israelite prophecy had a history of some three centuries behind it.

It is also noteworthy that the canonical prophets refer often, and almost always disparagingly, to a class of people they themselves called "prophets" *(n*b*î*îm)*, leaving us wondering whether they would have wished to be known by that title. One of them, Amos, appears to disavow it, though the passage in question has been interpreted otherwise (Amos 7:14). The explanation is, of course, that prophecy corresponded to an acknowledged institution and one which, as we shall see, functioned primarily within cultic religion. Hence the problem, which still awaits a satisfactory solution, of the relation of the canonical prophets to the institutional complex of Israel and early Judaism. We are reminded, at any rate, that the people we call *the* prophets formed only a small minority of the category at any given time. It is perhaps still necessary to add that the material contained in the Hebrew Bible has been selected and edited according to specific and ideological criteria, and that this fact must be borne in mind by anyone who wishes to use it for the purpose of historical reconstruction.

The first section of the tripartite Hebrew canon, the "five fifths of the law," or *Tôrāh*, contains a narrative of founding events from creation to the death of Moses together with a great deal of legal material, about one third of the whole. According to the traditional view, it was written by Moses and promulgated by Ezra and his Great Assembly. This body was thought to be composed of Ezra himself, Nehemiah, the last three prophets, and other worthies, one hundred and twenty in all. The second section, *Prophets, (N*bî*îm)*, takes in the historical books Joshua through Kings and the fifteen books ascribed to prophetic authors. These are known respectively as Former Prophets and Latter Prophets, a distinction that was unknown to Judaism of the biblical and classical periods. Latter Prophets includes the three lengthy scrolls of Isaiah, Jeremiah, and Ezekiel and a collection of twelve shorter books on a separate scroll of comparable length. The further distinction into Major and Minor is even later, indicates length rather than relative importance, and can be safely ignored. The third section, the *Writings (K*tûbîm)*, comprises all the remaining books in the Hebrew Bible, and an even greater number in the Old Greek translation known as the Septuagint (LXX).

Recent years have witnessed a revival of interest in the canon itself, especially the process leading to its final definition, the implications of its peculiar structure, and the nature of the claims implied in the shaping of the tradition that went into it (Blenkinsopp, Childs, Sanders). This renewed interest is due, in part, to the decline of confidence in a Bible-centered theology that failed to give an adequate account of the basic issue of authority, and at the same time insisted on the unity of the Bible in ways that are now seen to be indefensible. Study of the formative process that eventuated in a canon reveals a cumulative effort to give shape and significant form to a common tradition and, by implication, to mold the structure and self-understanding of the community within which the tradition functioned. But it also reveals that this process involved reconciling, or simply juxtaposing, interpretations and points of view that are often divergent and sometimes mutually exclusive. Critical attention to the formation of the tradition, therefore, has raised the issue of a plurality of interpretations and the mediating of conflicting authority claims in the religious sphere. Given the peremptory and sharply divisive claims advanced by prophets, or by others on their behalf, prophecy was bound to play a decisive role in this ongoing process.

It is generally agreed that Torah was the first part of the collection to achieve what we would now call canonical status. The promulgation of the lawbook, allegedly found in the Temple during the reign of Josiah (640-609), was certainly an important landmark, and modern scholarship has concurred in identifying this book with Deuteronomy, though not exactly as we have it today. For the first time Deuteronomy speaks not of laws *(tôrôt)* but of the law *(tôrāh)* presented as an official public document not to be tampered with (Deut. 4:2; 12:32). About two centuries later the priest-scribe Ezra was sent on an official mission to Jerusalem by either Artaxerxes I Longimanus or Artaxerxes II Mnemon[1] with the task of seeing that "the law of the God of heaven" was enforced among Jews in the Trans-Euphrates satrapy of the Persian empire (Ezra 7). While this law cannot simply be identified with our Pentateuch, it provides one of several indications that the Persian period was decisive for the formation of the legal tradition in its final written form. But even much later, in the Greco-Roman period, we find a surprising variety of approaches to that tradition—e.g., in Jubilees and the Temple Scroll. The division into five books, which is not attested in the legend of Aristeas (probably late second or early first century B.C.E.), is first stated in Josephus' treatise *Against Apion* at the end of the first century C.E.[2]

Allusion to "the Law and the Prophets," familiar to readers of the

New Testament, first occurs in writings of the second century B.C.E. (Prologue to Sir., II Macc. 15:9), but without the distinction between Former and Latter Prophets. Writing toward the beginning of that century, Jesus ben Sira traced the course of prophecy from Joshua, "the successor of Moses in prophesying" (Sir. 46:1), to Isaiah, Jeremiah, Ezekiel, and the Twelve Prophets, again covering both historical and prophetic books without distinction. It is widely agreed that the Deuteronomic history was written toward the end of the monarchy and was revised and expanded around the middle of the sixth century B.C.E. While it must have enjoyed great authority from the moment of its appearance, because of its connections with the Deuteronomic lawbook, it had to survive the challenge of later essays in historiography, including the Chronicler's work. Writing during the first century B.C.E., a historian informs us that both Nehemiah and Judah Maccabee assembled a library of books including some dealing with kings and prophets (I Macc. 2:13-15). This kind of activity, understandable at times of militant nationalism, should also be taken into account in tracing the process leading to the final form of the prophetic canon.

The rabbinic text dealing with the order and authorship of biblical books (*b. Baba Batra* 14b-15a) attributes Joshua to Joshua; Judges, Ruth, and Samuel to Samuel; and Kings to Jeremiah. Thus the designation "Former Prophets" was due not to content but to the tradition of prophetic authorship. Josephus (*Against Apion* I.37) also viewed the writing of sacred history as a prophetic prerogative, consonant with his own claim to prophetic gifts, transparently aimed at promoting his own publications.[3] Over four centuries earlier, the author of Chronicles names so many seers and prophets among his sources as to leave little doubt that even then the idea was well established.[4] Further implications of this interesting transformation of the prophet into the historian will be discussed in a later chapter.[5]

In relation to Torah, Former Prophets can be seen as the history of the prophetic succession to Moses, prophet *kat' exochēn*, beginning with Joshua who received a share in his charisma (Num. 27:18-23; Deut. 34:9; both P). Later Jewish tradition traced this prophetic succession to the death of Malachi, last of the prophets, who was also a member of the Great Assembly mentioned earlier. If, as is often alleged, Deuteronomy served at one time as a theological preface to the history, it must have been detached from it at the time of its incorporation into the P-edited history of founding events.[6] The relation of the Deuteronomic history to the collection of prophetic books is no less problematic. Two of the latter have been expanded with material drawn from the history.[7] Jonah, one of the Twelve Prophets, is a prophetic legend of a kind we would expect to find in the history, where, however, there is only a passing reference to a prophet of that name (II Kings 14:25). Curious, too, is the absence of any mention of the canonical prophets by the historian, with the sole exceptions of Isaiah and Jonah. Some have taken this to indicate that Latter Prophets was compiled as a supplement to the history, and confirmation has been sought in evidence of Deuteronomic redaction of several of the prophetic books, especially Jeremiah.[8] But it is also possible that the historian deliberately passed over some of them on the grounds that their message was inappropriate to the needs of his contemporaries.[9] In addition, the possibility cannot be excluded that some were simply unknown to him.

It is reasonable to suppose, and in fact explicitly attested,[10] that collections of sayings were made during the prophet's lifetime or shortly after his death. Where the prophet had come to the attention of the civil and religious authorities, such sayings would have been widely reported. Amaziah, priest-in-charge at Bethel, was able to quote an oracle of Amos—one which apparently was not fulfilled—as grounds for extraditing him (Amos 7:11). At his trial for sedition in 609 B.C.E., Jeremiah was saved from death when someone quoted an oracle of Micah delivered about a century earlier (Jer. 26:17-19; Micah 3:12). A scribe wrote down Jeremiah's sayings in mid-career, read them in public, and rewrote them from dictation when the first copy was destroyed (Jer. 36). In other cases, sayings would have circulated orally in the prophet's support group. Some others may have been preserved among the Temple records, as was the case elsewhere in the Near East. All in all, it is highly unlikely that prophetic words were transmitted orally over a long period of time without at any point being committed to writing.

The political disasters of the early sixth century B.C.E. would have provided a further stimulus to the preservation of prophetic sayings, and it would be surprising if efforts had not been made during the exile to put together a selective corpus of such sayings. The editorial history of the prophetic books, especially Jeremiah, suggests that Deuteronomic scribes played a significant role at that time.[11] The process of editing and expanding this material continued into the Second Temple period. By the early second century B.C.E. the division into three and twelve was already familiar (Sir. 48:20 to 49:10), and not much later we begin to hear references to "the Law and the Prophets" (Prologue to Sir.; II Macc. 15:9; cf. Dan. 9:2). The Isaiah scroll from Qumran (1QIsa^a), dated on epigraphic grounds to the second century B.C.E., shows that the fixing of the text was also well advanced by that time.

In addition to Torah and Prophets a wide variety of writings was in circulation in Palestinian Judaism and in the Diaspora from the second century B.C.E. down into the Roman period. Some of these were included in the Pharisaic-rabbinic collection and others disallowed, in some cases only after considerable debate. Several others found their way into the Old Greek translation, though it is inexact to speak of this as an alternative, diasporic canon. Different groups cherished their own collections. The Qumran community, for example, had all the books in the Hebrew canon with the probable exception of Esther,[12] as well as devotional, liturgical, and mystical works several of which originated in the group. Early Christians also, on occasion, cited books which did not gain admission into any authoritative collection (I Cor. 2:9; Heb. 11:37; Jude 9, 14-16). Disputes about the status of some books—Qoheleth, Song of Songs, Sirach—continued into the Yavnean period. There is, however, no evidence that the canon was "fixed" at Yavneh (Jamnia), and, in fact, we have no list of authoritative writings before the second century C.E., and none from Jewish sources prior to the Babylonian Talmud.[13] This situation, incidentally, has raised the question whether there is still justification for the exclusion from the Protestant canon of the apocryphal or deuterocanonical books (Sundberg).

The juxtaposition in the Hebrew Bible of law and prophecy inevitably raises the broad issue, which has been crucial in Old Testament studies since at least the nineteenth century, of the relation between these two entities. The traditional Jewish view is stated with admirable clarity and brevity in the opening paragraph of the Mishnaic treatise *Pirke Abot:*

> Moses received Torah from Sinai and delivered it to Joshua; then Joshua delivered it to the elders, the elders to the prophets, and the prophets delivered it to the men of the Great Assembly.

On this showing, the primary function of the prophet was to bridge the gap between the primordial revelation at Sinai and the rabbinic leadership. Like the sages who succeeded them (cf. *b. Baba Batra* 12a), the prophets were therefore in the first place custodians and traditioners of Torah, which implied that prophecy was clearly subordinate to law. Critical scholarship in the nineteenth century, however, arrived at the conclusion that the bulk of the legal material in the Old Testament dates from the end rather than the beginning of the history of Israel. In his influential *Prolegomena to the History of Ancient*

Israel (1883²) Julius Wellhausen summed up the work of many predecessors in arguing that the prophets antedated the law codes and that therefore they could not have discharged the function assigned to them by the tradition. On the contrary, it was the ethical and spiritual religion of the prophets which made the law codes possible. Moreover, it was precisely the codification of the laws, marking the transition from Israel to Judaism, which created a situation fatal to the exercise of prophecy.

While much of the exegetical work of Wellhausen has held up remarkably well, the overall understanding of the religious history of Israel and early Judaism looks very different after the passage of a century. The discovery of several collections of laws from the ancient Near East, beginning with the Code of Hammurapi in 1901, has opened up form-critical study of legal material in the Hebrew Bible and obliged us, among other things, to distinguish more carefully between the age of individual laws and that of the collections. Form criticism has also made possible a more precise understanding of prophetic sayings. It has shown, for example, how many literary types used by the prophets are rooted in ancient institutions, especially warfare, law, and worship. Quite apart from the issue, still under discussion,[14] of the antiquity of covenant formulations, prophetic indictments often follow quite closely stipulations of law in the Pentateuch, and verdicts of divine judgment pronounced by prophets often correspond to curses attached to laws. In this respect at least, the idea of the prophet as a radical, a religious individualist pitted against the "establishment," a proponent of a new morality, is in need of revision.

The relation between law and prophecy is clearly too complex to be explained solely in terms of which came first. The earliest collection of laws, contained in the so-called Covenant Code (Ex. 20:23 to 23:19), certainly antedates the canonical prophets. The Deuteronomic program, promulgated toward the end of the Judean monarchy, was certainly influenced by prophetic preaching. Much of the ritual law in Leviticus and Numbers is much older than the collections in which it is now found. Moreover, the canonical prophets must be distinguished in principle from the institution of prophecy, *a fortiori* from other institutions such as the priesthood. Their claim to an authority deriving in a direct way from their experience of God put them outside of acknowledged jurisdictions and introduced an element of deep conflict into the life of the community. The accusation of Jeremiah, directed against those who claimed to be wise on account of their possession of the law and who, at the same time, neglected the prophetic word (Jer.

8:8), is only one indication of conflict between different claims to authority in the religious sphere. It may also suggest that one reason for the redaction of the laws and their narrative context was precisely to counter the destabilizing influence of prophecy. The definition of a certain epoch in the past as normative could also be seen in the same light. The postscript to the Pentateuch (Deut. 34:10-12) establishes a clear demarcation at the death of Moses and denies parity between the revelation accorded to him and prophetic revelation. Unlike the Samaritans, and perhaps also the Sadducees, however, Pharisaic-rabbinic Judaism came to affirm both the Law and the Prophets. Christianity did too, with the difference that it shifted the center of gravity from the Law to the Prophets. Thereby both faiths found themselves caught up inescapably in the need to mediate continually between tradition and situation, the claims of the past and those of the present and the future.

2. MODERN CRITICAL STUDY OF PROPHECY

M. J. **Buss**, "Prophecy in Ancient Israel," *IDBS*, 1976, 694-697; R. E. **Clements**, *Prophecy and Covenant*, Naperville, Ill.: Alec R. Allenson, 1965, 11-26; *One Hundred Years of Old Testament Interpretation*, Philadelphia: Westminster Press, 1976, 51-75; O. **Eissfeldt**, in H. H. Rowley (ed.), *The Old Testament and Modern Study*, Oxford: Clarendon Press, 1951, 115-161; *The Old Testament: An Introduction*, 52-56, 77-81, 146-152, 301-443; G. **Fohrer,** *Introduction to the Old Testament*, 342-470; "Neuere Literatur zur alttestamentlichen Prophetie," *TR* 19, 1951, 277-346; 20, 1952, 192-271, 295-361; "Zehn Jahre Literatur zur alttestamentlichen Prophetie," *TR* 28, 1961, 1-75, 235-297, 301-374; "Neue Literatur zur alttestamentlichen Prophetie," *TR* 40, 1975, 337-377; 41, 1976, 1-12; H. F. **Hahn,** *The Old Testament in Modern Research*, Philadelphia: Fortress Press, 1970[3]; J. H. **Hayes**, "The History of the Form-Critical Study of Prophecy," SBL Seminar Papers 1, 1973, 60-99; E. **Jacob**, "Quelques travaux récents sur le prophétisme," *RHPR* 53, 1973, 415-425; 54, 1974, 523-550; H.-J. **Kraus,** *Geschichte der historisch-kritischen Erforschung des Alten Testaments von der Reformation bis zur Gegenwart*, Neukirchen-Vluyn: Verlag der Buchhandlung des Erziehungsvereins, 1956; W. E. **March**, "Prophecy," in J. H. Hayes (ed.), *Old Testament Form Criticism*, San Antonio: Trinity University Press, 1974, 141-177; B. D. **Napier**, "Prophet, Propheticism," *IDB* III, 1962, 896-919; P. H. A. **Neumann**, *Das Prophetenverständnis in der deutschsprachigen Forschung seit Heinrich Ewald*, Darmstadt: Wissenschaftliche Buchgesellschaft, 1979; M. X. **Ramlot**, "Prophétisme," *SDB* VIII, 1972, 811-1222; T. H. **Robinson**, "Neuere Prophetenforschung," *TR* 3, 1931, 15-103; H. H. **Rowley**, "The Nature of Old Testament Prophecy in the Light of Recent Study," *The Servant of the Lord, and Other Essays*, London: Lutterworth Press, 1952, 89-128 (= *HTR* 38, 1945,

1-38); J. **Scharbert**, "Die prophetische Literatur: Der Stand der Forschung," *ETL* 44, 1968, 346-406; C. **Westermann**, *Basic Forms of Prophetic Speech*, Philadelphia: Westminster Press, 1967, 13-89; R. R. **Wilson**, "Form-Critical Investigation of the Prophetic Literature: The Present Situation," SBL Seminar Papers 1, 1973, 100-121; H. W. **Wolff**, "Hauptprobleme alttestamentlicher Prophetie," *EvTh* 15, 1955, 446-468.

One of the most significant achievements of biblical scholarship in the nineteenth century was the rediscovery of prophecy as a distinctive religious category. The traditional Christian view, represented by conservative and apologetic theologians like E. W. Hengstenberg and J. C. K. Hofmann, saw the prophets as forerunners and foretellers of Christ. Wellhausen, on the other hand, argued that Christ, who inherited the religion and ethics of the prophets, was betrayed by the institutional church just as the prophets had been betrayed by Judaism. The new approach also broke with the traditional Jewish view according to which the prophet was essentially a tradent of law, both written and oral. Since, according to this view, everything necessary for Israel's life had been revealed at Sinai, the prophetic message could not contain anything new. At the most, it could render explicit what was only implicitly contained in the Sinaitic revelation. In this broader sense, the epoch of revelation came to an end with the death of the last prophet (*b. Sanh.* 11a; *b. Yoma* 9b; *b. Soṭah* 48b). With this position, incidentally, we may compare that of a more traditional dogmatic theology which brought Christian revelation to an end with the death of the last apostle.

Modern critical scholarship, which did not derive its mandate from ecclesiastical authority, studied the prophets independently of such traditional *loci communes*. Applying literary criticism to the task of identifying the actual words of the prophets, their "authentic" message as distinct from "secondary" editorial accretions, it claimed to find in them a unique class of religious individualists with a message focused on the present rather than the distant past or the distant future. Thus it seemed possible to arrive at a highly distinctive prophetic religion, at once spiritual and ethical, which could then be contrasted with the magical and materialistic propensities of popular religion centered on the sacrificial cult. This prophetic religion could then be seen clearly as the high point of Israel's developing religious consciousness, and the postprophetic period as one of progressive decline. One result has been the neglect or misrepresentation of Second Temple Judaism in theologies of the Old Testament and histories of the religion of Israel, a state of affairs which has not yet been overcome.[15]

Critical study in the nineteenth century, therefore, shifted the center of gravity decisively from the Pentateuch to the Prophets, and this move undeniably had a strong impact on Christian theology in general. It contributed, for example, to a new emphasis on the religious interpretation of history (in a quite different way from the *Heilsgeschichte* of J. C. K. Hofmann) and an enhanced appreciation for the social responsibility of the churches. These were real advances, but they were accompanied by severe limitations arising out of the presuppositions that colored much of the work done at that time. So, for example, the portrait of the prophet as "religious genius" generally went with a low esteem for religious institutions and ritual in particular. Deriving in good part from Herder and the Romantics, this one-sided view has since been rendered obsolete by progress in anthropology and the history of religions. Emphasis on the ethical and spiritual aspects of prophetic religion, while justified in principle, was too closely tied to the presuppositions of liberal theology and too strongly colored by the needs of confessional polemic—e.g., in the long-standing debate on prophetic opposition to the sacrificial cult.

The new perspective on prophecy can be conveniently dated to *Die Theologie der Propheten* which Bernhard Duhm published in 1875 at the age of twenty-eight. The full title of this book is significant: "The Theology of the Prophets as Foundation for the Inner Historical Development of Israelite Religion." Suspicion that the ghost of Hegel is hovering nearby is confirmed by the author's division of the history into Mosaism, prophetism, and Judaism. The ethical idealism of the prophets represents the essence of true religion stemming from their direct and intensely personal experience of God. The emphasis, therefore, is on the prophetic commissioning, the visions and other extraordinary experiences of these chosen intermediaries. In his commentary on Isaiah, published seventeen years later, the author demonstrated the method by which these conclusions were reached, and especially the exegetical procedures by which the genuine words of the prophet were sifted out from the bulk of editorial expansions. It was this method, applied with great skill, which makes his work the first genuinely modern commentary on a prophetic book.[16]

Duhm's publications did not, of course, constitute an absolute beginning, if indeed there is such a thing in the history of literature. His idealistic portrait of the prophet had already been sketched out in the work of H. G. A. Ewald (1803-1875), with whom both Budde and Wellhausen had studied at Göttingen. In his *Propheten des Alten Bundes* (1840), Ewald described the prophet, in Israel as elsewhere, as proclaiming and interpreting the thoughts of God, the eternal truths which were destined to prevail in history but which, for the most part, remained dormant in the human consciousness. The prophet of Israel proclaimed these truths fearlessly to his contemporaries as an apostle of spiritual renewal and embodied them in his own intense involvement in the political events of his time. Unlike many of his academic contemporaries in theological faculties, Ewald practiced what he taught, and did so with such conviction that he ended up, for a time, in one of Bismarck's prisons and was removed from his post in the University of Göttingen.

During much of the nineteenth century the understanding of prophecy remained under the influence of the philosophical currents of the time, especially Romanticism (Herder, Eichhorn), Idealism (Ewald, Duhm), and rationalism (Kuenen, Cornill). Common to all these approaches was an ignorance of, or indifference to, the broader political and cultural context of the history of Israel and the writings through which it was known. Knowledge of that context, which accumulated rapidly after the decipherment of cuneiform and hieroglyphic scripts around the middle of the century, inevitably called into question reconstructions and periodizations based on idealistic premises. The impact on the study of prophecy of these new data was not, however, appreciated until 1914 when Gustav Hölscher published an important monograph that attempted to incorporate them in a controlled way.[17] As the subtitle indicates, Hölscher set out to apply the methods of the History of Religions school to the study of prophetic phenomena in Israel. He was also deeply impressed by the pioneering study of Wilhelm Wundt on the social psychology of religious phenomena in general and ecstatic phenomena in particular (*Völkerpsychologie*, Vol. 2, 1906). Hölscher argued that ecstatic propheticism was characteristic not of nomadic societies, such as Israel was before the settlement in the land, but of the agrarian culture of Asia Minor, Syria, and Palestine. It could therefore be assumed that the kind of ecstatic prophecy attested most frequently in the early period and among the northern tribes was taken over from Canaanite practice. Examination of the relevant descriptions of these phenomena in the Hebrew Bible, helped out with the account of Wen-Amon's visit to Byblos[18] and other accounts in authors of late antiquity (Heliodorus, Lucian, Apuleius), also suggested the conclusion that ecstatic prophecy of this kind generally occurred in connection with cultic acts, especially sacrifice, and in holy places dedicated to the vegetation deities. It was also, for the most part, a communal phenomenon, with bands of ecstatics under a leader similar to the organization of the Dervish *tawaf* of a later time. It happened, however, that these bands produced from time to time an extraordinary figure—such as Samuel, Elijah, and perhaps some of the classical prophets—who detached himself from the group and acted on his own. At any event, orgiastic traits tended to recede with the passing of time, though they never entirely disappeared. The poetry in the prophetic books arose as a spontaneous expression of the prophet's transformed consciousness, and could therefore serve as a reliable criterion for distinguishing genuine prophetic sayings from editorial additions and embellishments.[19]

Something of the same shift in perspective was also apparent in the early work of Hermann Gunkel (1862-1932), who combined the methods of the History of Religions school with a knowledge of and sensitivity to literature exceptional for Old Testament scholars then or since. While Gunkel's main effort was directed at the Genesis narratives and the Psalms, he was able to show that the prophets made use of many literary types *(Gattungen)* originating in different social and institutional settings, including and especially worship.[20] Unlike many later practitioners of form criticism, however, Gunkel did not fall into the trap of locating the prophet in the setting to which the literary type could be traced. On the contrary, he made a clear distinction between the several literary types which were either employed in prophetic preaching or incorporated at a later time into prophetic books and those forms which were peculiar to prophecy. The most important of these were the prophetic indictment or commination and the pronouncement of judgment made in the name of God. The latter, which was invariably in the form of a brief oracular saying, was *the* characteristic prophetic speech form, though the former increased in length and importance with the passing of time. Genuine prophetic utterance of this kind proceeded from what Gunkel called the prophet's mysterious experience of oneness with God and identification with his purposes in history.[21] This incommunicable and ultimately inexplicable experience was, for Gunkel, the essence of prophecy.

The work of Hölscher and Gunkel moved the study of prophecy decisively away from the Idealist and Romanticist perspective that had dominated most of the critical work done since Herder and Eichhorn in the late eighteenth and early nineteenth centuries.[22] Despite what was said earlier about Hölscher, we would have to conclude that the impetus to change did not come primarily from new material—as was the case with the Genesis narratives (especially Gen. 1-11) and the laws—since little apart from the Wen-Amon narrative had come to light. The most significant developments for the future were Hölscher's study of ecstasy and its relation to cult and Gunkel's literary perceptions and intuitions about the character of prophetic utterance and his listing of traditional *Gattungen* in prophetic books. Gunkel's work was carried further by his student, the Norwegian scholar Sigmund Mowinckel (1884-1966), one of the most prolific and imaginative contributors to Old Testament studies of this century. Mowinckel began by applying Gunkel's conclusions about the original and characteristic form of prophetic speech (brief oracular sayings in verse) to Jeremiah.[23] On this basis, he distinguished between the original sayings of the prophet, most of them in Jer. 1-25, and the prose sermons in the Deuteronomic style scattered throughout the book, his source C, which has been a major feature of all subsequent studies of the book. To this extent Mowinckel continued in the nineteenth-century tradition of source criticism, though now based on a certain understanding of prophetic consciousness.

Right from the beginning of his career Mowinckel was never content with a merely mechanical division into sources but addressed himself, in this and later works,[24] to the dynamic process by which the oral message of the prophet was transmitted, eventually achieving the form in which it now appears in the canon. Emphasis on oral composition, delivery, and transmission of prophetic sayings was developed to its furthest point by Scandinavian scholars in the 1930s and 1940s. In its most extreme form, represented by the work of Ivan Engnell,[25] we have a radical rejection of source criticism and therefore of any attempt to reconstruct, however tentatively, the editorial history of a prophetic book. Some prophetic books (Nahum, Habakkuk, Joel, Second Isaiah) were transmitted in cultic circles, written down from the beginning and remaining unchanged thereafter. Others (Isa. 1-39, Amos, Jeremiah) came to be written down only after the text had reached a point of fixity as a result of oral tradition. In either case there was no room for the kind of literary criticism that aimed at sorting out earlier and later compositional levels in a prophetic book. A similar, if less categorical and rigid, rejection of source criticism was expressed by H. S. Nyberg[26] and H. Birkeland.[27] They too gave priority to schools of disciples, active over several generations, who preserved, adapted, and amplified the words of the master, but in such a way that it is now impossible to distinguish between "authentic" and "secondary" in the prophetic material that has been allowed to survive.

This one-sided emphasis on oral tradition did not go unchallenged then,[28] and has now been largely abandoned. As difficult and hypothetical as it is, the reconstruction of the editorial history of prophetic books remains of major importance: historically, since it provides essential data for religious developments in Israel and early Judaism;[29] theologically, since the final form of the text cannot be disregarded in favor of a hypothetical authentic and original nucleus. We shall have occasion to note both the importance of this task and the difficulties that attend it at several points in our study.

The reader will have noted that studies in the transmission of prophetic material were already beginning to suggest a prominent place for the cult which, for most nineteenth-century Old Testament scholars, was antithetical to prophecy. Following Gunkel's form-critical and comparative method, Mowinckel identified a group of psalms (e.g., Ps. 60; 65; 82; 110) which contain what appear to be prophetic oracles of assurance delivered in a service of worship.[30] This led him to a more thorough examination of the role of ecstatic prophets alongside priests in Israelite worship, and especially in the great New Year festival during which Mowinckel believed that the enthronement of Yahweh as king of Israel was somehow reenacted. There could be no doubt that cultic prophecy was a well-established institution during the time of the monarchy, and Mowinckel argued that it was continued during the period of the Second Temple by the Levitical singers whose tasks are described by the Chronicler as a form of prophecy. While distinguishing in principle between these cultic functionaries and the classical prophets, Mowinckel was led to conclude that some of the latter (Nahum, Habakkuk, Joel) were probably Temple prophets, while First Isaiah and Micah contained material composed by Jerusalemite cult prophets who were responsible for the transmission of these books.[31]

It was Mowinckel more than anyone else who brought the relation between prophecy and cult to prominence during the thirties and forties of this century. With the unfair advantage of hindsight, we can now see that much of the work of that time, including some of Mowinckel's writing, was vitiated by the methodological error of reducing phenomena in different cultures, similar in some respects, to a unitary pattern. There was also a tendency in some quarters to follow uncritically the lead of W. Robertson Smith, James Frazer, and others in deriving all myths from rituals.[32] With respect specifically to prophecy, there were those who held that all of the canonical prophets were cultic functionaries.[33] At the other end of the spectrum it was argued that the prophets were totally opposed to the cult in any shape or form.[34] It is safe to say that neither of these positions was able to give a satisfactory account of the texts in their entirety. Arguments for close association with the cult could be made, following Mowinckel, more convincingly with respect to *some* of the canonical prophets—Nahum, Habakkuk, and the postexilic authors of Haggai, Zechariah, and Joel.[35] In retrospect, however, it is clear that positions defended at both ends of the spectrum with respect to the others have not been sustained, though a satisfactory formulation has still not been reached.[36]

The same issue could be approached from a different direction, that of form criticism which, as we have seen, was initiated by Gunkel (Hayes, March, Westermann). Gunkel listed several speech forms used by prophets—songs, liturgies, parables, priestly torah, etc.—but distinguished these carefully from forms peculiar to prophecy of which he believed the most ancient to be the oracle against a foreign and hostile land. At this point the error noted earlier enters into play, in that several form critics of prophetic speech were led to assume that traditional liturgical forms, when used by prophets, could serve as evidence that these prophets held a cultic office.[37] H. E. von Waldow, for example, concluded from the salvation oracles in Second Isaiah that the author was a cult prophet, since such sayings feature in liturgies in which cult prophets participated.[38] On the well-established basis that the law was recited at the annual (or septennial) covenant festival in Israel, H. Reventlow drew the conclusion that prophets like Amos and Jeremiah, who condemned their contemporaries for failure to observe the laws, did so in an official capacity as law speaker or covenant mediator in the cult.[39] Somewhat more nuanced was the argument of E. Würthwein with respect to the problematic relationship of Amos to the *n'bî'îm*. In his discussion of Amos 7:14-15, certainly one of the most crucial and obscure passages in all the prophetic literature, Würthwein argued that Amos did not deny that he was a *nābî'*, i.e., a professional cult prophet, but wished to assert that, in spite of this office, he had been called to deliver a message entirely different from what might be expected from a cult prophet. On this basis Würthwein went on to argue that the authentic nucleus of the book testifies to a decisive change having occurred in the career of Amos. As a cult prophet he pronounced the curse on Israel's enemies (1:3 to 2:3) and interceded successfully for his own people (7:1-6). Subsequently, however, he was called directly by God to pronounce the sentence of death on Israel, and thus put himself outside of the ranks of his former colleagues.[40]

In a later study Würthwein went further and suggested that the typical prophetic judgment saying, pronounced in the divine first person, also originated in the cult. The basis for this conclusion lay in the similarity between the specific form of prophetic indictment (the so-called *rîb* pattern, as in Hos. 4:1-6 and Micah 6:1-5) and pronouncements of Yahweh as judge in certain of the psalms (e.g., Ps. 50).[41] Würthwein did not comment on how this conclusion would affect the argument in his earlier article about Amos, but it would seem to imply that Amos could have gone through his entire career as a cult prophet.

Whatever their intrinsic merits or demerits, these essays helped to intensify study of the individual units in the prophetic books and highlight problems in the use of the form-critical method.[42] Meanwhile, there was a noticeable waning of interest in deciding the question one way or the other as to the prophets' relationship to worship. More precisely focused studies on the traditions within which individual prophets stood seemed, in any case, to hold out better hope of clarifying, if not solving, this particular issue.[43] There have also been indications in recent years that the editorial history of prophetic books has once again come to the fore, though on a quite different basis and for quite different reasons than was the case in the early decades of critical study.[44] Closely related to the prophecy-cult question is the attempt to clarify and interpret the criteria for distinguishing between true and false prophecy and to establish more precisely the identity of these "false prophets," i.e., the opponents of the canonical prophets.[45] How important the issue of criteria is for understanding the historical development of prophecy, and how important it remains for understanding the nature of the claim staked by the canonical prophets, should become clear in the course of our study.

During the last two decades we have seen indications of a certain disillusionment with and reaction against not only the results of the historical-critical study of prophetic texts but also the historical-critical method itself. In itself such a reaction is understandable since methods no less than results are determined by the intellectual climate and ideological currents of the age in which they are elaborated. Indeed, the discipline itself has reacted against some of the more ideologically determined aspects of the method, especially its evolutionism and its tendency to explain phenomena primarily in terms of their origins. Studies appearing under the rubric of literary and rhetorical analysis may be welcomed insofar as they take seriously the text as we have it, its internal organization and its genuinely literary character. Bridging the gap between literary criticism as understood by literary critics and as understood and practiced by Old Testament scholars is also a legitimate and important goal.[46] Much of this work, however, unfortunately illustrates the difficulty for Old Testament scholars of being at the same time critical and literary. And, in addition, the prophetic books have proved much more resistant to such analysis than has narrative, no doubt because of the highly distinctive character of the material, the heavy editing it has undergone, and the difficulty of establishing literary units as a starting point.[47] The same problems help to explain why analyses of biblical material of a formalist or structuralist kind have been for the most part restricted to narrative genres.[48]

As things stand at the moment, we are still far from understanding prophecy, in the sense of "seeing it steadily and seeing it whole" (Matthew Arnold). We have moved away from the nineteenth-century portrait with its often prejudicial implications for other forms of religious life, and especially those which achieved prominence in the emergence of Judaism.[49] We are now aware of the need to relate canonical prophecy to structures and institutions in Israel and the culture area in general, but we are still none too sure how this is to be done. Progress has been made in understanding what is generally referred to as "the prophetic consciousness," not so much from the direction of psychology as by taking into account comparative data from other cultures and the social determinants of ecstasy.[50] There is still the unresolved problem involved in passing from the prophetic consciousness to the production of the literature, with the clear indications that it conveys of poetic craft, sometimes of a high order, and the conscious and often sophisticated use of established types of speech. This leads directly into the theological problem of the prophet's mediation and interpretation of the common traditions and symbols in the light of an intensely personal experience;[51] and this, in its turn, inevitably raises the issue of conflicting claims to authority in the religious sphere and the different possibilities for a resolution.

3. WORDS AND MEANINGS

W. F. **Albright,** *From the Stone Age to Christianity,* Garden City: Doubleday & Co., 1957[2]; E. R. **Dodds,** *The Greeks and the Irrational,* Berkeley: University of California Press, 1951; E. **Fascher,** *PROPHĒTĒS. Eine sprach- und religionsgeschichtliche Untersuchung,* Giessen: A. Töpelmann, 1927; H. **Krämer** and R. **Rendtorff,** *TDNT* VI, 1968, 781-861; T. J. **Meek,** *Hebrew Origins,* New York: Harper & Brothers, 1950[2]; C. **Westermann,** *Basic Forms of Prophetic Speech,* 98-115.

Prophecy has been so subjected to arbitrary and interested interpretations that it is absolutely essential to begin with a historical and phenomenological study. The primary aim of such study should be to identify the characteristic features of prophecy in Israel and its developments in early Judaism and in Christianity. Current usage has itself undergone quite a development, as one may see by consulting the

Oxford English Dictionary. The emphasis may be on prediction, emotional preaching, social activism, or the power to enlighten, to communicate insight, as with the leader of a cult group. The older meaning of biblical interpreter, in use among the Puritans of the sixteenth and seventeenth centuries, has survived among evangelicals, though here the stress is generally on millenarian and apocalyptic interpretation. Rather curiously, the term is also quite often used of millenarian cults by sociologists of religion.[52] In no case is a preferred connotation based on a critical-historical and typological study of the phenomenon in the Hebrew Bible.

Those who believe it possible to decide the issue by appeal to etymology point out that the word derives from the Greek *prophētēs,* meaning one who proclaims a message on behalf of another, generally a deity. While this point is useful symbolically, in that it locates prophecy in the order of communication, sign, and language, it should be obvious that etymology is not a sure guide to meanings in the language group to which the word belongs, much less in others. In ancient Greece "prophecy" could refer to the giving of oracles either in a state of trance or in a normal, rational way. Thus, the devotees of Zeus at the ancient shrine of Dodona in Epirus or of Apollo at Delphi obtained guidance in matters of small or great moment from a member of the temple staff called "the prophet," who interpreted the ecstatic and unintelligible language of the priestess of Zeus or the Pythia respectively. As in ancient Israel, "prophecy" could also refer to group ecstasy of the orgiastic kind, generally associated with the cult of Dionysos (Bacchus). There were also prophetic figures who foretold the future, of whom the best known is Cassandra as depicted by Aeschylus. In philosophical works from Plato to Philo prophecy could, finally, become the object of theoretical consideration as to its nature and origin, leading directly to early Christian theories of biblical inspiration.

Though ecstasy and soothsaying are amply attested in the Hebrew Bible, the Jewish scholars who translated it into Greek, beginning in the third century B.C.E., used the substantive *prophētēs* and the verb *prophēteuein,* avoiding such terms as *mantis* and *manteuomai,* which connote an ecstatic person and ecstatic behavior respectively. Such usage probably reflects the translators' enlightened suspicion of the more uncontrolled aspects of religious behavior as well as their desire to emphasize the more declarative aspects of Israelite prophecy. Their preferences will not, however, necessarily be the best guide to the meaning of the relevant Hebrew words. Of these by far the most frequent is *nābî'* (plural *n'bî'îm*). While the derivation of this word is still a matter of dispute, the majority opinion today would relate it to *nabi'um* in Akkadian, a passive form which means "the called one."[53] This would conveniently signal the importance of the prophetic commissioning, but we repeat that etymologies do not carry over into usage in a straightforward way. The decisive factor will always be context rather than etymology.

Verbal forms deriving from the noun occur in the nif'al *(nibbā')* and hitpa'el *(hitnabbē')* and it is sometimes asserted, or simply assumed, that the former refers to prophetic speech and the latter to ecstatic behavior. The hitpa'el is indeed used of wild and uncontrolled behavior (I Sam. 10:5-13; 19: 20-24; I Kings 18:29; 22:10), even where there is no question of anything prophetic—as when Saul, deranged by jealousy, tried to pin David to the wall with his spear (I Sam. 18:10-11). Even much later the ecstatic prophet *(mitnabbē')* could be bracketed with the madman *('îš m'šuggā')* who speaks and acts in an uncontrolled manner (Jer. 29:24-28). But the nif'al is also used of communal, orgiastic ecstasy (I Sam. 10:11; 19:20; I Kings 22:12), while the hitpa'el can refer to rational prophetic speech (I Kings 22:8; Ezek. 37:10). There is therefore no hard and fast distinction, though *nibbā'* came to be the standard word for prophetic speech, just as speaking came to be considered the normal expression of what it meant to be a prophet.[54]

Other terms for "prophet" occur, most importantly *hōzeh* (visionary), *rō'eh* (seer), and *'îš 'elōhîm* (man of God); and it goes without saying that the Israelites were familiar with a considerable range of "prophetic" phenomena in the broadest sense, e.g., dream interpretation, divination by various techniques, incubation in a shrine, necromancy, and the like (cf. Deut. 18:9-14). Even though many of the canonical prophets would probably not have used it of themselves, *nābî'* came to be the standard term since it referred to professional practitioners in Temple and court. An editor or glossator has added a note at I Sam. 9:9 (it should really follow v. 11) explaining that the word *rō'eh*, used in the story of the seer who found Saul's wayward donkeys, corresponds to the more usual and current *nābî'*. This too suggests that the latter became a catchall term and that therefore its meanings can be safely inferred only from the contexts in which it occurs.

These contexts are of different kinds and have to be interpreted according to their specific genres. There are prophetic legends in the historical books (I Kings 17 to II Kings 13) and occasionally in the prophetic books themselves (Isa. 36-39; Jonah). Much too can be learned from a form-critical study of sayings in *oratio recta*. The messages of Yahweh through his prophets, like those of the Delphic Apollo communicated through the Pythia, are couched in the first person. The standard introductory formula "Thus says Yahweh" is taken from the established protocol of official messages and letters in the ancient Near East, pointing to the prophetic self-designation as emissary of Yahweh.[55] The royal messenger was an important official, often a member of the court, whose task was to relay a message or command from the king verbatim, though he might add some words of an exhortatory, comminatory, or explanatory nature of his own. This may be taken as a simple but important clue to prophetic self-understanding, since several of the prophets claimed to have access to the presence of Yahweh and to have been sent out on a mission by him, while denying this privilege to others whom they considered pseudo prophets (I Kings 22:19-23; Isa. 6; Jer. 23:18). The conviction of acting under such a mandate is essential to understanding how the prophets thought of their authority and role in society, and can therefore provide a starting point for addressing the central issue of prophetic identity.

4. THE SOCIAL LOCATION OF THE PROPHET

P. L. **Berger,** "Charisma and Religious Innovation: The Social Location of Israelite Prophecy," *American Sociological Review* 28, 1963, 940-950; K. **Burridge,** *New Heaven, New Earth,* Oxford: Basil Blackwell, 1969; R. P. **Carroll,** *When Prophecy Failed: Cognitive Dissonance in the Prophetic Traditions of the Old Testament,* New York: Seabury Press, 1979; M. **Eliade,** *Shamanism: Archaic Techniques of Ecstasy,* Princeton: Princeton University Press, 1964; D. **Emmett,** "Prophets and Their Societies," *Journal of the Royal Anthropological Institute* 86, 1956, 13-23; L. **Festinger** et al., *When Prophecy Fails,* New York: Harper & Row, 1964; C. **Geertz,** "Religion as a Cultural System," in M. Banton (ed.), *Anthropological Approaches to the Study of Religion,* London: Tavistock Publications, 1966, 1-46; H. F. **Hahn,** *The Old Testament in Modern Research,* Philadelphia: Fortress Press, 1970³, 44-82, 157-184; E. **Hammershaimb,** *Some Aspects of Old Testament Prophecy from Isaiah to Malachi,* Copenhagen: Rosenkilde & Bagger, 1966, 91-112; J. A. **Holstein,** "Max Weber and Biblical Scholarship," *HUCA* 46, 1975, 159-179; A. **Jepsen,** *NABI. Soziologische Studien zur alttestamentlichen Literatur und Religionsgeschichte,* Munich: C. H. Beck, 1934; K. **Koch,** "Zur Entstehung der sozialen Kritik bei den Propheten," in H. W. Wolff (ed.), *Probleme biblischer Theologie,* Munich: Chr. Kaiser Verlag, 1971, 236-257; L. **Köhler,** "Der Botenspruch," *Kleine Lichter,* Zurich: Zollikon, 1945, 13-17; H.-J. **Kraus,** "Die prophetische Botschaft gegen das soziale Unrecht Israels," *EvTh* 15, 1955, 295-307; "Die Anfänge der religionssoziologischen Forschungen in der alttestamentlichen Wissenschaft," in *Biblisch-theologische Aufsätze,* Neukirchen-Vluyn: Neukirchener Verlag, 1972, 296-310; G. **van der Leeuw,** *Religion in Essence and Manifestation,* Gloucester, Mass.: Peter Smith, 1967, I,

191-241; I. M. **Lewis,** *Ecstatic Religion,* Harmondsworth: Penguin Books, 1971; B. O. **Long,** "Prophetic Authority as Social Reality," in G. W. Coats and B. O. Long (eds.), *Canon and Authority,* Philadelphia: Fortress Press, 1977, 3-20; T. W. **Overholt,** "Commanding the Prophets: Amos and the Problem of Prophetic Authority," *CBQ* 41, 1979, 517-532; S. B. **Parker,** "Possession Trance and Prophecy in Pre-exilic Israel," *VT* 28, 1978, 271-285; T. **Parsons,** *Societies: Evolutionary and Comparative Perspectives,* Englewood Cliffs: Prentice-Hall, 1966; D. L. **Petersen,** *The Roles of Israel's Prophets,* Sheffield: JSOT Press, 1981; N. H. **Ridderbos,** "Einige Bemerkungen über den Propheten als Boten von Jahwe," in M. H. van Voss et al. (eds.), *Festschrift für M. A. Beek,* Assen: Van Gorkum, 1974, 211-216; J. F. **Ross,** "The Prophet as Yahweh's Messenger," in B. W. Anderson and W. Harrelson (eds.), *Israel's Prophetic Heritage,* New York: Harper & Row, 1962, 98-107; S. L. **Thrupp,** *Millenarian Dreams in Action,* New York: Schocken Books, 1970; J. **Wach,** *Sociology of Religion,* Chicago: University of Chicago Press, 1944, 331-374; M. **Weber,** *Ancient Judaism,* New York: The Free Press, 1952 (first published 1917-19); *The Sociology of Religion,* Boston: Beacon Press, 1963 (first published 1922); *The Theory of Social and Economic Organization,* New York: The Free Press, 1964 (first published 1913), 324-392; J. **Williams,** "The Social Location of Israelite Prophecy," *JAAR* 37, 1969, 153-165; R. R. **Wilson,** "Prophecy and Ecstasy: A Reexamination," *JBL* 98, 1979, 321-337; *Prophecy and Society,* Philadelphia: Fortress Press, 1980; P. **Worsley,** *The Trumpet Shall Sound,* New York: Schocken Books, 1968[2].

The discussion on the identity of the prophet has, for the most part, been carried on without reference to the social location of the prophet and his teaching and to the social determinants of his states of mind and behavior. Where the issue has arisen, the emphasis has been on prophetic self-awareness and God-awareness; the terms of the discussion have therefore been those of psychology and theology. The issue of social location has, nevertheless, forced itself on the attention of scholars through form-critical study, an essential aspect of which is the relation of literary types to their social matrices. This was a significant advance, and no one now doubts the importance of establishing the social world of a text, prophetic or otherwise. We must repeat, however, that the *Sitz im Leben* of a literary form occurring in prophetic texts does not necessarily tell us anything about the social situation of the prophet who made use of it. The protracted debate about the prophet's relation to the cult came closest to raising the issue of social status and role in an explicit way. It has not, however, eventuated in a firm consensus and was in any case conducted without benefit of sound sociological theory.

In recent years some interesting moves have been made toward applying role theory, the sociology of knowledge, reference-group theory, and the results of fieldwork in millenarian and ecstatic cults to the study of Israelite prophecy. The effect so far has been not to solve long-standing points of dispute but to send us back to the texts with new questions, or old questions formulated in a new way. Some of the more important would be the following: To what extent was the self-awareness and behavior of the prophet determined by the society and its expectations? What were these expectations, and to what extent did the prophet fulfill them and thus play a socially supportive and corroborative role? What was the prophet's support group? Who listened to him and how would the audience have understood what he was saying? Along a different line we would be led to ask: how did one become a prophet? From what social classes were prophets recruited? What was the manner and effect of the prophetic commissioning and how was the prophet expected to legitimate his new status? And then, of course, the long-debated issue of the prophet's standing vis-à-vis those institutions which were understood to mediate well-being and salvation—especially the monarchy, the priesthood, and the complex of cultic acts that were carried out in the Temple.

The likelihood of giving satisfactory answers to such questions as these is, needless to say, restricted by the relative paucity of the data at our disposal. We have some few stories about prophets (prophetic legends) of very uneven value as source material. The prophetic books themselves contain some biographical and autobiographical passages, but consist for the most part of sayings attributed to prophets. Both kinds of material have undergone extensive editing over several centuries, with the result that we cannot be optimistic about the possibility of reconstructing the social world in which the prophet acted and spoke. This, however, is all that we have.

Some aspects of this tentative social history, to be discussed in greater detail in subsequent chapters, may be briefly mentioned here. In the early centuries, and to a limited extent in the later period, prophecy was closely connected with warfare and cult. Bands of dervish-like ecstatics settled in close proximity to sanctuaries (e.g., Gilgal, Bethel) under the leadership of a prestigious figure. But there were also peripatetic figures like the anonymous man of God from Judah (I Kings 13), Elijah, and Elisha. Some of these retained their links with the settled communities and may have originated in them. Of their social standing and station in life prior to embarking on a prophetic career we know practically nothing. Some, like Samuel, would have been dedicated to a sanctuary at an early age in the manner of the monastic oblates of the Middle Ages. Since the members of these communities were apparently not celibate (II Kings 4:1), others again may have belonged to them since birth. Of Elijah's origins we know only the name of his family or clan and place of birth (I Kings 17:1). Elisha seems to have farmed prior to his call (I Kings 19:19). Whatever their origins—probably low in the social scale—the ecstatics were not highly esteemed by most of their contemporaries, which is hardly surprising in view of their remarkable and at times bizarre behavior.

The problem of data is even more severe with most of the canonical prophets. The case of Amos is instructive since the information provided by the book (he is not mentioned elsewhere) is susceptible of more than one interpretation. The title describes him as one of the shepherds of Tekoa (Amos 1:1) and in the one brief biographical passage he speaks of himself as a herdsman and a dresser of sycamore figs (7:14). The Hebrew term corresponding to "shepherd" or "sheep breeder" *(nōqēd)* occurs only once elsewhere in the Hebrew Bible, where it refers to a king of Moab (II Kings 3:4). It therefore cannot be made to indicate a countryman of low estate. The occurrence of the same term in a Ugaritic text in connection with priests has also suggested the possibility of a cultic reference, i.e., keeper of the herds destined for sacrificial use. But since it is difficult to imagine how dressing sycamore figs could be a cultic activity, the observation is probably beside the point. Yet if Amos was, as he himself is reported to have said, called from following the sheep to become Yahweh's prophet, how are we to explain the extensive knowledge of religious tradition and of international affairs evidenced in the authentic sayings, knowledge which we do not normally associate with sheep rearers?

Little as we know of Amos, we know even less about most of the others in the collection apart from an occasional reference to the father or place of origin. In discussing Micah we shall see that his place of origin (Moresheth) may point to a significant distinction between Jerusalemite and provincial prophets. The situation is somewhat different with Isaiah and Jeremiah. Information on Isaiah in the sayings collections can be supplemented by biographical legends incorporated into the scroll (Isa. 36-39). Here he appears as a holy man, not unlike Elijah, who prays, intercedes, works miracles, and predicts the future. About his life prior to his call we know nothing and there is, in addition, a disturbing lack of harmony between the Isaiah of the sayings and the subject of the biographical legends. Jeremiah is the best known of the prophets and was clearly the object of considerable biographical interest. Raised in a Benjaminite priestly family in Anathoth about two miles north of Jerusalem, he seems to have been more at home in the traditions of the central highlands than in those of

Jerusalem. We have no reliable knowledge of his life prior to his prophetic commissioning, and the same is true of Ezekiel, also a priest or at least a member of a priestly family, who received his call about half a century later (Ezek. 1:1-3).

It appears, then, that little importance was attached to the prophet's life, activity, and station prior to the commissioning; a circumstance that severely limits our ability to answer some of the questions detailed above. Examination of the call narratives shows that a common understanding of what was involved in being a prophet emerged at a fairly early date. Rightly, then, the study of these passages has been seen to be crucial for understanding the central issue of prophetic identity. The characteristic message formula ("thus says Yahweh") also indicates the prophetic role of intermediary between God and people, and implies the image of the divine court presided over by Yahweh, to whose presence the designated messenger is admitted, and from which he sets out to discharge his mission. The claim implicit in this view of the prophetic status was a large one indeed, and would inevitably lead to conflict with socially sanctioned jurisdictions in the civil and religious sphere. Tracing the course of this conflict is an important aspect of the social context of prophecy during the time of the monarchy.

Few attempts at reconstructing this context have been as influential as that of Max Weber, whose earliest writing on the subject goes back to the second decade of the century. In dealing with the earliest period he stressed the importance of warrior ecstasy (similar to that of the early Germanic berserks), devotion to the warrior god of the tribal federation, and the close ties between prophet and Nazirite. He held that the passage to monarchy, with the substitution of a professional army for the tribal levy, led to the demilitarization of this primitive type of orgiastic prophecy, though the hallowed language of the holy war continued in use in the prophetic struggle against the monarchy. The prophets of this epoch, drawn from no one social class, were thrust into the role of political demagogues and pamphleteers. This kind of public activity, unthinkable in the great empires like that of Assyria, at least testified to the persistence of the archaic ideal of the confederacy. It was on this basis that the canonical prophets passed judgment on their contemporaries and elaborated their ethical teaching.

In his more general and theoretical studies Weber located prophecy in the context of charismatic authority. The prophetic-charismatic figure is legitimated not by virtue of a socially acknowledged office but solely through extraordinary personal qualities. He is not designated by a predecessor, installed or ordained in office, but called. The claims staked by him, or by others on his behalf, would tend to set him in opposition to dominant elites dedicated to maintaining the status quo. Prophecy would therefore play a destabilizing rather than a corroborative role in society.

Since Weber's analysis seems to confirm the "religious genius" view of the prophet, and may in fact have been influenced by it, since he read the specialist literature, it should be noted that several critics have not been happy with what they regard as an excessive emphasis on exceptional individuals in Weber's work nor with the impression which it gives that charisma is essentially a socially marginal phenomenon.[56] While there is some justification for these criticisms, it must be said that Weber allowed for charismatic succession and a certain degree of embodiment of charisma in institutions. Most importantly, this part of his work provided a theoretical context for understanding the conflict over authority in the religious sphere precipitated by prophetic activity.

Weber's definition of the prophet in terms of charisma[57] enabled him to distinguish this category of *homo religiosus* from others such as the priest, soothsayer, legislator, ethical teacher, philosopher, and mystic. The further distinction between exemplary and ethical or emissary prophecy, the former characteristic of India and the latter of the ancient Near East, is also useful as a rough guide, though both types occur in the history of Israel. Other sociologists and historians of religion have proposed somewhat different typologies (e.g., Van der Leeuw, Wach). Comparison between the different forms of Israelite prophecy and different types of mediation by religious specialists in traditional societies in the modern period has raised some interesting questions that call for further study and discussion. These include the nature and extent of the social support needed for mediation of this kind, the circumstances (social stress, political crisis, *anomie*) in which certain kinds of "prophetic" activity tend to emerge, and the role of society, or a limited segment of society, in the process by which an individual assumes the function of intermediary.

While it is still too early to evaluate the impact of "social world" studies on our understanding of prophecy in general, one respect in which progress has been made is in clarifying the social determinants of what is often referred to as "the prophetic consciousness." The debate on the relative importance of ecstasy (i.e., extraordinary states of consciousness and patterns of behavior) in the history of Israelite prophecy was, of course, well under way long before the results of anthropological fieldwork were available for comparative purposes. It had become something of an axiom in Old Testament scholarship that, while such conditions are clearly attested in the early period of Israelite history, they are in no way characteristic of "classical" prophecy. The fact that, with the exception of Ezekiel, these "classical" prophets speak little of the spirit and spirit activity was also often cited in support of this view. Given these assumptions, it is still important to ask whether the extraordinary state of consciousness and type of behavior known, for want of a better word, as ecstasy are of the essence of prophecy or whether they are characteristic of only one type or one phase of development. The issue has theological as well as historical implications since it involves the important matter of the prophet's legitimacy and authority.

Though imprecise and unsatisfactory, the term "ecstasy" appears to be unavoidable. Anthropologists tend to restrict it to the study of religious phenomena, on the assumption that it is a variation of the physiological and behavioral condition known as trance. It is important to note that it is not used to describe the means by which an individual obtains, or is believed to obtain, communication from the divine world or the world of the spirits. For the latter, expressions such as possession or soul loss, or others current in the societies in which the phenomena are attested, are deemed more appropriate. The distinction is not merely formal, since it alerts us to the possibility that a prophet may experience spirit possession, and thereby receive a communication from that other world, without manifesting physiological or behavioral changes. Yet there generally exists the expectation, in Israel as in other societies, that such extraordinary behavior *may* indicate possession and, consequently, the warrant to speak and be heard. The important issue then is whether the society, or some segment of it, accepts this interpretation of the phenomena, since it is clear that the ecstatic intermediary cannot function without some degree of social support.

Little need be said about the various forms that the condition of ecstasy or trance can assume. It is agreed that it can manifest itself in violent and orgiastic or lethargic and catatonic states, that it can affect individuals or groups (e.g., the ecstatic coenobia known as "the sons of the prophets"), that it can happen spontaneously or be induced by appropriate techniques (music, percussion, self-laceration, drugs, etc.). While some of these manifestations fall within the purview of clinical pathology—e.g., aphasia, catatonia—it is less important for our purpose to investigate "prophetic psychology" than it is to understand how such conditions were interpreted in the social contexts in which they occurred.

While it must be emphasized that the study of the social determinants of ecstatic phenomena is still in its infancy, some provisional observations may be put forward. It seems, for example, that they are often attested among socially peripheral, dispossessed, or deprived groups that come together to take part in ecstatic rites, speak in tongues, etc., as a sort of ritualized rebellion against the power structures of the society. Such exercises function to enhance the self-esteem and sometimes the status of the group, or at least make it visible to those in power. There also seems to be a correlation between the incidence of group ecstasy and situations of social or political stress, e.g., invasion or occupation by a foreign power. Hence it is no surprise that so much prophetic activity is attested in Israel during the Philistine wars in the eleventh and tenth centuries, the intermittent warfare with Damascus in the ninth, and during the more critical periods of Assyrian and Babylonian hegemony from the eighth to the sixth century.

Ecstasy, therefore, is characteristic of peripheral groups, serving to promote their interests and status in the society to which they belong. It can also serve to legitimate leadership in such groups. Elisha, for example, had to validate his position as successor to Elijah vis-à-vis such groups by deeds of power similar to those of his master. His first act, therefore, was to divide the waters of the Jordan using Elijah's mantle (II Kings 2:13-14; cf. v. 9). Less frequently it can also serve to reinforce the authority of central political or religious leaders, as Weber pointed out. More commonly, however, religious leadership, once firmly established, discourages ecstatic phenomena as a potential source of social disruption and heterodoxy. As I. M. Lewis puts it:

> The more strongly based and entrenched religious authority becomes, the more hostile it is towards haphazard inspiration. New faiths may announce their advent with a flourish of ecstatic revelations, but once they become securely established they have little time or tolerance for enthusiasm. For the religious enthusiast, with his direct claim to divine knowledge, is always a threat to the established order.[58]

We would probably agree that this tendency has been amply illustrated in the history of Christianity and, to a lesser extent, that of Judaism.

The close affinity between ecstatic phenomena and millenarian beliefs has suggested to some scholars in recent years that the results of fieldwork in millenarian cults (e.g., Melanesian cargo cults and the so-called "ghost dance" of the Plains Indians) may have a bearing on our understanding of Israelite prophecy.[59] This, in its turn, brings into play the long and fascinating string of millenarian movements throughout Jewish and Christian history.[60] Such comparisons, however, can be very misleading. At the most obvious level, there is a world of difference between the way such beliefs are formed and sustained in "primitive" societies and the social context of Israelite prophecy and early Jewish apocalyptic. It must also be borne in mind that millenarian movements throughout the history of Christianity (e.g., Anabaptists, Millerites) and of Judaism (e.g., Sabbatianism) are themselves deeply indebted to biblical prophecy and apocalyptic. Comparison is, perhaps, most appropriate in connection with the emergence of apocalyptic sects during the period of the Second Temple. In these, for example, as in several of the cults documented by anthropologists, we see a redefining and restructuring of the redemptive process by groups that do not dispose of power in the society to which they belong.[61]

Mention must also be made of attempts to work out the implications of unfulfilled prophecy by reference to the theory of cognitive dissonance, a term introduced into social psychology a quarter of a century ago. Cognitive dissonance deals with the stratagems by means of which an individual or group attempts to reduce the inconsistency created by the disconfirmation of well-established beliefs and convictions. Its application to unfulfilled prediction is obvious. Predictive prophecy, especially of the short-term variety, is always a risky business since it is subject to falsification (cf. Deut. 18:21-22, which states this as a criterion for separating false from true prophecy). It is noted that the effect of disconfirmation is not, as might be expected, the collapse of the belief system which gave rise to the prediction but explanations, sometimes very ingenious, of nonfulfillment, rescheduling of the predicted event, and a more intense campaign to persuade oneself and others of the truth of the original prediction (Festinger, Carroll). Here too the theory would seem to apply more appropriately to Jewish and early Christian apocalyptic than to prophecy correctly understood. Despite the Deuteronomic criterion of falsification, it seems that an unfulfilled prediction (e.g., Amos 7:11; Micah 3:12) did not necessarily result in loss of prophetic credentials or lead to the rationalizations and other effects required by the theory. And, more importantly, predicting future events was not a major concern of the canonical prophets.

It goes without saying that one must also explain the ethical teaching of the prophets with reference to specific social contexts in which the message was first spoken and heard. We will attempt to do this as we trace the history of Israelite prophecy in the chapters that follow.

Notes

1. The date, then, would be either 458 or 398 B.C.E. All that can and need be said here is that no decisive argument has been advanced to eliminate either

date, and there are some who believe neither is correct. On the basis of Ezra 7:14 it is probable, though not certain, that he brought the lawbook with him. See further below, p. 276, n. 32.

2. "Five are the books of Moses, comprising the laws and the traditional history from the birth of man down to the death of the lawgiver" (Josephus, *Against Apion* I.39).

3. J. Blenkinsopp, "Prophecy and Priesthood in Josephus," *JJS* 25, 1974, 239-262.

4. Samuel the seer (I Chron. 29:29); Nathan the prophet (I Chron. 29:29; II Chron. 9:29); Gad the seer (I Chron. 29:29); Shemaiah the prophet (II Chron. 12:15); the prophet Iddo, author of a midrash (II Chron. 13:22); Jehu ben Hanani (II Chron. 20:34); Isaiah (II Chron. 26:22); anonymous seers during the reign of Manasseh (II Chron. 33:19).

5. See below, p. 255.

6. Clues to this incorporation are: the P date at Deut. 1:3; the repetition, in revised form, of Num. 27:12-23—which originally recorded the death of Moses—at Deut. 32:48-52; the account of Moses' death at Deut. 34:1, 7-9. All of these passages are attributed to P.

7. Isa. 36-39 = II Kings 18:13 to 20:19; Jer. 52 = II Kings 24:18 to 25:30.

8. In addition to Freedman (1975, 182), see R. E. Clements, *Prophecy and Tradition*, Atlanta: John Knox Press, 1975, 8-23, 41-57.

9. E.g., Amos is not mentioned in the Deuteronomic historian's account of the reign of Jeroboam II, though a salvation prophet, Jonah ben Amittai, is (II Kings 14:23-29). II Kings 14:27, "But Yahweh had not said that he would blot out the name of Israel from under heaven," may be directed against the message of Amos, as argued by F. Crüsemann, "Kritik an Amos im deuteronomistischen Geschichtswerk" in H. W. Wolff (ed.), *Probleme biblischer Theologie*, Munich: Chr. Kaiser, 1971, 57-63.

10. Jer. 36:1-4; 45:1; probably also Isa. 8:16, though LXX has no reference to disciples.

11. See below, pp. 191-193.

12. The (probable) exception of Esther was due, perhaps, to the problematic nature of the festival of Purim, which is not mandated in the Pentateuch and which the Qumran community did not celebrate. Esther's marriage to the pagan king would also not have endeared the book to them. The fact that it is the only book in the Hebrew Bible that does not contain the name of God is probably beside the point.

13. The earliest lists are in Melito of Sardis (Eusebius, *Hist. Eccl.* IV.26) and in the Didache manuscript discovered by Bryennios in 1883. The latter may go back to the end of the first century c.e. See J.-P. Audet, "A Hebrew-Aramaic List of Books of the Old Testament in Greek Transcription," *JTS*, n.s., 1, 1950, 135-154. Later lists are preserved by Origen and Epiphanius. We are reminded that the biblical canon was originally a Christian idea.

14. G. E. Mendenhall, *Law and Covenant in Israel and the Ancient Near East*, Pittsburgh: Biblical Colloquium, 1955, argued that the form and substance of

the covenant were directly influenced by Hittite suzerainty treaties (fourteenth to twelfth centuries B.C.E.) and were therefore very ancient. At the other end of the spectrum is the position of L. Perlitt, *Bundestheologie im Alten Testament*, Neukirchen-Vluyn: Neukirchener Verlag, 1969, that the covenant idea goes back no further than the Deuteronomic movement.

15. For a closer analysis of this situation, see James Barr, "Le Judaïsme postbiblique et la théologie de l'Ancien Testament," *RTP* 18, 1968, 209-217; *Judaism: Its Continuity with the Bible*, Southampton: Camelot Press, 1968; J. Blenkinsopp, "Tanakh and the New Testament: A Christian Perspective," in L. Boadt et al. (eds.), *Biblical Studies: Meeting Ground of Jews and Christians*, New York: Paulist Press, 1980, 96-119.

16. B. Duhm, *Das Buch Jesaia*, Göttingen: Vandenhoeck & Ruprecht, 1968[5] (first published 1892).

17. G. Hölscher, *Die Propheten. Untersuchungen zur Religionsgeschichte Israels*, Leipzig: J. C. Hinrichs, 1914.

18. See below, p. 55.

19. Demonstrated in Hölscher's *Hesekiel. Der Dichter und das Buch*, Giessen: A. Töpelmann, 1924.

20. Gunkel's principal statement on prophecy was his introduction to Hans Schmidt, *Die grossen Propheten*, in *Die Schriften des Alten Testaments* II, 2, Göttingen: Vandenhoeck & Ruprecht, 1923[2]. His form-critical method is exemplified in "Nahum 1," *ZAW* 13, 1893, 223-244; "Der Micha-Schluss," *Zeitschrift für Semitistik und verwandte Gebiete*, 2, 1924, 145-178.

21. H. Gunkel, "Die geheimen Erfahrungen der Propheten," *Suchen der Zeit* 1, 1903, 112-153, reprinted in *Die grossen Propheten*, xvii-xxxiv (see n. 20).

22. It will be appreciated that our attempt to trace the main lines of development obliges us to oversimplify and omit much that was important at the time of writing and in some cases may still be read with profit. For the period in question we should at least list W. Robertson Smith, *The Prophets of Israel* (1895[2]), C. H. Cornill, *Der israelitische Prophetismus* (1920[13]), and J. Skinner, *Prophecy and Religion* (1926[2]).

23. S. Mowinckel, *Zur Komposition des Buches Jeremia*, Kristiania: Dybwad, 1914.

24. See especially Mowinckel's *Jesaja-Disiplene. Profetien frå Jesaja til Jeremia*, Kristiania: Dybwad, 1926; *Prophecy and Tradition: The Prophetic Books in the Light of the Study of the Growth and History of the Tradition*, Oslo: Dybwad, 1946.

25. I. Engnell, "Profetia och tradition," *SEÅ* 12, 1947, 94-123; *The Call of Isaiah*, Uppsala: Lundquist, 1949, 54-60; "Methodological Aspects of Old Testament Study," *SVT* 7, 1960, 21; *A Rigid* (sic) *Scrutiny: Critical Essays on the Old Testament*, Nashville: Vanderbilt University Press, 1969.

26. H. S. Nyberg, *Studien zum Hoseabuch*, Uppsala: Lundquist, 1935.

27. H. Birkeland, *Zum hebräischen Traditionswesen. Die Komposition der prophetischen Bücher des Alten Testaments*, Oslo: Dybwad, 1938.

28. G. Widengren, *Literary and Psychological Aspects of the Hebrew Prophets*, Uppsala: Lundquist, 1948, appealed to early Islamic texts to make the opposite

point, i.e., that prophetic texts could have been, and probably were, written down shortly after they were delivered. See also the criticism of J. van der Ploeg, "Le rôle de la tradition orale dans la transmission du texte de l'Ancien Testament," *RB* 54, 1947, 5-41, and the sober and tentative reconstruction of the editorial history of prophetic books by T. H. Robinson, *Prophecy and the Prophets in Ancient Israel,* London: Gerald Duckworth & Co., 1953[2], 50-59.

29. This has been especially apparent in attempts to use this material to bridge the gap between prophecy and apocalyptic; see below, n. 44.

30. S. Mowinckel, *Psalmenstudien III. Die Kultprophetie und prophetische Psalmen,* Kristiania: Dybwad, 1923; *The Psalms in Israel's Worship,* Nashville: Abingdon Press, 1967, II, 53-73.

31. See above, n. 24. The most substantial studies in cult prophecy are those of A. Haldar, *Associations of Cult Prophets Among the Ancient Semites,* Uppsala: Almqvist & Wiksell, 1945; A. R. Johnson, *The Cultic Prophet in Ancient Israel,* Cardiff: University of Wales Press, 1962[2]; and, most recently, *The Cultic Prophet and Israel's Psalmody,* Cardiff: University of Wales Press, 1979.

32. The British branch of the "Myth and Ritual School," as it is sometimes called, is represented by collections of essays edited by S. H. Hooke: *Essays on the Myth and Ritual of the Hebrews in Relation to the Culture Pattern of the Ancient Near East,* London: Oxford University Press, 1933; *The Labyrinth,* London: Oxford University Press, 1935; *Myth, Ritual and Kingship,* Oxford: Clarendon Press, 1958. The Scandinavian branch is represented by I. Engnell, *Studies in Divine Kingship in the Ancient Near East,* Uppsala: Almqvist & Wiksell, 1943; the second edition of this work was published by Basil Blackwell in 1967.

33. Especially A. Haldar (see above, n. 31).

34. Representing this position, quite widely held, were J. P. Hyatt, "The Prophetic Criticism of Israelite Worship," in H. M. Orlinsky (ed.), *The Library of Biblical Studies,* Cincinnati: Hebrew Union College Press, 1969, 201-224; and C. F. Whitley, *The Prophetic Achievement,* London: A. R. Mowbray, 1963, 63-92.

35. P. Humbert, "Le Problème du livre de Nahoum," *RHPR* 12, 1932, 1-15; *Problèmes du livre d'Habacuc,* Neuchâtel: Neuchâtel Université, 1944; A. S. Kapelrud, *Joel Studies,* Uppsala: Almqvist & Wiksell, 1948; G. W. Ahlström, *Joel and the Temple Cult of Jerusalem,* Leiden: E. J. Brill, 1971.

36. Comparatively little attention has been given to this issue since the surveys of H. H. Rowley, "Ritual and the Hebrew Prophets," *JSS* 1, 1956, 338-360 (= *From Moses to Qumran,* New York: Association Press, 1963, 111-138), and R. Hentsche, *Die Stellung der vorexilischen Schriftpropheten zum Kultus,* Berlin: A. Töpelmann, 1957.

37. The point is made succinctly by William McKane: "The assumption that there is an indissolubility of form and setting, on which the transition from form-critical observations to conclusions about the cultic functions of prophets sometimes rests, appears particularly fragile." "Prophecy and the Prophetic Literature," in G. W. Anderson (ed.), *Tradition and Interpretation: Essays by Members of the Society for Old Testament Study,* Oxford: Clarendon Press, 1979, 164.

38. H. E. von Waldow, *Anlass und Hintergrund der Verkündigung des Deuterojesaja*, Dissertation, Bonn, 1953. However, in *Der traditionsgeschichtliche Hintergrund der prophetischen Gerichtsreden*, Berlin: A. Töpelmann, 1963, Von Waldow derived the prophetic pronouncement of judgment formally from the secular practice of law.

39. H. Reventlow, "Prophetenamt und Mittleramt," *ZTK* 58, 1961, 269-284; *Das Amt des Propheten bei Amos*, Göttingen: Vandenhoeck & Ruprecht, 1962; *Liturgie und prophetisches Ich bei Jeremia*, Gütersloh: Gütersloher Verlagshaus, 1963. A similar position was taken by J. Muilenberg, "The 'Office' of the Prophet in Ancient Israel," in J. P. Hyatt (ed.), *The Bible in Modern Scholarship*, Nashville: Abingdon Press, 1965, 74-97.

40. E. Würthwein, "Amos-Studien," *ZAW* 62, 1950, 10-52.

41. E. Würthwein, "Der Ursprung der prophetischen Gerichtsrede," *ZTK* 49, 1952, 1-15; cf. F. Hesse, "Wurzelt die prophetische Gerichtsrede im israelitischen Kult?" *ZAW* 65, 1953, 45-53.

42. Special attention has been paid to the indictment and pronouncement of judgment, the so-called *rîb* pattern, reports of commissionings and visions; in addition to Hayes, March, and Westermann see K. Koch, *The Growth of the Biblical Tradition*, New York: Charles Scribner's Sons, 1969. Some of the problems are dealt with by G. Fohrer, "Remarks on Modern Interpretation of the Prophets," *JBL* 80, 1961, 309-319.

43. E.g., H. W. Wolff, "Hoseas geistige Heimat," *TZ* 81, 1956, cols. 83-94, connecting Hosea's sayings with northern Levitical preaching. In *Amos' geistige Heimat*, Neukirchen-Vluyn: Neukirchener Verlag, 1964 (= *Amos the Prophet: The Man and His Background*, Philadelphia: Fortress Press, 1973), the same author derived significant aspects of Amos' message from the sapiential tradition with its roots in the old clan ethos; cf. S. Terrien, "Amos and Wisdom," in B. W. Anderson and W. Harrelson (eds.), *Israel's Prophetic Heritage*, New York: Harper & Brothers, 1962, 108-115. While much has been made of Jerusalemite cultic traditions in Isaiah (e.g., Mowinckel and Engnell, nn. 24 and 25, above), others have argued in addition that he was influenced by the tradition of scribal learning at the court and may himself have been a scribe prior to his prophetic calling; see J. Fichtner, "Jesaja unter den Weisen," *TLZ* 74, 1949, cols. 73-79, and, more recently, J. W. Whedbee, *Isaiah and Wisdom*, Nashville: Abingdon Press, 1971. For a summary of recent traditio-historical work on Second Isaiah, see W. Rast, *Tradition History and the Old Testament*, Philadelphia: Fortress Press, 1972, 57-71.

44. The theological issues involved have been touched on in the first section of this chapter. But it is also obvious that the redactional history of prophetic books should yield data relevant to developments in the later period, e.g., the emergence of apocalyptic, as assumed by O. Plöger, *Theocracy and Eschatology*, Richmond: John Knox Press, 1968; P. D. Hanson, *The Dawn of Apocalyptic*, Philadelphia: Fortress Press, 1975; J. Vermeylen, *Du Prophète Isaïe à l'apocalyptique*, 2 vols., Paris: J. Gabalda, 1977-78.

45. See P. H. A. Neumann, *Das Prophetenverständnis in der deutschsprachigen*

Forschung seit Heinrich Ewald, 33-39, for a bibliographical survey of German-language contributions. Among the more significant studies in English in recent years are: J. L. Crenshaw, *Prophetic Conflict: Its Effect Upon Israelite Religion,* Berlin: Walter de Gruyter, 1971; J. A. Sanders, "Hermeneutics in True and False Prophecy," in J. W. Coats et al. (eds.), *Canon and Authority,* Philadelphia: Fortress Press, 1977, 21-41; S. J. De Vries, *Prophet Against Prophet,* Wm. B. Eerdmans Publishing Co., 1978 (a study of I Kings 22).

46. D. Robertson, "Literature, the Bible as," *IDBS,* 1976, 547-551; *The Old Testament and the Literary Critic,* Fortress Press, 1977; J. F. A. Sawyer, "A Change of Emphasis in the Study of the Prophets," in R. Coggins et al. (eds.), *Israel's Prophetic Tradition: Essays in Honour of Peter R. Ackroyd,* Cambridge: Cambridge University Press, 1982, 233-249.

47. L. Alonso Schökel, *Estudios de poética hebrea,* Barcelona: Herder, 1963; *La Palabra inspirada. La Biblia a la luz de la ciencia del lenguaje,* Barcelona: Herder, 1966.

48. R. M. Polzin, *Biblical Structuralism: Method and Subjectivity in the Study of Ancient Texts,* Philadelphia: Fortress Press, 1977.

49. See n. 15, above. On Jewish interpretations of prophecy (as distinct from explanations of the traditional view) see H. M. Orlinsky (ed.), *Interpreting the Prophetic Tradition,* New York: KTAV Publishing House, 1969, especially the contributions of B. J. Bamberger, "The Changing Image of the Prophet in Jewish Thought," 301-323, and J. A. Agus, "The Prophet in Modern Hebrew Literature," 43-80. The most distinctive Jewish treatments of prophecy are those of M. Buber, *The Prophetic Faith,* New York: Macmillan Co., 1949, and numerous other publications; A. J. Heschel, *The Prophets,* New York: Harper & Row, 1962; *Faith and Reason: Essays in Judaism,* New York: KTAV Publishing House, 1973, 33-39; Y. Kaufmann, *The Religion of Israel from Its Beginnings to the Babylonian Exile,* New York: Schocken Books, 1972, 341-451. On Buber, see most recently U. E. Simon, "Martin Buber and the Interpretation of the Prophets," in R. Coggins et al., *Israel's Prophetic Tradition,* 250-261.

50. See below, pp. 43-46.

51. More problematic are those instances where prophets deliberately reverse the accepted understanding of traditional motifs, e.g., the Day of Yahweh (Amos 5:18-20; Isa. 2:12-17); on which see McKane in *Tradition and Interpretation,* 172-173 (n. 37, above). A major thesis of G. von Rad's *Old Testament Theology* II, *The Theology of Israel's Prophetic Traditions,* New York: Harper & Row, 1965, is that prophetic preaching broke decisively with the traditions of earlier Israelite religion.

52. E.g., L. Festinger et al., *When Prophecy Fails,* New York: Harper & Row, 1964.

53. Others defend the active sense: "one who calls out," and therefore "speaker"; see Meek, *Hebrew Origins,* 150-151.

54. Thus the nif'al *(nibbā')* occurs some 70 times in Jeremiah and Ezekiel referring to prophetic speech, while hitpa'el *(hitnabbē')* is attested only 7 times. The nif'al form is parallel to *ntp* (hif'il) in Amos 7:16 *(lō' taṭṭîp* = do not preach).

55. See J. Ross, "The Prophet as Yahweh's Messenger," in B. W. Anderson and W. Harrelson (eds.), *Israel's Prophetic Heritage,* New York: Harper & Row, 1962, 98-107.

56. See Berger, 948-949; Emmett and Parsons, 75-76; and D. Little, "Max Weber and the Comparative Study of Religious Ethics," *JRE* 2, 1974, 5-40.

57. "We shall understand 'prophet' to mean a purely individual bearer of charisma, who by virtue of his mission proclaims a religious doctrine or divine commandment" (Max Weber, *The Sociology of Religion,* 46).

58. I. M. Lewis, *Ecstatic Religion,* 34.

59. In addition to Carroll and Wilson, see T. W. Overholt, "The Ghost Dance of 1890 and the Nature of the Prophetic Process," *Ethnohistory* 21, 1974, 37-63.

60. For the medieval period and the Anabaptists, see N. Cohn, *The Pursuit of the Millennium,* New York: Oxford University Press, 1970².

61. One of the best analyses of the goals of millenarian movements is that of Burridge, who stresses the importance of control of the "redemptive media" in a society.

II
FROM THE BEGINNINGS
TO AMOS

1. NEAR EASTERN PROPHECY AND THE PROBLEM
OF ORIGINS

K. **Baltzer,** *Die Biographie der Propheten,* Neukirchen-Vluyn: Neukirchener Verlag, 1975; R. **Coggins** et al. (eds.), *Israel's Prophetic Tradition: Essays in Honour of Peter R. Ackroyd,* Cambridge: Cambridge University Press, 1982; D. **Conrad,** "Samuel und die Mari- 'Propheten.' Bemerkungen zu 1 Sam 15, 27," *ZDMG* 43, 1969, Suppl. 1, 273-280; S. **Daiches,** "Balaam—a Babylonian Bārū," *Bible Studies,* London: Edward Goldston, 1950, 110-119; H. **Donner,** "Balaam pseudopropheta," in H. Donner et al. (eds.), *Beiträge zur alttestamentlichen Theologie,* Göttingen: Vandenhoeck & Ruprecht, 1977, 112-123; G. **Dossin,** "Sur le prophétisme à Mari," in *La Divination en Mésopotamie ancienne et dans les régions voisines,* Paris: Presses universitaires de France, 1966, 77-86; F. **Ellermeier,** *Prophetie in Mari und Israel,* Herzberg am Harz: Erwin Jungfer, 1977²; J. C. **Greenfield,** "The Zakir Inscription and the Danklied," *Proceedings of the Fifth World Congress of Jewish Studies,* Jerusalem: World Union of Jewish Studies, 1969, 1, 175-176; A. **Guillaume,** *Prophecy and Divination Among the Hebrews and Other Semites,* London: Hodder & Stoughton, 1938; A. **Haldar,** *Associations of Cult Prophets Among the Ancient Semites,* Uppsala: Almqvist & Wiksell, 1945; J. H. **Hayes,** "Prophetism at Mari and Old Testament Parallels," in *Trinity University Studies in Religion* 9, San Antonio: Trinity University Press, 1971, 31-41; J.-G. **Heintz,** "Prophetie in Mari und Israel," *Bib* 52, 1971, 543-555; S. **Herrmann,** "Prophetie in Israel und Ägypten: Recht und Grenze eines Vergleichs," *SVT* 9, 1963, 47-65; H. B. **Huffmon,** "Prophecy in the Mari Letters," *BA* 31, 1968, 101-124; "Prophecy in the Ancient Near East," *IDBS* 697-700; "The Origins of Prophecy," in F. M. Cross et al. (eds.), *Magnalia Dei,* Garden City: Doubleday & Co., 1976, 173-186; R. **Largement,** "Les Oracles de Bile'am et la mantique suméro-akkadienne," in *Travaux de l'Institut Catholique de Paris. Ecole des Langues Orientales Anciennes de l'Institut Catholique de Paris,* Paris: Blond & Gay, 1964, 37-50; J. **Lindblom,** "Zur Frage des kanaanäischen Ursprungs des altisraelitischen Prophetismus," in J. Hempel and L. Rost (eds.), *Von Ugarit nach Qumran,* Berlin: A. Töpelmann, 1961, 89-104; *Prophecy in*

Ancient Israel, Oxford: Basil Blackwell, 1962, 29-46; A. **Malamat,** "Prophetic Revelations in New Documents from Mari and the Bible," *SVT* 15, 1966, 207-227; "Mari," *BA* 34, 1971, 2-22; W. L. **Moran,** "New Evidence from Mari on the History of Prophecy," *Bib* 50, 1969, 15-56; P. H. A. **Neumann,** *Das Prophetenverständnis in der deutschsprachigen Forschung seit Heinrich Ewald,* 15-24; M. **Newman,** "The Prophetic Call of Samuel," in B. W. Anderson and W. Harrelson (eds.), *Israel's Prophetic Heritage,* 86-97; F. **Nötscher,** "Prophetie im Umkreis des alten Israel," *BZ,* n.s., 10, 1966, 161-197; E. **Noort,** *Untersuchungen zum Gottesbescheid in Mari. Die "Mariprophetie" in der altestamentlichen Forschung,* Neukirchen-Vluyn: Neukirchener Verlag, 1977; J. R. **Porter,** "The Origins of Prophecy in Israel," in R. Coggins et al., *Israel's Prophetic Tradition,* 12-31; R. **Rendtorff,** "Reflections on the Early History of Prophecy in Israel," *Journal for Theology and the Church* 4, 1967, 14-34; J. F. **Ross,** "Prophecy in Hamath, Israel and Mari," *HTR* 63, 1970, 1-28; L. **Rost,** "Fragen um Bileam," in H. Donner and L. Rost (eds.), *Beiträge zur alttestamentlichen Theologie,* Göttingen: Vandenhoeck & Ruprecht, 1977, 377-387; W. **von Soden,** "Verkündigung des Gotteswilles durch prophetisches Wort in den altbabylonischen Briefen aus Mari," *WO* 1, 1947-50, 397-403; S. D. **Walters,** "Prophecy in Mari and Israel," *JBL* 89, 1970, 78-81; C. **Westermann,** *Basic Forms of Prophetic Speech,* 115-128.

The Hebrew Bible itself attests that prophecy was not confined to Israel. Jeremiah (27:1-15) referred to prophets and other religious specialists in the neighboring lands of Edom, Moab, Ammon, and the Phoenician cities who, like their counterparts in Israel but unlike Jeremiah himself, were supporting plans for a rebellion against Nebuchadrezzar in 594 B.C.E. This raises some interesting questions. Was Israelite prophecy one of several more or less similar national varieties of the one phenomenon in that area? If a corpus of religious texts had survived from, say, Edom, at all comparable to what we have from Israel, how would the one have differed from the other? What factors dictated the particular direction in which prophecy developed in Israel?

Unfortunately we have practically no data from these neighboring lands that would enable us to answer these questions. We may surmise that commands relayed from the god Chemosh to King Mesha of Moab to attack Israelite cities, reported on the Moabite Stone (*ANET,* 320-321), came through ecstatic prophets in the service of court or cult. This, however, is not explicitly stated, and there are other possibilities. From somewhat farther afield, the northern Syrian city-state of Hamath, we have an inscription set up by Zakir its king which dates from the eighth century and is therefore not far removed from the time of Amos. It tells how, during the siege of a dependent city, Zakir prayed to the local Baal and received assurance of divine assistance through seers and other inspired individuals. The message is couched in the divine first person, as are those of Israelite prophets, and it is a message of assurance: "Do not fear, for I made you king, and I shall stand by you and deliver you."[1] Also from Syria, but about a millennium earlier, a cultic functionary of the shrine of the god Adad in or near Aleppo had a divine message for Zimrilim, last king of Mari, which contained conditional promise and threat in some respects comparable to Nathan's dynastic oracle (II Sam. 7).[2]

The Elijah and Elisha legends, to be discussed later on in this chapter, testify to the importation of ecstatic prophecy from the Phoenician cities to the Northern Kingdom as a result of Ahab's marriage with Jezebel (I Kings 18:19, 26-29; II Kings 10:19). There was probably little to distinguish the four hundred and fifty prophets of the Phoenician Baal on Mount Carmel, who performed their limping dance, slashed themselves with knives, and cried ecstatically to their god, from the "sons of the prophets" associated with Samuel, Elijah, and Elisha. About two and a half centuries earlier an Egyptian text tells the story of a temple official called Wen-Amon who visited Byblos to purchase timber and was ill received by the prince of that city. Just when it seemed he would have to return empty-handed, a youth, presumably at the court, went into trance during sacrificial rites and revealed to the city ruler that the visitor had been sent by the god Amon (*ANET,* 26).

The situation is quite different in Egypt, especially because of the dominance of the priestly and scribal classes and the learned tradition of which they were the guardians. Discussion has tended to focus on a narrative set during the Old Kingdom, at the time when the pyramids were being built. A skilled speaker, one Neferti, priest-scribe of the goddess Bastet, is introduced to Pharaoh Snefru of the fourth dynasty and utters a prophecy of social and political chaos to come which will be brought to an end by a king who will come from the south, destroy the enemies of Egypt, and restore justice and order in the land (*ANET,* 444-446). The prediction of disaster to be followed by an age of well-being ushered in by a king is certainly reminiscent of certain "messianic" prophecies in the Hebrew Bible. The "prophecy of Neferti" is, however, a *vaticinium ex eventu* since it dates to the reign of Amen-em-het, first ruler of the twelfth dynasty (ca. 1990-1785 B.C.E.), who brought to an end the political and social chaos of the First Intermediate Period and is the "king from the south" alluded to in the "prophecy."

More to our purpose, the author of the prediction is neither ecstatic nor charismatic, but is introduced into the narrative as scribe and rhetorician. In that capacity he may well have drawn on a well-established literary tradition of speaking about a golden age in the future. As late as the Ptolemaic period the Demotic Chronicle and the so-called Potter's Oracle predict the destruction of foreign rulers, the coming of a savior-king, and the inauguration of a new age of well-being.[3] But it is tolerably clear that whatever historical links can be discerned between Israelite prophecy and types of mediation in the great urban centers of the Near East are with Syria and Mesopotamia rather than with Egypt. On the other hand, it is entirely possible, even probable, that the ethical teaching contained in Egyptian admonitions and instructions, of which many have survived, influenced the prophetic protest against social injustice during the Assyrian and Babylonian periods.[4]

Among the Hittites in Asia Minor the state priesthood also exercised control over the various forms of divination and dream interpretation by means of which messages were received from the gods. One text, however—the Plague Prayer of Mursilis II from the fourteenth century B.C.E.—enjoins recourse to an ecstatic "man of god" in addition to omens, dreams, and incubation to discover the cause of a plague which was ravaging the kingdom (*ANET*, 394-396). In this respect, as in others, the Hittites were dependent on the religious traditions and practices of Mesopotamia, where ecstasy had always been an acknowledged form of possession and communication with the gods. If, as appears likely, Balaam's homeland was in Upper Mesopotamia (Num. 22:5; 23:7), we would have an example of the Mesopotamian ecstatic seer in the Hebrew Bible itself. For although the Balaam cycle (Num. 22-24) has been made to serve as political and religious propaganda during the period of the early monarchy, the lineaments of the ecstatic seer, "enraptured and with eyes unveiled," can still be discerned.

The most interesting and impressive parallels to some forms of Israelite prophecy have come to light among the royal archives of the Amorite kingdom of Mari in Upper Mesopotamia (Tell Hariri, just inside the Syrian border with Iraq). These are letters reporting communications from several deities (Dagan, Adad, the goddesses Annunitum and Diritum) to Zimrilim, last king of the city (ca. 1730-1697 B.C.E.) (*ANET*, 623-632). In some cases the intermediary, male or female, appears to be a private person holding no office. In others the message was delivered through an ecstatic (*muḫḫûm*, fem. *muḫḫutûm*) or oracle-giver (*āpilum, aplûm,* fem. *apiltûm*) employed in a temple, especially that of Dagan, chief god of the area, in the city of Terqa near Mari. In these instances the message was communicated in the temple and was often accompanied by sacrificial rites. One of the texts speaks of an oracle specialist who guarded a tent sanctuary, somewhat reminiscent of Joshua in the oracle tent in the wilderness.[5] It is not always clear whether a particular message was solicited (e.g., by incubation) or came spontaneously and unannounced.

Several of the communications were received in dreams, a form of revelation not unambiguously endorsed in the Hebrew Bible. Doubts about the divine origin of such communications could be laid to rest when the dream was repeated either on the following day or after a long period of time. Others came in visions, others again in a state of trance, no doubt induced by appropriate techniques by temple ecstatics. There are indications that at Mari, as elsewhere, the latter were under the jurisdiction of the temple priesthood (cf. Jer. 29:26-27). The letters show evident concern to authenticate the message, especially by seeking independent confirmation, e.g., consultation of the omens. The mediator's identity often required authentication by forwarding a lock of hair and fringe of an outer garment to the recipient.

Since the messages are generally part of reports by public officials to the palace the actual words of commissioning by the god are not always given. We do, nevertheless, find formulae similar to those employed by Israelite prophets, e.g., "Dagan sent me," "Thus spoke Annunitum." Less frequently, the words of the god are reported in *oratio recta*, as in the commissioning of a certain Malik-Dagan by the god Dagan: "Now go, I send you. Thus shall you speak to Zimrilim saying: 'Send me your messengers and lay your full report before me . . .'" The letters, however, throw no light on the process by which a man or woman came to be recognized and acknowledged as an intermediary.

More important than the form is, of course, the content of the messages delivered to the king. Most of them have to do with military affairs—warnings about revolt and the possibility of assassination, injunctions against undertaking certain expeditions or entering into certain alliances. In some instances the warnings—e.g., about fortifying a gate or not rebuilding a house—are accompanied by threats of unpleasant consequences. Others have to do with cultic matters such as holding sacrificial rites for the dead or building a temple for a deity who feels he has been slighted by the king. There are complaints explicit or otherwise as, for example, when the goddess Annunitum addresses the king: "O Zimrilim, even though you for your part have spurned me, I for my part shall embrace you" (*ANET*, 630). The god Adad of Aleppo, where Zimrilim had taken refuge before returning to reestablish his father's kingdom in Mari, gave him a dynastic oracle not unlike that of Nathan to David (II Sam. 7):

Am I not Adad the lord of Kallassu who reared him between my
thighs and restored him to the throne of his father's house? After
restoring him to the throne of his father's house, I again gave him a
dwelling-place. Now, since I restored him to the throne of his
father's house, I should receive from him an hereditary property
[for a temple]. If he does not give it, I am the lord of throne,
territory, and city, and what I gave I will take away. If on the other
hand he grants my request, I will give him throne upon throne,
house upon house, territory upon territory, city upon city; even
the land from east to west will I give him. (*ANET*, 625)

In general, however, the messages are supportive of the king and his
political and military goals. It should be noted that two, and possibly
three, of them are directed against Hammurapi the Babylonian king
and his allies, predicting their defeat at the hands of Zimrilim. Since it
was Hammurapi who was to conquer and destroy Mari, and thus bring
Zimrilim's reign to an end, we have a situation remarkably similar to
that of the last days of Judah more than a millennium later when
salvation prophets like Hananiah were predicting the defeat of
Nebuchadrezzar, king of the same city (e.g., Jer. 28:2-4).

There are sufficient indications from other sites in Syria and
Mesopotamia to suggest that, in this respect, the situation at Mari was
fairly typical of the entire area. And while we are in no position to trace
the history of Mesopotamian "prophecy," the personnel, practices, and
types of oracles seem to remain fairly constant over a very long period
of time. From the period of Assyrian supremacy in the eighth and
seventh centuries B.C.E.—the high period of prophetic activity in
Israel—we have collections of oracles delivered by "proclaimers" and
"revealers" in the name of the national god Ashur in Nineveh, the
goddess Ishtar in her temple at Arbela, and other deities. Here too the
inspired persons, male and female, give directions on political and
military issues—e.g., the discovery of traitors—assure the king of
success in his undertakings and indulge occasionally in mild scolding.
From a collection of oracles addressed to or referring to Esarhaddon
(680-669 B.C.E.) it also appears that such oracles were written down
shortly after they were delivered orally and arranged in collections
according to the deity from whom they originated or the "prophet"
who delivered them (*ANET*, 449-450).[6] We therefore have a process
comparable in some respects to the compilation of prophetic books in
Israel at that time and later.

The material that we have briefly surveyed does not allow us to solve
the problem of the origins of Israelite prophecy. At the most, it enables
us to pose it in a more satisfactory way and to put forward a working

hypothesis that can be checked as we work through the historical development of prophecy in Israel. It will be apparent, to begin with, that a Canaanite origin, as proposed by Hölscher, Jepsen, and others, is oversimplified. Where we find the more violent and orgiastic type of ecstatic phenomena, generally attested in prophetic groups and coenobia,[7] we may suspect influence from the vegetation cults of Canaan and the Phoenician cities and the practices associated with them. But it is also possible that we are dealing here with a type of war prophecy that some of the early settlers brought with them and that was contaminated by the Canaanite-Phoenician type with the development of urban life and the adoption of much of Canaanite cult and culture. The persistence of such extremist elements as Nazirites and Rechabites, with their rejection of Canaanite culture and their attachment to the holy war of the tribal federation, would certainly be consistent with this explanation. Unfortunately, we know nothing directly about "prophetic" phenomena among the Hebrews prior to the settlement, and are therefore forced to rely on analogies drawn from what we do know about nomadic institutions and practices.[8]

Enough has been said about the Mari reports dealing with ecstatic intermediaries to indicate what must have been a standard pattern in the urban centers of Northern Mesopotamia and Syria with which Israel had close ties from the earliest days. These intermediaries were generally, but not invariably, associated with sanctuaries where they pronounced oracles accompanied by sacrificial rituals. Their revelations were generally, but not invariably, supportive of the ruler and his political and military undertakings. One of their principal functions was to further these undertakings by pronouncing the curse on foreign enemies. Despite the seven centuries which separate the reign of Zimrilim from that of David, there seems no reason to deny that Israel was familiar with the same pattern. The important questions, however, have to do not with origins but with development, and especially the emergence of the kind of prophecy represented by Amos, Isaiah, Jeremiah, and the other canonical prophets.

It must not be overlooked that reflection on the origins of prophecy arose in the course of time in Israel itself. According to one view, prophecy was God's answer to the people's request for mediation made at Mt. Sinai (Deut. 18:15-18; cf. Ex. 20:18-20). The "prophet like Moses" of this much-quoted text came to be interpreted eschatologically of an individual figure, but it is generally, and correctly, taken to refer to the prophetic succession as a whole. It assumes that prophecy originated with, and is embodied paradigmatically in, Moses, and that it functions throughout the history in the service of the covenant.

Another passage (Num. 11:10-30) deals with the creation, during the wandering in the wilderness, of a new office the purpose of which was to assist Moses in governing the people. He was instructed to select seventy from among the elders and officers of the community and present them at the tent of meeting. When he did so Yahweh came down in the cloud, took some of the spirit that was on Moses and put it on the seventy, with the result that they "acted like prophets" for that one time only (Num. 11:25).[9] Two of their number, however, were not presented at the tent and yet manifested the same symptoms. Joshua thereupon objected, but Moses refused to prevent them, with the words, "would that all Yahweh's people were prophets, that Yahweh would put his spirit upon them!"

This is one of several traditions about the wilderness period which deal with different aspects of the institutional life of Israel and which have undergone rather heavy editing.[10] As it stands, it cannot be interpreted as simply legitimating the Israelite "presbyterate," since the narrative assumes that this office was already in existence. It does seem to intend to legitimate ecstatic prophecy by deriving it from the spirit of Moses which is unquestionably of divine origin. In that case, the two—Eldad and Medad—who were not "ordained" and who yet prophesied would most naturally stand for those prophets who stood outside the institutional framework, which in effect means the cult. We are reminded once again that the canonical prophets made up only a small and anomalous minority of the prophets of Israel at any point in the history.

A quite different tradition suggests that the call of Samuel at Shiloh (I Sam. 3:1 to 4:1) marked the beginning, or at least a new beginning, of prophetic activity. Before that time revelations and visions were infrequent, but the situation was quite different after Samuel's call (I Sam. 3:1, 21; 4:1). At this point we are on firmer historical ground since prophecy was always intimately associated with the monarchy, beginning with Saul, for whose downfall, according to the tradition, one of the principal reasons was loss of prophetic support. It is also well attested that times of political crisis, such as then existed with the struggle against the Philistines, elicit the kind of prophetic activity of which we are speaking. We shall go on to see that during Israel's "heroic age" and the early monarchy, prophecy was intimately associated with warfare. Hence, whatever its links with the indigenous culture and cults of Canaan, Israelite prophecy in its earliest manifestations had a character of its own dictated by the unique situation—the struggle for survival and the emergence of the monarchy—in which Israel was then engaged.

2. WAR PROPHECY AND THE PASSAGE TO MONARCHY

G. W. **Ahlström,** "Der Prophet Nathan und der Tempelbau," *VT* 11, 1961, 113-127; W. F. **Albright,** "Samuel and the Beginnings of the Prophetic Movement," in H. M. Orlinsky (ed.), *Interpreting the Prophetic Tradition,* New York: KTAV Publishing House, 1969, 149-176; K. **Baltzer,** *Die Biographie der Propheten,* 13-105; J. **Blenkinsopp,** "The Quest of the Historical Saul," in J. W. Flanagan and A. W. Weisbrod (eds.), *No Famine in the Land: Studies in Honor of John L. McKenzie,* Missoula, Mont.: Scholars Press, 1975, 75-99; N. P. **Bratsiotis,** " 'ish," *TDOT* 1, 1977, 233-235; D. L. **Christensen,** *Transformations of the War Oracle in Old Testament Prophecy,* Missoula, Mont.: Scholars Press, 1975; V. **Eppstein,** "Was Saul Also Among the Prophets?" *ZAW* 81, 1969, 287-304; H. **Haag,** "Gad und Nathan," in A. Kuschke and E. Kutsch (eds.), *Archäologie und Altes Testament. Festschrift für Kurt Galling,* Tübingen: J. C. B. Mohr (Paul Siebeck), 1970, 135-143; "bēn," *TDOT* 2, 1977, 152-153; R. **Hallevy,** "Man of God," *JNES* 17, 1958, 237-244; M. **Haran,** "From Early to Classical Prophecy: Continuity and Change," *VT* 27, 1977, 385-397; J. H. **Hayes** and J. M. **Miller** (eds.), *Israelite and Judaean History,* Philadelphia: Westminster Press, 1977, 285-380; J. **Lindblom,** "The Political Background of the Shiloh Oracle," *SVT* 1, 1953, 78-87; *Prophecy in Ancient Israel,* 47-104; "Saul inter prophetas," *ASTI* 9, 1974, 30-41; P. D. **Miller, Jr.,** *The Divine Warrior in Ancient Israel,* Cambridge, Mass.: Harvard University Press, 1973; J. **Muilenburg,** "The 'Office' of the Prophet in Ancient Israel," in J. P. Hyatt (ed.), *The Bible in Modern Scholarship,* Nashville: Abingdon Press, 1965, 74-97; H. M. **Orlinsky,** "The Seer in Ancient Israel," *OA* 4, 1965, 153-174; S. B. **Parker,** "Possession Trance and Prophecy in Pre-exilic Israel," *VT* 28, 1978, 271-285; L. **Perlitt,** "Mose als Prophet," *EvTh* 31, 1971, 588-608; A. **Phillips,** "The Ecstatics' Father," in P. R. Ackroyd and B. Lindars (eds.), *Words and Meanings: Essays Presented to David Winton Thomas,* Cambridge: Cambridge University Press, 1968, 183-194; O. **Plöger,** *Die Prophetengeschichten der Samuel- und Königsbücher,* Greifswald: E. Panzig, 1937; J. R. **Porter,** *"Bene hannebî'îm,"* *JTS,* n.s., 32, 1981, 423-428; R. **Smend,** *Yahweh War and Tribal Confederation,* Nashville: Abingdon Press, 1970; F. **Stolz,** *Jahwes und Israels Kriege,* Zurich: Zollikon, 1972; J. **Sturdy,** "The Original Meaning of 'Is Saul Also Among the Prophets?' " *VT* 20, 1970, 206-213; M. **Weber,** *Ancient Judaism,* 90-117; J. J. **Williams,** "The Prophetic 'Father': A Brief Explanation of the Term 'Sons of the Prophets,' " *JBL* 85, 1966, 344; A. **Weiser,** *Samuel. Seine geschichtliche Aufgabe und religiöse Bedeutung,* Göttingen: Vandenhoeck & Ruprecht, 1962; R. R. **Wilson,** "Early Israelite Prophecy," *Int* 32, 1978, 3-16.

We noted at the beginning that prophecy is generally defined with reference to the Latter Prophets. Variously described as "canonical," "writing," or "classical" prophecy—none of which terms is entirely satisfactory—this material corresponds to a phase in the historical development of prophecy beginning with the great Assyrian expansion in the eighth century. The earliest of these prophets—Amos and Hosea in the Northern Kingdom, and Micah and Isaiah in the Southern Kingdom—represent a critical point in the history of prophecy and in the history of Israel in general; so much so that we are inclined to underestimate the lines of continuity with the past that are essential for understanding the significance of this high period of prophetic activity.

It was also noted that these "classical" prophets are aware of a prophetic tradition already well established and refer explicitly to prophetic predecessors. The confrontation between Amos and Amaziah (Amos 7:10-17) shows, for example, that *nᵉbîʾîm* were employed in state sanctuaries under royal jurisdiction exercised through the priesthood. Another passage (Amos 2:11-12) speaks of prophets and Nazirites encountering opposition even before the time of the monarchy.[11] The bracketing of prophets with Nazirites—a dervish-like order dedicated to the militant defense and propagation of the Yahweh cult—also stresses the connections between prophecy and warfare which were of decisive importance in the early period. The involvement of prophetic groups and individuals in the political life of the country inevitably spelled opposition. Prophecy was, in any case, an ambiguous phenomenon right from its first appearance. The extraordinary behavior of ecstatic prophets could always be interpreted as sickness or madness (e.g., II Kings 9:11; Hos. 9:7; Jer. 29:26), to which should be added accusations of venality (e.g., Micah 3:5-12) and of leading the people astray (e.g., Hos. 4:5; 9:7-9). Yet despite these ambiguities, Amos, Hosea, and their successors appealed to a prophetic tradition with which they could identify, one which Hosea does not hesitate to trace back to Moses himself (Hos. 12:13).

Our knowledge of prophecy during the early period depends mainly on the Deuteronomic history (Joshua through Kings), with minor contributions from the Pentateuch and the Chronicler's history. In view of the theological purposes determining the selection and presentation of events in these writings, our data will inevitably be patchy and incomplete. Abraham is described as a prophet in a passage generally attributed to the Elohist (E) source of the Pentateuch (Gen. 20:7). While this notice reflects the importance of intercessory prayer as a characteristic prophetic activity—to which we may add Abraham's pleading for the doomed city of Sodom (Gen. 18:22-33)—it cannot be used as evidence for the existence of a certain type of prophecy during the time of the ancestors. All it tells us is that the Elohist source, to the extent that we can reconstruct it, seems to have been deeply influenced by the prophetic movement. The attribution of oracles to such founding fathers as Jacob (Gen. 49) and Moses (Deut. 33) has to be understood along the same lines, though the individual tribal sayings undoubtedly are ancient.

Hosea seems to have been the first to describe Moses as a prophet:

> By a prophet Yahweh brought Israel up from Egypt,
> And by a prophet he was preserved. (Hos. 12:13)

This characterization was taken up and developed by the Deuteronomic school (Deut. 18:15-18; 34:10). But Deuteronomy and the Deuteronomic history are concerned to present prophecy according to their own understanding of the history of Israel and its institutions. This led them to stress the "Mosaic" character of prophecy, in the sense that prophecy was intended to make available throughout history a mediation comparable to that of Moses. Eventually the entire Pentateuch came to be ascribed to Moses as a kind of prophetic legacy committed to Israel just before his death.[12] At that point Moses emerged as *the* prophet, in something of the way in which the term is applied to Mohammed in Islam.

If we were able to unravel all the traditions about Moses, tracing the different threads back to their beginnings, we might well find that this view of Moses is historically well founded. Kaufmann and Buber in particular have argued that, together with Miriam and Aaron, Moses belonged to a family of seers comparable to the Arabic *kāhins*.[13] The earliest traditions about the tent of meeting (*'ōhel mô'ēd*) or oracle tent, pitched outside the camp in the wilderness, would certainly be consistent with this hypothesis, since it was there that Moses received divine communications on behalf of the group (Ex. 33:5-11). The tent was also the scene of the ecstatic prophesying of the elders (Num. 11:16-17, 24-30) and the vindication of Moses' unique status as prophet (Num. 12:1-8). It should be noted, however, that it was Joshua not Moses, who is represented, in a tradition of equal antiquity, as the permanent minister of the oracle-deity in the tent (Ex. 33:11); in which respect he discharged a function similar to that of Samuel in the Shiloh sanctuary.[14] We have here, at any rate, a tradition meriting the greatest respect which traces the origins of prophecy in Israel to native roots in the remote period before the settlement in the land.

The Deuteronomic history was written to explain the disasters that overcame both kingdoms as the result of failure to heed the prophetic warning. The fact that no prophets are mentioned during the period preceding the monarchy (i.e., in Joshua and Judges) is to be explained by the author's clearly structured ideas about charismatic succession:

Joshua was appointed as charismatic mediator for the period of the conquest (Num. 27:15-23; Deut. 34:9; Josh. 1:1-9), and after his death "judges" were "raised up," the last of whom was Samuel (Judg. 2:16-23; I Sam. 12:11). For this source there is a close link between prophet and king. From the death of Solomon to the fall of Jerusalem prophets make frequent appearances to predict the fall of kings and dynasties for failure to observe the Mosaic law. Hence the pattern of prophecy-fulfillment is structurally decisive, providing the key to interpreting the history and leaving no doubt as to who was responsible for the disasters that had overtaken the writer's contemporaries.

We have already suggested the problems involved in working back from the great narrative complexes to historically reliable data on early prophecy in Israel. That the ancestors are recorded as having visions and other supranormal experiences (e.g., Gen. 15), or giving oracles (e.g., Gen. 49), or that they are posthumously honored with the title of prophet (Gen. 20:7), does not authorize us to reclassify them as seers in the manner of Balaam or the Arabic *kāhin*. One possible approach is by way of Deuteronomy and Hosea to Ephraimite traditions preserved in the Pentateuch, one of which provides fascinating if obscure glimpses of the oracle tent and its resident seer. Miriam, sister of Moses and member of the Levi clan, is called a prophetess (*n^ebî'āh*, Ex. 15:20), in which capacity she provided encouragement in battle by singing, dancing, and music. During the conquest another prophetess, Deborah, issued the call to arms, accompanied the tribal levy into battle, gave instruction on when to attack, and also took part in singing and playing musical instruments (Judg. 4-5). In both cases the closest parallel is the female seer *(kāhina)* among the pre-Islamic tribes of the Arabian peninsula. The foreign seer Balaam, discussed briefly at an earlier point, is also employed in warfare, though his connections seem to be with Mesopotamia rather than with Arabia (Num. 22-24).

We have seen that, in the scheme of the Deuteronomic history, prophecy in the strict sense begins with Samuel. Before his call the word of Yahweh was rare; after it, divine revelations were frequent (I Sam. 3:1; 3:19 to 4:1). The call itself, which took place in the Shiloh sanctuary, perhaps during an incubation ritual (3:2-18), resulted in no commission to speak or act (cf. Isa. 6) but rather in the authentication of Samuel as prophet to all Israel and the acknowledgment by the people of his new status (I Sam. 3:20). We may note, too, the intimate connection in this entire passage between prophecy and cult. The historian himself introduces an anonymous "man of God" who condemns the corruption of cult at Shiloh and the Eli priesthood responsible for it (2:27-36). The same message is delivered to Samuel

(3:11-14) and yet, subsequent to his call, Shiloh remains the designated place for divine communications (3:21). Samuel, correspondingly, is a cultic prophet in the sense that he ministered in the sanctuary and received divine revelations there. This, however, did not prevent him from condemning the cult and its personnel and it certainly did not prevent him from operating outside the sanctuary. To say the least, then, the Shiloh narrative reflects ideas about prophecy current at different times throughout the history: the process by which the prophet was commissioned and subsequently acknowledged as such by his public, and the relation between the prophet and the cultic institutions of Israel, especially the sacrificial ritual.

In these and similar respects the narratives about Samuel have certainly been influenced by later developments in the history of prophecy. So overlaid with theological interpretation are these narratives, in fact, that it is now practically impossible to say anything certain about Samuel as a historical figure. He is represented as judge, in both the military (I Sam. 11:11) and judicial sense (7:15-17), as seer (9:11, 19), sacrificing priest (7:10; 13:8-15), man of God (9:3-10), and paradigm of prophetic opposition to kingship (13:8-15; 15:1-31); and in this last capacity he pronounces a message indistinguishable from that of later prophets (I Sam. 15:22-23; cf. Hos. 6:6). A further complication is that the birth story clearly implies that he is to be a Nazirite, an implication that becomes explicit in one of the Samuel fragments from Qumran (4QSam[a]): "I will give him as a Nazirite for ever, all the days of his life," corresponding to I Sam. 1:22. The name etymology, however, would refer more naturally to Saul than to Samuel (1:20); and it is noticeable how often the verb *š'l* occurs in the birth story, including the passive form *šā'ûl* (1:28). It is Saul moreover, and not Samuel, who acts the part of the Nazirite by his violent and spirit-driven participation in Israel's holy war. It therefore seems reasonable to conclude that a birth and conception story of a familiar type which referred originally to Saul has been transferred to Samuel and conflated with a prophetic commissioning narrative which, for the Deuteronomic historian, marked the beginning of the history of prophecy under the monarchy.

One pericope in I Samuel which deals primarily with Saul but features Samuel provides, for that reason, a surer clue to the latter's identity. A fugitive from Saul's men, David took refuge in an ecstatic coenobium directed by Samuel in Ramah (I Sam. 19:18-24). After the troops sent ahead by Saul to arrest David were caught up in the communal ecstasy, Saul himself arrived, was similarly affected, and ended up tearing off his clothes and lying naked on the ground in a catatonic state for an entire day and night. According to this tradition, then, Samuel was the leader or "father" of an ecstatic brotherhood, not unlike the sheik presiding at a later day over the Sufi dervish community. Another tradition exists about Saul's appointment as military overlord by Samuel (I Sam. 9:1 to 10:16). Since the ecstatic brotherhoods were active in warfare, and since we have several instances of n'bî'îm designating or anointing leaders and kings (Judg. 4:6-9; I Kings 11:29-40; 16:2; II Kings 9:4-10), these two traditions are not mutually exclusive. Yet a careful reading of the story of Kish's straying donkeys leads to the probable conclusion that it dealt originally with an anonymous "man of God" or clairvoyant who only at a later stage of editing was identified with Samuel the kingmaker.[15] Seers of this kind should be distinguished from the ecstatic dervishes over whom Samuel presided, and it does not seem likely that he fulfilled both roles.

The condition of trance or mental dissociation so often attested in this early period is derived from the spirit of Yahweh (e.g., I Sam. 10:6, 10; 19:20, 23; I Kings 22:21-23). Whatever the archaic, magical connotations of rûaḥ—a word that can also mean wind or breath—it refers in these narratives to a force deriving from Yahweh and driving the inspired one to a certain course of action. The case of Saul, whose association with the ecstatic brotherhoods is mentioned more than once (I Sam. 10:11; 18:10; 19:24), serves to illustrate one of the ambiguities from which prophecy is rarely free. For here was a man who appears to have been psychologically predisposed to "stand outside himself," as may be seen in the way he called the tribes to war in support of Gilead (I Sam. 11:6-7), and in the spear-throwing incident (18:10-11; 19:9-10). On his way to designation as tribal leader he fell in with a prophetic band and at once, in the telling phrase used at that point, "became another man" (I Sam. 10:5-6). Violent behavior of this kind might nowadays result in a diagnosis of manic depression or dementia praecox, and even in ancient Israel could be interpreted as a form of sickness or madness (cf. II Kings 9:11; Hos. 9:7; Jer. 29:26). Such extraordinary behavior, therefore, was susceptible of more than one interpretation. Since prophecy could not function without a degree of social acceptance, there had to be a "discerning of spirits" by the society or that segment of it addressed by the prophet.

Whatever view one takes of the conquest narrative in Joshua and the process of settlement in the land, it seems clear that Israel was forged as a nation in the crucible of warfare. As Wellhausen put it, war was the cradle of the nation. We noted earlier that the Deuteronomist saw the prophets as successors to the "judges," with Samuel a transitional figure. There are indeed obvious similarities, but the differences cannot be overlooked. One of the most historically trustworthy of the traditions about Samuel presents him as leader of a band of ecstatic prophets, and there can be no doubt that both he and they were involved in the political and military events of that critical period in the consolidation of the tribes.[16] Saul's connections with ecstatic prophets have already been noted, and it is particularly significant that his career as charismatic warlord followed the spectacular encounter with an ecstatic troupe *(ḥebel n'bî'îm)* near a town occupied by a Philistine garrison.[17] It is also clear from the subsequent narrative that his political failure was due in considerable measure to his loss of prophetic support (I Sam. 13:8-15; 15:1-35; 28:6).

With David's establishment of a dynasty, creation of a professional army in place of the tribal levy, and subjugation of the tribal structures to a complex state system, these older forms of prophecy were bound to undergo change. The secession of the northern and central tribes after the death of Solomon, though judged negatively in the dominant Judean tradition, was in reality a protest against these innovations and a reaffirmation of the archaic pattern. It is for this reason that ecstatic war prophecy continued to thrive in the Northern Kingdom and is unattested in Judah, at least until the resurgence of Assyria posed a direct threat to its existence in the eighth century.

Under the United Monarchy in Judah we find, nevertheless, a type of court prophecy similar in some respects to that of the Mari "prophets" discussed earlier. Wishing to build a temple to Yahweh in Jerusalem, David consulted with Nathan, his court seer, who at first gave a favorable reply but then, after a night vision, forbade him to do so (II Sam. 7:4-17). In keeping with a conservative aversion to Canaanite cult places, the original form of this oracle opposed the building of a temple without qualification. In the following reign, however, an editor added a qualification—"he (i.e., Solomon) shall build a house for my name" (v. 13)—in acknowledgment of the fact that the Temple actually was built. The point is made by a play on the word *bayit* (house), which can signify "temple" or "dynasty": David will not build me a house (temple); I will build him a house (dynasty). Appropriately, therefore, it was Nathan who named David's heir by Bathsheba (II Sam. 12:25), and we find him active at her side in the palace intrigues leading to the ousting of the pretender Adonijah (I Kings 1). Another court seer, Gad, was associated with David even before his accession (I Sam. 22:3-5) and continued to play an important part thereafter, guiding him in such crucial decisions as choosing the site of the future sanctuary (II Sam. 24:18-19; I Chron. 22:1). Other prophetic oracles predicting the expansion of David's kingdom (II Sam. 3:9-10; 5:2; Gen. 49:8-12; Num. 24:15-19)[18] probably emanated from the circle of court prophets with which David surrounded himself.

3. PROPHECY IN THE NORTHERN KINGDOM: ELIJAH AND ELISHA

R. A. **Carlson,** "Elie à l'Horeb," *VT* 19, 1969, 416-439; R. P. **Carroll,** "The Elijah-Elisha Sagas," *VT* 19, 1969, 400-415; F. M. **Cross,** *Canaanite Myth and Hebrew Epic,* Cambridge, Mass.: Harvard University Press, 1973, 223-229; G. **Fohrer,** *Elia,* Zurich: Zwingli Verlag, 1968²; F. S. **Frick,** "Rechabites," *IDBS,* 726-728; J. H. **Hayes** (ed.), *Old Testament Form Criticism,* 173-175; J. H. **Hayes** and J. M. **Miller** (eds.), *Israelite and Judaean History,* 381-414; G. **Hentschel,** *Die Elija-erzählungen,* Leipzig: St. Benno Verlag, 1977; A. **Jepsen,** "Elia und das Gottesurteil," in H. Goedicke (ed.), *Near Eastern Studies in Honor of W. F. Albright,* Baltimore: Johns Hopkins University Press, 1971, 291-306; K. **Koch,** *The Growth of the Biblical Tradition,* 195-200; B. O. **Long,** "2 Kings III and Genres of Prophetic Narrative," *VT* 23, 1973, 337-348, J. M. **Miller,** "The Elisha Cycle and the Accounts of the Omride Wars," *JBL* 85, 1966, 441-454; "The Fall of the House of Ahab," *VT* 17, 1967, 307-324; M. **Noth,** *The History of Israel,* New York: Harper & Brothers, 1960², 225-250; M. **Pope,** "Rechabites," *IDB* IV, 1962, 14-16; A. **Rofé,** "The Classification of Prophetic Stories," *JBL* 89, 1970, 427-440; "Classes in the Prophetic Stories: Didactic Legenda and Parable," *SVT* 26, 1974, 143-164; H. H. **Rowley,** "Elijah on Mount Carmel," *BJRL* 43, 1960-61, 190-219 (= *Men of God,* London: Thomas Nelson & Sons, 1963, 37-65); H.-C. **Schmitt,** *Elisa,* Gütersloh: Gütersloher Verlagshaus Gerd Mohn, 1972; H. **Schweizer,** *Elischa in den Kriegen,* Munich: Kösel Verlag, 1974; H. **Seebass,** "Zur Königserhebung Jeroboams I," *VT* 17, 1967, 325-333; "Die Verwerfung Jeroboams I und Salomos durch die Prophetie des Ahia von Silo," *WO* 4, 1968, 166-169; "Elia und Ahab auf dem Karmel," *ZTK* 70, 1973, 121-136; "Der Fall Naboth in 1 Reg xxi," *VT* 24, 1974, 474-488; "Tradition und Interpretation bei Jehu ben Chanania und Ahia von Silo," *VT* 25, 1975, 175-190; K. **Seybold,** "Elia am Gottesberg," *EvTh* 33, 1973, 3-18; R. **Smend,** "Das Wort Jahwes an Elia," *VT* 25, 1975, 525-543; J. J. **Stamm,** "Elia am Horeb," *Studia Biblica et Semitica Theodoro Christiano Vriezen,* Wegeningen: H. Veenman, 1966, 327-334; O. H. **Steck,** *Überlieferung und Zeitgeschichte in den Elia-Erzählungen,* Neukirchen-Vluyn: Neukirchener Verlag, 1968; R. **de Vaux,** "The Prophets of Baal on Mount Carmel," *The Bible and the Ancient Near East,* Garden City: Doubleday & Co., 1971, 238-251; S. J. **De Vries,** *Prophet Against Prophet,* Grand Rapids: Wm. B. Eerdmans Publishing Co., 1978; E. **Würthwein,** "Zur Komposition von 1 Reg 22:1-38," *Das Ferne und Nahe Wort,* Berlin: A. Töpelmann, 1967, 245-254; "Elijah at Horeb: Reflections on I Kings 19:9-18," in J. Durham and J. R. Porter (eds.), *Proclamation and Presence: Old*

Testament Essays in Honour of Gwynne Henton Davies, London: SCM Press, 1970, 152-166; "Die Erzählung vom Gottesmann aus Juda in Bethel," in H. Gese and H. P. Rüger (eds.), *Wort und Geschichte. Festschrift für Karl Elliger zum 70. Geburtstag,* Kevelaer: Batzon & Bercker, 1973.

During the two centuries from the death of Solomon (ca. 925) to the fall of Samaria (722 B.C.E.) references in the history to prophets and prophecy are restricted entirely to the Northern Kingdom. Our first reaction would be to explain this in terms of the historian's purpose, namely, to apply the lesson of Samaria's fate to Judah: if you ignore your prophets as they did theirs, the same will happen to you (II Kings 17:7-18).[19] It should be noted, however, that the idea of charismatic leadership, which remained strong in the territory of the Northern Kingdom, acted as a counterforce to hereditary kingship. This left more room for the involvement of prophets in public affairs, and we shall find them playing an important role in the making and unmaking of rulers, especially in the half century preceding the establishment of the Omrid dynasty.

It may be useful, first, to sketch in the political situation. The unification of the tribes, brought about by the political genius of David, lasted only through the lifetime of Solomon his successor. The basis for David's rule over the tribes of the Central Highlands and the north was an agreement or covenant between himself and their elders (II Sam. 5:1-3). Despite opposition and sporadic attempts to repudiate this agreement—for example, by the Benjaminite Sheba ben-Bikri (II Sam. 20)—it survived throughout his reign and must have been renewed at the accession of Solomon. After the latter's death his successor Rehoboam duly betook himself to Shechem, the ancient shrine of the Joseph tribes, to seek renewal of the agreement. This time, however, the tribal leaders were no longer content to go through with a purely formal ratification but laid down conditions which Rehoboam unwisely rejected out of hand (I Kings 12:1-15). The outcome was the accession of Jeroboam, one of Solomon's officials, as ruler of a separate kingdom to the north. The revolt against Solomon was, in effect, a reaffirmation of the traditional pattern of tribal separatism as against the innovation of hereditary and dynastic kingship. The result was that, while the Davidic dynasty lasted for well over three centuries in Judah, the Northern Kingdom witnessed the rapid rise and fall of petty dynasts, with the army playing a dominant role as in some Latin American countries today. In this situation the old war prophecy continued to flourish while in Judah it was, in effect, "demilitarized" and forced to take different directions.

In describing the rise to power of the Ephraimite Jeroboam ben-Nebat, the historian assigned a role of the greatest importance to a Shiloh prophet named Ahijah who, following the example of Samuel, designated Jeroboam king of the ten tribes (I Kings 11:29-39). After enjoying prophetic support, possibly also from Judah (12:22-24), he was condemned by Ahijah, who also predicted the death of his son who was sick (14:1-16). The same pattern continued with the prophet Jehu ben-Hanani, who first supported and then condemned the equally short-lived dynasty of Baasha (16:1-4, 7, 12-13). Elijah, Elisha, Micaiah, and others were, in different ways and to different degrees, in conflict with the Omrids. They predicted their collapse and were even involved in the coup that brought their dynasty to an end and Jehu to the throne (I Kings 20:33-43; 21:19, 21-24; 22:28; II Kings 1:6; 9:1-10). The history of prophetic involvement is then carried forward by Amos and Hosea, who condemned the dynasty of Jehu and predicted its collapse (Amos 7:9, 11; Hos. 1:4-5). While there are clear indications that the Deuteronomic historian has substantially edited these reports—e.g., by extending prophetic predictions to cover the fall of the Northern Kingdom and by emphasizing prophetic opposition to the cult of Bethel and Dan—there can be no doubt that prophetic circles played a major role as brokers of political power in the Northern Kingdom.

With the successful coup of the army commander Omri (ca. 876) an era of relative stability was inaugurated for the first time in half a century. One of Omri's first moves was to found a new capital city, Samaria, though the city of Jezreel at the foot of Mt. Gilboa also served as a royal residence. Peaceful relations with Judah allowed the Omrids to pursue a vigorous policy of expansion to the north and east, a policy which included commercial alliances with the prosperous Phoenician cities. To further these ends Omri arranged a marriage between his son Ahab and Jezebel, daughter of the Tyrian king Ittobaal. A typical *mariage de convenance* of this kind would hardly have merited comment had she not turned out to be a zealous devotee of the Tyrian Baal. Using her position to advantage, she actively promoted the Baal cult during the reign of her husband and their two children, Ahaziah and Jehoram, who succeeded him. Her influence even spread to Judah, where her daughter Athaliah engineered a palace coup and spent the five years of her reign attempting to impose a new political and religious direction on Judah, an attempt which was thwarted by the Temple priesthood.

The partisan point of view of the historian makes it difficult for us to get a correct picture of the religious situation in Israel during the reign of Ahab (ca. 869-850). He gave his children Yahwistic names, supported Yahwistic prophets (I Kings 22:5-12) and, at least initially, showed respect for native Israelite custom (21:1-4). Yet he built sanctuaries in Samaria for the Tyrian Baal and Asherah, the Canaanite mother goddess, staffed by hundreds of male and female ecstatics. He seems to have given his wife a free hand, since we hear of prophets of Yahweh suffering persecution and altars to Yahweh being demolished (18:4, 22, 30; 19:10, 14). Even the majordomo of the court had to act secretly in rescuing prophets of Yahweh from death (18:3-4). The Deuteronomic historian represents the "golden calves" set up at Bethel and Dan as genuine cult objects whose worship implied rejection of the Yahweh cult (I Kings 12:28-30; cf. Ex. 32:1-6). More probably, however, the bull icon served as a pedestal for Yahweh, and its choice was dictated by the desire to reconcile the surviving Canaanite enclaves to the dynasty. It is also likely that by the time of Ahab much of the population of the kingdom had accommodated the cult of Yahweh to that of the vegetation deities. The arrival of Jezebel, clearly a quite exceptional individual, precipitated a violent struggle between conservative Baalist and Yahwist elements at both ends of the spectrum. It is in this context that the narratives about Elijah have to be read and understood.

The abrupt introduction of Elijah into the chronicles of the kingdoms (I Kings 17:1) suggests that the historian has excerpted stories and legends about this powerful figure from a large deposit of hagiographical material in circulation. The chance reference to "Beersheba which belongs to Judah" (19:3) also suggests that much of this material was written down before the fall of Samaria. The historian has inserted what suited his purpose into his chronicle of kings, adding only comments here and there to bring it into line with his own interpretation of the history.[20] Elijah's role as covenant mediator is therefore stressed in keeping with Deuteronomic views on prophecy, and the Baalist prophets are put to death in keeping with the Deuteronomic law (Deut. 18:20).

Like the *Legends of the Saints,* a good part of the Elijah material belongs to the genre of hagiography. As in other examples of the genre (e.g., Anthony the Hermit, Hanina ben-Dosa, Apollonius of Tyana) certain motifs tend to recur: the saint is fed miraculously by birds (I Kings 17:2-7) or by angels (19:5-8), he controls the weather (17:1), multiplies food (17:8-16), raises the dead to life (17:17-24), levitates (18:12; II Kings 2:1-12, 16) and performs preternatural feats of endurance (I Kings 18:46; 19:8). Legendary elements have certainly played an important part in the growth of this tradition, and yet through the legends an impression of enormous spiritual power still comes to us from that remote time in the past.

The narrative opens with Elijah bringing drought on the land through the curse and then taking refuge outside Ahab's jurisdiction. While his act was designed to emphasize a central religious issue, namely, control of rainfall and therefore of the basis of economic life, it would also have precipitated a political crisis, since a disaster of this magnitude would tend to raise questions about the legitimacy of the dynasty (cf. the three-year drought at the beginning of David's reign, II Sam. 21:1-14). The denouement, with the confrontation on Carmel (I Kings 18:20-40), has undergone considerable editing. The site, a prominent cult center from at least the second millennium, may have changed hands following on treaties between Israel and the Phoenician cities. At any rate, the demolition and rebuilding of the altar to Yahweh (I Kings 18:30) suggest a dispute over ownership of this piece of real estate, since the erection of an altar was a conventional way of staking a claim to disputed territory.[21] The Deuteronomic historian has expanded the episode into a pan-Israelite convocation around an altar built of twelve stones. The occasion was also taken for a little satire at the expense of the Phoenician deity, and the sober prayer of Elijah is contrasted with the orgiastic delirium of the Baalist prophets with their limping dance and self-laceration.[22] The episode ends grimly with more bloodletting and, in due course, the first rain in three years.

In view of this rather complete triumph we are surprised to find that Elijah had subsequently to flee for his life into the Negeb, whence he made a forty-day pilgrimage to Horeb (I Kings 19:1-18). This unexpected juxtaposition may be due to the way originally independent narratives have been arranged, or it may suggest that Elijah's triumph was less complete than the historian gives us to believe. Baalist prophets, in fact, continued to flourish (II Kings 10:19) and it was left to Jehu to exterminate the Baal cult in an unprecedented bloodbath shortly after his seizure of power (ca. 845 B.C.E.). It is also possible that the visit to Horeb served originally as the call and commissioning of Elijah, and that the account of the drought and its termination came from a quite different source and was placed first for dramatic effect.

The editorial expansions to which the Horeb episode has been subjected will help to explain the bewildering variety of interpretations in the commentaries. The main problem is to reconcile the "still, small voice" (NEB: "a low murmuring sound") with the giving of a commission that would lead to bloodshed and destruction. The contrast between wind, earthquake, and fire on the one hand and the quiet voice or sound on the other has also given rise to numerous homiletic variations on a theme, some of them decidedly bizarre. One proposed explanation refers to the contrast between orgiastic and lethargic ecstasy.[23] Another would regard the theophany (I Kings 19:11-13a) as an insertion, the purpose of which is to contrast the primordial theophany at Sinai (Ex. 19:16-19) with indirect revelation addressed to the prophet's inner ear.[24] If this interpolation is bracketed, we have Elijah describing a situation of almost total apostasy and Yahweh, in response, commanding the destruction of unfaithful Israel through Hazael king of Damascus, Jehu the fanatical army commander, and Elisha, all three to be anointed by Elijah.[25] Only a remnant of seven thousand will survive as the nucleus of a new and faithful community. We have here already, in essence, the message of the great prophets of the eighth and seventh centuries who passed the sentence of death on their contemporaries.

Other somewhat different traditions about Elijah set him in opposition to the Omrid dynasty in the manner of Samuel's opposition to Saul. Ahab's attempt to push through a forced sale of a vineyard next to the royal palace at Jezreel was thwarted by the owner's appeal to ancient Israelite legal custom forbidding perpetual alienation of family property (I Kings 21:1-19). Though obviously displeased, Ahab did not, to his credit, insist. Jezebel, however, suborned two ruffians to bring capital charges against Naboth the owner, as a result of which he was executed and his property confiscated by the crown. Typically, Elijah's condemnation of Ahab has been expanded to take in the fall of the dynasty, the fulfillment of which is duly noted at the appropriate point (II Kings 10:10, 17). Ahab's son and successor, Ahaziah, also fell foul of Elijah, being condemned for recourse to foreign gods after suffering an accident at the palace. His death was also interpreted as resulting from the prophet's curse (II Kings 1:2-17).

These traditions, of varying historical, religious, and ethical value, tend to give the impression of a figure who emerges abruptly from nowhere in particular and, after a stormy career, disappears in a flaming chariot into the sky. We have the impression, above all, of a *solitary* figure. This impression may, however, be misleading. Both he and his disciple Elisha are addressed as "father" (II Kings 2:12; 13:14), and the title implies leadership of the prophetic coenobia which he appears to have visited for the last time shortly before his mysterious disappearance from the scene (2:2-12). In this respect he reminds us of Samuel presiding over an ecstatic group in Ramah (I Sam. 19:18-24), a function which did not exclude a wide range of other activities. The chronicles of the Syrian wars waged by the Omrids testify to the political and military roles of the ecstatic prophets, operating either

singly or collectively.[26] Most if not all of these, not excluding Elijah and
Elisha, were probably familiar at first hand with the coenobitic life of
small prophetic communities which engaged in ecstatic exercises and
led an economically very ascetic existence. Like certain peripheral
groups in our own culture, they expressed their rejection of the
dominant urban culture, heavily Canaanized as it was, by a distinctive
attire (cf. II Kings 1:8), simple diet, and physical segregation from the
amenities of city life. While the Nazirites, closely related to the *nᵉbî'îm* as
we have seen, let their hair grow long, others may have shaved their
heads like Buddhist monks.[27] They remind us that prophecy can consist
not just in a commission to speak but in the adoption of a certain style of
living that dramatizes the rejection of what passes for reality in the
society as a whole.[28]

A constant feature of prophecy during this period is association with
warfare and religious crusades. At a certain point in the Syrian wars
Elisha saw, and caused his disciple to see, the mountain full of horses
and fiery chariots (II Kings 6:17). As he lay dying the same prophet was
visited by King Joash, who called out, "My father, my father! The
chariots of Israel and its horsemen!" (13:14), recalling the vision seen
by Elisha when his master was taken up (2:11-12). An ancient poem
describes Yahweh as "charioteer on the clouds" (Ps. 68:5, *rōkēb bā'ᵉrāpôt*,
emended text), a title attributed to Baal in the Ugaritic texts.[29] The
connotation is that of heavenly warrior, lord of chariotry (cf. Ps. 68:18),
consonant with the title "Yahweh of the hosts" which first appeared
during the Philistine wars. These "primitives" of the ninth century B.C.E.
acted under the orders of Yahweh the warrior god. In his anti-Baalist
crusade Jehu was aided by a certain Jonadab ben-Rechab, founder of
the Rechabites (II Kings 10:15-16). Marked by a radical rejection of
Canaanite culture and cult, they lived in tents, refused to engage in
agriculture, and abstained from wine. Two and a half centuries later
Jeremiah recommended them to his countrymen as models of religious
fidelity during the last days of Judean independence (Jer. 35:2-19).
The term "Rechabite" has some relation to "charioteer" and may mean
"devotee of the chariot god" (cf. the Syrian deity Rakkab-el or
Rakkub-el). It is difficult to avoid the suspicion that the connections
between Elijah, Elisha, and the Rechabites may have been closer than
appears. The latter also was known as "father" (Jer. 35:6), and all three
were fanatical Yahwists committed to the destruction of the Baal cult.
That Elijah began and ended his life in the Transjordanian region of
Gilead may also be a significant factor in "locating" him, but if so, we do
not have the means of elucidating it.

The "acts" of other prophetic figures of the ninth century may have been in circulation, but the only one apart from Elijah and Elisha known to us by name is Micaiah ben-Imlah. His confrontation with the mantics of Ahab's court,[30] led by a certain Zedekiah (I Kings 22:1-36), is a classic example of interprophetic conflict. The rulers of the two kingdoms agreed on a campaign to recover Ramoth-Gilead from Syria, but first there had to be confirmation by prophetic oracle. Given the Judean redaction of the narrative, it is not surprising that it was the king of Judah who suggested inquiring of Yahweh and then expressed dissatisfaction with the enthusiastic approval of the court prophets. Under the direction of Zedekiah the court prophets put on an ecstatic performance—the analogy of a pep rally is alluring but deceptive—before the two kings in the plaza by the city gate. Zedekiah himself acted out the promised victory proleptically by putting on iron horns and uttering an oracle of assurance introduced by the standard formula "Thus says Yahweh." Micaiah also foresaw success in the campaign but went on to relate two visions in which he saw the people leaderless on the hills and was admitted to the heavenly court with Yahweh on his throne and the hosts around him. At the request of Yahweh one of his attendants, called simply "the Spirit," offered to deceive the king of Israel into making the wrong decision by becoming a lying spirit in the mouth of his prophets; and so it happened.

This incident is particularly significant for understanding how the problematic aspects of prophecy were handled in Israel. The crucial question was that of resolving conflicting claims to revelation. How discriminate between true and false prophetic claims? This test case juxtaposes two quite different types of prophecy. Theologically, only the prophet who has been admitted to the divine presence can claim a hearing. But since this claim is obviously unverifiable, other criteria were needed. It is not enough to speak in the name of Yahweh, using familiar forms of address, for Zedekiah also did that. It is implied, though not stated, that visions and rational discourse are more authentic expressions than the ecstatic behavior and sympathetic magic of the court prophets. Predictions are also important diagnostically, especially when they can be verified or falsified (i.e., proved true or false) shortly after they have been uttered. But there is also the sense that the onus of proof falls on the prophet who reassures rather than the one whose message contradicts the expectations of the hearers. We shall see later on how this problem of discrimination, the Achilles' heel of prophecy, came to a head during the last days of the monarchy.[31]

The metaphor of fatherhood and sonship current in prophetic groups lies behind the conferring of a double share of Elijah's spirit on Elisha (II Kings 2:9-10) since, according to law, the first son received a double share of the estate by virtue of primogeniture (Deut. 21:17). Following on his call to discipleship (I Kings 19:19-21) Elisha was therefore appointed to succeed Elijah as head of the prophetic communities, a position which was authenticated in their presence by miracles (II Kings 2:13-14, etc.). The call of Elisha was to become something of a paradigm for charismatic succession, since it appears to lie behind the commissioning of the seventy elders (Num. 11) and the succession of Joshua to Moses (Num. 27:15-23; Deut. 34:9). It also served as a model for discipleship in early Christianity.[32] For the rest, the narrative tradition about Elisha has had a long and complex history, its interaction with the Elijah tradition being particularly problematic. It is possible, for example, that some of the miracles of Elisha have been attributed to Elijah,[33] and that the revolutions fomented by Elisha in Samaria and Damascus (II Kings 8:7-15; 9:1-13) were given firmer legitimation by reference back to the more prestigious figure (I Kings 19:15-16). Elisha, from Abel-meholah in the Jordan Valley, is more closely associated with the ecstatic communities, several of which were located in that region. He is, in all respects, a more "primitive" figure, embodying the more destructive forces that could be concentrated in that kind of personality. It was he who, through a prophetic deputy, set in motion the revolution of Jehu with the massacres, unparalleled in Israelite history, that went with it: the same revolution that would later be condemned by Amos and Hosea. Not untypically, he ended his life urging the king to another campaign against Syria and venting his anger at what he considered a less than total dedication to seeing it through (II Kings 13:14-19).

Apart from Elisha's active involvement in the Syrian wars, the Elisha tradition has concentrated on his role as charismatic wonderworker. The core of the narrative is a chain of miracles that exhibit the power transferred to him in his calling. Some are works of healing and resuscitation (II Kings 4:8-37; 5:1-19), one of them posthumous (13:20-21). Others demonstrate control over the forces of nature (2:12-14, 19-22; 4:38-41; 6:1-7), including the multiplication of food (4:1-7, 42-44). Others again would be classified today as examples of clairvoyance and extrasensory perception (6:8-10, 12, 17). There are, finally, what we might call punitive miracles of the kind encountered in the apocryphal gospels (6:18; 2:23-25). Comparison with miracles attributed to other saints—including the Gospel miracles—would reveal certain common structural features that would in turn provide valuable clues to the function and intent of the genre. To pursue these suggestions further would, however, take us away from our main line of inquiry.

Elisha died in the early years of the eighth century, during the reign of Joash (ca. 801-786 B.C.E.). Jeroboam II, the son of Joash, succeeded him and led Israel to a high point of political success and economic prosperity, a situation reflected in the book of Amos. This prophet, who was most probably born while Elisha was still alive, was to pass judgment on the second-from-last representative of the dynasty set up with Elisha's backing. At this point we must break off the story to take it up again in the following chapter.

NOTES

1. *ANET*, 655-656. See Ross, 1-8, for a discussion of the terms *ḥzyn* and *'ddn* used for the intermediaries in this text.

2. See A. Malamat, "A Mari Prophecy and Nathan's Dynastic Oracle," in J. A. Emerton (ed.), *Prophecy: Essays Presented to Georg Fohrer on His Sixty-fifth Birthday*, Berlin: Walter de Gruyter, 1980, 68-82.

3. Discussed by M. Hengel, *Judaism and Hellenism*, Philadelphia: Fortress Press, 1974, I, 184-185.

4. This suggestion of Herrmann calls for a thorough comparison between the social teaching of Israelite sages, with its indubitable contacts with Egyptian wisdom (e.g., Prov. 22:17 to 24:22), and the prophetic demand for social justice.

5. *ANET*, 625, and the note on *maškanum;* cf. Hebrew *miškān,* "tent-shrine."

6. See H. B. Huffmon, "Prophecy in the Ancient Near East," *IDBS*, 699-700.

7. I Sam. 10:5, 10; I Kings 20:35-43; 22:10-12; II Kings 3:15-16.

8. See Lindblom, *Prophecy in Ancient Israel*, 8-12; G. Fohrer, *History of Israelite Religion*, Nashville: Abingdon Press, 1972, 223-229, who makes a clear-cut distinction between nomadic seerdom and ecstatic prophecy.

9. The last phase, *w'lō' yāsāpû,* may be intended to acknowledge that elders were not known subsequently to act ecstatically.

10. See M. Noth, *Numbers, A Commentary,* Philadelphia: Westminster Press, 1968, 87-90; G. von Rad, *Old Testament Theology* II, New York: Harper & Row, 1965, 8-9.

11. The passage in question (Amos 2:11-12) is sometimes understood to be a later insertion, perhaps from a Deuteronomic source, but the arguments do not appear to be decisive; see W. Schmidt, "Die deuteronomistische Redaktion des Amosbuches," *ZAW* 77, 1965, 178-183; H. W. Wolff, *Joel, Amos,* Neukirchen-Vluyn: Neukirchener Verlag, 1967, 137-138, 204-207 (= *Joel and Amos,* Philadelphia: Fortress Press, 1977, 170-171).

12. The date at the beginning (1:3) and the account of Moses' death at the end (34:1, 7-9) of Deuteronomy, both attributed to P, reflect the process by which this book was incorporated into the P-edited narrative of founding events.

13. Y. Kaufmann, *The Religion of Israel from Its Beginnings to the Babylonian*

Exile, tr. and abridged by Moshe Greenberg, New York: Schocken Books, 1972, 227-228; M. Buber, *Moses: The Revelation and the Covenant,* New York: Harper & Brothers, 1958, 162-171.

14. On the oracular character of this tent, see M. Haran, "From Early to Classical Prophecy: Continuity and Change," *VT* 27, 1977, 385-397. He takes I Sam. 2:22b, which refers to the sons of Eli lying with the women who served at the entrance to the tent of meeting (at Shiloh!), to be a P editorial addition. It should be noted that the term *mᵉšārēt,* "minister," is used of Joshua (Ex. 33:11) and Samuel (I Sam. 2:11). It may not be mere coincidence that both are also described as *na'ar.* This term, in addition to the usual meaning "youth," may have stood for "prophetic disciple"; see the curious repetition *uᵉhanna'ar na'ar* (I Sam. 1:24), with reference to Samuel, and *wayyēlek hanna'ar hanna'ar hannābî'* (II Kings 9:4) with reference to one of the "sons of the prophets" commissioned by Elisha to anoint Jehu. The latter may contain a lemma and gloss explaining the unfamiliar usage; cf. *n'rm,* Ugaritic, with the meaning "members of a guild," C. H. Gordon, *Ugaritic Manual,* Rome: Pontifical Biblical Institute, 1955², 297.

15. I Sam. 9:1-10 speaks only of a "man of God," a term that is not used in the rest of the narrative, which speaks of a seer *(rō'eh)* and identifies him with Samuel. The explanatory gloss at v. 9, which would follow more naturally v. 11, is designed to assure Samuel's status as prophet *(nābî').*

16. I Sam. 19:18-24, where the community *(lahᵃqāh* or, more probably, *qᵉhillāh)* was established in Ramah. The place is more specifically designated as Naioth (Qere; cf. Navoth at 20:1), unless this is a common noun; cf. *nāweh,* dwelling, with a cultic sense as in Ex. 15:13; II Sam. 15:25; Jer. 25:30; and Ps. 74:8. If it were a sanctuary, it would be easier to understand why David would seek refuge there, and ecstatics are associated with a sanctuary elsewhere.

17. The phrase "Do whatever your hand finds to do" (I Sam. 10:7) would naturally connote a military exploit, especially in view of his commissioning by Samuel (10:1). His first military exploit appears to have been against the Ammonites rather than the Philistines (11:1-11). The connection could, however, be with the attack on the Philistine garrison (or the assassination of a Philistine commander) at Geba, 13:4 (cf. Gibeah, 10:5, 10), with the ecstatic rapture constituting a parallel tradition to the hewing up of the oxen and sending the parts to all the tribes in 11:6-7.

18. Indirectly, perhaps, also Gen. 3:15 and 9:25-26.

19. We are speaking, of course, of the first redaction of the Deuteronomic history in the last decades of Judah's independence; see especially F. M. Cross, *Canaanite Myth and Hebrew Epic,* 274-285.

20. I Kings 18:18, 31-32, 36-37; 21:20-26; 22:37-53; II Kings 1:17-18.

21. E.g., I Sam. 14:35; Saul builds his first Yahweh altar after winning back territory from the Philistines. In Gen. 12:7-8 and 13:18, Abraham's altars at Shechem, Bethel, and Mamre may be understood in the same sense. For the Carmel altar, see A. Alt, "Das Gottesurteil auf dem Karmel," *Kleine Schriften zur Geschichte des Volkes Israel* II, Munich: C. H. Beck, 1953, 135-149.

22. For the view that the taunt is directed specifically at the Phoenician Baal, see R. de Vaux, *Les Livres des Rois,* Paris: Editions du Cerf, 1958, 13-16, and *The Bible and the Ancient Near East,* 238-251.

23. J. Lindblom, *Prophecy in Ancient Israel,* 49.

24. E. Würthwein, *Proclamation and Presence,* 152-166.

25. II Kings 8:7-15; 9:1-13; I Kings 19:19-21; II Kings 2:9-12. Hazael was designated king by Elisha, and Jehu by one of Elisha's prophetic disciples.

26. I Kings 20:13-22, 28, 35-43; 22:1-28; II Kings 6:8 to 7:20; 8:7-15.

27. Perhaps indicated in the incident of the boys who mocked Elisha because of his shaven head or tonsure and were mauled by bears—a classic case of overreaction (II Kings 2:23-25).

28. Parenthetically, the communal prophecy of this early period provided a model for some of the sects of the late Second Temple period that regarded themselves as the heirs of the prophetic tradition; a model that may help explain some of the more encratic and enthusiastic elements in early Christianity. The ideal of a prophetic fellowship keeping alive the charismatic impulse of the beginnings keeps on emerging throughout Christian history, sometimes assuming forms as strange and bewildering as the "primitives" who looked to Elijah and Elisha for leadership.

29. For the incidence of *rkb 'rpt,* see the glossary in C. H. Gordon, *Ugaritic Manual,* 324.

30. That the king in question is Ahab is assumed by the historian (see v. 39). Ahab, however, is named only once, v. 20, though here LXX and Vulgate have "the king of Israel." Elsewhere MT has "the king of Israel" (17 times), though Jehoshaphat king of Judah is named.

31. See below, p. 187.

32. E.g., Luke 9:57-62 and Acts 1:6-11, where the taking up of Jesus and giving of the Spirit are modeled on the Elijah narrative. (The same vocabulary occurs as in the LXX version in Kingdoms.) The disciples are to be clothed with power and work miracles, reminiscent of the miraculous cloak of Elijah, and it is emphasized that they see Jesus being taken up, as Elisha must see his master, in order to receive the spirit.

33. II Kings 4:1-7; cf. I Kings 17:14-16; II Kings 4:18-37; cf. I Kings 17:17-24.

III

THE PERIOD
OF ASSYRIAN EXPANSION

1. THE INTERNATIONAL SITUATION

ANET, 282-301 (Assyrian royal annals); 532-541 (Assyrian vassal treaties); J. **Bright,** *A History of Israel,* Philadelphia: Westminster Press, 1981[3], 267-309; B. S. **Childs,** *Isaiah and the Assyrian Crisis,* Naperville, Ill.: Alec R. Allenson, 1967; H. **Donner,** *Israel unter den Völkern,* Leiden: E. J. Brill, 1964; "The Beginning of the Assyrian Period of the History of Israel and Judah," in J. H. Hayes and J. M. Miller (eds.), *Israelite and Judaean History,* 415-434; N. K. **Gottwald,** *All the Kingdoms of the Earth,* New York: Harper & Row, 1964, 93-217; S. **Herrmann,** *A History of Israel in Old Testament Times,* Philadelphia: Fortress Press, 1975, 243-262; J. W. **McKay,** *Religion in Judah Under the Assyrians,* Naperville, Ill.: Alec R. Allenson, 1973; M. **Noth,** *The History of Israel,* 253-269; B. **Oded,** "Judah and the Exile," in J. H. Hayes and J. M. Miller (eds.), *Israelite and Judaean History,* 435-458.

During the period covered in the previous chapter, the ninth century B.C.E., the international context of events in Israel and Judah was for the most part restricted to the other states of comparable size in the Syro-Palestinian corridor, and among them Damascus in particular. The Assyrians had begun to impinge on the area under Ashurnasirpal II (884-859) and Shalmaneser III (858-824), but their forward movement had been halted by a rare coalition of these Aramean states, including Israel, at the battle of Karkar on the Orontes (853 B.C.E.). With the accession of Tiglath-pileser III in 745, however, a century of sustained imperial expansion by the Assyrians resulted in the subjugation of the entire area and even, for a time, the occupation of Egypt. This created an entirely new situation for the kingdoms of Israel and Judah, one which was bound to leave an indelible mark on their traditional religious beliefs and cult. It signaled the beginning of the great world empires whose rise and fall is depicted in impressive symbolism by the writers of apocalyptic.[1] Though the implications were not grasped at once, it was to call into question all national cults and local deities, forcing them to come to terms with an entirely new situation at the risk of disappearing from the scene.

The period to be discussed begins a few decades before the accession of Tiglath-pileser and ends with the death of Ashurbanipal about 627 B.C.E., after which point the Assyrian empire rapidly came to an end. As far as the two kingdoms are concerned, it corresponds to the period from the last years of the dynasty of Jehu in the Kingdom of Samaria to the religious reforms of Josiah in Judah. If we speak of it as the age of "classical" prophecy, we must bear in mind the lines of continuity with the past alluded to earlier. To be more specific, the first of the oracles against foreign nations in Amos concerns Damascus and its king Hazael (Amos 1:3-5), who was designated by Elisha (II Kings 8:7-15). The oracle, moreover, condemns Damascus for its barbarous treatment of Gilead, no doubt during campaigns recorded in the history (II Kings 10:32-33). The conventional distinction between "primitive" and "classical" should therefore give rise to some searching questions. To what extent are the differences due to the new situation confronting the two kingdoms from about the middle of the eighth century? Are these differences substantial or due rather to the adoption of different literary expressions and a different mode of transmission? More specifically, why beginning about that time do we have collections of prophetic material rather than biographical and hagiographical narratives about prophetic figures?

Before attempting to answer these questions,[2] we must first briefly sketch the course of events during that fateful period of the eighth and early seventh centuries. Whatever we may think of Max Weber's assertion that the primary concern of the prophets was with foreign politics, in that international affairs constituted the theater of their god's activity,[3] it is at least clear that they cannot be understood apart from these events. In what follows we shall limit ourselves to those movements and events which impinged more or less directly on the kingdoms of Israel and Judah.

After a brief surge forward in the ninth century, the Assyrians experienced a half century of decline during which the Syro-Palestinian states were able to pursue their own policies unmolested. The dynasty founded by Jehu was therefore able to consolidate itself, reaching a high-water mark of political success and economic expansion under Jeroboam II (786-746). In Judah much the same situation obtained during the long reign of Uzziah (783-742).[4] The

assassination of Jeroboam's son and successor Zechariah after less than
a year's reign coincided with the accession of Tiglath-pileser and may
not have been unconnected with it. Thereupon the dynasty came to an
end and there followed in the Northern Kingdom a period of chaos
(745-722) during which five kings ascended the throne, of whom three
were assassinated and another, the last, was deported by the Assyrians.

The accession of the usurper Tiglath-pileser III ushered in a century
of achievement that brought Assyria to the apogee of its power. The
Assyrian success was built on a highly organized standing army which,
unlike the forces put into the field by the smaller powers, did not have
to return home at intervals to sow and bring in the crops. The Assyrians
are not noted for their contribution to literature and the arts. As one
scholar has put it, they have left behind texts remarkable for their
linguistic difficulty and intellectual poverty.[5] In warfare, however, they
were technologically far ahead of anything seen previously, and
especially in the art of siege warfare. They were also the first we know
of to use atrocities against civilian populations as a deliberate
instrument of policy and, in the event of rebellion, mass deportations.
Most important, for the first time in history Tiglath-pileser set up an
imperial administration comprising provinces governed by Assyrian
officials and, especially at the periphery, vassal states bound by treaties
some of which are extant. By these means Assyria managed during the
following century to extend its rule from the Caucasus to the Persian
Gulf and from the Tigris to the Mediterranean.

The "king of the world," as Tiglath-pileser modestly called himself,
began to campaign in North Syria in 738, occupying Hamath and
reducing Damascus and Israel to vassalage. Assyrian annals record that
the kings of these two states, Raṣunnu (Rezin, Isa. 7:1) and Menahem
respectively, were obliged to pay tribute (cf. II Kings 15:19-20). Four
years later he was back campaigning against the Philistine cities,
occupied Gaza, whose king Hanno fled to Egypt, and reached as far as
the Wadi el-'Arish, the traditional boundary with Egypt. During or
shortly after this campaign, probably in the summer of 734, Damascus
and Israel, the latter now ruled by the usurper Pekah (737-732), tried
to force Ahaz of Judah into an anti-Assyrian alliance. When the latter
very understandably demurred, the allies to the north invaded Judah
with the intention of replacing Ahaz with a puppet of their own (II
Kings 16:5; Isa. 7:1 to 8:15; 17:1-6; Hos. 5:8-14; 8:7-10). Against
prophetic advice Ahaz appealed to the Assyrians for help, a fateful
move that was to inaugurate a long period of vassalage. In the following
year Tiglath-pileser annexed Galilee and the upper Transjordan
region, carving out of these regions the provinces of Megiddo and

Gilead respectively. There were the usual deportations, and all that was left was the rump state around the city of Samaria in the Central Highlands. Pekah was assassinated and Hoshea, the last king of Israel, ascended the throne as an Assyrian vassal. By this time Damascus had also been incorporated into the Assyrian imperial system. Sometime after the accession of Shalmaneser V, Hoshea broke his oath of allegiance by conspiring with one of the rival dynasts in Egypt at that time. The outcome of this rash act was the siege and reduction of Samaria, the deportation of over 27,000 of the population and the creation of yet another Assyrian province, that of Samerina (722). Foreign groups were moved in—and continued at later intervals to be moved in (Ezra 4:2, 10; Isa. 7:8b)—to take the place of the deportees, and for all practical purposes the ten tribes disappeared from history.

As noted a moment ago, the outcome of Ahaz' appeal to Tiglath-pileser was that for somewhat more than a century, to the death of Ashurbanipal (627), Judah remained both de jure and de facto an Assyrian vassal. While not always easy to assess in detail, the bearing of this situation on the traditional forms of religious life could not have been positive. Judeans and, later, Jews were not the only ones to discover that subjection to a great empire rarely leaves local cults unchanged. The Assyrian chronicles and vassal treaties assign pride of place to Ashur, principal deity of the imperial pantheon, in whose name the vast conquests around the Near East were undertaken. He was "lord of all lands"; vassal treaties such as bound Judah to the imperial court were made in his name, the vassal assuming "the yoke of Ashur." Assyrian imperial policy with respect to local cults does not appear to have been entirely consistent. There are instances of such cults being dismantled and even, in rarer cases, restored. The Israelite historian, for example, records that after the fall of Samaria the local administration sent for a priest of Yahweh to teach the settlers the law of the land (II Kings 17:24-28), in much the same way as the Persians sent Ezra to teach "the law of the God of heaven" in the Trans-Euphrates province of their empire (Ezra 7). There were also occasions when the Assyrian imperial cult was imposed, though this does not seem to have been the regular practice. All vassals, however, had to support this cult by way of annual tribute.

From the Israelite side, it must have seemed to many that Yahweh had been defeated by Ashur, and that the disasters were due to the abandonment of the native vegetation deities, a situation that is explicitly attested for the period after the fall of Jerusalem (Jer. 44:15-19). At the very least, the tendency to syncretism, already well developed, would have been strengthened; and this is exactly what we find happening. Conversely, the periodic attempts to purify the Yahweh cult and repristinate the tradition attested during this century were inevitably associated with attempts to throw off the yoke of the oppressor and his ubiquitous god.

Shalmaneser V, conqueror of Samaria, died soon after the fall of that city, but the same expansionist policy was pursued by his successor Sargon II (722-705). Shortly after his accession he had to put down a rebellion in Gaza supported by the Egyptians, and eight years later it was the turn of Ashdod, another of the Philistine cities. The annals of his reign inform us that Judah, now ruled by Hezekiah (715-689), took part in this revolt, but with what results we are not told. The biblical historian also suggests that he was involved in rebellion with the Babylonian king Marduk-apla-iddin (Merodach-baladan, II Kings 20:12-19), a move which was also supported by Elamites and Arabs. The accession of Sennacherib in 705, accompanied by prolonged internal disturbances, was the signal for further unrest in the empire. Hezekiah's purification of the cult in the Jerusalem Temple and throughout the country (II Kings 18:1-4; II Chron. 30:14; 31:1), as well as the fortifying of the capital and the securing of its water supply (II Kings 20:20; II Chron. 32:5, 30; Isa. 22:9-11),[6] were almost certainly carried out with a view to profiting by this situation. Sennacherib, however, came out on top and by 701 had reasserted his hold on the Phoenician and Philistine cities, which again had been backed by Egypt, and after reducing those cities of Judah which stood in his way he invested Jerusalem.

At this point the Assyrian annals are quite clear. Shut up in Jerusalem like a bird in a cage, the rest of his country ravaged, Hezekiah had to submit and pay an even heavier tribute. The biblical narrative, however, seems to have conflated two versions of what happened. One of these is in essential agreement with Assyrian records (II Kings 18:13-16), while the other appears to be a rather legendary account of the mysterious annihilation of the Assyrian army investing the city followed soon after by the death of the tyrant (19:35-37). This last, memorialized in Byron's poem about the Assyrian coming down like a wolf on the fold, continues to be the subject of inconclusive debate among biblical scholars. The outcome, however, is tolerably clear: Judah was not, for whatever reason, incorporated into the Assyrian empire, and this fact in itself may have given rise to the tradition of a miraculous deliverance. Judah continued to be a vassal state and, despite several attempts, never succeeded in regaining full independence.

Sennacherib lost his life in a palace revolt, not soon after the campaign of 701, as the biblical history suggests (II Kings 19:37), but some twenty years later. He was succeeded by Esarhaddon (680-669), who not only held on to the strategically crucial Syro-Palestinian land bridge, in spite of the occasional rebellion, but even succeeded in conquering Egypt in 671. As for the surviving vassal state of Judah, little is known from that time (701) to the accession of Josiah (640). Among the western vassal kings mentioned in the annals of Esarhaddon is Manasseh, whose long reign (689-642) followed that of his father Hezekiah. The Deuteronomic historian has absolutely nothing good to say about him (II Kings 21:1-18). By undoing the work of his predecessor, reintroducing the chthonic cults, and even setting up altars for the Host of Heaven in the Temple precincts, he incurred responsibility for the exile and deportation that Judah was to suffer less than a half century after his death. It is indeed likely, as suggested earlier, that there was a recrudescence of Canaanite religion during this time of vassalage, and it is also possible, even likely, that Assyrian cults were introduced into the country if they were not there already. But it is not a coincidence that our principal source praises Hezekiah and Josiah, who were active in resisting the Assyrian overlord, and denounces Manasseh, who was not. The Chronicler, however, not generally considered a reliable historical source when he diverges from Kings, records that Manasseh was deported to Babylon and then, after repenting, was allowed to return home (II Chron. 33:10-13). He also informs us that Manasseh went on to strengthen the defenses of his capital and carried out a reform of the cult (33:14-17). These notices are often interpreted as the Chronicler's way of explaining why Manasseh managed to reign so long in apparent defiance of divine retributive justice, whereas Josiah, obviously a good king, came to an untimely and violent end. But the notice about the deportation and the fortification of the city does not look like a fabrication, so that the possibility must be left open that Manasseh actually did rebel, perhaps in support of Shamash-shum-ukin, brother of Ashurbanipal (669-627), who claimed the throne of Babylon in 652.

Of Manasseh's son Amon, who reigned for two years or less (642-640), we know only that he was assassinated as the result of a palace conspiracy and that his assassins were shortly thereafter eliminated by a group known as "the people of the land" who put Amon's eight-year-old son Josiah on the throne (II Kings 21:19-26). We can only speculate as to what instigated these disturbances. It is not unlikely that during Amon's short reign, as during that of his father (II Kings 21:16), violence erupted between those in favor of acquiescing in the status quo and those calling for rebellion. The success of the

Assyrians in suppressing revolt in Babylon and in conquering Elam two years later (646) suggests that the prudent alternative was that of acquiescence. A favorable opportunity would present itself only after the death of Ashurbanipal, with the rapid decline of Assyrian power during the minority of the new king Josiah.

2. AMOS

K. **Budde,** "Zur Text und Auslegung des Buches Amos," *JBL* 43, 1924, 46-131; R. B. **Coote,** *Amos Among the Prophets: Composition and Theology,* Philadelphia: Fortress, 1981; J. F. **Craghan,** "Amos in Recent Literature," *Biblical Theology Bulletin* 2, 1972, 242-261; G. **Farr,** "The Language of Amos, Popular or Cultic?" *VT* 16, 1966, 312-324; F. C. **Fensham,** "Common Trends in Curses of the Near Eastern Treaties and Kudurru-Inscriptions Compared with the Maledictions of Amos and Isaiah," *ZAW* 75, 1963, 155-175; R. **Fey,** *Amos und Jesaja,* Neukirchen-Vluyn: Neukirchener Verlag, 1963; H. **Gese,** "Kleine Beiträge zum Verständnis des Amosbuches," *VT* 12, 1962, 417-438; R. **Gordis,** "The Composition and Structure of Amos," *HTR* 33, 1940, 239-251; H. **Gottlieb,** "Amos und Jerusalem," *VT* 17, 1967, 430-463; W. R. **Harper,** *A Critical and Exegetical Commentary on Amos and Hosea,* Edinburgh: T. & T. Clark, 1905; A. S. **Kapelrud,** *Central Ideas in Amos,* Oslo: Oslo University Press, 1961[2]; K. **Koch,** *The Prophets* I, *The Assyrian Period,* London: SCM Press, 1982, 36-75; S. **Lehming,** "Erwägungen zu Amos," *ZTK* 55, 1958, 145-169; J. L. **Mays,** *Amos, A Commentary,* Philadelphia: Westminster Press, 1969; L. **Monloubon,** "Amos," *SDB* VIII, 1972, 706-724; J. **Morgenstern,** "Amos Studies," *HUCA* 11, 1936, 19-140; 12/13, 1937-38, 1-53; 15, 1940, 59-305; 32, 1961, 295-350; H. **Reventlow,** *Das Amt des Propheten bei Amos,* Göttingen: Vandenhoeck & Ruprecht, 1962; W. H. **Schmidt,** "Die deuteronomistische Redaktion des Amosbuches," *ZAW* 77, 1965, 168-193; L. A. **Sinclair,** "The Courtroom Motif in the Book of Amos," *JBL* 85, 1966, 351-353; J. D. **Smart,** "Amos," *IDB* I, 1962, 116-121; S. L. **Terrien,** "Amos and Wisdom," in B. W. Anderson and W. Harrelson (eds.), *Israel's Prophetic Heritage,* New York: Harper & Row, 1962, 106-114; J. M. **Ward,** *Amos and Isaiah: Prophets of the Word of God,* Nashville: Abingdon Press, 1969; "Amos," *IDBS,* 21-23; J. D. W. **Watts,** *Vision and Prophecy in Amos,* Leiden: E. J. Brill, 1958; H. W. **Wolff,** *Amos the Prophet: The Man and His Background,* Philadelphia: Fortress Press, 1973; *Joel and Amos,* Philadelphia: Fortress Press, 1977; E. **Würthwein,** "Amos-Studien," *ZAW* 62, 1949-50, 10-52.

It has become part of the conventional wisdom to date the beginnings of "classical" prophecy to Amos around the middle of the eighth century B.C.E. As noted earlier, however, this position may lead us to overlook elements of continuity with earlier prophecy and to accept certain presuppositions about the nature of prophecy in general that can be misleading if not actually false. The distinction between "primitive" and "classical," for example, generally goes with a negative evaluation of ecstasy and is meant to prepare for the assertion that genuine prophetic authority rests on the word rather than the manifestations of the spirit. This way of emphasizing the "protestant" character of prophecy, however, fails to take adequate account of evidence for ecstatic experiences among prophets of the eighth to the sixth century and the frequency with which verbal communications are described as rooted in extraordinary personal experience; witness the remarkable opening line, "The words of Amos . . . which he saw *in vision*" (Amos, 1:1; cf. Isa. 1:1; Micah 1:1; Hab. 1:1).

It should also be noted that the impression of a complete break has much to do with the change in literary form from stories about prophets that contain sayings attributed to them to collections of sayings in which the biographical element, where present, is minor and incidental. In the Elijah material, for example, divine communications are introduced by the formula, "The word of Yahweh came to him" (I Kings 17:2, 8; 18:1; 19:9; 21:17, 28). In prophetic books this is transposed into the first person (e.g., Hos. 1:1). When transmitted to others by Elijah, such communications are prefaced with the standard prophetic introduction, "Thus says Yahweh" (I Kings 17:14; 21:19; II Kings 1:4, 6, 16) or the somewhat less common, "as Yahweh the God of Israel lives" (I Kings 17:1; cf. 18:15). On the other hand, biographical "legends" occur in the prophetic books (e.g., Isa. 36-39; Jer. 52; Jonah) and in some cases we have what appear to be parallels, one in the third and the other in the first person, of the same event (Hos. 1:2 to 2:1; 3:1-5; Jer. 7:1-20; 26:1-6). The account of Amos' confrontation with the priest of Bethel (7:10-17) is the only biographical passage in the book, and it will be important for us to consider its relation to the collected sayings and to the Deuteronomic account of the reign of Jeroboam II in II Kings 14:23-29.

The question still awaits an answer why we have collections of sayings attributed to prophets from this point in time or, to put it differently, why we have a Book of Amos and not a Book of Elijah. Perhaps the simplest answer will be that, beginning with the eighth-century prophets, more importance was attributed to what the prophet actually said rather than to what kind of a person he was or what he did. This, in its turn, may have something to do with the fact that, beginning with Amos, the prophets direct their message for the most part to the entire people rather than to an individual; and they do so because of the entirely new situation then coming into existence on the international scene.[7] Once events had run their course and the two kingdoms had been swallowed up by the great empires, attention would once again focus on the person and work of the prophet, a situation that can be observed with respect to Jeremiah, the Isaian Servant, and the Deuteronomic portrait of Moses.[8]

Amos is third (second in LXX) in the Book of the Twelve or *Dodekapropheton,* a collection which was already in existence by the time of Ben Sira in the early second century B.C.E. (Sir. 49:10). The principle of arrangement appears to be chronological, though critical scholarship has found it necessary to revise it in some respects. The juxtaposition of Joel with Amos may be due to the many themes which the two books have in common: a plague of locusts, drought represented as fire, ritual lamentation, the Day of Yahweh, cosmic disturbances, the promise of miraculous fertility. The motto at the beginning of Amos (1:2) also occurs, in a slightly different form, toward the end of Joel (3:16 [MT 4:16]), and it appears that the books have been linked intentionally by the theme of Yahweh's presence in the Temple. These and other indications suggest a Jerusalemite recension of the prophetic books sometime during the period of the Second Temple. And this brings us to the crucial issue of the editorial history of Amos.

The book falls fairly easily into three parts. After the superscription (Amos 1:1) and the motto (1:2) there are eight sayings against various nations, the last being Israel, condemning them for different atrocities and crimes (1:3 to 2:16). The central part of the book contains a collection of mostly short sayings attributed to Amos (3-6) while the last section (7-9) consists in five vision reports (7:1-3, 4-6, 7-9, 8:1-3; 9:1-4) with expansions and interpolations. We shall deal with these briefly in order.

The syntax of the first verse, with its double relative clause, suggests that the phrase "who was among the shepherds of Tekoa" has been inserted into a title which read, "Words of Amos which he saw in vision concerning [or: against] Israel in the days of Uzziah king of Judah and in the days of Jeroboam the son of Joash, king of Israel." This type of introduction, which prefaces other prophetic books (Isaiah, Jeremiah, Hosea, Micah, Zephaniah), is reminiscent of the Deuteronomic historian, especially his practice of synchronizing reigns in the two kingdoms (cf. Hos. 1:1). It will therefore suggest the conclusion that the Deuteronomic school was responsible for a collection of prophetic books, perhaps restricted to those listed above which have this characteristic title.[9] We have already noted the motto (Amos 1:2) which has the effect of deriving the divine judgment pronounced by Amos from the Jerusalem Temple as its ultimate source. Rooted in age-old ritual practice that could be adapted to changing historical circumstances, the condemnations of foreign nations take in a broad circle of Israel's neighbors, which is to say enemies, moving counterclockwise from north to east.[10] It is generally agreed that the sayings against Tyre, Edom, and Judah are later than Amos' day, leaving a series of five ending—in crushing paradox—with Israel itself.[11] The Judah saying (2:4-5) is couched in typical Deuteronomic language, while the other two could have been added—or updated—anytime during the exilic or early Second Temple period (cf. Joel 3:4-8 [MT 4:4-8]). It also seems likely that the historical reproach against Israel (Amos 2:9-12), again reminiscent of well-known Deuteronomic themes, has been inserted between the indictment (2:6-8) and the verdict (2:13-16), which usually come together in Amos.[12]

The opening apostrophe of the sayings source (Amos 3:1-2), of Deuteronomic character, applies the prophet's message to all Israel, not just the northern tribes, and therefore reinforces the point made by the insertion of the anti-Judah saying. The poem about prophetic inspiration (Amos 3:3-8), often taken as evidence of sapiential influence on Amos,[13] has received a very telling Deuteronomic interpolation—the most obvious in the book—at v. 7:

> Surely Yahweh God does nothing,
>   without revealing his secret
>   to his servants the prophets.

The preceding verse,

> Does evil befall a city,
> Unless Yahweh has done it?

could easily have been read as an indictment of Israel's God for actually willing the destruction of Samaria—and indeed also of Jerusalem. The interpolation, therefore, served as an apologia, in keeping with one of the dominant themes of the Deuteronomic history, i.e., that God was not to be held responsible for the disasters that had overtaken the kingdoms since he had warned the people through "his servants the prophets."[14] We may see here the first indication of disquietude at certain aspects of the message of Amos; others will be noted as we read further in the book.

Less certain, though by no means improbable, is the view that one or more of the references to Bethel (Amos 3:14 and especially the gloss "concerning Bethel" at 5:6[15]) reflect the extension of Josiah's reforms into the territory of the Northern Kingdom absorbed into the Assyrian empire (cf. II Kings 23:15-20). If we grant a Deuteronomic redaction of the book at all, this would be predictable. The Deuteronomic historian never tires of condemning the setting up and perpetuation of the apostate cult at Bethel and included a prophetic legend about a man of God who came from Judah during the reign of an earlier Jeroboam to predict its ignominious end (I Kings 13).[16]

The origin of the hymn stanzas or "doxologies" has long been discussed, with most scholars denying them to Amos.[17] It should be noted nevertheless that they aptly fit one of the major themes of the prophet, i.e., that Israel's warrior god, the god of the ecstatic prophets of the earlier period, has now declared war against his own people. The first in particular (Amos 4:13), coming directly after the threatening "prepare to meet your God, O Israel"—referring to a warlike encounter —closes out admirably the preceding five reproaches (4:6-11).[18]

A special problem is posed by the series of three exhortations to seek Yahweh rather than the provincial sanctuaries or, alternatively, to seek good rather than evil (Amos 5:4-5, 6, 14-15). While certainty about their origin is not attainable, they are not easily reconciled with the prospect of irreversible doom that prevails in the sayings as a whole. They seem, rather, to substitute a "perhaps" (v. 15) for the unconditional "no" that Amos addressed to the Kingdom of Israel.[19] The exhortatory and homiletic form, moreover, is much more characteristic of the Deuteronomic style than it is of Amos. The Deuteronomists often enjoin the "seeking" *(drš)* of Yahweh, especially in connection with the cult at the one legitimate sanctuary. It would therefore seem plausible to suggest that here too sayings have been added to the book in response to the new hope for the irredentist northern territories awakened by the religious and political aspirations of Josiah and his men in the late seventh century.[20]

The nucleus of the third part of the book of Amos is the series of five vision reports in the first person. The first two (7:1-3, 4-6), threatening locusts and drought respectively, are constructed in the same way and record the successful intercession of the prophet. The third, the vision of the plumb line (7:7-9), threatens earthquake, the destruction of the high places, and the violent end of the dynasty. At this point the time for intercession has passed, and the last two visions (8:1-3; 9:1-4) presuppose that divine judgment on Israel is now final and irreversible. It is possible, even likely, that the visions formed a separate collection originating with the prophet himself and transmitted by a disciple. They have been expanded here and there,[21] a particularly important case being the prediction of the violent end of the Jehu dynasty, probably added after the coup of Shallum in 745 B.C.E.[22]

The only biographical narrative in the book (7:10-17) has been inserted between the third and the fourth vision. It records how Amaziah, priest-in-charge at Bethel, forwarded to the king an accusation against Amos of conspiracy, based on the prophet's public prediction that Jeroboam would die by the sword and the people would go into exile. In consequence, Amaziah ordered Amos to leave the state sanctuary and find employment in Judah—a surprisingly mild sentence in view of what might have been expected and a testimony to the fear which such individuals were capable of generating. In replying, Amos denied that he was a prophet or a member of a prophetic fraternity, asserted that he had his own occupation which provided the needed support, and informed Amaziah that he had been called by Yahweh to carry out an ad hoc commission to prophesy to the people of Israel.[23] Not content with this, he went on to predict an atrocious fate for Amaziah and his family, assuring him that both he and the whole people were destined to end up in exile.

This passage, of different provenance from that of the sayings and the visions, has been inserted at this point because of the immediately preceding reference to the impending fate of the dynasty (7:9). It has the appearance of having been excerpted from a longer narrative, but any attempt to determine its identity is bound to be speculative. Some scholars have suspected a connection with the confrontation recorded in I Kings 13 between an anonymous Judean prophet and an earlier Jeroboam that also took place at Bethel.[24] It has also been suggested that it may derive from an alternative account of the reign of Jeroboam II which was in circulation before the fixing of the text as we have it in II Kings (MT). It is noticeable that, despite the conventional condemnation passed on all the rulers of the Northern Kingdom ("he did what was evil in the sight of Yahweh," II Kings 14:24), the historian is on the whole favorable to Jeroboam, who saved Israel with the backing of the prophet Jonah ben-Amittai and who, after all, reigned for forty-one years. As pointed out earlier, he goes to the trouble of denying that Yahweh had passed final and complete judgment on Israel (II Kings 14:27), which leaves one wondering whether he had Amos in mind, especially in view of the fact that he passes over his activity in silence.[25] All we can say is that, if the tradition in Amos 7:10-17 was known to the Deuteronomic historian, we can easily conjecture why he passed it over in favor of a different and more benign judgment on this king. There is also the fact, not unimportant in view of the Deuteronomic criteria for true prophecy (Deut. 18:21-22), that Amos' prediction of the violent end of Jeroboam did not come true.[26] In the context of the book as a whole, the passage functions not only to legitimate the mission of Amos but to show what happens when the prophetic message is disregarded.[27]

The fourth and fifth visions have been separated by a supplementary collection of sayings (Amos 8:4-14; 9:7-10) that includes several variants of sayings in the main corpus.[28] The strong saying putting Israelites on the same level in the eyes of God as Nubians and Philistines (Amos 9:7-8) has been quite radically modified by a later editor who, like the author of II Kings 14:27, was not prepared to accept the verdict of unconditional and total destruction ("except that I will not utterly destroy the house of Jacob," v. 8b). The eschatological finale, promising the restoration of the Davidic dynasty, the reintegration of dispersed Israel, and a golden age in which ancient curses would be turned into blessings (Amos 9:11-15), matches the hopes entertained by different circles during the exilic and early Second Temple period and could not have belonged to the book before that time.[29]

Without underestimating the difficulties attending this kind of reconstruction, we can summarize our conclusions as follows. While we do not hear of disciples of Amos, he must have had a support group that preserved his words and some memory of his activities. It was in such a group, during his lifetime or shortly afterward, that the sayings were brought together and the visions recorded. The initial impetus may have been the great earthquake (1:1), which Amos appears to have predicted (see especially 4:11; 6:11; 7:7-8; 8:8; and 9:1). Further editorial activity may well have followed the coup of Shallum in 745 which brought the dynasty to an end. The addition to the third vision ("I will rise against the house of Jeroboam with the sword," 7:9) looks like a revision of the saying of Amos announcing Jeroboam's death by the sword (7:11). Inevitably, the message of Amos would have been applied to Judah after the fall of the Northern Kingdom in 722 B.C.E., and this too has left some traces in the book (6:1, 5). The extension of the reforming activity of Josiah into the territory of the central and northern tribes, and especially his destruction of the cult center at Bethel, are reflected in those editorial editions which bear the hallmark of the Deuteronomic school. We have suggested that the same school, still active during the exilic period, brought out a collection of prophetic material as a kind of supplement to the history, and that an updated version of this was published about the middle of the sixth century B.C.E.[30] At this stage the title was expanded into the typically Deuteronomic form, the oracle against Judah added (Amos 2:4-5), the diatribe against the cult expanded (and its meaning rather radically modified, 5:25-27), and other additions introduced to make the book serviceable for the needs of that age. At the same time, or later, the eschatological finale transformed the grim harbinger of doom into a messenger of hope and a herald of a new age about to dawn (9:11-15).

The book, therefore, has had an editorial history of several centuries, and it is illusory to suppose that we can come by any information on the man and his message without working our way back through that history. The superscription dates his activity to the reigns of Uzziah in Judah (ca. 783-742) and Jeroboam in Israel (ca. 786-746). The additional information that his revelation came to him two years before the earthquake would be helpful if we knew when this earthquake took place. Since it was still being talked about centuries later (Zech. 14:5) it must have been a major catastrophe, and it may be the same one which left its mark on stratum VI at Hazor, dated by pottery finds to the eighth century, more probably the first half of the century.[31] Allusions to historical events in the sayings—especially the invitation to inspect Calneh, Hamath, and Gath (Amos 6:2)—have led some scholars to date his activity after the westward drive of Tiglath-pileser had begun, and therefore after the death of Jeroboam. The historical reference is, however, quite uncertain, and there is the problem that the book in no way reflects the chaotic situation in the Kingdom of Samaria in the decades following the death of Jeroboam. We may therefore date his activity in the north, which was probably quite brief, to about the middle of the eighth century B.C.E.

The expanded form of the superscription describes Amos[32] as one of the sheep breeders of Tekoa, a fortified town about eight miles south of Jerusalem in the Judean wilderness.[33] In the account of his arrest at Bethel he himself describes his profession as tending herds and dressing sycamore fig trees (7:14).[34] As meager and uncertain as it is, this information does not warrant the image, common in popular presentations, of an uneducated rustic visionary. Any interpretation must allow for the knowledge of international affairs, acquaintance with sacred tradition and poetic skill attested by the authentic sayings. On the other hand Amos was not, on his own admission, a "professional" *nābî*, but a private individual who, like certain of the Mari ecstatics, had visions and communicated messages directly or indirectly to the ruler.[35]

The biographical memoir records Amos' mission to the Kingdom of Samaria and arrest in the state sanctuary at Bethel on a charge of sedition (7:10-17). If, as seems likely, Jeroboam's expansionist policy involved him in warfare with Judah, as was the case during the previous reign (II Kings 14:11-15), it would have been natural to interpret Amos' sayings as an attempt by the agent of a hostile power to undermine morale.[36] The command to "prophesy to my people Israel"

(Amos 7:15) probably came to him accompanied by the visions
recorded in the third part of the book (cf. Isa. 6:1-13; Jer. 1:4-19),
though it is impossible to say whether they were spread over a period of
time or occurred in rapid succession, as was the case with Zechariah in
the late sixth century (Zech. 1:7 to 6:15). As we have seen, the first two
threaten disasters, which were averted by prophetic intercession. The
third, the vision of the plumb line, appears to predict the earthquake,
which could no longer be averted, while in the last two Amos could only
look on helplessly as the panorama of destruction by earthquake and
military action, the piles of corpses and the deadly harvesting,
unfolded before his eyes. The sayings of Amos remain incomprehen-
sible unless we assume the absolute certitude of one who has seen it
happen; who, as has been said, walks among people condemned to
death who do not know it.

While the original nucleus of the sayings reveals a remarkable variety
of forms, a constant structural feature, already apparent in the sayings
against foreign nations, is the sequence indictment-verdict, the latter
element generally introduced by the particles "therefore" (lākēn) or
"behold" (hinnēh).[37] Though exact parallels are lacking, there are good
grounds for believing that this presentation has borrowed from the
language of international relations, especially between suzerain and
vassal. The different forms taken by the verdict correspond quite
closely, in any case, to curses incorporated into treaties, with special
reference to the threat of exile in Assyrian vassal treaties.[38] The theme
of calamitous military defeat, occupation by a foreign power, and
eventual exile is taken up into the traditional language of the holy war,
with the difference that the war is now one in which Yahweh takes up
arms against his people (see especially Amos 4:12). In keeping with this
reversal, a point at which Amos decisively parts company with his
prophetic predecessors, the traditional theme of the Day of Yahweh is
turned upside down: not salvation in battle but destruction, not light
but darkness.[39]

Certainly the most remarkable feature of Amos' preaching is this
systematic reversal of the traditional symbols and images that sustained
the common life and self-perception of the political community and
were focused in its cult. It is apparent right from the beginning with the
inclusion of Israel among the nations that fall under the curse, a move
that not only distorts the sense of a traditional oracle of salvation but
prepares for the climactic annulment of Israel's special status:

> "Are you not like the Ethiopians to me,
> O people of Israel?" says Yahweh.

"Did I not bring up Israel from the land of Egypt,
 and the Philistines from Caphtor and the Syrians from Kir?
Behold, the eyes of Yahweh God are upon the sinful kingdom,
 and I will destroy it from the surface of the ground."

(Amos 9:7-8a)

It was only logical that the same reversal of expectations would be applied to the cult, especially the great fall festival of the ingathering, with the prospect of disaster taking the place of salvation and mourning that of joy.[40] One of the most astonishing aspects of the book is the presentation of worship as the expression of a radically sinful way of life (Amos 4:4-5). The entire apparatus of festivals, sacrifice, religious music, and tithing is rejected as hateful to Yahweh (5:21-24),[41] a rejection that will be repeated often in the prophetic books (e.g., Hos. 6:6; 8:13; Isa. 1:10-17; Jer. 6:20). Much of the critical discussion of these passages has been clouded by denominational assumptions about what are thought to be appropriate or inappropriate forms of *Christian* worship. Yet it is simply inconceivable that Amos rejected worship as such in favor of a purely spiritual and ethical religion. The point is rather that for his contemporaries, as he believed, worship had become a way of validating their own values and assumptions. The cult, moreover, was the means of keeping alive the historical memories and sustaining (through the laws whose recital was part of the cult) the moral values that constituted them as a community with certain definite characteristics and goals. Amos was convinced that it was no longer serving this purpose.

The justification for the death sentence passed on the society by Amos is to be found in the accumulated indictments on which the case for the prosecution is built.[42] Amos is speaking as a layman affronted by the negligence and indifference of the priests and Temple personnel, a provincial who detests the life-style of the idle rich in the capital (Amos 3:15; 4:1-3; 6:1-7), a conservative who sees the old order passing away. While this particular perspective is limiting and in some respects distorting, it was not without a basis in the social realities of that time. Increasing centralization, the need to subsidize a royal court and an elaborate cult, heavy taxation ("exactions of wheat," 5:11) that forced many farmers off their lands, large estates with absentee landlords, military service, and forced labor were the major factors undermining the old order. The great expansion of trade with the Phoenician cities and the wealth confiscated during successful military campaigns brought about a new prosperity which did not trickle down to the lower social levels.[43] In this situation Amos, like Hesiod a little over half a century later, took up the cause of the dispossessed and excluded, and did so in the name of traditional values.

It is still necessary to insist that for the prophets the sphere of morality is the social and political domain, and therefore includes what for us falls under international law, social justice, and civil rights. Amos is much less concerned than Hosea with forms of worship—he mentions apostate cults only once (8:14)—and much more concerned to excoriate a violent, oppressive, and exploitative society. He also itemizes: selling into slavery for trivial debts (2:6; 8:6), excessive fines (2:8), falsifying weights and measures (8:5), dishonest trade practices (8:6), corrupting the legal process (2:7; 5:10, 12), and so on. These accusations are not random, or based simply on his own ethical perceptions. It can be shown that they correspond in most cases with stipulations of the so-called Covenant Code (Ex. 20:23 to 23:19) and therefore cohere in an ideal of a society willed by God to be just and righteous. One example will suffice. The refusal to return a pawned cloak to a poor man by evening (Amos 2:8) violates a precise stipulation of law, one of several in the code designed to protect the disadvantaged:

> If ever you take your neighbor's garment in pledge, you shall restore it to him before the sun goes down; for that is his only covering, it is his mantle for his body; in what else shall he sleep? And if he cries to me, I will hear, for I am compassionate.
>
> (Ex. 22:26-27)

By providing the reason for the verdict, which was to be carried out through natural events (locusts, drought, earthquake), but even more through political events, and specifically the Assyrian campaigns in the west,[44] Amos' indictment laid the basis for a certain understanding of divine action in history that was to be immensely influential but also very problematic.[45] His is only one prophetic voice, and some of the limitations of his vision were already apparent to those who preserved and transmitted his words. But there is no going back on his basic message, that a society which neglects justice and righteousness does not deserve to survive.

3. HOSEA

P. R. **Ackroyd,** "Hosea and Jacob," *VT* 13, 1963, 245-259; F. I. **Andersen** and D. N. **Freedman,** *Hosea: A New Translation with Introduction and Commentary,* Garden City: Doubleday & Co., 1980; E. **Baumann,** " 'Wissen um Gott' bei Hosea als Urform von Theologie?" *EvTh* 15, 1955, 416-425; M. J. **Buss,** *The*

Prophetic Word of Hosea, Berlin: Walter de Gruyter, 1969; J. F. **Craghan,** "The Book of Hosea: A Survey of Recent Literature," *Biblical Theology Bulletin* 1, 1971, 81-100, 145-170; O. **Eissfeldt,** *"Ba'alšamēm* und Jahwe," *ZAW* 57, 1939, 1-31; G. **Fohrer,** *Die symbolischen Handlungen der Propheten,* Zurich: Zwingli Verlag, 1968²; A. **Gelston,** "Kingship in the Book of Hosea," *OTS* 19, 1974, 71-85; J. **Gray,** *The KRT-Text in the Literature of Ras Shamra,* Leiden: E. J. Brill, 1964²; *The Legacy of Canaan,* Leiden: E. J. Brill, 1965²; W. R. **Harper,** *A Critical and Exegetical Commentary on Amos and Hosea,* Edinburgh: T. & T. Clark, 1905; E. **Jacob,** "L'Héritage cananéen dans le livre du prophète Osée," *RHPR* 43, 1963, 250-259; A. W. **Jenks,** *The Elohist and North Israelite Traditions,* Missoula, Mont.: Scholars Press, 1977, especially 112-117; A. S. **Kapelrud,** *Baal in the Ras Shamra Texts,* Copenhagen: Gad, 1955; G. A. F. **Knight,** *Hosea: Introduction and Commentary,* London: SCM Press, 1960; K. **Koch,** *The Prophets* I, *The Assyrian Period,* 76-93; C. **van Leeuwen,** *Hosea,* Nijkerk: G. F. Callenbach, 1968; H. G. **May,** "The Fertility Cult in Hosea," *AJSL* 48, 1932, 73-98; J. L. **Mays,** *Hosea, A Commentary,* Philadelphia: Westminster Press, 1969; H. S. **Nyberg,** *Studien zum Hoseabuch,* Uppsala: Almqvist & Wiksell, 1935; H. W. **Robinson,** *The Cross of Hosea,* Philadelphia: Westminster Press, 1949; H. H. **Rowley,** "The Marriage of Hosea," *BJRL* 39, 1956, 200-223 (= *Men of God,* London: Thomas Nelson & Sons, 1963, 66-97); W. **Rudolph,** *Hosea,* Gütersloh: Gütersloher Verlagshaus Gerd Mohn, 1966; M. **Scott,** *The Message of Hosea,* London: S.P.C.K., 1921; J. D. **Smart,** "Hosea," *IDB* II, 648-653; J. A. **Soggin,** "Hosea und die Aussenpolitik Israels," in J. A. Emerton (ed.), *Prophecy,* 131-136; H. **Utzschneider,** *Hosea—Prophet vor dem Ende,* Göttingen: Vandenhoeck & Ruprecht, 1980; J. M. **Ward,** *Hosea: A Theological Commentary,* New York: Harper & Row, 1966; "The Message of the Prophet Hosea," *Int* 23, 1969, 387-407; "Hosea," *IDBS,* 421-422; H. W. **Wolff,** " 'Wissen um Gott' bei Hosea als Urform der Theologie," *EvTh* 12, 1952-53, 533-554; "Hoseas geistige Heimat," *TLZ* 91, 1956, 83-94; *Dodekapropheton 1: Hosea,* Neukirchen-Vluyn: Neukirchener Verlag, 1965² (= *Hosea,* Philadelphia: Fortress Press, 1974); *Die Hochzeit der Hure,* Munich: Chr. Kaiser Verlag, 1979; T. **Worden,** "The Literary Influence of the Ugaritic Fertility Myth on the Old Testament," *VT* 3, 1953, 273-297.

The title of Hosea is similar to that of Amos, but with the addition of the three Judean kings Jotham, Ahaz, and Hezekiah (Hos. 1:1). This would imply that the prophet's public activity spanned a period of more than thirty years, from before the death of Jeroboam II (ca. 746) to after the accession of Hezekiah (ca. 715), and therefore after the fall of Samaria (722). But according to the Deuteronomic historian, Hezekiah came to the throne during the reign of the last king of Israel, who happened to have the same name as the prophet (Hoshea ben-Elah, II Kings 18:1). Since there are good reasons for doubting this synchrony,[46] and since nothing in the book suggests that Hosea commented on this event, we should date his activity from about the middle of the eighth century to the effective end of the reign of his namesake in 724 B.C.E. He was therefore a contemporary of Amos but his public activity lasted much longer.

Uncertain as most of them are, the historical references in the book support, or at least are not inconsistent with, this dating. The early chapters (Hos. 1-3) presuppose a period of political stability, and the condemnation of the Jehu dynasty (1:4-5) would most naturally be understood as preceding the coup of Shallum in 745 B.C.E. The frequent denunciations of the monarchy and of those who "devour their rulers" (7:7) in the rest of the book fit the last quarter century of the Northern Kingdom, during which four out of six kings were assassinated. The allusion to Ephraim going to Assyria (5:13) may refer to the submission of Menahem (II Kings 15:19-20), or possibly that of Hoshea (II Kings 17:3), and there is also a reference to overtures in the direction of Egypt (Hos. 7:11; cf. 9:3; 11:5; 12:1 [MT 12:2]), a standard response to danger from the north. It seems likely that the long passage 5:8 to 6:6 reflects the fateful events of 734-733 B.C.E., when Israel and Damascus attempted to force Judah into an anti-Assyrian coalition, resulting in Ahaz of Judah calling in the Assyrians and, in consequence, the extension of Tiglath-pileser's empire into Damascus and the northern and eastern regions of the Kingdom of Samaria.[47] The last reference is to the deposition of Hoshea and the end of the monarchy (13:9-11) two or three years before the fall of Samaria and the incorporation of the entire kingdom into the Assyrian empire. Whether that means that Hosea died, or was killed, during the siege of Samaria and the military occupation of the country we do not know.

We have noted more than once how the distinctive character of our sources in the Hebrew Bible can mislead us into a sense of total discontinuity between the first of the canonical prophets and their predecessors. It is therefore particularly necessary to emphasize Hosea's links with a prophetic tradition of opposition to monarchy in the Northern Kingdom represented by Ahijah of Shiloh, Micaiah, Elijah, and no doubt others. His description of the prophets as the instruments by which the divine decree of judgment is carried out (Hos. 6:5) would very naturally refer to these predecessors. Since it follows a passage that probably refers to the disastrous effects of the Syro-Ephraimite war it could also include Amos, whose prediction of disaster was proving only too correct.[48] Elsewhere Hosea quotes an opinion, no doubt shared by many to whom his message was unwelcome, that "the prophet *(nābî')* is a fool, the man of the spirit *('îš hā-rûaḥ)* is mad" (Hos. 9:7), and goes on to state that, nevertheless, the prophet is the watchman *(ṣōpeh)* of Ephraim (9:8).[49] It is clearly an essential part of his own self-image to be within a tradition of chosen intermediaries that has unbroken links with the past:

> I spoke to the prophets;
> it was I who multiplied visions,
> and through the prophets gave parables.
> (Hos. 12:10 [MT 12:11])[50]

It is only in the context of this tradition, assumed by Hosea and those who gave him a hearing, that we can hope to understand what was genuinely new in the message he addressed to his contemporaries.

Discussion of the tradition within which Hosea stood has focused in recent decades on the thesis of Hans Walter Wolff that the prophet was closely associated with Levites in the Northern Kingdom who not only formed part of his support group but took a leading role in transmitting his sayings.[51] This association, Wolff claimed, provides the best explanation of several features of the book that have long been acknowledged: Hosea's concern for the cult and the sacred traditions of the old tribal federation, his opposition to the established priesthood (Hos. 4:4-10), his identification of Moses the Levite as prophet (12:13 [MT 12:14]) and fountainhead of "amphictyonic" prophecy,[52] and the close linguistic and thematic links between the book and Deuteronomy. Wolff does not say that Hosea himself was a Levite but, given his arguments, it is difficult to see how that possibility could be excluded.

While it has the advantage of highlighting several dominant themes in Hosea, Wolff's hypothesis suffers from a severe and possibly fatal weakness arising out of the obscurity which shrouds the early history of the priesthood in Israel. One of the earliest narratives about an individual Levite locates him in Judah (Judg. 17:7), and there are other indications of Levitical connections with that tribe in the early period.[53] The same narrative ends with the Levitical descendants of Moses in charge of the "graven and molten image" (*pesel ûmassēkāh*, Judg. 17:4) at Dan, later to become one of the two principal sanctuaries of the Northern Kingdom. The cult at Shiloh, equally suspect and more explicitly condemned (I Sam. 2:12-17, 27-36; 3:11-14), was also directed, at least in the Deuteronomic historian's view, by Levitical priests (I Sam. 2:27-28). It is therefore questionable to assume that those priests who claimed descent from Moses the Levite (Ex. 2:1) were the bearers of the authentic Yahwistic traditions of the earliest period. It is perhaps unnecessary to add that we have no historically reliable evidence for Levites as minor clergy earlier than the Second Temple. Deuteronomy distinguishes between priests employed at the state sanctuary and those in the towns, but makes no distinction in principle between them with respect to status and prerogatives—they are all Levitical priests (Deut. 18:6-7).[54] The Deuteronomic historian blames Jeroboam for appointing *some* priests who were not of Levitical descent (I Kings 12:31), and it is possible that those who were excluded from employment joined the ranks of the opposition (as Wolff suggests) or emigrated to Judah (as II Chron. 11:14 states). In either case they are never mentioned in Hosea, and those features of the book to which Wolff alludes can be explained without recourse to a Levite hypothesis.[55]

Further clarification of this important issue will be possible only after a more careful look at the contents of Hosea. Like Amos, it contains both biographical and autobiographical passages and ends with the prospect of ultimate salvation. The biographical memoir with which the book opens (Hos. 1:2 to 2:1 [MT 1:2 to 2:3]), presumably written up by a disciple, has its own title, "The beginning of Yahweh's speaking with Hosea," which already suggests a rather long prophetic activity. It has been expanded, sometime after the fall of Samaria, by a statement exempting Judah from the same fate (1:7) and a final note promising reunification of north and south under a Davidic ruler (1:10 to 2:1 [MT 2:1-3]). The brief autobiographical passage dealing with the treatment of an unfaithful wife (3:1-5) has also been expanded, at least by the addition of the phrase "and David their king" (v. 5), more likely by the addition of the entire passage dealing with the reintegration of the tribes under a Davidic ruler (vs. 4-5). Like certain editorial expansions in Amos, these probably reflect the extension of Josiah's activity into the Central Highlands and the north in the last decades of the Assyrian empire. We also assume, as the most probable hypothesis, that the first-person narrative is an alternative version of the biographical memoir, but that it has been subsequently reinterpreted as a sequel to the memoir by the simple expedient of adding the adverb "again" (*'ôd*): "Go *again*, love a woman . . ." (3:1). The effect of this rereading of the text is to bring the prophet's marital vicissitudes—if that is what is being described—more into line with a historical perspective on Yahweh's dealings with Israel, a perspective which is developed elsewhere in the book.[56]

If this reading of the two passages is correct, the allusion to the "children of Israel" (*benê yiśrā'ēl*, Hos. 3:1) has probably suggested the extension of the marital metaphor in the first chapter to include the three named offspring of Hosea's union with the "harlot wife" (1:2). The explanation is provided in the central panel of this triptych (2:2-23 [MT 2:4-25]), which consists in a legal indictment of the *land* of Israel (*'ereṣ*, a feminine noun) represented as an unfaithful wife. The forensic metaphor was particularly appropriate at a time when confederate and vassal treaties were being made and unmade and oaths sworn and foresworn (cf. 6:7; 8:1; 10:4; 12:2 [MT 12:3]). The sustained homiletic style of Hosea, quite different from that of Amos, has also contributed notably to the high cadence of the Deuteronomic school, which also developed Hosea's theme of the broken covenant.[57] At the end of the section there are two editorial expansions, both introduced by the phrase "in that day" *(bayyôm hahû')*, which promise the end of idolatry, freedom from the ravages of wild beasts, fertility, and a secure and permanent relationship between Israel and its God (Hos. 2:16-20, 21-23 [MT 2:18-22, 23-25]). The same reversal from curse to blessing has been noted in Amos and will be seen to be a regular feature of preexilic prophetic books.

From the remainder of the book (Hos. 4-14) it is clear that the process of transmission followed different lines from that of Amos, in part because of the much longer time span of Hosea's activity. These chapters appear to fall into two sections (Hos. 4:1 to 12:1 [MT 12:2]; 12:2 to 14:9), both of them presented as legal indictments of an unfaithful people.[58] The individual "kerygmatic units"[59] are not always easy to distinguish since there are few "lead-in" formulae of the kind that are characteristic of Amos. They appear to be transcriptions of sayings or, more frequently, discourses delivered on different occasions over a period of at least two decades. We have the distinct impression that those who gathered them together aimed at a chronological order, ending with the deposition of Hoshea and the prospect of military occupation (Hos. 13:9-16 [MT 13:9 to 14:1]). In addition, some of the discourses are organized around dominant metaphors such as harlotry (4:11-19) or a heated oven (6:11b to 7:7). The style is remarkably homogeneous with relatively few indications of editorial reworking. Apart from the passage that speaks of the Syro-Ephraimite war (Hos. 5:8 to 6:6), allusions to Judah are cautionary, if not condemnatory (4:15; 5:5; 6:11; 8:14),[60] and may be explained by the overriding need for the Southern Kingdom to learn from the fate of its neighbor to the north. These editorial adjustments may be from disciples of Hosea who went south after the fall of Samaria. It is even possible that they came to the attention of Hezekiah, who was inclined to listen to prophets (II Kings 19:2-7, 20-34; 20:1-19) and whose reforms aimed at preventing Judah from suffering the same fate as its northern neighbor. This, at any rate, would help to explain the connections between Hosea and the development of the Deuteronomic reform movement in the Kingdom of Judah.[61]

Looking back over the process of transmission by which the books of

Amos and Hosea reached their present form, we see that the first collections of sayings and discourses (or sermons) were probably put together during the careers of the prophets. Oral transmission (as opposed to oral composition) probably played a very limited role at this or any later stage; indeed, the generally bad state of the text of Hosea may be due in part to the difficulty of transcribing relatively long discourses delivered over several decades and certainly not always under ideal conditions. Almost inevitably their indictments of the Northern Kingdom would have been applied, with the necessary modifications, to Judah after the disaster of 722 B.C.E. This may have happened as early as Hezekiah, who carried out extensive reforms (II Kings 18:4, 22; II Chron. 29:3 to 31:21) and sponsored literary activity (Prov. 25:1). The revived hope of reunification inspired by Josiah's activity in the north almost a century later (II Kings 23:15-20) gave added impetus to the study of the books and marked an important stage in their editorial history. The publication of a Deuteronomic edition during the Babylonian exile, which has left traces in both books, did not prevent further expansions and glosses during the Second Temple, though these are much less in evidence in Amos and Hosea than in Isaiah and other prophetic collections of Judean origin. We are reminded again that during this entire period there were those who felt authorized not only to reinterpret prophetic sayings in the light of new situations but to incorporate their commentary in the text itself.

Whether they circulated separately or not, the first three chapters of the book comprise a quite distinct unit with its own internal logic. The marriage of Hosea[62] has given rise to more questions and hypotheses than any other passage in Latter Prophets: is it a real event or an allegory, a vision or a metaphor? Were two women involved or only one? If one, was she sexually promiscuous when the prophet married her or did she become so only afterward? If she was not a woman of notorious morals whom the prophet was commanded to "make respectable," was she perhaps a cult prostitute or hierodule or did she engage in this profession at some time after the marriage? Or finally, since one cannot go on indefinitely, was she just one of the many Israelite women who played the role of the hierodule once only before marriage to ensure fertility?[63]

We have already taken one step in the direction of a solution (which can claim nothing more than plausibility) by arguing that the short autobiographical version in Hos. 3:1-3 should be read as originally parallel to 1:2-6, 8-9, a position which makes it possible to use it to elucidate the structure and meaning of the symbolic act. In 3:1-3 Hosea records that he was commanded to love a woman who had a paramour (or, with LXX: who loved evil) and was an adulteress. He did so, paid the marriage price, and laid down conditions under which he agreed to remain with her. In the biographical report he is commanded to take a "wife of harlotry" (*'ēšet z°nûnîm*)[64] to bear him children. He therefore took a certain Gomer bat-Diblaim,[65] who bore him three children to whom he gave names of increasing ill omen. The name of the first, Jezreel (punningly close to Israel), refers back to the bloody coup of Jehu in the city of that name (II Kings 9-10) and forward to the end of the dynasty (II Kings 15:10), and indeed the end of the kingdom. The name of the second, a daughter Lo Ruhama (Not pitied), meant that the period of divine mercy and forgiveness, and therefore of prophetic intercession, had run out. We are reminded of the fateful point in time between the second and third visions of Amos when the word of mercy (*niham YHWH 'al-zō't*, Amos 7:3, 6) is no longer heard:

I will no longer pass by them. (Amos 7:8)

I will no longer have pity on the house of Israel. (Hos. 1:6)

The third child's name, Lo Ammi (Not my people), marked the end of the special relationship established long ago in the wilderness between Yahweh and Moses: "You are not my people and I am not your I AM."[66] Here too we have a transposition of the verdict pronounced by Amos after the last vision, one in which the conviction of being an elect people was based on the exodus from Egypt rather than the theophany in the burning bush: "Are you not like the Ethiopians to me, O people of Israel . . . ?" (Amos 9:7-8).

It is obvious but important to note that these brief narratives contain elements of their own interpretation. Thus, in Hos. 3:1 the love that Hosea is *commanded* to bestow on the woman corresponds to the love of Yahweh for his people whose sin is false worship, and specifically the cult of vegetation deities.[67] As noted earlier, the allusion here to the sons of Israel has probably suggested the extension of the symbolism to the three named children. We would conclude that, although the structure of such symbolic acts strongly suggests a basis in the personal history of Hosea, the children's names constitute a purely literary development. These "children of harlotry" (*yaldê z°nûnîm*, 1:2) are the "alien children" (*bānîm zārîm*, 5:7) whose parents are castigated for dealing faithlessly with Yahweh, that is to say, the present generation of Israelites which has abandoned its ancient commitments. And the principal cause of the alienation, as is apparent from the indictment in 2:2-15 (MT 2:4-17), is the false worship of the vegetation deities.

The referent of the symbolic act, then, is the relationship between Yahweh and Israel established at a certain point in its history. As we read farther in the book, it becomes apparent that for Hosea this took place in the wilderness where Yahweh *found* Israel (Hos. 9:10a; see also 2:14 [MT 2:16]; 11:3-4; 12:9 [MT 12:10]; 13:5-6). It was only later, at the point of entry into the land, that Israel abandoned Yahweh for another partner (Hos. 9:10b; cf. Num. 25:1-18). For the symbolism to really work, therefore, it would be necessary for Hosea to marry a woman who only subsequently "went wrong." The allegory of the unfaithful spouse in Ezek. 16, certainly based on Hos. 1-3, confirms this reading since it presents Yahweh's betrothal to a young girl who only later became a prostitute.[68] It would also be more consonant with the dominant theme of the book to suppose that the prostitution in question was of the cultic variety, a prominent feature of the Baal cult (Hos. 4:12-14). Whatever the state of mind of the priests or laymen who frequented those "holy ones" (*q'děšôt*, 4:14), on which it is hardly necessary to speculate, the practice was intended to reenact the marriage between the fertility deity and his consort and thus ensure the fertility of the fields, the cattle, and the womenfolk. The woman, therefore, whether she existed only as a literary figure or, as seems more likely, as the real wife of the prophet, corresponds to Israel in the phase of its existence which began with the settlement on the land, with all that that entailed.

Following the lead of Elijah, as well as the ecstatic conventicles, the Rechabites, and other groups that rejected any form of cultural accommodation, Hosea presented the religious practices of most of his contemporaries as nothing more or less than a rejection of Yahweh, a form of paganism. In this respect we would have to say that the book is tendentious in its depiction of pagan priests (*k'mārîm*, Hos. 10:5) servicing the state sanctuary, worshipers kissing calves (13:2), and so on.[69] A closer reading of relevant biblical texts, together with the evidence from archaeology[70] and the Ugaritic material, would lead us to a different conclusion. The dominant religion, not only in Israel but in Judah, and not only then but throughout almost all of the history into the period of the Second Temple, was a syncretic blend of the Yahweh cult of the pre-state period with elements of the immemorial vegetation cult involving El, Asherah, Baal, Anath, and other deities of the Syro-Palestinian pantheon. The basic motivation behind this option was not so much an addiction to sexual excess but the need to come to terms with the economic conditions of people, the vast majority of whom worked the land. No defense of this other "religion of Israel" has been allowed to survive, and therefore it is not so easy to see that

Hosea represented a minority position that came to prevail, and that put its stamp on the historical record, only at a much later time.

For Hosea false worship, "turning to other gods" (Hos. 3:1), is at the root of moral failure and social disintegration. But false worship began when Israel abandoned its traditions upon entry into the land (9:10) and passage to monarchy (8:4; 9:15). Hence any prospect of reformation will depend on recovering and reappropriating the traditions of the pre-state period. In Hosea, for the first time, we find the outline of the Hexateuch narrative, if in fragmentary and rudimentary form. He is familiar with one version of the fate of the twin cities by the Dead Sea (Hos. 11:8; cf. Gen. 19:24-29; Deut. 29:23) and the Jacob saga (Hos. 12:3-4, 12 [MT 12:4-5, 13]).[71] The liberation from Egypt under the prophetic leadership of Moses (Hos. 2:15 [MT 2:17]; 11:1; 12:13 [MT 12:14])[72] is for him of unique significance since it, rather than the phenomena of nature, displays the character of the God whom Israel is to worship ("your God from the land of Egypt," 12:9 [MT 12:10]; 13:4). In spite of the "murmurings" (13:5-6), the wilderness period was the time of Israel's innocence and intimacy with its God (2:14 [MT 2:16]; 9:10; 11:3-4; 12:9 [MT 12:10]), and it was there that Yahweh revealed himself as Ehyeh, he who is with his people (1:9). Appeal to these normative events and disclosures implies a drastic relativization of the present sociopolitical structures. In perceiving them for what they were and condemning them, Hosea demonstrated the revolutionary strength of the prophetic movement of the eighth century B.C.E. In his inability to propose an alternative, other than the utopian and unrealistic option of a return to nomadic existence, he demonstrated one of the fundamental weaknesses of Israelite prophecy in general. In the Deuteronomic school, in several (but not all) respects the heir of Hosea, we find the utopianism blended with a realistic appraisal of the realities of institutional living.

Hosea concentrates so much upon false worship ("harlotry," "whoredom") that, unlike Amos, he has relatively little to say about social justice and the civil rights of the disadvantaged. If justice *(mišpāt)* and righteousness *(ṣᵉdāqāh)* are key words for Amos (5:24), Hosea prefers to speak of fidelity *(ḥesed)* and the knowledge of God *(da'at ᵉlōhîm)*, the latter term implying fidelity to the traditions with all that that implied.[73] In the indictment with which the second section of the book begins there is what appears to be an earlier form of the Decalogue (Hos. 4:2; cf. Jer. 7:9), with the perhaps significant omission of the Sabbath precept. This does not necessarily imply that the Decalogue was already there to be quoted, as it were, since it is equally possible that the prophets contributed to its mature formulation as we have it in Deuteronomy (5:6-21).

A similar problem is at hand with Hosea's allusion to a divine covenant *(bᵉrît)* which Israel had broken.[74] It is often said that Hosea's marriage was intended to symbolize the covenant between Yahweh and the people of Israel. This is true at least to the extent that Hosea knew of such a covenant at the beginning of Israel's history and to the extent that much of what he says presupposes it. It is arguable, however, that rather than drawing on a set of traditional formulations associated with such a covenant, Hosea himself contributed significantly to the language and thematic of covenant as we find it in its mature form in Deuteronomy. In view of the frequent making and breaking of treaties at that time (cf. Hos. 10:4 and 12:1 [MT 12:2]), and the parallels with Assyrian vassal treaties alluded to earlier, it would not be surprising if the language of international relations found its place in prophetic teaching at that crucial passage of history. At the same time the metaphor of sexual union represented a real breakthrough in the use of language, opening up new and rich veins of meaning throughout the history of both Judaism and Christianity.

4. ISAIAH OF JERUSALEM

P. R. **Ackroyd**, "Isaiah I-XII: Presentation of a Prophet," *SVT* 29, 1977, 16-48; P. **Auvray**, *Isaïe 1-39*, Paris: J. Gabalda, 1972; H. **Barth**, *Die Jesajaworte in der Josiazeit. Israel und Assur als Thema einer produktiven Neuinterpretation der Jesajaüberlieferung*, Neukirchen-Vluyn: Neukirchener Verlag, 1977; W. H. **Brownlee**, *The Meaning of the Qumran Scrolls for the Bible, with Special Attention to the Book of Isaiah*, New York: Oxford University Press, 1964; M. **Burrows**, *The Dead Sea Scrolls of St. Mark's Monastery* I, New Haven: American Schools of Oriental Research, 1950; B. S. **Childs**, *Isaiah and the Assyrian Crisis*, Naperville, Ill.: Alec R. Allenson, 1967; R. E. **Clements**, *Isaiah and the Deliverance of Jerusalem: A Study of the Interpretation of Prophecy in the Old Testament*, Sheffield: JSOT Press, 1980; W. **Dietrich**, *Jesaja und die Politik*, Munich: Chr. Kaiser Verlag, 1976; G. R. **Driver**, "Linguistic and Textual Problems: Isaiah I-XXXIX," *JTS* 38, 1937, 36-50; "Notes on Isaiah," *BZAW* 77, 1958, 42-48; B. **Duhm**, *Das Buch Jesaia*, Göttingen: Vandenhoeck & Ruprecht, 1968⁵ (first published 1892); J. H. **Eaton**, "The Origin of the Book of Isaiah," *VT* 9, 1959, 138-157; R. **Fey**, *Amos und Jesaja*, Neukirchen-Vluyn: Neukirchener Verlag, 1963; J. **Fichtner**, "Jesaja unter den Weisen," *TLZ* 74, 1949, 75-80; G. **Fohrer**, "The Origin, Composition and Tradition of Isaiah I-XXXIX," *ALUOS* 3, 1961-62, 29-32; *Das Buch Jesaja*, Zurich: Zwingli Verlag, 1966-67²; H. L. **Ginsberg**, "Isaiah in the Light of History," *Conservative Judaism* 22, 1967, 1-18;

G. B. **Gray,** *The Book of Isaiah,* Edinburgh: T. & T. Clark, 1912 (reprint 1947); G. F. **Hasel,** *The Remnant,* Berrien Springs, Mich.: Andrews University Press, 1972; J. H. **Hayes,** "The Tradition of Zion's Inviolability," *JBL* 82, 1963, 419-426; A. S. **Herbert,** *The Book of the Prophet Isaiah, Chapters 1-39,* New York: Cambridge University Press, 1973; H. W. **Hoffmann,** *Die Intention der Verkündigung Jesajas,* Berlin: Walter de Gruyter, 1974; F. **Huber,** *Jahwe, Juda und die anderen Völker beim Propheten Jesaja,* Berlin: Walter de Gruyter, 1976; J. **Jensen,** *The Use of Tôrâ by Isaiah: His Debate with the Wisdom Tradition,* Washington, D.C.: Catholic Biblical Association of America, 1973; D. **Jones,** "The Traditio of the Oracles of Isaiah of Jerusalem," *ZAW* 67, 1955, 226-246; O. **Kaiser,** *Isaiah 1-12, A Commentary,* Philadelphia: Westminster Press, 1972; *Isaiah 13-39, A Commentary,* Philadelphia: Westminster Press, 1974; K. **Koch,** *The Prophets* I, *The Assyrian Period,* 105-156; E. A. **Leslie,** *Isaiah,* Nashville: Abingdon Press, 1963; L. J. **Liebreich,** "The Compilation of the Book of Isaiah," *JQR* 46, 1955-56, 259-277; 47, 1956-57, 114-138; S. **Mowinckel,** "Die Komposition des Jesaiabuches Kap. 1-39," *AcOr* 11, 1933, 267-292; C. R. **North,** "Isaiah," *IDB* II, 731-744; G. **von Rad,** *Old Testament Theology* II, 147-175; R. B. Y. **Scott,** "The Literary Structure of Isaiah's Oracles," in H. H. Rowley (ed.), *Studies in Old Testament Prophecy Presented to T. H. Robinson,* Edinburgh: T. & T. Clark, 1950, 175-186; I. L. **Seeligmann,** *The Septuagint Version of Isaiah,* Leiden: E. J. Brill, 1948; P. W. **Skehan,** "Some Textual Problems in Isaiah," *CBQ* 22, 1960, 47-55; J. **Skinner,** *Book of the Prophet Isaiah,* Cambridge: Cambridge University Press, 1925²; J. A. **Soggin,** *Introduction to the Old Testament,* 255-269; C. C. **Torrey,** "Some Important Editorial Operations in the Book of Isaiah," *JBL* 57, 1938, 109-139; J. **Vermeylen,** *Du Prophète Isaïe à l'apocalyptique,* 2 vols., Paris: J. Gabalda, 1977-78; T. C. **Vriezen,** "Essentials of the Theology of Isaiah," in B. W. Anderson and W. Harrelson (eds.), *Israel's Prophetic Heritage,* 128-146; J. M. **Ward,** *Amos and Isaiah,* Nashville: Abingdon Press, 1969; "Isaiah," *IDBS,* 456-461; J. W. **Whedbee,** *Isaiah and Wisdom,* Nashville: Abingdon Press, 1971; H. **Wildberger,** *Jesaja,* Neukirchen-Vluyn: Neukirchener Verlag, 1978- (3 vols. have appeared thus far, covering chs. 1-39); R. R. **Wilson,** *Prophecy and Society in Ancient Israel,* 213-219, 270-274; J. **Ziegler,** "Die Vorlage der Isaias-Septuaginta (LXX) und die erste Isaias-Rolle von Qumran (1QIsa)," *JBL* 78, 1959, 34-59; W. **Zimmerli,** "Jesaja und Hiskia," in H. Gese and H. P. Rüger (eds.), *Wort und Geschichte. Festschrift für Karl Elliger zum 70. Geburtstag,* Kevelaer: Butzon & Bercker, 1973, 199-208.

The Isaiah scroll, one of the longer units in the Hebrew Bible, comprises prophetic material collected over a period of about half a millennium. While the nucleus of this collection goes back, directly or indirectly, to Isaiah ben-Amoz, to whom the entire book is attributed (1:1), at least two thirds of the text derives from anonymous disciples, seers, scholiasts, and interpreters of either the First or the Second Temple period. From the late eighteenth century, critical readers of the book have known that most of chs. 40-66 cannot be dated earlier than the Babylonian exile, and therefore two centuries after the lifetime of the Jerusalemite prophet. Following Bernhard Duhm (in his commentary published in 1892) most scholars would also argue that 56-66 forms a distinct unit which, even if it includes earlier sayings, dates from the Persian period. But literary analysis has also revealed that the first part of the scroll (1-39) is an aggregate of different compilations, not all of the same age and provenance, and each having its own editorial history prior to its incorporation into the book. Literary analysis alone cannot go beyond a hypothetical reconstruction of the stages by which the book, or a part of it, reached its present form, and so no two attempts will be in entire agreement. But since there is no other way back into the world of Isaiah and his discipleship, the attempt must be made; and we shall see that, while much is uncertain, some conclusions are less uncertain than others.

The discovery of the Qumran Isaiah scroll (1QIsaᵃ), dated on epigraphic grounds to the second century B.C.E., and the Greek translation, of unknown date but probably made about the same time, give us a *terminus ad quem* for its editorial history. Therefore up to that time, or shortly before, exegetical activity could be incorporated in the book itself. Writing in the early second century B.C.E., Jesus ben-Sira was familiar with at least the biographical "legends" in Isa. 36-39 and all or part of Isa. 40-55 (Sir. 48:22-25). The biographical or hagiographical tradition about Isaiah, which goes back to these "legends" incorporated in the scroll and the Deuteronomic history (II Kings 18-20), was taken up and amplified by the Chronicler (II Chron. 32), Ben Sira, Josephus (*Ant.* X.11-35), and the Martyrdom of Isaiah.[75] It made its contribution to the pattern of prophetic biography, which was well developed by the Greco-Roman period and left its mark on the Gospel portrait of Jesus, especially in Luke's Gospel.

This biographical material is the last of several distinct compilations that make up Isa. 1-39. The first (1-12) consists for the most part of judgment on Israel and is followed by sayings directed against several hostile foreign nations (13-23). This leads into a section (24-27) known, since Duhm, as "the Isaian apocalypse," including songs or psalms celebrating the downfall of an unnamed city. There follow sayings pronouncing judgment on Israel (Judah), many of them in the form of woe oracles (28-31). These are then rounded off with miscellaneous poems and prayers dealing with the coming age of judgment and redemption (32-35) which have connections with 40-55, the so-called Second Isaiah of the exilic period.

The biographical "legends" about Isaiah in 36-39 deal with three incidents: his intervention in favor of the king and the beleaguered city during the campaign of Sennacherib in 701 B.C.E. (36-37), oracles delivered to Hezekiah during his sickness (38), and Isaiah's prediction of exile in Babylon delivered during the embassy of Merodach-baladan (39). These have also been incorporated, with some relatively minor differences, into the Deuteronomic history (II Kings 18-20). It seems likely that they were brought into the scroll at a rather late date since they break the connection between 35 and 40-48 which belong together.[76] At the same time, the prediction of exile in Babylon (39:5-7) contrasts well with the promise of return from captivity with which Second Isaiah begins. Whatever the source of these narratives (perhaps the court of Hezekiah where a great deal of writing was going on), they represent a tradition remarkably different from that of the sayings in other sections of the scroll. Only here is Isaiah called a *nābî'* (37:2; 38:1; 39:3) and presented as a miracle worker, somewhat in the manner of Elisha (38:7-8, 21). What is even more significant, he is presented here essentially as an optimistic prophet working closely in tandem with the king. It is probably for this reason that the historian wove this material into his account of Hezekiah's reign while passing over in silence the quite different Isaiah of the sayings collections.[77]

Isaiah's intervention in the Assyrian campaign brought on by Hezekiah's revolt (Isa. 36-37), which must have happened toward the end of his career, has come down to us in more or less parallel versions that have been conflated. One of these describes an Assyrian official's boastful challenge to the king and his ministers, following which Hezekiah went to the Temple and sent a delegation to request Isaiah's intercession, with the result that the prophet gave an oracle of assurance ("Do not fear," 37:6) predicting the retreat and death of Sennacherib (36:1 to 37:7). The other has the Assyrian king himself challenging Hezekiah, who went to the Temple, prayed, and received assurance from Isaiah that his prayer had been heard. This version too ends with an assurance of Assyrian failure backed up with a confirmatory sign which, in the present state of the text, precedes the oracle (37:9-35). The second version gives more prominence to the king, whose prayer averts disaster, and presents the oracle (37:33-35; cf. 37:6-7), or at least its conclusion, in Deuteronomic language (". . . for my own sake and for the sake of my servant David," v. 35). It may represent an exilic expansion of a short narrative in which Isaiah played a sustaining role vis-à-vis Hezekiah comparable to the Mari ecstatics vis-à-vis Zimrilim.[78]

Comparable in some respects is the chronistic account of Isaiah's intervention in the Syro-Ephraimite war thirty-three years earlier (Isa. 7:1-25). Here too the narrative has affinities with the history of the monarchy (II Kings 16:5, 7-9) in describing a critical situation that faced Ahaz, the father of Hezekiah, in 734 B.C.E. with the prospect of invasion by the armies of Damascus and Israel. The prophet's intervention follows the same pattern with an oracle of assurance ("Do not fear," Isa. 7:4) and a sign that the crisis will be resolved within a relatively short period of time (7:10-16; cf. 37:30-32).[79] There are, however, some interesting differences. One is that the fulfillment of the oracle is dependent on the king's faith ("If you will not believe, surely you shall not be established," 7:9b). The other is the role of his child to whom, following Hosea, he gave the symbolic name Shear Yashub ("A remnant will return"). In his company he met the king at the precise place where, thirty-three years later, the Assyrian officials would demand the surrender of the city (7:3; cf. II Kings 18:17). The sign which would assure Ahaz that the prophet was to be trusted was to be the birth of a child called Immanuel (God with us) of a mother cryptically alluded to as the Young Woman (Isa. 7:14). While the symbolic structure would best be satisfied if this child of good omen, like the other two, were Isaiah's (cf. the three children of Hosea), the earliest interpretation appears to have a king in mind who must be none other than Hezekiah, son and heir to Ahaz (8:8), and this identification has been widely accepted.[80] The third child, with the improbable name Maher-shalal-hash-baz (Speed spoil, hasten plunder), presaged the devastation of Damascus and Israel by the Assyrians (8:1-4), which in fact happened during the campaigns of 734-733 B.C.E. The decisive political fact was that Ahaz, against the prophet's advice, invited in the Assyrians to stave off the threat from the Damascus-Samaria axis at the cost of accepting vassal status, a situation that remained unchanged during the following century.

This report, then, like Isa. 36-37, deals with king and prophet at a fateful moment of the nation's history, the beginning of vassalage to Assyria. It has been sandwiched between two first-person narratives (6:1-13; 8:1 to 9:1a [MT 8:1-23a]) in what we must assume is an intentional and meaningful arrangement. The first is dated to the death of Uzziah, which took place sometime between 742 and 735.[81] In exalted language, it describes how Isaiah received a commission in a vision to speak to an unresponsive audience. The structure of the vision-report is almost exactly parallel to that of Micaiah ben-Imlah during the reign of Ahab (I Kings 22:19-23). Yahweh is seated on his throne surrounded by his attendants, the seraphs or "burning ones" (cf. "all the host of heaven," I Kings 22:19). After the chant to Yahweh of the hosts and the purging of guilt (not attested in Micaiah's vision), Yahweh calls for a volunteer to perform a mission, in the one case to deceive Ahab and in the other to harden the hearts and obfuscate the senses of the people.[82] In the earlier narrative the response comes from one of the attendants, called simply "the spirit," *(hārûaḥ)*, who will make use of false prophets to achieve his end, while in Isa. 6 the prophet himself volunteers and is commissioned.

Isaiah's vision, which lives on in the liturgical forms of Kedushah, Trisagion, and Sanctus, has become a classical locus for the study of religious experience (e.g., in Rudolf Otto's influential *The Idea of the Holy*). But if we give due importance to its structural role in the section (the first person/third person/first person unit, Isa. 6:1 to 9:1a) we shall be led to the conclusion that it refers to the rejection of the prophet's message by Ahaz and those who supported his pro-Assyrian policy.[83] In the last section of the unit Isaiah describes the symbolic act of writing and notarizing a deed handing over the territory of Damascus and Samaria to the Assyrians, followed by his cohabiting with "the prophetess"[84] and, in due time, the birth of the child with the ominous name. The force of the act and the name corresponds to that of the Immanuel sign (7:14-16), namely, that the enemies threatening invasion from the north will be discomfited without the need for Judah to bring in the Assyrians. The sequel, however, reflects the actual course of events: subjection to the Assyrians (8:5-8, perhaps from the time of Hezekiah), accusations of sedition and conspiracy leveled at the anti-Assyrian party with which Isaiah was identified (8:11-15), and the retirement of Isaiah and his group into the wings, taking with them a copy of the prophet's sayings against the day of their fulfillment and vindication (8:16 to 9:1a [MT 8:16-23a]).[85]

This central section, dealing with the events of the critical year 734-733, forms the centerpiece of the first collection in the book (Isa. 1-12), which is rounded off with psalms of thanksgiving for salvation *(yᵉšû'āh)* that allow for play on the name Isaiah *(yᵉša'yāhû,* Yahweh is salvation) and thus recall the three children with the names of good omen (12:1-2, 4-6).[86] Since, however, this prose narrative breaks into the poem on the divine anger (5:24-25; 9:8 to 10:4) and a series of sayings about Assyria (5:26-30; 10:5-19, 27b-34), it seems that it has been spliced into a compilation that was already in existence. The entire scroll bears the title Vision of Isaiah, the same term used by the Chronicler for the writings of the prophet (II Chron. 32:32) and probably a familiar one in Jerusalemite cultic circles (cf. Obadiah and Nahum). It has been combined with the standard Deuteronomic superscription listing the reigns during which Isaiah was active and thus indicating a career of between thirty and forty years. The presence of a second title at the beginning of Isa. 2 obliges us to read the first

chapter as a separate small collection of sayings that has been
incorporated into the first of the larger compilations (chs. 1-12) of
which the scroll is composed.

These sayings of Isa. 1, which, for the most part, certainly go back to
Isaiah himself,[87] describe a situation of devastation in Judah overrun by
foreign armies with only Jerusalem intact. Several attempts have been
made to match them with what little we know of the history of the
kingdom during the prophet's career.[88] On the whole, it seems more
likely that they come from the time of the short war with Damascus and
Israel rather than from that of the Assyrian crisis under Hezekiah. The
savage denunciation of the "rulers of Sodom" (Isa. 1:10) is difficult to
reconcile with Isaiah's attitude to Hezekiah in the biographical material
(36-39), and the rejection of the cult would be hard to understand after
the religious reforms carried out in that reign. Besides, one hears clear
echoes of Amos here, not least in the contrast between the sacrificial
cult and the demands of social justice (1:12-17), and this would be more
likely in the early stages of Isaiah's career.[89] The description of the
devastated land, with only Jerusalem holding out, also corresponds
with what we know of events in 734 B.C.E., when the armies of Israel and
Damascus invaded the country and laid siege to the capital (cf. II Kings
16:5-6; Isa. 7:1-2).

The next section (Isa. 2-4) is also reminiscent of Amos in its
condemnation of the ruling classes who "grind the face of the poor"
(3:15) and of the society women of Jerusalem whose life-style reflects a
lack of concern for traditional values (3:16-17, 24-26; cf. Amos 4:1-3).
The great poem on divine judgment (Isa. 2:6-22) restates for the
benefit of Judah the central message of Amos: that the God of Israel
has now abandoned his people and left them at the mercy of history.
The importance of this poem can be gauged by the amount of
exegetical activity that it has occasioned (2:9-11, 17-22), including
expansions and comments of a clearly apocalyptic character.[90] But the
last word is not one of judgment, for the Jerusalemite circles which
preserved and meditated on the words of the prophet have also
enclosed the poem and its accompanying diatribe in the promise of new
life arising out of judgment. The theme of Jerusalem as center of
pilgrimage for the nations with which the section opens, and which is
also found with slight variations at Micah 4:1-5,[91] is matched with a final
word of promise for the exiles at the end (4:2-6), either shortly before
or shortly after their return to the devastated city.[92]

That Isaiah was also familiar with the sayings of Hosea is suggested
by echoes and allusions here and there (e.g., Isa. 9:18; cf. Hos. 7:6), and
it was perhaps Hosea who suggested the theme of the unfaithful sons

(Isa. 1:2-3) and the harlot city (1:21-26). The love song of the vineyard, with its undertones of the fertility cult and vintage festivals (5:1-7), may also have been inspired by Hosea (Hos. 10:1).[93] The series of woes (Isa. 5:8-23) is modeled on those of Amos (Amos 5:7, 18; 6:1, 4) and indicts the upper classes for the same kind of social irresponsibility—sometimes using the same language: the practice of enclosure, bribery, denying the poor their rights, drinking, reveling, and so on. The poem on the divine anger (Isa. 5:24-25; 9:8 [MT 9:7] to 10:4), each of the five stanzas of which ends with the refrain,

> For all that his anger is not turned away,
> and his hand is stretched out still,

is directed against the Kingdom of Samaria and opens with what is very probably an indirect allusion to Amos:

> Yahweh has sent a word against Jacob,
> And it will light upon Israel.
>
> (Isa. 9:8)

The refrain itself,[94] the use of quotations (Isa. 9:9-10; cf. Amos 6:13), the condemnation of social oppression and judicial corruption (Isa. 10:1-2), even what appears to be an allusion to the earthquake (5:25), suggest that Isaiah has taken up where Amos left off and that his intent is to apply the message of his older contemporary to the Kingdom of Judah. Other denunciations of the Northern Kingdom reproduce themes found in the earlier prophet (17:1-6; 28:1-4), and the same criteria by which Israel is judged and found wanting are applied to Judah. This will serve to show once again that prophecy is not explicable purely in terms of personal experience, but requires that we take account of an active prophetic tradition by which events are interpreted and through which the personal experience is mediated.

Isaiah is more explicit than Amos in referring to the Assyrians and the role they were destined to play in Israel's future (Isa. 5:26-30; 10:5-34). It was common practice in antiquity to explain or justify conquest by referring to the anger of the native deities at their negligent or impious devotees. If the historian has reported it correctly, Sennacherib used this argument to justify his campaign against Judah, even claiming to have received an oracle of Yahweh commanding him to destroy that kingdom (II Kings 18:22, 25). Isaiah, for his part, described the Assyrians as an instrument—an ax, a saw, or an overseer's rod—in the hands of Yahweh (Isa. 10:5-19). Adopting familiar mythological themes, he depicted the irresistible hordes descending from the north like a swarm of locusts at the signal to advance (5:26-29; 10:27-34). With the passing of time, however, his attitude hardened, especially after Judah entered into voluntary vassalage to the superpower of that day (10:7-11, 13-19; 14:24-27; 37:6-7, 22-35). We have to remind ourselves that Isaiah was not an intellectual elaborating a political theory or a theology of history but was actively engaged in politics, taking sides and giving advice that was meant to be translated into political action. We may be sure that he was identified with the anti-Assyrian party, which continued to oppose the official policy after Ahaz made his fateful decision. We hear accusations of conspiracy (8:11-15), sarcastic allusions to the plan of Yahweh (as proposed by the prophet, 5:19), and prophetic voices in support of both positions (29:10; 30:10). The replacement of Shebna by Eliakim as majordomo of the palace (22:15-24; cf. II Kings 18:18) may also have been brought about by differences of opinion or policy shifts on the Assyrian issue. It seems reasonable to assume that for the balance of the reign of Ahaz, Isaiah was no longer *persona grata* at the court, even if he did not, as is often alleged, retire from public life (8:1-22).

Ahaz died ca. 715 B.C.E. and an oracle against the Philistines is dated to that year (Isa. 14:28-32) presaging the campaigns against the cities of the Pentapolis waged by Hezekiah (II Kings 18:8).[95] The first years of Hezekiah's reign saw much plotting and scheming between the Philistine cities and Egypt, whose ambitions in Asia were reviving under Shabaka (716-701) of the twenty-fifth or Ethiopian dynasty (see Isa. 18:1 to 19:15). The chronological sequence of events for the first decade of Hezekiah's reign is not well known. In spite of the fact that the Assyrian empire now reached to within a few miles of Jerusalem, Hezekiah conducted an aggressive policy of expansion, attacking Edomites to the south (Isa. 21:11-17; I Chron. 4:42-43) and Philistines to the west. This new nationalism, inspired perhaps by the example of a resurgent Egypt and abetted by a vigorous lobby of sages and prophets at the court (Isa. 29:9-10, 14; 30:10), was evidently dangerous. The sayings that can be plausibly dated to that period (22:1-8, 12-14; 30:8-17) show that Isaiah's main concern was to dissuade the young king from being drawn into an anti-Assyrian alliance that would predictably lead to disaster. In the year 712, Sargon II conducted a successful campaign against the Philistine city of Ashdod (*ANET*, 286) during which the promised help from Egypt did not materialize. Isaiah took the occasion, which certainly had repercussions in Jerusalem, to walk naked through the capital (perhaps accompanied by his followers) to simulate the fate of the Egyptians, and those foolish enough to rely on them, as prisoners of war being led off into captivity (20:1-6). This kind of protest, characteristic of peripheral groups, confirms the impression that during the three decades from the beginning of vassal status under Ahaz to the revolt of Hezekiah, Isaiah and his support group[96] were deprived of power and opposed to official policies. This would help to explain not only the vehemence of his invective (e.g., 28:7-8, directed against priests and prophets) and the counter invective of those whom he attacked (e.g., 28:9-10), but also the remarkably contrasting tone of the biographical narrative in 37-39.

Looking back over the material in Isa. 1-35 that can with probability be traced back to Isaiah and his immediate discipleship,[97] we note again what little interest there is in providing information on the prophet himself. We know his name and that of his father; he was married (perhaps to a prophetess, but we have seen that that is uncertain) with at least two children. We have no indication of his profession prior to his prophetic commission, nor of what he did for a living after that point. Occasional use of scribal literary conventions does not make him a scribe any more than the vision in the Temple (if that is where it took place) makes him a member of the Temple staff.[98] It is even less likely that he was the official historian of that time as the Chronicler (II Chron. 26:22; 32:32) appears to suggest. He was certainly a well-known public figure with access to leading members of the court (22:15-25; cf. II Kings 18:18; 19:2-7) and to the king, at least in times of national crisis. While obviously a well-educated person and a gifted poet, he and his followers (probably a very small group) were actively engaged in political life over a period of at least three decades. While still resolutely opposed to foreign alliances, and especially the Egyptian connection on which Hezekiah set such store (e.g., 30:1-5), Isaiah played a leading role in the resistance to the Assyrians during Sennacherib's campaign of 701 B.C.E. After this point, on which the biographical tradition has focused, we hear no more of him. He must have died later in Hezekiah's reign or in the early years of Manasseh his successor.

While the sayings provide few clues on Isaiah's own perception of his prophetic role, we learn enough to be sure that he saw himself continuing a well-established tradition of prophetic mediation. We have seen that in the early phase of his career he took over from Amos and, to a lesser extent, Hosea, applying their message to the Kingdom of Judah. He was familiar with the tradition of the true prophet silenced and ignored (Isa. 30:10-11; cf. Amos 2:12) and saw it still at work in his own career. There are few if any indications in the genuine sayings of a specifically Judean, as opposed to Ephraimite, understanding of the prophetic function. Such intermediaries can be known as either prophets *(n'bî'îm)* or seers *(hōzim)* (Isa. 29:10; 30:9-10); they are bracketed with priests (28:7; cf. Hos. 4:4-5); they receive their call in the same way, through vision; and they deal in the spoken word (5:24; cf. 9:8 [MT 9:7]).[99] The prophet who stands in this tradition tends to identify optimistic prophets in the service of the court (the speakers of "smooth things," 30:10) with questionable forms of mediation such as divining, soothsaying, and necromancy (2:6; 3:2-3; 8:19) more characteristic of foreign lands (such as Egypt, 19:3). The only mark that might be considered distinctive is the identification of the prophet's message as a form of teaching *(tôrāh,* 5:24; 30:9).[100] It also seems to have been seen in that way by his opponents who satirized him as a pedantic schoolmaster repeating the same lesson over and over again (28:9-10). Isaiah replied in kind: since you are unwilling to learn your lesson from me you will have to learn it from the Assyrians who don't even speak your language (vs. 11-13).

Since Isaiah is presumed to have been a native of Jerusalem (though we are never told this), it has often been concluded that he inherited a religious tradition different in several important respects from that of Ephraimite prophets. The latter drew freely on the memory of the founding events before the occupation of the land, events memorialized in the religious centers of the Joseph tribes, while in Judah and Jerusalem it was the dynastic promise to the Davidites (II Sam. 7) and Yahweh's choice of Jerusalem as his dwelling place (II Sam. 6; etc.) which were of decisive importance. We must bear in mind, however, that Isaiah had a very long career during much of which he was in opposition to the monarchy, the court, and the Jerusalem cult, which by its very nature and constitution was designed to sustain official policies. It was therefore natural, as we have just seen, that he should draw on patterns of prophetic opposition that had developed in the Northern Kingdom during the two centuries of its existence. His interest in the fate of the northern and central tribes, indeed of Israel in the inclusive sense, is also noteworthy, and is reflected in the appellative "house of Jacob" (Isa. 2:5, 6; 8:17; 9:8 [MT 9:7]; 10:20, 21) and the corresponding divine title "the Holy One of Jacob" (29:23).

The use of divine titles in Isaiah is only one indication of the need for caution in making these distinctions between Judean and Ephraimite traditions. By far the most common one is "Yahweh of the hosts" *(YHWH ṣ'bā'ôt)* which almost certainly originated at Shiloh, and therefore among the Joseph tribes, and is first attested during the Philistine wars. While it was firmly established in cultic usage in Jerusalem before the time of Isaiah, it also serves to link Isaiah, and

Amos before him, with the old war prophecy that flourished in the north. The title "the Holy One of Israel," also favored by Isaiah,[101] occurs previously only in the Ephraimite prophet Hosea (Hos. 11:9; perhaps also 11:12 [MT 12:1]), while "the Mighty One (*'abîr*) of Israel" (Isa. 1:24) and "the Rock of Israel" (30:29) are found in practically the same form in the oracle on Joseph in Gen. 49:24. Too much should not be made of these observations, but they at least suggest that the liturgical usage on which Isaiah drew was not as highly distinctive as has sometimes been thought.

Most, if not all, of the exalted language about Jerusalem as the city of the divine presence, the center of world pilgrimage, the inviolable "daughter of Zion," and the like does not go back to Isaiah himself, or even to his immediate discipleship (Isa. 2:2-4; 4:2-6). While Isaiah was probably well aware of such language, and while he never confronted Jerusalem with the absolute threat which the provincial Micah directed at it (Micah 3:12), he does not hesitate to compare it with Sodom (1:10), denounce it as a harlot city (1:21), and hold out the prospect of ruin and destruction (8:5-8, etc.). Only in one saying, probably from the time of Hezekiah's rebellion (31:4-5), does he speak of Yahweh fighting for and protecting his city.[102]

His attitude to the Davidic dynasty is certainly positive, though tempered with political realism, and he never condemns the institution of monarchy as did Hosea during the last decades of the Northern Kingdom. The major difficulty here is to understand how the "royal poems" (9:2-7 [MT 9:1-6]; 11:1-9) fit into the book as a whole and the thinking of Isaiah insofar as we can reconstruct it. The first celebrates the birth of an heir to the throne or the accession of a king as the inauguration of a new era of well-being and peace. The language, found also in psalms that have a similar theme (Ps. 2; 72; 110), embodies an ancient royal titulary and ideology borrowed from Egypt and the Canaanite city-states as early as the United Monarchy. Attempts to identify the "son" have been inconclusive. If it comes from Isaiah himself, one would most naturally think of Hezekiah, whose accession Isaiah may well have greeted, prematurely as it happened, as the beginning of a more hopeful era. Since, however, the actual context (9:1 [MT 8:23]; 9:8-12 [MT 9:7-11]) deals with the fate of the Northern Kingdom, we would be more inclined to assign it to the time of Josiah when hopes for reunification were high.[103] The dating of the second poem is equally problematic. On the basis of its strong thematic affinity with the first of the "Servant Songs" (Isa. 42:1-4), and with those passages which speak of the Davidic scion as "the branch," an exilic origin seems plausible.[104] If this is so, it does not alter the fact that, unlike Hosea, Isaiah himself thought of the monarchy as an institution through which God mediated salvation to his people.

In the last analysis, what is most characteristic of Isaiah is his overwhelming sense of the reality of God. The attribution of holiness to God (the Holy One of Israel, the Holy God) implies not so much ethical character as absolute otherness. The reaction of Isaiah in the vision in which he received his commission illustrates the fact that sin is understood not so much in the act of ethical reflection as rather when the reality of that Other breaks through into consciousness—"Woe is me! For I am lost; for I am a man of unclean lips, and I dwell in the midst of a people of unclean lips" (Isa. 6:5). The activity of God follows from this intuition of his being, and so Isaiah is able to communicate with remarkable immediacy the sense of divine power acting on the world and the reality of judgment. Yahweh has a plan, a purpose, which does not necessarily conform to political feasibility (14:24-27; 28:23-29; 37:26). Isaiah does not believe in *Realpolitik,* since he does not take with ultimate seriousness those who appear to be the movers and shakers in national or international affairs (29:7-8; 31:3). The reason is not that he keeps his private world of religious experience separate from public affairs. On the contrary, the vision which is at the core of the prophet's experience must take over and transform political life, the cost of failure being nothing less than total disaster.

Isaiah makes it clear that the appropriate response to this perception of reality is an attitude of positive and active acceptance or, in other words, faith. He does not try to prove that this will work out well in the life of the individual or the community, but simply states that it is so:

> If you are willing and obedient,
>   you shall eat the good of the land.
>   (Isa. 1:19)

> If you will not believe *(ta'ᵃmînû),*
>   surely you shall not be established *(tē'āmēnû).*
>   (Isa. 7:9)

> In quietness and trust shall be your strength.
>   (Isa. 30:15)

5. MICAH

W. **Beyerlin,** *Die Kulttraditionen Israels in der Verkündigung des Propheten Micha,* Göttingen: Vandenhoeck & Ruprecht, 1959; M. **Collin,** "Recherches sur l'histoire textuelle du prophète Michée," *VT* 21, 1971, 281-297; O. **Eissfeldt,**

The Old Testament: An Introduction, 406-413; A. **George,** "Le Livre de Michée," *SDB* IV, 1952, 1252-1263; H. **Gunkel,** "Der Micha-Schluss," *Zeitschrift für Semitistik und verwandte Gebiete* 2, 1924, 145-178 (= "The Close of Micah: A Prophetic Liturgy," in *What Remains of the Old Testament,* London and New York: Griffin, 1928, 115-149); E. **Hammershaimb,** "Einige Hauptgedanken in der Schrift des Propheten Micha," *ST* 15, 1961, 11-34; P. **Haupt,** "The Book of Micah," *AJSL* 27, 1911, 1-63; K. **Jeppesen,** "New Aspects of Micah Research," *JSOT* 8, 1978, 3-32; J. **Jeremias,** "Die Bedeutung der Gerichtsworte Michas in der Exilzeit," *ZAW* 83, 1971, 330-353; A. S. **Kapelrud,** "Eschatology in the Book of Micah," *VT* 11, 1961, 392-405; K. **Koch,** *The Prophets* I, *The Assyrian Period,* 94-104; T. **Lescow,** "Redaktionsgeschichtliche Analyse von Micha 1-5," *ZAW* 84, 1972, 46-85; E. A. **Leslie,** "Micah the Prophet," *IDB* III, 1962, 369-372; J. L. **Mays,** *Micah, A Commentary,* Philadelphia: Westminster Press, 1976; B. **Renaud,** *Structure et attaches littéraires de Michée IV-V,* Paris: J. Gabalda, 1964; *La Formation du livre de Michée,* Paris: J. Gabalda, 1977; W. **Rudolph,** *Micha-Nahum-Habakkuk-Zephanja,* Gütersloh: Gütersloher Verlagshaus Gerd Mohn, 1975; L. P. **Smith,** "The Book of Micah," *Int* 6, 1952, 210-227; B. **Stade,** "Bemerkungen über das Buch Micha," *ZAW* 1, 1881, 161-172; B. **Vuilleumier,** *Michée, Nahoum, Habacuc, Sophonie,* Neuchâtel: Delachaux et Niestlé, 1971; J. M. **Ward,** "Micah," *IDBS,* 592-593; J. T. **Willis,** "The Structure of the Book of Micah," *SEÅ* 34, 1969, 5-42; H. W. **Wolff,** "Wie verstand Micha von Moreschet sein prophetisches Amt?" *SVT* 29, 1978, 403-417; A. S. **van der Woude,** "Micah in Dispute with the Pseudo-prophets," *VT* 19, 1969, 244-260; "Deutero-Micha: ein Prophet aus Nord-Israel?" *NTT* 25, 1971, 365-378.

The Deuteronomic title to Micah puts him within much the same time span as Isaiah, that is, the second half of the eighth century B.C.E. At the end of the following century it was known that he prophesied the destruction of Jerusalem under Hezekiah (Jer. 26:18), which again makes him a contemporary of Isaiah. The book itself offers few clues to the date of the prophet's activity. The title states that he spoke against Samaria (Micah 1:1), and his prediction of the destruction of that city (1:5-7) must be earlier than 722 B.C.E. The lament over towns in the Lachish area (1:8-16) assumes the reality or prospect of military conquest. It is generally referred to Sennacherib's campaign in 701, during which, as we have seen, Isaiah played a leading role in Jerusalem. This, however, is not the only possibility. One could think, for example, of Sargon II's campaign against the Philistine cities in 712 B.C.E., during which Isaiah walked naked through Jerusalem (cf. Micah 1:8, "For this I will lament and wail; I will go stripped and naked"). Gath, the first town in Micah's list, about six miles as the crow flies from Moresheth-gath, was occupied by the Assyrians during the campaign (*ANET,* 286), which must have made a deep impression in Jerusalem and the Judean countryside.[105] In addition, sayings against Judah in chs. 1-3 would fit quite well the first decade of Hezekiah's reign, though some of them may date from the reign of Ahaz or even earlier.

The possibility of getting at reliable information on Micah himself is diminished by the extraordinarily difficult problems involved in reconstructing the editorial history of the book.[106] The following summary, therefore, can claim to be no more than tentative and provisional. There is broad agreement that the eight or nine sayings in Micah 1-3 go back to Micah himself with only minor editorial expansions and glosses.[107] They are, for the most part, easy to identify on the basis of introductory forms standard in prophetic writings—the call to listen (1:2; 3:1, 9), the woe saying (2:1) and, with notable infrequency, "Thus says Yahweh" (3:5). The second section in the book (chs. 4-5) deals in a cluster of themes encountered in the literature of the exilic and restoration periods: the ascendancy of Jerusalem and divine rule in the city (4:1-8), exile in Babylon and return (4:9-10), the eschatological battle at the gates of Jerusalem (4:11-13), the Davidic ruler (5:2-4 [MT 5:1-3]),[108] and the destruction of idolatry (5:10-15 [MT 5:9-14]).[109] While sayings transmitted from Micah and his disciples may have provided the impetus to this collection (e.g., 5:5-6 [MT 5:4-5], the defeat of Assyria by a coalition of princes), indications of a later time are quite clear. First, if the prediction, central to the book, of the destruction of Jerusalem (3:12) were to have had any effect when quoted at Jeremiah's trial in 609 B.C.E. (Jer. 26:17-19), it could not have been followed then, as it is now, by the glowing prospect of future well-being in 4:1-8. Second, there are the indications that Micah and Isaiah have passed through the hands of the same tradents,[110] and, finally, there is explicit allusion to exile in Babylon and eventual liberation (4:9-10).[111]

The provenance and literary form of the last section (Micah 6-7) have proved much more elusive. The opening indictment *(rîb)* and reproach (6:1-5), strongly reminiscent of Amos and Hosea, may well be from Micah himself or his immediate discipleship. The criticism of animal sacrifice divorced from ethical concern (6:6-8) is in the same prophetic tradition (cf. Amos 5:21-24; Isa. 1:12-17) and should also be attributed to him. The difficulty with the last part of the chapter (6:9-16) has always been the allusion to the statutes of Omri and the deeds of Ahab's house (v. 16), leading some scholars to assign it to a prophet from the Northern Kingdom, perhaps even earlier than Micah.[112] The Deuteronomic historian, however, accuses two Judean kings, Jehoram and Ahaziah, of following the example of the kings of

Israel as the house of Ahab had done (II Kings 8:18, 27). Manasseh is also condemned for following Ahab's example in making an Asherah (II Kings 21:3). There is therefore no reason why a Judean prophet could not address such a reproach to a Judean king, and it is perhaps along these lines that we are to explain Micah's indictment of Lachish for leading Jerusalem into sin by imitating "the transgressions of Israel" (Micah 1:13).[113] The city addressed in this passage is therefore undoubtedly Jerusalem (6:9), and while the form of the accusation is consonant with Deuteronomic rhetoric, it could as well be an example of Deuteronomic dependence on Micah or his disciples as the reverse.[114]

The last chapter is quite different in character and has a distinctly liturgical flavor. It consists of a lament in the first person singular (Micah 7:1-10) with a response in the form of prophecies of well-being (vs. 11-17). This structure, identified in several psalms (e.g., Ps. 60 and 108), suggests the role of the cult prophet in worship.[115] By its nature this kind of material is almost impossible to date, but it is highly unlikely that it was written up before the Persian period and may even be later.

The only biographical information provided by the book is the name—a common one—and the place of origin, Moresheth (1:1) or Moresheth-gath (1:14), a town about twenty miles southwest of Jerusalem near the important administrative and military center of Lachish (Tell ed-Duweir).[116] We therefore at least know that he was a provincial, and this information may help to explain his sharp criticism of the capital (1:5, 9; 3:9-12). Micah is a fierce defender of the rights of the small farmers whose ancestors had been working the same plot of land, distributed and guaranteed by ancient custom (2:5), for centuries. His indictment is therefore directed against the ruling classes in the capital which, in his view, were breaking up the old order and driving the independent farmer off his land. The means were no different from those employed by the bureaucrats and *nouveaux riches* of all ages: enclosure of fields (2:2, 4); foreclosure resulting from unpaid debts (2:2, 9)—literally stripping the clothes off their backs (2:8; cf. Amos 2:8); forced labor (3:10); the falsification of weights and measures (6:11); bribery (3:11); and so on. It must also be borne in mind that the strain of resentment expressed by Micah and others against the endless round of animal sacrifice (6:6) had probably less to do with religious conviction than with the economic burden that it imposed on the agrarian class. No one, in short, not even Amos, equals Micah in protesting the exploitation of the powerless:

> You who hate the good and love the evil,
> who tear the skin from off my people,
>   and their flesh from off their bones;
> who eat the flesh of my people,
>   and flay their skin from off them,
> and break their bones in pieces,
>   and chop them up like meat in a kettle,
>   like flesh in a cauldron.
>
> (Micah 3:2-3)

Aware of the general direction of his diatribe, the more perceptive of the commentators have noted the element of personal involvement in his attack on the perpetrators of social injustice. Several have suggested that he himself belonged to the class of free farmers whose whole way of life was threatened by the irresponsibility and greed of the ruling classes. We can, perhaps, be more specific and suggest that he belonged to those known during the monarchy as "the people of the land" (*'am hā'āreṣ*), that is, independent landowners outside the capital who, typical of this social stratum everywhere, were conservative, traditionalist, and suspicious of the civil and religious bureaucracy that controlled their lives. In the ninth century these people had played a leading role in the overthrow of the Baalist queen Athaliah and the subsequent accession of the Davidite Jehoash (II Kings 11:18-20). About a half century later it was again "the people of the land" who secured the accession of Uzziah after his predecessor had been assassinated in Lachish, whither he had no doubt fled in the hope of finding protection and support (II Kings 14:21). And once again, in 640, they were to play a leading part in punishing the Jerusalemite assassins of Amon and putting the child Josiah on the throne (II Kings 21:24). It is noteworthy that it was "the elders of the land" who, a century later, were able to remember and quote a saying of Micah (Jer. 26:17-19), a circumstance that may be significant for the transmission of his sayings in general.[117]

At a later point[118] we shall suggest that the preaching of Micah contributed either directly or indirectly to the Deuteronomic reform movement in Judah, and that the connection is apparent especially in the Deuteronomic agrarian legislation and the conservative attitude to institutions. The fact that, unlike other prophets, Micah does not attack the monarchy can be explained by the attachment of the *'am hā'āreṣ* to the dynasty, and it links up with the Deuteronomic ideal of a constitutional monarchy (Deut. 17:14-20). Use of the terms "heads" (*rā'šîm*) and "rulers" (*q'ṣînîm*), from the tribal past (Micah 3:1, 9, 11), together with insistence on their responsibility to promote justice (3:1), is only one example of the strong conservatism that fed the reform movement reflected in Deuteronomy.

We can learn something about Micah as prophet from the criticism that he leveled at the professional prophets who supported state policies and were employed in the Jerusalem Temple. Like Amos (Amos 7:12-13, 16; cf. 2:12), he was commanded not to preach that disaster will overtake the kingdom, or that Yahweh's patience has come to an end, or that he (Yahweh) is responsible for such evils as are threatened (Micah 2:6-7).[119] The message of the *n'bî'îm* is quite different. It is one of well-being (*šālôm*, 3:5), meaning that "disgrace will not overtake us" (2:6), and "no evil shall come upon us" (3:11), and the reason is that Yahweh is in our midst (3:11). Thus the *n'bî'îm* expounded the official theology based on the doctrine of the divine election of people, dynasty, and city, a theology that found expression in the Temple cult and generated a high level of confidence and morale.[120] We can perhaps discount Micah's accusations of venality (3:5, 11), which are standard in this kind of polemic, and his linking prophecy (their kind of prophecy) with divination (3:6, 7, 11). His main point was that they were deceiving the people by feeding their need for reassurance and telling them what they wanted to hear (2:11; 3:5). It is clear that Micah wanted nothing to do with this kind of prophecy, and it is highly unlikely that he would even have wished to be known as a *nābî'*.

In contrast to this understanding of the prophetic office he makes a statement, of a kind rare in the prophetic writings, about himself: "but as for me, I am filled with power and justice and strength, to declare to Jacob his transgression and to Israel his sin" (Micah 3:8).[121] The contrast is somewhat parallel to that of Amos when he was silenced by the "religious establishment": "I am no prophet nor a prophet's son; *but* I am a herdsman . . . and Yahweh took me from following the flock, and Yahweh said to me, 'Go, prophesy to my people Israel' " (Amos 7:14-15). In both cases association with the institution of prophecy is disavowed, yet full authorization is claimed for a mission that is essentially the same for both.

Starting out from this avowal, Hans Walter Wolff has argued that Micah was one of the elders of Moresheth who took up the cause of his own constituency, the people who worked the land, with the authorities in Jerusalem on those occasions when the elders of the country towns were summoned to the capital. He therefore does not fit the prophetic profile, has left no account of a calling, hardly ever uses the "standard" messenger form ("thus says Yahweh"), and almost always speaks in his own name rather than that of Yahweh. It is particularly significant, continues Wolff, that when he speaks of "my people" he is not speaking for God, as is almost always the case elsewhere in prophetic writings, but really means his own constituency, the people back home on the land around Moresheth (Micah 2:4, 8, 9; 3:2, 3). It is therefore no surprise that, in contrasting himself with the prophets, he speaks of being "filled with justice," that is, equipped to fight for justice on behalf of the oppressed who have no voice.[122]

Wolff, who has a reputation for probing beneath the anonymity of individual prophetic figures, has made a particularly valuable contribution in his essay to our understanding of Micah and of the canonical prophets in general. If, as he argues, both Micah and Amos held the office of elder, it would be easier to explain several aspects of their teaching, e.g., the use of language related to the old clan wisdom and the distancing from cultic forms and traditions.[123] One aspect that would not be so well explained by means of this hypothesis would be the range of interest manifested in these books. Both prophets condemn Samaria, and Amos ranges much farther afield into the world of international politics. Most important, however—and this is by no means a criticism—we would have to ask whether what Wolff says about Micah is not the case, *mutatis mutandis,* with all of the canonical prophets who define their identity and mission over against the contemporary phenomenon of prophecy. And finally, however diverse their respective origins, the canonical prophets inherit and contribute to a specific prophetic tradition even when, as is generally the case, they do not refer to their predecessors by name.[124]

Micah, or one of his disciples, formulates for his contemporaries the fundamental religious question in order to show how the prophetic word provides the answer (Micah 6:6-8). The question is not one of theological or philosophical understanding but of *doing:* What must I do in order to approach God? In the normative religion of Israel the answer is clear. God can only be approached, which means, in effect, that sin can only be removed, through the sacrificial system: "Without the shedding of blood there is no forgiveness of sins" (Heb. 9:22). Hence the rhetorical questions in ascending hyperbole: Shall I offer burnt offerings, thousands of rams, rivers of oil, even my own son in order to bridge the gap? The answer is communicated through the prophetic message. These are things that *you* choose to do. What *God* demands of you is to fulfill the requirements of justice, be faithful to commitments, and live your life in humble and attentive openness to God. This sentence has rightly been prized as one of the best summaries of the teaching of the great eighth-century prophets. And in no way does it detract from its value that, in its very formulation, it raises but does not solve the crucial issue of the relation between prophecy and institution.

NOTES

1. N. Gottwald, *All the Kingdoms of the Earth*, 94, has even referred to Tiglath-pileser as "the father of Israelite eschatology."

2. See below, pp. 86-88.

3. Max Weber, *The Sociology of Religion*, 51.

4. While the dates of Assyrian rulers will generally have a margin of error of no more than a year or two, the chronology of the kings of Israel and Judah is still subject to debate and dates should be considered approximate; see the options listed in J. H. Hayes and J. M. Miller, *Israelite and Judaean History*, 682-683.

5. Morton Smith in J. A. Garraty and Peter Gay (eds.), *The Columbia History of the World*, New York: Harper & Row, 1972, 153.

6. See *ANET*, 321, for the Siloam inscription, cut after Hezekiah's engineers had completed the tunnel bringing water from the Gihon spring to the pool of Siloam.

7. J. S. Holladay, Jr., "Assyrian Statecraft and the Prophets of Israel," *HTR* 63, 1970, 29-51, argues a connection with the Assyrian practice of holding the entire people rather than the ruler alone responsible for maintaining treaty obligations.

8. See G. von Rad, *Old Testament Theology* II, 273-277, and further discussion below, pp. 157-160, 168.

9. See the remarks of E. Auerbach, "Die grosse Überarbeitung der biblischen Bücher," *SVT* 1, 1953, 8-9, on redactional activity during the exile; and, with reference to Amos, W. H. Schmidt, "Die deuteronomistische Redaktion des Amosbuches," *ZAW* 77, 1965, 168-193. The subject is discussed further below, p. 192.

10. On the cultic background of the sayings against the nations see, in addition to the commentaries, A. Bentzen, "The Ritual Background of Amos i 2 – ii 16," *OTS* 8, 1960, 85-99, and M. Weiss, "The Pattern of the "Execration Texts" in the Prophetic Literature," *IEJ* 19, 1969, 150-157. Other aspects are discussed by M. Fishbane, "The Treaty Background of Amos 1:11 and Related Matters," *JBL* 89, 1970, 313-318; S. M. Paul, "Amos 1,3-2,3, a Concatenous Literary Pattern," *JBL* 90, 1971, 397-403; W. Rudolph, "Die angefochtenen Völkersprüche in Amos 1 und 2," in K.-H. Bernhardt (ed.), *Schalom. Studien zu Glaube und Geschichte Israels. A. Jepsen zum 70. Geburtstag*, Stuttgart: Calwer Verlag, 1971, 45-49 (defends the authenticity of the sayings).

11. The arguments for the later origin of the three are laid out by J. L. Mays, *Amos, A Commentary*, 33-36, 40-42. Corresponding to the five (original) sayings against the nations there are five sayings beginning "Hear [this word]" (Amos 3:1, 13; 4:1; 5:1; 8:4), five reproaches (4:6-11), and five visions; there may also

have been originally a series of five woe sayings (5:7, 18; 6:1, 4); cf. the poem with the fivefold refrain in Isa. 5:24-30 + 9:8 to 10:4, which has definite associations with Amos, and the opening verse of which ("Yahweh has sent a word against Jacob," Isa. 9:8 [MT 9:9]) may refer to the preaching of Amos. See R. Fey, *Amos und Jesaja,* Neukirchen-Vluyn: Neukirchener Verlag, 1963, 89-104.

12. H. W. Wolff, *Joel and Amos,* 168-171, and Schmidt, "Die deuteronomistische Redaktion," 172-174, assign vs. 10-12 to a Deuteronom(ist)ic editor, but the allusion in v. 9 to the destruction of the gigantic Transjordanian Amorites is also a Deuteronomic theme; cf. Deut. 2:10, 20-21.

13. H. W. Wolff, *Amos the Prophet,* 6-16 (= *Amos' geistige Heimat,* Neukirchen-Vluyn: Neukirchener Verlag, 1964, 5-12); S. Terrien, "Amos and Wisdom," in B. W. Anderson and W. Harrelson (eds.), *Israel's Prophetic Heritage,* 106-114; J. L. Crenshaw, "The Influence of the Wise upon Amos," *ZAW* 79, 1969, 42-52.

14. "His servants the prophets" *(ᵃbādāyw hannᵉbîʾîm)* is the standard term for the prophetic succession in Deuteronomic writings (I Kings 14:18; 15:29; 18:36; II Kings 9:7, 36; 10:10; 14:25; 17:13, 23; 21:10; 24:2; Jer. 7:25; 25:4; 26:5; 29:19; 35:15; 44:4).

15. In context, a more appropriate translation of *lamed* than RSV "for Bethel."

16. See below, pp. 186-187.

17. On the "doxologies" (Amos 4:13; 5:8-9; 9:5-6—the term is not entirely appropriate), see, in addition to the commentaries, F. Horst, "Die Doxologien im Amosbuch," *ZAW* 47, 1929, 45-54; J. D. W. Watts, "An Old Hymn Preserved in the Book of Amos," *JNES* 15, 1956, 33-39; J. L. Crenshaw, "Amos and the Theophanic Tradition," *ZAW* 80, 1968, 203-215.

18. G. W. Ramsey, "Amos 4 12—A New Perspective," *JBL* 89, 1970, 187-191, suggests the (implausible) translation, "Prepare to call your gods, O Israel!" On the reproach form in vs. 6-11, see J. Blenkinsopp, "The Prophetic Reproach," *JBL* 90, 1971, 267-278, and on its relation to the covenant, see W. Brueggemann, "Amos IV 9-13 and Israel's Covenant Worship," *VT* 15, 1965, 1-15, following on Reventlow, *Das Amt des Propheten bei Amos,* 120-124.

19. Cf. the account given by F. Hesse, "Amos 5,4-6, 14ff.," *ZAW* 68, 1956, 1-17.

20. See especially Deut. 4:27-31, seeking Yahweh in exile, and Deut. 12:2-7, which enjoins seeking him at the place that he shall choose rather than frequenting the native sanctuaries, which are to be destroyed (cf. 12:30). One should also bear in mind the typically Deuteronomic motivation clause, "that you may live . . ." (Deut. 4:1; etc.).

21. At Amos 8:3 a slight alteration has changed "the female singers of the temple" *(šārôt)* to "the songs of the temple" *(šîrôt),* more in keeping with the proprieties of worship in the Second Temple.

22. The words at 7:9 may have served to correct Amos' prediction of the violent death of Jeroboam (7:11).

23. The interpretation of Amos 7:14 has long been a matter of dispute. There is a strongly represented opinion that the context calls for an affirmative statement by Amos in one of the following senses: *(a)* "I was not a prophet . . . , but now I am"; see especially H. H. Rowley, "Was Amos a Nabi?" in J. Fück (ed.), *Festschrift Otto Eissfeldt,* Halle: Max Niemeyer, 1947, 191-198; *(b)* "Am I not a prophet . . . ?" See especially G. R. Driver, "Amos VII,14," *EvTh* 67, 1955-56, 91-92; P. R. Ackroyd, "Amos VII,14," *EvTh* 68, 1956-57, 94; "A Judgment Narrative Between Kings and Chronicles," in G. W. Coats and B. O. Long (eds.), *Canon and Authority,* 83-84; *(c)* "Certainly I am a prophet . . . ," assuming emphatic *lamed;* S. Cohen, "Amos Was a Navi," *HUCA* 32, 1961, 175-178; H. N. Richardson, "A Critical Note on Amos 7,14," *JBL* 85, 1966, 89; H. Schmid, " 'Nicht Prophet bin ich, noch bin ich Prophetensohn.' Zur Erklärung von Amos 7,14a," *Judaica* 23, 1967, 73. There is also the question whether the nominal sentence (i.e., with the verb understood) should be translated in the past (as Rowley above) or the present, as, e.g., H.-J. Stoebe, "Der Prophet Amos und sein bürgerlicher Beruf," *Wort und Dienst* 5, 1957, 160-181; S. Lehming, "Erwägungen zu Amos," *ZTK* 55, 1958, 145-169; and many of the commentators. See also J. MacCormack, "Amos VII,14," *EvTh* 67, 1955-56, 318; A. H. J. Gunneweg, "Erwägungen zu Amos 7,14," *ZTK* 57, 1960, 1-16. I have assumed that the most natural reading is in the present: "I am not a *nābî',* nor am I a *ben-nābî',* for I am a herdsman and a dresser of sycamore fig trees." The second part of the statement, "Yet Yahweh took me . . . ," does not contradict this. Amos is saying that he received an ad hoc commission even though he was a layman, i.e., not one of those employed and recognized as *neb̂î'îm* (prebendary prophets).

24. See J. L. Crenshaw, *Prophetic Conflict,* Berlin: Walter de Gruyter, 1971, 41-42; P. R. Ackroyd, "A Judgment Narrative," 78-80.

25. See above, p. 47, n. 9, and n. 9 of this chapter.

26. The most interesting recent conjecture on the relation between Amos 7:10-17; II Kings 14:23-29; and I Kings 13 is that of P. R. Ackroyd, "A Judgment Narrative" (see n. 23).

27. H. Schulte, "Amos 7, 15a und die Legitimation des Aussenseiters," in H. W. Wolff (ed.), *Probleme biblischer Theologie, G. von Rad zum 70. Geburtstag,* Munich: Chr. Kaiser, 1971, 462-478; G. M. Tucker, "Prophetic Authenticity: A Form-Critical Study of Amos 7:10-17," *Int* 27, 1973, 423-434.

28. These variants include Amos 8:4 (cf. 2:7; 5:11); 8:6 (cf. 2:6); 8:7 (cf. 4:2; 6:8); 8:8 (cf. 9:5); 8:9 (cf. 5:18); 8:10 (cf. 5:16-17); 8:13-14 (cf. 5:2). As H. W. Wolff, *Joel and Amos,* 325, puts it, "Those who formulated these oracles still had Amos' own words ringing in their ears."

29. See below, p. 192.

30. See above, p. 23.

31. See, most recently, Y. Yadin, "Hazor," in M. Avi-Yonah (ed.), *Encyclopedia of Archaeological Excavations in the Holy Land* II, Jerusalem: Israel Exploration Society & Massada Press, 1976, 485, 495. The more precise date of 760 B.C.E. suggested earlier by Yadin was presumably based on the practice of

several commentators of so dating Amos' ministry and not on the basis of archaeological data; see J. L. Mays, *Amos, A Commentary,* 20.

32. On the name, see J. J. Stamm, "Der Name des Propheten Amos und sein sprachlicher Hintergrund," in J. A. Emerton (ed.), *Prophecy: Essays Presented to Georg Fohrer on His Sixty-fifth Birthday,* Berlin: Walter de Gruyter, 1980, 137-142.

33. The hypothesis of a northern origin for the prophet, while not ruled out by anything in the book, is inadequately supported; see H. Schmidt, *Die Herkunft des Propheten Amos,* Berlin: Walter de Gruyter, 1920, 158-171; S. N. Rosenbaum, "Northern Amos Revisited: Two Philological Suggestions," *Hebrew Studies* 18, 1977, 132-148.

34. The term *bôqēr* (Amos 7:14), though *hapax legomenon,* would most naturally mean one who has the care of cattle or oxen. Its incompatibility with "Yahweh took me from following the flock" (*ṣō'n,* sheep and goats, v. 15) should not be pressed, since this may be a conventional way of describing a call (cf. II Sam. 7:8). In Amos 1:1 he is described as one of the *nōqᵉdîm* of Tekoa. The most probable meaning of this term is still "herdsman" or "sheep rearer," and its only other occurrence in the Hebrew Bible, at II Kings 3:4 with reference to the king of Moab, and its use in a Ugaritic text (*ANET,* 141) in association with priests, do not suggest a lowly social status. Even if Amos did look after livestock destined for sacrifice, as suggested by Kapelrud, *Central Ideas in Amos,* 5-7, this would hardly make him a "cultic official," and no one, to my knowledge, has suggested that dressing sycamore figs was a cultic function. For the meaning of *nōqēd,* see S. Segert, "Zur Bedeutung des Wortes nōqēd," *SVT* 16, 1967, 279-283. The conjecture of M. Bič, "Der Prophet Amos—ein Haepatoskopos," *VT* 1, 1951, 293-296, that *nōqēd* refers to an inspector of livers, was refuted by A. Murtonen, *VT* 2, 1952, 170-171.

35. See above, pp. 56-58.

36. The account of Jeroboam's reign in II Kings 14:23-29 records his success in restoring Israel's boundaries to the north and the east as far as the Dead Sea (cf. Amos 6:13-14, which refers to victories east of the Jordan). While there is no mention of hostilities with Judah, Uzziah was also pursuing an expansionist policy in various directions including the Tranjordanian region (II Chron. 26:6-8), increasing the likelihood of friction. The historian also notes that Jeroboam's campaigns had prophetic support (II Kings 14:25).

37. Amos 2:13; 3:11; 4:12; 5:11, 16; 6:7, 14; 8:11; 9:8, 9.

38. This can be seen especially in the vassal treaties of Esarhaddon, *ANET,* 537-538. It was the prediction of exile which brought Amos to the attention of the authorities (Amos 7:11), but it occurs as a major theme throughout the book (1:5, 15; 4:2-3; 5:27; 6:7; 7:17; 9:4). Another standard form of the curse occurs at 5:11b (cf. 9:14 and Deut. 28:30, 39): "You have built houses of hewn stone but you shall not dwell in them; you have planted pleasant vineyards, but you shall not drink their wine." Also noteworthy in this respect is *pšᶜ* (rebel, rebellion) for "sin" (1:3, 6, 9, 11, 13; 2:1, 4, 6; 3:14; 4:4; 5:12). See D. R. Hillers, "Treaty-Curses and the Old Testament Prophets," *BibOr* 16, 1964, 1-101; F. C.

Fensham, "Common Trends in Curses of the Near Eastern Treaties and kudurru-Inscriptions Compared with the Maledictions of Amos and Isaiah," *ZAW* 75, 1963, 155-175; M. Fishbane, "The Treaty Background of Amos 1:11 and Related Matters," *JBL* 89, 1970, 313-318; J. S. Holladay, "Assyrian Statecraft and the Prophets of Israel," *HTR* 63, 1970, 29-51.

39. For a convenient summary of recent discussion see A. J. Everson, "Day of the Lord," *IDBS*, 209-210, and for an exhaustive analysis see S. J. De Vries, *Yesterday, Today and Tomorrow,* Grand Rapids: Wm. B. Eerdmans Publishing Co., 1975, 55-331. Given the nature of the holy war in ancient Israel, there is no need to choose between a military and a cultic connotation. The war context of Amos 5:18-20, the first passage in the prophetic literature dealing explicitly with the "Day of Yahweh," is supported by 1:14 ("the day of battle") and 2:16 ("on that day," i.e., of defeat in battle).

40. Allusions to the fall and harvesting (Amos 4:9; 5:16-17; 8:1-3), cultic rejoicing and lamentation (5:16-17; 8:3, 10), and the hymn of praise to the creator God (4:13; 5:8-9; 9:5-6) have been taken to indicate that Amos addressed the people at Bethel gathered for the great autumnal festival of ingathering. In itself quite plausible, this should not be taken to provide a key for interpreting the entire book, as J. Morgenstern, "Amos Studies," *HUCA* 11, 1936, 19-140.

41. Amos 5:25-27 appears to be an attempt to reinterpret the diatribe against the cult by representing it as non-Yahwistic and by referring to the quite different worship of the pre-state period (cf. II Sam. 7:4-7). On this last, see H. Junker, "Amos und die 'opferlose Mosezeit,' " *Theologie und Glaube* 27, 1935, 686-695.

42. See L. A. Sinclair, "The Courtroom Motif in the Book of Amos." *JBL* 85, 1966, 351-353, and on the *rîb* pattern (i.e., statement of the case against the accused): B. Gemser, "The *Rîb*- or Controversy-Pattern in Hebrew Mentality," *SVT* 3, 1955, 120-134; H. B. Huffmon, "The Covenant Lawsuit in the Prophets," *JBL* 78, 1959, 285-295; G. E. Wright, "The Lawsuit of God: A Form-Critical Study of Deuteronomy 32," in B. W. Anderson and W. Harrelson (eds.), *Israel's Prophetic Heritage,* 26-67; H.-J. Boecker, "Anklagereden und Verteidigungsreden im Alten Testament," *EvTh* 20, 1960, 398-412; *Redeformen des Rechtsleben,* Neukirchen-Vluyn: Neukirchener Verlag, 1964; J. Harvey, "Le '*Rîb*-Pattern,' réquisitoire prophétique sur la rupture de l'alliance," *Bib* 43, 1962, 172-196; *Le Plaidoyer prophétique contre Israël après la rupture de l'alliance,* Bruges and Montreal: Desclée de Brouwer, 1967; J. W. Limburg, "The Root *ryb* and the Prophetic Lawsuit Speeches," *JBL* 88, 1969, 291-304; J. Blenkinsopp, "The Prophetic Reproach," *JBL* 90, 1971, 267-278; S. Amsler, "Le Thème du procès chez les prophètes d'Israël," *RTP* 3.24, 1974, 116-131; K. Nielsen, *Yahweh as Prosecutor and Judge: An Investigation of the Prophetic Lawsuit (Rîb-Pattern),* Sheffield: JSOT Press, 1978.

43. See especially H. Donner, "Die soziale Botschaft der Propheten im Lichte der Gesellschaftsordnung in Israel," *OA* 2, 1963, 229-245.

44. It is noteworthy that Assyria is not mentioned in Amos, unless one

accepts LXX "Assyria" for MT "Ashdod" at 3:9. The oppressor is simply referred to as an enemy (*ṣar*, 3:11) and "a nation" (*gôy*, 6:14). Assuming that Amos was active several years before the accession of Tiglath-pileser III, it is remarkable that he should have foreseen conquest by the Assyrians, since we know of no significant military threat from that quarter after the last western campaign of Adad-Nirari III in 796 B.C.E. (*ANET*, 281-282). We must also bear in mind that we know very little of the long reign of Jeroboam II, and can only speculate on the historical events which, according to the historian (II Kings 14:26), reduced Israel to desperate straits at that time.

45. This has been true not just for the present-day theologian and philosopher; see below, pp. 186-188.

46. II Kings 18:1 puts Hezekiah's accession in the third year of Hoshea, but 18:13 dates Sennacherib's campaign (701 B.C.E.) in the fourteenth year of Hezekiah, which means he came to the throne in 715 B.C.E. (with a margin of error of no more than a year).

47. A. Alt, "Hosea 5,8–6,6. Ein Krieg und seine Folgen in prophetischer Beleuchtung," *Kleine Schriften* II, 1953, 163-187; H. Donner in J. H. Hayes and J. M. Miller (eds.), *Israelite and Judaean History*, 421-434; H. W. Wolff, *Hosea*, 103-121.

48. See especially Amos 3:11; 6:14; and the forecast of the end of Damascus, 1:3-5. It is otherwise probable that Hosea was acquainted with Amos' sayings: the preference for loyalty and knowledge of God over sacrifice (6:6) is reminiscent of Amos 5:21-24 though verbally not very close; 10:2b echoes the language of the last vision (Amos 9:1), and it is particularly significant that the only mention in Amos of false or syncretic cults (8:14) appears to have evoked a response in Hosea (4:15). The latter speaks of Gilgal and Beth-aven (= Bethel) and those who swear "as Yahweh lives!" while Amos 8:14 refers to Ashimah of Samaria, a deity also mentioned at II Kings 17:30 and probably in the Elephantine papyri, an unnamed deity worshiped at Dan by whom its devotees swear, "as your god lives, O Dan!" and "the way of Beersheba." The latter probably conceals an allusion to a fertility deity (cf. Prov. 31:3, *d^erākêkā*, parallel with *ḥêlekā*, with the meaning "sexual potency"). Hos. 8:14 (cf. Amos 1:4, etc.) and Hos. 12:5 (cf. Amos 4:13, etc.) may be due to editorial affinities rather than direct dependence.

49. The text is, however, obscure; see H. W. Wolff, *Hosea*, 151, 157-158. The term is used of the prophetic office in Jer. 6:17; Ezek. 3:17; 33:2, 6, 7; Isa. 52:8; 56:10. See below, pp. 151-152.

50. Translating "give" and not "gave" as in RSV, since *^adammeh* is frequentative or iterative imperfect; see Gesenius-Kautsch, *Hebrew Grammar*, §112dd. Hosea, therefore, sees the prophetic process as still going on and presumably not just in his own person.

51. H. W. Wolff, "Hoseas geistige Heimat," and *Hosea*, 75.

52. Wolff: "amphictyonisch orientierte Propheten" ("Hoseas geistige Heimat," 85).

53. For indications and arguments, see A. Cody, *A History of Old Testament Priesthood,* Rome: Pontifical Biblical Institute, 1969, 56-58.

54. The only exception is Deut. 27:14, in a late stratum; cf. "Levitical priests," v. 9, and the tribe Levi, v. 12. See J. Blenkinsopp, *Prophecy and Canon,* 30.

55. It may be added that the hypothesis of a prophetic covenant mediator, whose functions included the reading of the law in a solemn cultic assembly, has not been established. Deut. 18:15-18 is not the description of an actual office but an attempt to fit prophecy into an ideal institutional "grid." The hypothesis was advanced by H.-J. Kraus, *Worship in Israel,* Richmond: John Knox Press, 1966, 102-112, and expanded by J. Muilenburg, "The 'Office' of the Prophet in Ancient Israel," in J. P. Hyatt (ed.), *The Bible in Modern Scholarship,* Nashville: Abingdon Press, 1965, 74-97. It has often been criticized, e.g., by R. E. Clements, *Prophecy and Covenant,* 1965, 80, and *Prophecy and Tradition,* Atlanta: John Knox Press, 1975, 8-14.

56. It is a noteworthy feature of Hosea's sayings, and one that distinguishes them from those of Amos, that each of the three sections of the book ends on a note of promise and hope (see Hos. 3:1-3; 11:8-11; 14:1-8).

57. Hos. 6:7 (textually uncertain) and 8:1; cf. Deut. 17:2; 29:11; Josh. 7:11, 15; 23:16; Judg. 2:20; II Kings 18:12; in all of which the expression "transgress the covenant" (*la%bōr bºrît,* or other verbal form) occurs.

58. In Hos. 12:2 (MT 12:3) it seems tolerably clear from the content of the indictment that "Israel" has been replaced by "Judah"; see Wolff, *Hosea,* 211.

59. Wolff, *Hosea,* xxx.

60. Cf. the references in Amos 6:1, 5.

61. The connection would be between the teaching of Hosea and his disciples on the basic cause of the disaster and the anti-Canaanite measures of Hezekiah (II Kings 18:4, 22). In view of the linguistic and thematic associations between the "golden calf" episode in Ex. 32 (especially the allusion to orgiastic rites in v. 6) and the cult of the Northern Kingdom, it is plausible to see a reflection of Hezekiah's measures in the so-called "cultic decalogue" of Ex. 34:12-26.

62. On the name Hosea, see Wolff, *Hosea,* 4-5; Andersen and Freedman, 151-153. The patronymic, Beeri, has suggested to some a Benjaminite origin on the inadequate grounds that the town Beeroth is situated in the territory of that tribe. We know nothing of the prophet's occupation prior to his call, and so cannot say whether he was a priest (Duhm), sage (Fohrer), or even baker (Knight).

63. H. H. Rowley, "The Marriage of Hosea," *BJRL* 39, 1956, 200-223 (= *Men of God,* New York: Thomas Nelson & Sons, 1963, 66-97) covered the spectrum of opinions up to a quarter of a century ago; see further the leisurely discussion in Andersen and Freedman, *Hosea,* 115-309, and, for Wolff's hypothesis of the premarital sexual rite (somewhat analogous to the medieval *jus primae noctis*), see Wolff, *Hosea,* 13-15. The hypothesis is contested by W. Rudolph, "Präparierte Jungfrauen?" *ZAW* 75, 1963, 65-73.

64. For this type of phrase, cf. *rûaḥ zᵉnûnîm* (Hos. 4:12; 5:4); the plural abstract denotes a quality or disposition; if the woman had been a prostitute, cultic or otherwise, at the time of marriage, one would have expected *zōnāh* or *'iššāh zōnāh.*

65. The name Gomer has resisted attempts to wrest a symbolic meaning out of it. The dual form Diblaim is unusual as a patronymic, which has led some commentators to the conclusion that it conceals a no longer clearly understood allusion to the cult of Asherah or Anath, since *dᵉbēlāh* means "fig cake" and cakes made of figs or raisins seem to have featured in the cult of these deities (cf. 3:1; Jer. 7:18; Isa. 16:7). This, however, is improbable to say the least, if for no other reason than that a feminine dual form would be required.

66. This translation should not be emended as in RSV; cf. *'ehyeh ᵃšer 'ehyeh,* Ex. 3:14.

67. The raisin cakes *(ᵃšîšê ᵃnābîm)*, as noted above (n. 65), belonged to the cult of Asherah, consort of El and "Queen of Heaven," cf. Jer. 7:18 and 44:19. The last passage is of special interest since it is the only place in the Hebrew Bible where women speak on the subject of religious practice.

68. Note also the provision of gold and silver, oil, flour, etc. (Ezek. 16:17-19; cf. Hos. 2:8-9 [MT 10-11]).

69. The deity is designated only as Baal (Hos. 2:8, 13, 16 [MT 2:10, 15, 18]; 9:10; 11:2; 13:1), sometimes in the plural, and there is allusion to the worship of calves *(ᵃgālîm,* 8:5; 10:5; 13:2), more properly, bulls *(šᵉwārîm,* 12:11 [MT 12:12]), Canaanite festivals (2:11, 13 [MT 2:13, 15]), sacrificial rites on hills and under trees (4:13), and cultic steles *(maṣṣēbôt,* 10:1-2).

70. In addition to numerous figurines of the fertility goddess and *maṣṣēbôt,* we now have the inscriptions from Kuntillet 'Ajrud, a religious center in the Sinai from the ninth and eighth centuries B.C.E., excavated in 1975-1976. Some of these contain blessings in the name of Baal and Yahweh and his Asherah *(brkt. 'tkm. lyhwh. šmrn. wl'šrt; brktk. lyhwh. wl'šrth.).* Pending publication of the material see Zeev Meshel, *Kuntillet 'Ajrud: A Religious Centre from the Time of the Judaean Monarchy on the Border of Sinai,* Jerusalem: Israel Museum, 1978 (Catalogue no. 175). Archaeological evidence for the survival of syncretism in the exilic and postexilic periods is briefly surveyed by Morton Smith, *Palestinian Parties and Politics That Shaped the Old Testament,* New York: Columbia University Press, 1971, 90-93.

71. In addition to the commentaries see P. R. Ackroyd, "Hosea and Jacob," *VT* 13, 1963, 245-259; E. M. Good, "Hosea and the Jacob Tradition," *VT* 16, 1966, 137-151; C. Jeremias, "Die Erzväter in der Verkündigung der Propheten," in H. Zimmerli (ed.), *Festschrift für W. Zimmerli,* Göttingen: Vandenhoeck & Ruprecht, 1977, 206-222; and the exhaustive study of F. Diedrich, *Die Anspielungen auf die Jakob-Tradition in Hosea 12,1–13,3,* Würzburg: Echter Verlag, 1977.

72. L. Perlitt, "Mose als Prophet," *EvTh* 31, 1971, 588-608.

73. H. W. Wolff, " 'Wissen um Gott' bei Hosea als Urform der Theologie," *EvTh* 12, 1952-53, 533-554; E. Baumann, " 'Wissen um Gott' bei Hosea als

Urform von Theologie?" *EvTh* 15, 1955, 416-425; G. von Rad, *Old Testament Theology* II, 142-143.

74. Hos. 8:1. The covenant with the animal world in 2:18 (MT 2:20) is of a different kind and occurs in a passage that we have taken to be editorial; the covenant transgressed at Adam (6:7) may refer to an event in the recent past unknown to us; 10:4 and 12:2 clearly refer to contemporary treaties. Hos. 8:1 may therefore be the earliest datable allusion to the covenant in the Hebrew Bible.

75. O. Eissfeldt, *The Old Testament: An Introduction,* 609-610.

76. See below, pp. 209-210.

77. Thus the Deuteronomic history omits any allusion to the opposition prophets of the eighth and seventh centuries, while giving information on Jonah ben-Amittai, an optimistic prophet who supported Jeroboam II and who was condemned by Amos! This rather odd circumstance may be explained on the hypothesis of a history of the kingdoms written during the reign of Josiah and perhaps ending at II Kings 23:25a: "Before him (i.e., Josiah) there was no king like him . . . according to all the law of Moses" (cf. the similar praise of Hezekiah, II Kings 18:5). Interest of the reform party—to which the historian belonged—in the territory of the northern tribes and the euphoria accompanying the reforms would explain the strand in the history favorable to the Northern Kingdom (e.g., II Kings 13:23; 14:27) and the historian's silence on Amos, Hosea, the Isaiah of the sayings, and Micah. The publication of separate collections of their sayings during the exilic period would have rendered their inclusion in the later edition of the history unnecessary. For the two editions of the history see especially F. M. Cross, *Canaanite Myth and Hebrew Epic,* 274-289; R. D. Nelson, *The Double Redaction of the Deuteronomistic History,* Sheffield: JSOT Press, 1981.

78. See the analysis of R. R. Wilson, *Prophecy and Society in Ancient Israel,* 213-219, somewhat vitiated by his determination to make a clear-cut distinction between Ephraimite and Judean types of prophecy on the basis of criteria some of which are debatable. E.g., since *nābî'* is the characteristic title for Ephraimite and *ḥōzeh* for Judean intermediaries, and since Nathan is always referred to as *nābî',* he must have been originally Ephraimite, a conclusion for which there is not the slightest supporting evidence and much that speaks against it (especially in I Kings 1). On Isa. 38-39, see P. R. Ackroyd, "An Interpretation of the Babylonian Exile: A Study of 2 Kings 20, Isaiah 38-39," *SJT* 27, 1974, 329-352.

79. The editorial insertion at Isa. 7:8b refers to Esarhaddon's settling of a foreign ruling class in Samaria in 669 B.C.E. (cf. Ezra 4:2). It was inevitable that the message of assurance would be followed by threats after Ahaz invited in the Assyrians, and also, perhaps, at the time of Hezekiah's revolt, 705-701 B.C.E. (Isa. 7:17-25; cf. 8:5-10).

80. Among recent commentaries see those by P. Auvray, *Isaïe 1-39,* Paris: Editions du Cerf, 1972, 104-108, and H. Wildberger, *Jesaja* I, 289-293; for other references see Wildberger and J. Vermeylen, *Du Prophète Isaïe à*

l'apocalyptique, 216-221. O. Kaiser, *Isaiah 1-12,* 96-106, defends the quite different hypothesis that *hā'almāh* (v. 14) refers to any young woman in Judah of marriageable age, in the sense that "the danger will disappear so rapidly that women who are now with child will name their sons, in thankfulness for being saved, 'Immanuel,' 'God with us' " (103). The article with *'almāh* and the parallelism with the other symbolic names which attach to specific individuals create serious problems for this hypothesis; and Kaiser disposes far too rapidly of the chronological objections against an identification with Hezekiah. If we follow II Kings 18:13, against 18:1, Hezekiah came to the throne in or near 715. If he was conceived in 734, the year of the Syro-Ephraimite crisis, he would then be eighteen or nineteen at his accession.

81. After Uzziah contracted leprosy (II Kings 15:5), Jotham (ca. 750-735) is presumed to have acted as regent while Uzziah lived on in retirement outside the city, perhaps on the site of Ramat Raḥel, excavated in 1954 and 1959-62. Jotham may not have outlived Uzziah by very long; indeed, it is not out of the question that Uzziah outlived him and that therefore Ahaz was regent at the time.

82. On the "hardening" (literally, "fattening") of hearts, see E. Jenni, "Jesajas Berufung in der neueren Forschung," *TZ* 15, 1959, 321-339 and O. Kaiser, *Isaiah 1-12,* 82-83. It can best be understood as arising out of later reflection on the failure of the mission in 734 B.C.E.

83. On Isa. 6, see, in addition to the commentaries, M. M. Kaplan, "Isaiah 6.1-11," *JBL* 45, 1926, 251-259; I. Engnell, *The Call of Isaiah,* Uppsala: Lundquist, 1949; L. J. Liebreich, "The Position of Chapter Six in the Book of Isaiah," *HUCA* 25, 1954, 37-40; R. Knierim, "The Vocation of Isaiah," *VT* 18, 1968, 47-68; O. H. Steck, "Bemerkungen zu Jesaja 6," *BZ* 16, 1972, 188-206. The position of this chapter in the unit to which it belongs (6:1 to 9:1a [MT 6:1 to 8:23a]), rather than at the beginning of the book, means that it describes Isaiah's commissioning for a specific task, not necessarily the absolute beginning of his prophetic activity. J. Milgrom, "Did Isaiah Prophesy During the Reign of Uzziah?" *VT* 14, 1964, 164-182, may therefore be right (he believes Isaiah did, and that the sayings from that time are to be found in chs. 1-5), but the matter cannot be decided.

84. On the prophetess, *hann'bî'āh,* of Isa. 8:3, see the commentaries and A. Jepsen, "Die Nebiah in Jes 8:3," *ZAW* 72, 1960, 267-268. If she was not a prophetic figure in her own right, she may have been a Temple singer. It is perhaps prudent to add that we are not told that she was Isaiah's wife.

85. K. Budde, "Zu Jesaja 8, Vers 9 und 10," *JBL* 49, 1930, 423-428; K. Galling, "Ein Stück judäischen Bodenrechts in Jes. 8," *ZDPV* 56, 1933, 209-218; T. Lescow, "Jesajas Denkschrift aus der Zeit des syrisch-ephraimiti-schen Krieges," *ZAW* 85, 1973, 315-331; H.-P. Müller, "Glauben und Bleiben. Zur Denkschrift Jesajas Kapitel vi 1 – viii 18," *SVT* 26, 1974, 25-54.

86. See also "thy anger has turned away" (*yāšōb 'app'kā,* Isa. 12:1), and cf. the refrain of the poem in 5:24-25 + 9:8 to 10:4, "his anger is not turned away" (*lō'-šāb 'appô*).

87. Apart from the gloss *nāzōrû 'āḥôr*, Isa. 1:4, only the last section, vs. 27-31—including the theme of the redemption of Zion, the allusion to *šābîm* (those who have "turned," converts), and the reference to cult under oaks and in gardens (cf. Isa. 57:5; 66:17)—points to a Second Temple milieu.

88. See H. Donner and B. Oded in Hayes and Miller (eds.), *Israelite and Judaean History*, 421-451.

89. This is especially apparent in the Woes and the poem on the divine anger; see below, p. 113.

90. The most recent study is J. Blenkinsopp, "Fragments of Ancient Exegesis in an Isaian Poem (Jes 2 6-22)," *ZAW* 93, 1981, 51-62.

91. G. von Rad, "Die Stadt auf dem Berge," *EvTh* 8, 1948-49, 439-447 (= "The City on the Hill," *The Problem of the Hexateuch and Other Essays*, London: Oliver & Boyd, 1965, 232-242); H. Wildberger, "Die Völkerwallfahrt zum Zion," *VT* 7, 1957, 62-81. On the preceding title, see P. R. Ackroyd, "A Note on Isaiah 2,1," *ZAW* 75, 1963, 320-321.

92. See O. Kaiser, *Isaiah 1-12*, 53-57.

93. In addition to the commentaries, see A. Bentzen, "Die Erläuterung von Jes. 5,1-7," *AfO* 4, 1927, 209-210; H. Junker, "Die literarische Art von Is. 5,1-7," *Bibl* 40, 1959, 259-266.

94. I.e., *lō'-šāb 'appô* ("his anger is not turned away," Isa. 9:11 [MT 9:12], etc.); cf. *lō' ᵃšîbennû* ("I will not cause it to turn back," Amos 1:3, etc.), the implicit object of the verb is probably *'ap*, the divine anger, as argued by R. P. Knierim, in G. W. Coats and B. O. Long (eds.), *Canon and Authority*, 163-175.

95. Some refer the saying to the death of Sargon II in 705 and the accession of Sennacherib, who would thus be the serpent and the adder respectively (Isa. 14:29). In that case the most recent "smiting" that we know of would be Sargon's campaign in 712 against Ashdod (*ANET*, 286).

96. *limmudîm*, disciples, Isa. 8:16; MT *b'limmudāy* should be retained in preference to LXX and suggested emendations, e.g., *b'yaldāy*. They may have been Temple prophets, as suggested by A. R. Johnson, G. Widengren, and O. Kaiser; for references see the latter's *Isaiah 1-12*, 120.

97. For the later origin of several of the oracles against foreign nations (Isa. 13-23), the so-called "Isaian apocalypse" (24-27), and much if not all of the material in 32-35, see below, pp. 264-266.

98. J. Fichtner, "Jesaja unter den Weisen," *TLZ* 74, 1949, 75-80; R. T. Anderson, "Was Isaiah a Scribe?" *JBL* 79, 1960, 57-58; J. W. Whedbee, *Isaiah and Wisdom*, Nashville: Abingdon Press, 1971.

99. Cf. R. R. Wilson, *Prophecy and Society in Ancient Israel*, 253-274.

100. J. Jensen, *The Use of tôrâ by Isaiah: His Debate with the Wisdom Tradition*, Washington, D.C.: Catholic Biblical Association, 1973.

101. Isa. 1:4; 5:19, 24; 10:20; 12:6; 17:7; 29:19; 30:11, 12, 15; 31:1 ("the Holy One of Jacob" [29:23], occurs in a passage [29:22-24] that is not Isaian); cf. "the Holy God," 5:16; "the Holy One," 5:19; 10:17. On God's holiness see W. Eichrodt, *Theology of the Old Testament*, I, Philadelphia: Westminster Press, 1961, 270-282.

102. It should be added, however, that this interpretation of Isa. 31:4 is not entirely secure since the metaphor could mean that the lion (Yahweh) fights *against* (*'al*) Mt. Zion and will not surrender his prey (Jerusalem) to the shepherds (Egyptians) who have come out to rescue it; see O. Kaiser, *Isaiah 13-39,* 315-317, who, however, comes out in favor of a different meaning.

103. In addition to the commentaries, see M. B. Crook, "A Suggested Occasion for Isaiah 9,2-7 and 11,1-9," *JBL* 68, 1949, 213-224; A. Alt, "Jesaja 8,23–9,6. Befreiungsnacht und Krönungstag," *Kleine Schriften* II, 1953, 206-225; S. Mowinckel, *He That Cometh,* Oxford: Basil Blackwell, 1959, 102-110; H. von Reventlow, "A Syncretistic Enthronement Hymn in Isa. 9.1-6," *UF* 3, 1971, 321-325.

104. With Isa. 42:1-4 it has in common the endowment with the spirit and the emphasis on justice; but cf. especially Jer. 23:5-6 and 33:14-16, which attribute to the Davidic scion (*ṣemaḥ*) wisdom, justice, righteousness, and represent him as bringing about peace and security. See below, 183-184.

105. See Isa. 20 and perhaps also 22:1-14.

106. Discussion has being going on since Stade's *ZAW* article of 1881; for the most recent stages see the commentaries of Rudolph (1975) and Mays (1976) and the articles of Willis (1969), Lescow (1972), and Jeppesen (1978).

107. Micah 2:3-4 has been expanded editorially, and 2:12-13, dealing with the theme of the reunification of the remnant (*š<ʾ>ērît*) under a king, is almost certainly exilic or early postexilic. Van der Woude (1969) takes it to be a quotation from Micah's prophetic opponents, with Micah's answer, beginning "but I said," in 3:1. This, however, is quite improbable since 3:1-4 is not addressed to prophets and the pattern of thought in 2:12-13 is not typical of optimistic prophecy, to judge by the little we know of it under the monarchy.

108. On the ruler from Bethlehem, or Ephrathah, or Beth-ephrat, see J. Coppens, "Le Cadre littéraire de Michée V,1-5," in H. Goedicke (ed.), *Near Eastern Studies in Honor of W. F. Albright,* Baltimore: Johns Hopkins University Press, 1971, 57-62; M. Crook, "The Promise in Micah 5," *JBL* 70, 1951, 313-320.

109. J. T. Willis, "The Structure of Micah 3-5 and the Function of Micah 5.9-14 in the Book," *ZAW* 81, 1969, 191-214.

110. Micah 4:1-5; cf. Isa. 2:2-5; Micah 5:10-15 (MT 5:9-14); cf. Isa. 2:6-11; Micah 5:2-4 (MT 5:1-3); cf. Isa. 9:2-7 (MT 9:1-6); 11:1-9.

111. For a more detailed discussion of these chapters, see B. Renaud, *Structure et attaches littéraires de Michée IV-V,* Paris: J. Gabalda, 1964.

112. A. S. van der Woude, "Deutero-Micha: ein Prophet aus Nord-Israel?" *NTT* 25, 1971, 365-378.

113. The discovery of an incense altar and a fertility stele in an Israelite sanctuary could perhaps be seen as confirmation; see Y. Aharoni in M. Avi-Yonah (ed.), *Encyclopedia of Archaeological Excavations in the Holy Land* III, 747-749.

114. See further below, pp. 143-146.

115. First suggested by B. Stade, "Micha 1,2-4 und 7,7-20, ein Psalm," *ZAW*

23, 1903, 163-177, the liturgical character of the chapter was developed by H. Gunkel (1928); see also B. Reicke, "Liturgical Traditions in Micah 7," *HTR* 60, 1967, 349-368, and, for the section in general, T. Lescow, "Redaktionsgeschichtliche Analyse von Micha 6-7," *ZAW* 84, 1972, 182-212.

116. The prophet's birthplace is tentatively identified with Tell el-Judeideh, thirty-five kilometers southwest of Jerusalem; see J. Jeremias, "Moreseth-Gath, die Heimat des Propheten Micha," *PJB* 29, 1933, 42-53; Y. Aharoni, *The Land of the Bible*, rev. ed., Philadelphia: Westminster Press, 1979, 58.

117. On the meaning of the elusive term *'am hā'āreṣ* during the monarchy, see S. Daiches, "The Meaning of 'Am-haaretz' in the Old Testament," *JTS* 30, 1929, 245-249; J. A. Soggin, "Der judäische 'am-ha'ares und das Königtum in Juda," *VT* 13, 1963, 187-195; R. de Vaux, "Les Sens de l'expression 'peuple du pays' dans l'Ancien Testament et le rôle politique du peuple en Israël," *RA* 58, 1964, 167-172; E. W. Nicholson, "The Meaning of the Expression ' 'Am-ha'areṣ' in the Old Testament," *JSS* 10, 1965, 59-66; S. Talmon, "The Judean 'am ha'ares in Historical Perspective," *Fourth World Congress of Jewish Studies* I, 1967, 71-76; M. H. Pope, " 'Am Ha'arez," *IDB* I, 1962, 106-107.

118. See below, pp. 143-146.

119. A. S. van der Woude, "Micah in Dispute with the Pseudo-Prophets," 247, on 2:7a, translates the difficult *he'āmûr bēt-ya*ᵃ*qōb:* "He [i.e., Yahweh] affirmed [what has been undertaken by] the house of Jacob," taking *he'āmûr* as a hif'il, *he*ˣ*mîr*, as in Deut. 26:17-18, and the reference to be to Yahweh's covenant fidelity, in which the people blindly trusted. They may have done so, but this improbable emendation does not prove it.

120. See Van der Woude (n. 119), who attempts to reconstruct elements of mainline Israelite religion through quotations attributed to the "false prophets."

121. We take *'et-rûaḥ YHWH* (Micah 3:8), absent in Symmachus, to have been inserted at a later time, as a gloss on *kōaḥ*, by an editor more familiar with the idea of an inspired person being filled with the Holy Spirit than the endowment as described here. The phrase is syntactically awkward and breaks up the rhythm of the line; cf. H. W. Wolff, "Wie verstand Micha von Moreschet sein prophetisches Amt?" 406-407.

122. The content of Micah's indictment and his preference for archaic terms that go back to the pre-state period (*rā'šîm, qᵉṣînîm, ḥēleq, ḥebel bᵉgôrāl, qᵉhal YHWH*) would seem to support Wolff's hypothesis. It is also interesting, as he points out, that Num. 11:16-25 combines ecstatic prophecy with the institution of the elders (Wolff, 416).

123. Cf. H. W. Wolff, *Amos' geistige Heimat*, Neukirchen-Vluyn: Neukirchener Verlag, 1964 (= *Amos the Prophet: The Man and His Background*, Philadelphia: Fortress Press, 1973). For a different view of Micah's relation to the cult, see W. Beyerlin (1959).

124. Points of contact between Micah and Amos are many: e.g., Micah 1:2-7; cf. Amos 1:2; Micah 1:3; cf. Amos 4:13; Micah 2:3; cf. Amos 5:13. We noted earlier the parallels between Micah 2:6-7 and Amos 7:15-16, both using the verb *nṭp* (hif.), preach, for what the prophet does. On this verb, see below, p. 145.

IV

THE END OF NATIONAL INDEPENDENCE

1. THE LAST ATTEMPT AT EMANCIPATION AND REFORM

J. **Blenkinsopp,** *Prophecy and Canon,* 24-53; C. C. **Carmichael,** *The Laws of Deuteronomy,* Ithaca: Cornell University Press, 1974; H. **Cazelles,** "Sophonie, Jérémie et les Scythes en Palestine," *RB* 74, 1964, 24-44; J. H. **Eaton,** *Obadiah, Nahum, Habakkuk and Zephaniah,* London: SCM Press, 1961, 119-159; O. **Eissfeldt,** *The Old Testament: An Introduction,* 423-425; F. C. **Fensham,** "Zephaniah, Book of," *IDBS,* 983-984; G. **Gerleman,** *Zephaniah textkritisch und literarisch untersucht,* Lund: S. W. K. Gleerup, 1942; J. **Gray,** *I & II Kings, A Commentary,* Philadelphia: Westminster Press, 1970², 713-748; J. P. **Hyatt,** "The Date and Background of Zephaniah," *JNES* 7, 1948, 156-173; A. S. **Kapelrud,** *The Message of the Prophet Zephaniah: Morphology and Ideas,* Oslo: Universitetsforlaget, 1975; C. **Kuhl,** *The Old Testament: Its Origins and Composition,* Edinburgh: Oliver & Boyd, 1961, 219-221; G. **Langohr,** "Redaction et composition du livre de Sophonie," *Le Museon* 89, 1976, 51-73; E. W. **Nicholson,** *Deuteronomy and Tradition,* Oxford: Basil Blackwell, 1967; G. **von Rad,** *Studies in Deuteronomy,* Naperville, Ill.: Alec R. Allenson, 1944; *Deuteronomy, A Commentary,* Philadelphia: Westminster Press, 1966; J. M. P. **Smith,** *Micah, Zephaniah, Nahum, Habakkuk, Obadiah and Joel,* Edinburgh: T. & T. Clark, 1912, 159-263; L. P. **Smith** and E. L. **Lacheman,** "The Authorship of the Book of Zephaniah," *JNES* 9, 1950, 137-142; D. L. **Williams,** "The Date of Zephaniah," *JBL* 82, 1963, 77-88.

Under Ashurbanipal (669-627 B.C.E.) the Assyrian empire, which had reached its greatest extent with the conquest of Egypt by Esarhaddon, began to disintegrate. The central government was finding it increasingly difficult to hold down the subject provinces, and its difficulties were compounded by pressure from new enemies, including Elamites from the Iranian highlands and Scythians from the Caucasus region. A few years into the reign Egypt regained its independence under the twenty-sixth Saitic dynasty, and in 650 the king's brother Shamash-shum-ukin, viceroy of Babylon, raised the standard of revolt in that city in concert with other vassals, including perhaps the Judean king Manasseh. Ashurbanipal managed to hold on, but after his death events moved rapidly to their inevitable conclusion. The Kingdom of Babylon, founded by Nabopolassar in 625, pressed home its attack in alliance with Medes to the east and Scythians to the north. In 614 the ancient capital of Ashur was captured and two years later it was the turn of Nineveh. Ashur-uballit, last of a long line of Assyrian kings, held out for a short time in the Haran region in northern Mesopotamia where the Egyptians, now alarmed at the rapid shift in the balance of power, tried unsuccessfully to come to his assistance. With the decisive defeat of the Egyptian army at Carchemish in 605 it was clear that an entirely new chapter in the Near East was about to begin.

The decline and fall of Assyria, and the subsequent struggle between Babylon and Egypt to fill the vacuum, bore decisively on the vassal provinces and states of the Syro-Palestinian corridor obliging them to make decisions which, in view of the uncertain outcome, could not have been free of danger. It is safe to assume, for example, that the assassination of Amon, successor of Manasseh (II Kings 21:23), had something to do with the struggle between pro-Assyrian and emancipationist factions in the capital. The group described as "the people of the land"[1] avenged the death of Amon and put his son Josiah on the throne. This move must have put them in a commanding position during the regency, and it seems that they maintained this position even after Josiah's reign (II Kings 25:15; Jer. 1:18; 37:2; Ezek. 7:27; 22:29). But at that time (640 B.C.E.) it was still too early to make a clear bid for independence by denying the annual tribute, which weighed most heavily on the agrarian class that the "people of the land" represented.

According to the Chronicler (II Chron. 34:3), a thoroughgoing religious reform was launched in the twelfth year of Josiah's reign. While we do not have the means to fine-tune our chronology of the period enough to answer the question, the date is close enough to that of Ashurbanipal's death to suggest the possibility of a connection. The Deuteronomic historian, however, dates the reform six years later, after the discovery of the lawbook in the Temple (II Kings 22:3-8). But since it is easier to explain why he would want to suggest that the reform was inspired by this discovery than to suppose that the Chronicler simply invented an earlier reform, most scholars are now inclined to accept a connection between religious reform and political emancipation.

The situation in Judah during the two decades preceding the reforms is reflected in a small collection of sayings attributed to Zephaniah, a prophet active during the reign of Josiah (Zeph. 1:1). The Deuteronomic editor who gave the collection its title also, quite exceptionally, supplied the prophet with a genealogy, going back four generations to a certain Hezekiah. Since Zephaniah seems to be familiar with activities at the court and refers to the king's sons (1:8), it is still common to assume that the Hezekiah in question must be the Judean king who ruled before Manasseh. While this is chronologically possible, it is by no means certain. Given the Deuteronomic provenance of the title, it seems more likely that the genealogy was occasioned by the father's name, Cushi (meaning "Ethiopian" or "Sudanese"), and therefore had the purpose of demonstrating native rather than foreign descent—an essential requirement for prophets according to the Deuteronomic school (Deut. 18:15, 18).[2] It would therefore be hazardous to draw any biographical conclusions on the basis of the superscription, and the rest of the book is no more forthcoming on the prophet himself than are most of the other books in Latter Prophets.

The structure of the book corresponds fairly clearly to perspectives and aspirations of the Judean postexilic Temple community. Threat of an overwhelming divine judgment on the Judah of the prophet's day (Zeph. 1:2 to 2:3) is therefore balanced by the prospect of the conversion of Gentiles to the cult of Yahweh (3:9-10), final judgment on the unrepentant (3:8), and the restoration and final salvation of a purified Israel (3:11-13, 14-20). Sayings directed against foreign nations also occur (2:4-15) and, whatever their origin, it is clear that they too have been reformulated in accord with the changing political situation during the Neo-Babylonian and early Persian periods.[3] The similarity between the anti-Assyrian saying (2:13-15) and Nahum justifies the suspicion that Zephaniah was at one time a member of the Temple staff, a possibility that is not excluded by his condemnation of Jerusalem alongside Nineveh (3:1-7). The political circumstances of the time made party strife in the capital inevitable, and it was equally inevitable that the different parties would seek prophetic support.

Zephaniah's diatribe is directed at the syncretist party at the court who were engaging in the cult of Baal, the heavenly bodies (probably Assyrian), and the Ammonite deity Milcom alongside Yahweh (1:4-6).[4] The guilty ones are further identified as members of the aristocracy and the royal family who have adopted foreign customs and dress and profess an enlightened skepticism about the traditional religion and its prophetic representatives (1:7-13). Judges, prophets, and priests are also included in the indictment (3:3-5).[5] Allowing for the kind of extrapolations common in prophetic diatribe, the object of attack would appear to be the pro-Assyrian party at the court during the minority of Josiah. On the other side, that of Zephaniah himself, are ranged the "humble of the land" who fulfill the requirements of divine justice, seek righteousness, and live in obedient submission to Yahweh (2:3). The thought and language are remarkably close to the well-known "program" in Micah 6:8 announced through the prophetic word: the divine requirement is to act justly, love fidelity, and walk humbly with God. This, in effect, summarizes the ethical and religious ideal of the "humble of the land" with whom Zephaniah identifies.

The influence of Amos, apparent at several points in the book,[6] demonstrates the strength and consistency of the tradition of prophetic preaching against social and political corruption. As in Amos, these evils are seen as premonitory hints of a universal judgment described in the traditional language of the "Day of Yahweh"—a final reckoning that will involve not just Israel, or even the nations, but the entire cosmos in a catastrophic act of uncreation (Zeph. 1:2-3; cf. Jer. 4:23-26). There are also hints of the traditional theme of the "foe from the north" (Zeph. 1:10-11), which will play an important part in the early preaching of Jeremiah (Jer. 1:13-15; 4:6, etc).[7] Zephaniah is not one of the most original of prophetic spokesmen, but he contributed, with others, to keeping alive the alternative vision during a protracted dark period of Israelite history. This vision was to find a degree of realization in the reforms of Josiah and more permanent embodiment in the Deuteronomic program.

At this point it would be appropriate to refer back to what was said about Micah and his disciples[8] in order to make the further point that the last part of the book (Micah 6-7) shows signs of having been edited and brought up to date during the time of Zephaniah's activity. This is especially the case with Micah 6:9-16, which reflects a situation of social disorder such as obtained during the reign of Manasseh and probably also during the early years of Josiah's reign (II Kings 21:16; 24:4). Allusion to "statutes of Omri" and "deeds of Ahab" (Micah 6:16) recalls the condemnation of Manasseh for imitating the hated Ahab in setting up syncretist cults (II Kings 21:3; cf. 23:4-14). Micah 6:9-16 also runs parallel to Zephaniah in several respects. In both there is condemnation of an unnamed city, which must be Jerusalem (Micah 6:9; Zeph. 3:1), and much emphasis on the evils of idolatry in general and the cult of Baal in particular. The contrast between pride and humility is also noteworthy, in which respect it has already been noted that the much-quoted summary of the divine requirement at Micah 6:8 could have served as a program for the "humble of the land" of Zeph. 2:3.[9]

Here too, then, we have evidence for the persistence of a prophetic tradition of ethical teaching adopted by pietist groups which, in spite of the paucity of evidence, shows signs of increasing consolidation and formalization. We would not be mistaken in finding here one line of development leading to the Deuteronomic program.

As described in II Kings 23 and II Chron. 34, the reforms of Josiah dealt only in cultic matters and did not take issue with the social ills condemned in prophetic preaching. After the discovery of the lawbook in the Temple the young king is said to have consulted with the prophetess Huldah, wife of a member of the royal household. She confirmed his worst fears by predicting that, on account of neglect of the laws contained in the book, disaster would come on the kingdom, though the king himself would be spared a violent end. This prediction, similar to the one addressed by Isaiah to Hezekiah (II Kings 20:16-18), was mistaken with respect to Josiah's death (II Kings 23:29-30), suggesting that this part of it at least is historically trustworthy. It is noteworthy, at any rate, that the prophetess explains the disaster as the result not of social injustice but of idolatrous cults (II Kings 22:17).[10] The reforms that followed consisted in the purification of Temple worship, wholesale destruction of non-Yahwistic cult objects, and the disestablishment of cult centers outside Jerusalem. Taking advantage of the weakened Assyrian hold on the outlying provinces, Josiah also extended these activities into the territory of the northern tribes, destroying the rival sanctuary at Bethel and executing its priests. The reforms culminated in the celebration of a great Passover in Jerusalem.

Since the cultic reforms of Josiah closely parallel stipulations in the Deuteronomic lawbook (Deut. 12-26),[11] it has been recognized since late antiquity and widely acknowledged since the early nineteenth century that some historical connection must be postulated. It is also quite certain that the historian who reported the finding of the book in the Temple in the eighteenth year of Josiah's reign (i.e., 622 B.C.E.) intended to suggest that the law which it contained was the one (editorial additions apart) now preserved in our book of Deuteronomy. This law is presented as having been promulgated by Moses on the last day of his life and on the eve of Israel's entry into Canaan. Modern critical scholarship, however, is unanimous in recognizing Deuteronomy as a pseudepigraphal writing, implying that the book came into existence at a rather later time, though its individual laws may have had a long prehistory before being incorporated into the book. On the matter of dating, no similar unanimity has emerged, though there is increasing recognition of the possibility, even probability, of successive stages of development beginning earlier than Josiah's reign and extending into the Second Temple period.

It was noted earlier that the Chronicler dated the Josian reform several years *before* the finding of the book in the Temple. About three quarters of a century earlier Hezekiah had carried out the same kind of cultic reform by purifying the Temple, abolishing the "high places," and, according to the Chronicler at least, holding a plenary Passover in Jerusalem.[12] There seems no reason to doubt the essential accuracy of this information, especially in view of the fact that Hezekiah took advantage of the death of Sargon II in 705 to assert his independence, thus creating a situation propitious for religious reform. Confirmation of both stages of reform (under Hezekiah and Josiah) has also been proposed on the basis of excavation at Tel Arad, an important Judean city in the Negeb. The Yahwistic temple built during the United Monarchy, with its altar still covered with the residue of animal fat, and with its small "high place" *(bāmāh)* and stele *(maṣṣēbāh)*, was not rebuilt during the time of Josiah (stratum VI), and the altar appears not to have been in use after the time of Hezekiah.[13]

Short lived as they both were, these attempts at reform are important for our theme since they represent points at which prophetic preaching had some effect on official state policy. This is explicitly attested for Hezekiah, who was influenced by Isaiah (Isa. 37-39) and Micah (Jer. 26:16-19), but it can also be inferred from a comparison between the genuine sayings of some eighth- and seventh-century prophets and the earlier strata of the Deuteronomic lawbook. Like several of the prophetic books (Jer. 1:1; Amos 1:1), Deuteronomy is presented as "the words of Moses" (Deut. 1:1) and in the form of a prophetic address to the entire people. Moses himself is described as a prophet in the book (Deut. 18:15-18; 34:10), and the true prophet, who continues the mission and work of Moses, is invested with the highest authority. There can be no doubt that Deuteronomy was profoundly influenced by the prophetic movement.

The social legislation of Deuteronomy is in many respects quite advanced. Though marked by a certain utopian character—apparent in its abolition of poverty in principle (Deut. 15:4)—it laid down precise provisions in favor of the disadvantaged elements in society including resident aliens, the fatherless, widows, and unemployed clergy. Examples are the triennial tithe (14:28-29; 24:17-22; 26:12-15), remission of debts every seventh year (15:1-3) with appropriate safeguards against abuses (15:7-11), the prohibition of usury (23:19-20) and abusive debt collection (24:6, 10-13, 17), and insistence on the proper administration of justice (16:18-20). There are also enlightened provisions for the protection and, in some cases, the emancipation of slaves (15:12-18; 23:15-16; 24:7), and for fair treatment in the case of involuntary homicide (19:1-13).

One of the most distinctive characteristics of the legislation is the concern to preserve a traditional agrarian way of life together with the rights of the free farmer. Care for property, one's own and that of others, even extends to birds' nests (Deut. 22:6-7). The prohibition against removing boundary marks (19:14) struck at the practice of enclosure denounced by the prophets (e.g., Micah 2:2), and the provisions for release from military service (Deut. 20:5-9; 24:5) highlight a long-standing source of bitterness between the agrarian class and the monarchy. It is also noteworthy that the priestly tithe is quite restricted (18:1-8) and that support of the cult, an increasingly onerous burden as its operation became more and more complex, is to be proportionate to the individual's means (16:16-17). The monarchy itself is not condemned, but it is to be subject to the law and therefore, in effect, a constitutional monarchy (17:14-20).

It will be clear from these examples that Deuteronomy contains not a law code in the strict sense but a program for the future, and it is equally clear that such programs emanate from distinct parties or interest groups. Few issues in Old Testament studies have been debated so intensely and inconclusively as the provenance of the Deuteronomic program of cultic and social reform. At one time it seemed well established that its origins were to be sought in the Northern Kingdom, either in the period of its independent existence or during the century between the fall of Samaria and the finding of the lawbook in the Temple.[14] Arguments advanced in support of this hypothesis, however, either do not stand up under close scrutiny or call for substantial revision. One of the main props, affinity between Deuteronomy and the Elohist source in the Pentateuch (E), is problematic not only because of the rather elusive nature of this strand but also on account of the difficulty of establishing its "northern" character with a reasonable degree of probability. Deuteronomy certainly has affinity with Hosea, an Ephraimite prophet, but that is true of other prophets who are not Ephraimite. Moreover, Hosea shows little interest in the social abuses against which Deuteronomy legislates.[15]

A more promising approach, first explored by Bentzen and given wide currency by Von Rad,[16] concentrates on the Levites as the category responsible for both the homiletic form and the content of the Deuteronomic lawbook. While this line of inquiry has proved to be productive in several respects, its Achilles' heel is the need to rely almost exclusively on information provided by the Chronicler, who, in his version of the history, introduces the Levites at several points as instructors in Torah, judges, and reformers—in other words, as discharging the functions that were theirs in the Second Temple period. It remains true that our principal sources, the Deuteronomic history and the preexilic prophets, never mention the Levites for the period of the two kingdoms with the sole exception of their exclusion from gainful employment in the sanctuaries set up by Jeroboam (I Kings 12:31). This may indeed provide a useful clue since it is quite likely that, as the Chronicler informs us (II Chron. 11:13-17; 13:9), these dispossessed priests found their way into the Kingdom of Judah. But it would not follow that they brought with them a distinctive tradition that left its mark on Deuteronomy.[17]

In view of the emphasis that modern commentators have placed on the homiletic style of Deuteronomy, it should also be said that we have no reliable evidence for Levitical preaching during the preexilic period. While there are some obvious problems involved in the use of this term—not least the pejorative associations that have come to weigh it down—the Hebrew verb that it usually translates, *ntp* (hif.), refers invariably to prophetic activity and is generally used in parallelism with "prophesy." During the period in question, therefore, it is the prophet, not the Levite, who is the preacher *(maṭṭîp)*.[18]

Bearing in mind that certainty is beyond our reach, we may still attempt to summarize this important chapter in the religious history of Israel as follows. Movements of reform had been a constant feature of the history at least since the time of Asa and his son Jehoshaphat in the late tenth and early ninth centuries (I Kings 15:11-15; 22:43-46). The attempt to disestablish the provincial sanctuaries was first made by Hezekiah (II Kings 18:4, 22) as part of a reform whose purpose was to avoid a repetition of the fate that had befallen the Northern Kingdom. Impressive parallels between the preaching of Micah and the Deuteronomic legislation[19] suggest further that the class referred to as "the people of the land," whose interests and ethos found expression in Micah's preaching, played a significant role in this reform movement both then and in the next century under Josiah. We should also allow for a significant contribution from a pietist group responsive to prophetic preaching, the "humble of the land" of Zephaniah, especially under Manasseh and during the minority of Josiah. The scribal or sapiential character of Deuteronomy, to which several scholars have rightly drawn attention,[20] does not contradict this conclusion, since Deuteronomy was an official state document drawn up by specialists trained in the scribal tradition. There are indications that these scribes were particularly active during Hezekiah's reign and that by the time of Josiah they had begun to assume responsibility for the writing and probably also the interpreting of the laws.[21]

Since Deuteronomy also reflects aspirations for political independence under Josiah,[22] it was natural that it should emphasize the specifically Israelite character of prophecy. Prophecy, therefore, is contrasted with foreign modes of mediation (18:14) and it is insisted that the prophet must be a native Israelite (18:15, 18). The prophet who speaks in the name of a foreign deity is guilty of sedition and subject to the death penalty (13:1-5; 18:20), a stipulation that is readily intelligible in the context of the anti-Assyrian measures pursued by Josiah and his court.

2. THE PERSPECTIVE OF CULT PROPHECY ON INTERNATIONAL AFFAIRS: NAHUM AND HABAKKUK

W. F. **Albright,** "The Psalm of Habakkuk," in H. H. Rowley (ed.), *Studies in Old Testament Prophecy,* Edinburgh: T. & T. Clark, 1950, 1-18; W. **Brownlee,** *The Text of Habakkuk in the Ancient Commentary from Qumran,* JBL Monograph Series 11, Philadelphia: *Society of Biblical Literature and Exegesis,* 1959; K. **Budde,** "Habakuk," *ZDMG* 84, 1930, 139-147; K. J. **Cathcart,** *Nahum in the Light of the North-west Semitic,* Rome: Biblical Institute Press, 1973; "Treaty Curses in the Book of Nahum," *CBQ* 35, 1973, 179-187; "More Philological Studies in Nahum," *JNSL* 7, 1979, 1-12; O. **Eissfeldt,** *The Old Testament: An Introduction,* 413-416, 416-423; A. **George,** "Nahoum, Le Livre de," *SDB* VI, 291-301; N. K. **Gottwald,** *All the Kingdoms of the Earth,* 229-233; D. E. **Gowan,** "Habakkuk and Wisdom," *Perspective* 9, 1968, 157-166; *The Triumph of Faith in Habakkuk,* Atlanta: John Knox Press, 1976; H. **Gunkel,** "Nahum 1," *ZAW* 13, 1893, 223-244; A. **Haldar,** *Studies in the Book of Nahum,* Uppsala: Lundequist, 1947; P. **Haupt,** "The Book of Nahum," *JBL* 26, 1907, 1-53; P. **Humbert,** "Le Problème du livre de Nahoum," *RHPR* 12, 1932, 1-15; *Problèmes du livre d'Habacuc,* Neuchâtel: Secrétariat de l'Université, 1944; J. **Jeremias,** *Kultprophetie und Gerichtsverkündigung in der später Königszeit Israels,* Neukirchen-Vluyn: Neukirchener Verlag, 1969; P. **Jöcken,** *Das Buch Habakuk,* Cologne: Peter Hanstein, 1977; C.-A. **Keller,** "Nahoum," "Habacuc," in R. Vuilleumier and C.-A. Keller (eds.), *Michée, Nahoum, Habacuc, Sophonie,* Paris: Delachaux et Niestlé, 1971, 101-176; "Die theologische Bewältigung der geschichtlichen Wirklichkeit in der Prophetie Nahums," *VT* 22, 1972, 399-419; "Die Eigenart des Propheten Habakuks," *ZAW* 85, 1973, 156-167; J. L. **Mihelic,** "The Concept of God in the Book of Nahum," *Int* 2, 1948, 199-208; E. **Nielsen,** "The Righteous and the Wicked in Habaqquq," *StTh* 6, 1953, 54-78; E. **Otto,** "Die Stellung der Wehe-Worte in der Verkündigung des Propheten Habakuk," *ZAW* 89, 1977, 73-107; D. **Petersen,** "The Oracles Against the Nations: A Form-critical

Analysis," *SBL Seminar Papers,* 1975, 1.39-46; W. **Rudolph,** *Micha—Nahum—Habakuk—Zephanja,* Gütersloh: Gütersloher Verlagshaus Gerd Mohn, 1975, 143-254; H. **Schulz,** *Das Buch Nahum,* Berlin: Walter de Gruyter, 1973; J. M. Powis **Smith,** in J. M. P. Smith, W. H. Ward, and J. A. Bewer (eds.), *Micah, Zephaniah, Nahum, Habakkuk, Obadiah and Joel,* Edinburgh: T. & T. Clark, 1911, 267-360; C. C. **Torrey,** "Alexander the Great in the Old Testament Prophecies," *BZAW* 41, 1925, 281-286; H. H. **Walker** and N. W. **Lund,** "The Literary Structure of the Book of Habakkuk," *JBL* 53, 1934, 355-370; A. S. **van der Woude,** "The Book of Nahum: A Letter Written in Exile," *OTS* 20, 1977, 108-126.

Max Weber's contention that prophecy in Israel was essentially concerned with international affairs[23] is amply confirmed by the history of the last decades of Judean independence. The prophetic material in the books attributed to Nahum and Habakkuk spans the period of the decline and fall of Assyria and the resurgence of Babylonian power under Nebuchadrezzar or, in other words, from the death of Ashurbanipal (627) to the first deportation (598). Both the title and the actual contents of Nahum suggest that it is a composite work. The centerpiece is the oracle *(maśśā')*[24] against Nineveh (Nahum 1:15 to 2:12 [MT 2:1-13]) followed by a short prose comment (2:13 [MT 2:14]) and a long woe saying (3:1-19). These are introduced by an incomplete acrostic hymn (1:2-8) and three short sayings (1:9-14). The matter of authorship cannot be decided, as is generally the case with sayings against foreign countries and compositions of a liturgical character. The acrostic hymn can be traced, with the help of slight emendations,[25] from *aleph* to *kaph*. It celebrates the theophany of the national warrior god using familiar motifs in a well-established tradition of cultic hymnography.[26] At what point it was added as an appropriate introduction to the anti-Assyrian poems we cannot say.

The three short sayings that follow (Nahum 1:9-14), the text of which is generally in a sorry state, may represent surviving fragments of cultic prophecy from the period of nationalistic revival that followed the death of Ashurbanipal. It is now impossible to say whether they come from the prophet of the title, Nahum of Elkosh, about whom nothing is known.[27] As far as can be made out, the first of these sayings (vs. 9-11) takes issue with a group that opposed the anti-Assyrian policy of Josiah and his supporters and, in that group, one who is described as an "evil counselor," presumably a high official at the court. The next (vs. 12-13) is addressed to Jerusalem and, in the manner characteristic of official intermediaries, promises an end to Assyrian rule. The last (v. 14) is addressed to an individual, probably Ashurbanipal, recently deceased, predicting the destruction of his gods and the end of his line.

The anti-Assyrian poem is introduced by the herald *(mᵉbaśśēr)* and bringer of good news *(maśmîaʿ śālôm)*. These terms would be particularly appropriate for the kind of optimistic prophet that Nahum is taken to be, though their occurrence in Second Isaiah (Isa. 40:9; 52:7) suggests rather a shared editorial history.[28] The poem describes with quite brutal realism the capture and sack of Nineveh, though the kind of language used does not exclude the possibility that the poem was written before the actual event (612 B.C.E.). In that case, however, it is difficult to see how it could have preceded it by more than a few years, given the real danger of such inflammatory material coming to the attention of local Assyrian officials.[29] The most likely explanation is that it emanated from a cult prophet after the movement for emancipation had actually begun, that it was published openly for the benefit of king and court, and that Josiah responded to the call to keep the festivals and renew vows by convoking a great Passover of liberation a few years later (II Kings 23:21-23).

The woe saying against the "bloody city" (Nahum 3:1-19)[30] continues the description of its annihilation, and with this the book comes to an end. The tone of these poems will not easily find an echo in the mind of the modern reader, or at least the modern reader who has not suffered under such conditions as the Assyrians imposed on their subject provinces. But it is well to recall that what was at stake for the poet and his audience was the reality of divine power and the possibility of justice in the world of international affairs. These issues will come to clearer expression in Habakkuk, to be considered shortly.

Before leaving Nahum we must ask where he is to be situated on the spectrum of prophetic phenomena in Israel. The decisive clue is, of course, the oracle against a foreign nation, the issuance of which is one of the oldest and best established of prophetic functions. While it is used in different contexts by prophets, it may be accepted that it originated, and continued in use, as part of the official cult and as a function of national policy. It seems reasonably certain that Nahum was a central intermediary[31] and that therefore in his book we encounter cultic and nationalistic prophecy in a fairly pure state. The mythological language of theophany (Nahum 1:4; cf. Amos 1:2; Joel 3:16 [MT 4:16]), the title "Yahweh of the hosts" (Nahum 2:13; 3:5), and the absence of criticism of the cult and other state institutions suggest that Nahum represents an aspect of Josiah's policies quite different from those of which we learn from the historian of the reign. While, therefore, the book cannot be read as a coherent liturgy, it seems that Nahum was the spokesman for the Temple cult in the service of nationalistic revival after a century of subjugation to Assyria.[32]

In spite of the impressive territorial gains resulting from Josiah's bid for independence,[33] a perceptive observer of the international scene would have been obliged to make a rather cautious assessment of future possibilities. Egypt, which had regained its independence in 655 B.C.E., was already on its way to bringing Syria and Palestine back into its sphere of influence a decade before the death of Ashurbanipal with the conquest of the Philistine city of Ashdod in 639. Once it became apparent that Assyria was finished as a great power, this goal was pursued more vigorously by Psammeticus I and Necho II of the twenty-sixth Saitic dynasty. Josiah decided, correctly in the event, that the future lay with the Babylonians; but his attempt to win their favor by opposing the Egyptian penetration into Syria cost him his life (II Kings 23:29-30). The "people of the land" chose as his successor his younger son Jehoahaz (or Shallum, I Chron. 3:15 and Jer. 22:11), no doubt because he opposed the new oppressor. The Egyptians, however, deposed him after only three months on the throne and put Eliakim, Josiah's oldest son, in his place. Eliakim, renamed Jehoiakim by the Egyptians, ruled as an Egyptian puppet with the task of keeping the peace, suppressing movements of independence, and collecting the annual tribute routinely levied by the great empires (II Kings 23:35). These tasks did not make for popularity, and it is no surprise to hear of bloodshed, the execution of dissidents including prophets (Jer. 26:20-23), and the opposition of those, including Jeremiah (Jer. 22:13-19; 26:1-19), who had supported the policies of Josiah.

After the decisive defeat of the Egyptians at Carchemish on the Upper Euphrates in 605 B.C.E., control of the region passed to the Babylonians, and Jehoiakim was forced to submit to a new master. Shortly thereafter he made the mistake of withholding tribute, probably as a result of the Babylonian failure to conquer Egypt in 600 B.C.E. Assisted by levies from neighboring states (II Kings 24:2), the Babylonians invested Jerusalem but Jehoiakim died, or was killed, before they could occupy the city.[34] After a brief siege his son Jehoiachin was forced to submit and was deported together with the royal family, members of the court, and a significant number of the professional classes. Many in Judah continued to regard the exiled king as *de jure* monarch, and the Babylonians themselves may have encouraged this as a means of keeping their appointee, Mattaniah, renamed Zedekiah, in line. During the latter's reign the struggle between the pro-Babylonian and anti-Babylonian parties in Jerusalem reached a level of great intensity, creating a situation that Zedekiah was clearly unable to control. The outcome was a further bid for independence that predictably failed and led to the destruction of the capital city and the Temple, another deportation, and the final loss of national independence (586 B.C.E.).

Shortly after the death of Josiah a Jerusalemite prophet proclaimed, in the manner of Amos and Isaiah, the advent of a new world conqueror as the instrument of Yahweh's purposes in history. The proclamation comes as part of a dialogue between the prophet and his god (Hab. 1:2 to 2:5), an innovation in the prophetic literature that will be used by Second Isaiah (Isa. 40:1-11; 49:1-18) but which occurs in or is presupposed by cultic hymns.[35] Like the lamentation psalms, it begins with a complaint that the wicked and violent appear to triumph while the innocent are persecuted (Hab. 1:2-4). Using traditional language to describe an invading force (cf. Isa. 5:26-30), the divine response points to a new initiative of Yahweh in world history, the rousing of the Babylonians (*kaśdîm*, Chaldeans, Hab. 1:6), who, though themselves reprobates, will serve as instruments of punishment for the "wicked" in Judah (1:5-11). This reply does not entirely still the prophet's doubts, since he continues to complain about the triumph of the wicked over the righteous, and in a way which suggests that he himself is personally involved. As he continues, however, the object of his denunciation shifts to the pitiless conqueror who devours nations, so that a satisfactory divine answer still lies in the future (1:12 to 2:1). The final response from Yahweh does not provide this answer. It will come, but in the meantime the righteous must persevere, believing that salvation, promised through prophetic revelation, will eventually be theirs (2:2-5).

This brief summary of the first part of Habakkuk has passed over some serious problems of interpretation that have proved remarkably resistant to solution and that must be briefly mentioned.

The first concerns the date and historical reference of the dialogue. Beginning with Duhm, who read "Kittim" for "Chaldeans" at Hab. 1:6, commentators have from time to time speculated that *hakkaśdîm* is a gloss.[36] If this were so, the text would provide no clue to the identity of the "bitter and hasty nation" and its leader, especially in view of the conventional language of the *Völkerkampf* theme that is employed. Speculation has therefore been free to range from the Assyrians toward the end of the seventh century to the Macedonians and Alexander the Great in the fourth.[37] Closely related is the identity of "the wicked" (vs. 4, 13), which oscillates between internal opponents of the prophet and the new aggressors on the international scene.[38] We take the view that the text has certainly undergone development and may well have been reapplied to changing political situations, but that it best fits the years following the death of Josiah, a time of profound political and religious disorientation in Judah. "The wicked" would then be the supporters of Jehoiakim (609-598), who, according to our sources, shed innocent blood, executed prophets, and disregarded the claims of social justice.[39] The threat from the Babylonians and their leader (Nebuchadrezzar) would make best sense sometime between the battle of Carchemish (605) and the first deportation (598). We have an exact thematic parallel in Jer. 25:8-14 dated to that time. Yahweh is sending for the tribes of the north and for Nebuchadrezzar his servant as an instrument of Judah's chastisement. In due course, however, these two will be punished for their iniquity in fulfillment of prophetic prediction.

Habakkuk is the only preexilic prophet identified as a *nābî'* in the title, which could plausibly be taken to imply that he was a professional or prebendary prophet, probably connected with the Temple cult. The same conclusion is suggested by the term *maśśā'*, oracle, used more often than not for curses or comminations against hostile nations, which also featured in Temple liturgies when the occasion called for them (cf. Ps. 60; 83; 108). We have seen further that the dialogue in the first section is based on a liturgical model and the psalm in Hab. 3 has its own liturgical rubrics. As a central intermediary, Habakkuk would be expected to deliver oracles especially at a time of political crisis, and the process by which such oracles were solicited is described in the course of the dialogue. The passage in question (Hab. 2:1) may be translated as follows:

> At my guard post let me take my stand
>   and station myself on the watchtower[40]
> to watch and see what he will say through me,
>   and what answer he will give to my complaint.

An anonymous seer, probably during the Babylonian exile, has left behind a similar account of soliciting an oracle announcing the fall of Babylon (Isa. 21:6-8):

> Go, set a watchman,
>   let him announce what he sees.
> When he sees horsemen, riders in pairs,
>   riders on asses, riders on camels,
> let him listen hard, very hard.
> Then the seer cried out:
> "On a watchtower, O Lord, I stand
>   continually by day;
> at my guard post I take my station every night."

While the precise significance of the terms "watchtower" and "guard post" escapes us, the passages provide a valuable glimpse of a process analogous to incubation rituals (e.g., Gen. 28:11; I Sam. 3:3) whereby oracles were solicited. Habakkuk's patience was rewarded when he received a reply, doubtless in an ecstatic state, in which he was commanded to write the vision on tablets in large characters, like a highway sign, so that it could be read, as it were, on the run. The reply, therefore, was not the kind that the analogy of the lamentation psalms would lead us to expect. And it leaves us asking what was the vision that the prophet was commanded to write so large that it could not be ignored even by those who hurried past without stopping.

From the answer of Yahweh it is at least clear that the vision writ large contained a prediction of well-being the truth of which many, the prophet among them, were beginning to doubt (Hab. 3:3). No such vision has been mentioned in the book up to this point, so that some commentators have wondered whether the psalm in Hab. 3, describing in magnificent language the coming of the warrior-god to save his people, is intended. It does indeed speak of the defeat of the wicked, the enemies of Israel (Hab. 3:13-14). It describes in impressive terms the onset of prophetic ecstasy and records the prophet waiting quietly, that is, without doubt or perturbation, for the divine intervention (Hab. 3:16). Since, however, we have no assurance that the dialogue and the psalm come from the same hand, we would have to take account of the possibility that the vision and prediction are those of an earlier prophet which remained unfulfilled and thus gave rise to the crisis of faith through which Habakkuk and his contemporaries were passing. In that case we would have to consider the prophecy which Isaiah was commanded to write as a warranty of its truth against a future fulfillment (Isa. 8:16-17; 30:8-10; cf. 29:11-12). Isaiah too spoke of the need for a positive endurance, in faith, when present circumstances seemed to contradict the prophetic promise of divine intervention (Isa. 7:9; 30:15). And since the words of Isaiah seem to have been given a new life with Josiah's reforms and the expectation of freedom from the Assyrian yoke, which inspired them, a crisis of faith in prophecy, and therefore in the possibility of divine intervention, may well have occurred when those hopes died with Josiah.[41]

The faith that is called for in the interim between prophecy and fulfillment is faith in the possibility and reality of divine intervention in human affairs (Hab. 2:4; cf. 1:5). By means of a rather different reading—"he who is righteous by faith shall live" (Rom. 1:17; Gal. 3:11)—Paul made this celebrated text serve as scriptural backing for his polemic about the respective roles of faith and works. The Qumran

Habakkuk *pesher,* on the contrary, referred it to both observance of the laws and faith in the Teacher of Righteousness (1QpHab VIII.1-3). Habakkuk's differentiation between the wicked and the righteous on the basis of faith does in fact constitute a bridge between earlier prophetic teaching, especially that of Isaiah, and certain developments during the Second Temple that would lead to the emergence of the sects, including early Christianity.

The second and quite distinct section of the book consists in five woes against an unnamed tyrant (Hab. 2:6-20).[42] While it would be natural to identify him with the Babylonian king spoken of earlier, the language used provides no certain clues. He is a ruler guilty of plunder, bloodshed, and violence; he has founded a city on blood, has brought shame on his house, and inhabits a high and inaccessible fortress. Such a description could fit any one of several candidates throughout the history of the book's transmission. We must recall that prophetic books were not copyrighted and that sayings against foreign nations and rulers were particularly subject to reinterpretation in the light of new situations.

If it is true, as it seems to be, that Habakkuk represents central rather than peripheral prophecy,[43] it is equally true that by that time such prophets were finding themselves increasingly in the position of having to take sides: witness the contrast between the wicked and the righteous that occurs more than once in the first section (Hab. 1:4, 13; 2:4). Also indicative of a changing situation in the prophet's solicitation not of an oracle of salvation, which would be expected of a central intermediary, but of divine assurance in a crisis of faith. While the psalm in ch. 3 is not the original answer to the prophet's complaint, in the final arrangement of the book it serves the same purpose as the theophany in Ps. 73 and in Job, both of which raise the question of the reality and, by implication, the ethical character of the god of traditional religion. Such questioning increased in intensity following on the cumulative disasters of the late seventh and early sixth centuries B.C.E. It also featured prominently in the career of one of the most remarkable individuals in the history of Israel, to which we now turn.

3. JEREMIAH

P. R. **Ackroyd,** *Exile and Restoration,* Philadelphia: Westminster Press, 1968, 50-61; H. **Bardtke,** "Jeremia der Fremdvölkerprophet," *ZAW* 53, 1935, 209-239; 54, 1936, 240-262; J. M. **Berridge,** "Jeremia und die Prophetie des Amos," *TZ* 35, 1979, 321-341; J. **Bright,** *Jeremiah,* Garden City: Doubleday &

Co., 1965; R. P. **Carroll,** *From Chaos to Covenant: Uses of Prophecy in the Book of Jeremiah,* London: SCM Press, 1981; T. R. **Hobbs,** "Some Remarks on the Composition and Structure of the Book of Jeremiah," *CBQ* 34, 1974, 257-275; W. L. **Holladay,** "The Background of Jeremiah's Self-Understanding," *JBL* 83, 1964, 153-164; *Jeremiah: Spokesman Out of Time,* Philadelphia: United Church Press, 1974; *The Architecture of Jeremiah 1-20,* Lewisburg, Pa.: Bucknell University Press, 1976; J. P. **Hyatt,** "Torah in the Book of Jeremiah," *JBL* 60, 1941, 381-396; "The Book of Jeremiah: Introduction and Exegesis," *IB* V, 777-1142; E. A. **Leslie,** *Jeremiah Chronologically Arranged, Translated and Interpreted,* Nashville: Abingdon Press, 1954; G. C. **Macholz,** "Jeremia in der Kontinuität der Prophetie," in H. W. Wolff (ed.), *Probleme biblischer Theologie. Gerhard von Rad zum 70 Geburtstag,* Munich: Chr. Kaiser Verlag, 1971, 306-334; H. G. **May,** "The Chronology of Jeremiah's Oracles," *JNES* 4, 1945, 217-227; J. W. **Miller,** *Das Verhältnis Jeremias und Hezekiels sprachlich und theologisch untersucht,* Assen: Van Gorcum, 1955; S. **Mowinckel,** *Zur Komposition des Buches Jeremia,* Kristiania: Dybwad, 1914; P. K. D. **Neumann,** "Das Wort das geschehen ist . . . Zum Problem der Wortempfangstheologie in Jer. 1-25," *VT* 23, 1973, 171-217; E. W. **Nicholson,** *Deuteronomy and Tradition,* Philadelphia: Fortress Press, 1967; *Preaching to the Exiles,* New York: Schocken Books, 1970; *The Book of the Prophet Jeremiah: Chapters 26-52,* Cambridge: Cambridge University Press, 1975; T. W. **Overholt,** "Remarks on the Continuity of the Jeremiah Tradition," *JBL* 91, 1972, 457-462; "Jeremiah and the Nature of the Prophetic Process," in *Essays in Honor of J. Coert Rylaarsdam,* Pittsburgh: Pickwick Press, 1977, 129-150; K.-F. **Pohlmann,** *Studien zum Jeremiabuch,* Göttingen: Vandenhoeck & Ruprecht, 1978; T. M. **Raitt,** "The Prophetic Summons to Repentance," *ZAW* 83, 1971, 30-49; *A Theology of Exile: Judgment/Deliverance in Jeremiah and Ezekiel,* Philadelphia: Fortress Press, 1977; H. H. **Rowley,** "The Early Prophecies of Jeremiah in Their Setting," *BJRL* 45, 1962-63, 198-234 (= *Men of God,* London: Thomas Nelson & Sons, 1963, 133-168); M. B. **Rowton,** "The Chronology of Jeremiah's Oracles," *JNES* 10, 1951, 128-130; W. **Rudolph,** *Jeremia,* Tübingen: J. C. B. Mohr (Paul Siebeck), 1968; G. **Seitz,** *Redaktionsgeschichtliche Studien zum Deuteronomium,* Stuttgart: W. Kohlhammer, 1971; M. **Sekine,** "Davidsbund und Sinaibund bei Jeremia," *VT* 9, 1959, 47-57; J. **Skinner,** *Prophecy and Religion: Studies in the Life of Jeremiah,* Cambridge: Cambridge University Press, 1922; W. **Thiel,** *Die deuteronomistische Redaktion von Jeremia 1-25,* Neukirchen-Vluyn: Neukirchener Verlag, 1973; J. **Thompson,** *The Book of Jeremiah,* Grand Rapids: Wm. B. Eerdmans Publishing Co., 1980; H. **Weippert,** *Die Prosareden des Jeremiabuches,* Berlin: Walter de Gruyter, 1973; A. **Weiser,** *Das Buch Jeremia,* Göttingen: Vandenhoeck & Ruprecht, 1966; A. C. **Welch,** *Jeremiah: His Time and His Work.* Oxford: Basil Blackwell, 1951; C. F. **Whitley,** *The Exilic Age,* Philadelphia: Fortress Press, 1957; "Carchemish and Jeremiah," *ZAW* 80, 1968, 38-49; R. R. **Wilson,** *Prophecy and Society in Ancient Israel,* 231-251; W. **Zimmerli,** "Visionary Experience in Jeremiah," in R. Coggins et al., *Israel's Prophetic Tradition,* 95-118.

While we have more biographical information on Jeremiah than on any other prophet, the origin and transmission of the different kinds of material in the book raise serious problems for its evaluation and use. To begin at the end, the Greek version (LXX) not only is shorter than the Hebrew by about an eighth but also arranges the material differently. The differences can often be explained either as omissions due to orthographic error or as editorial decisions to lighten the text. But it is also possible that additions were made to the Hebrew text at a late date which were unknown to the Greek translator.[44] The discovery of several fragments of Jeremiah in the fourth cave of Qumran (4QJer[b]) that are closer to LXX than to MT will also serve to remind us that LXX contains genuine Palestinian textual tradition and is therefore not to be read as aberrant where it diverges from MT.[45]

Another significant difference between the Hebrew and Greek texts is that the sayings against foreign nations, toward the end of the book in the Hebrew (Jer. 46-51), occur after Jer. 25:13 and in a different order in the Greek. This latter position is not surprising, given the allusion to a book containing prophecies against nations (25:13), and it is also not uncommon for judgment on the nations to follow judgment on Israel in prophetic books (e.g., Isa. 13-23). This chapter (Jer. 25) is, in general, extremely important for understanding the organization of the book as a whole. It has long been assumed that the Deuteronomic school has played an important part in the production of the book, though there are differences of opinion as to the extent of their activity and the criteria for determining what is and is not Deuteronomic.[46] In this chapter, in which the prophet looks back over twenty-three years of unheeded prophesying, characteristic Deuteronomic ideas are not difficult to detect. The people have refused to listen to "his servants the prophets" who called them to repentance, and especially to the abjuration of idolatry; loss of independence followed by exile is the price to be paid for ignoring prophetic warnings; eventually judgment will be passed on the oppressing nation and Israel will have a new lease on life. This is a familiar pattern in the Deuteronomic history,[47] and it explains why the cup of wrath is to be offered to both Judah and the foreign nations (25:15-29). In order to make this point, the editor brought together a collection of Jeremiah's sayings against Judah assembled by the prophet himself in 605/4 B.C.E. with the help of Baruch (subsequently expanded as we are explicitly told, 36:32) and a compilation of sayings against foreign nations that must be of later date.

This view of the matter will explain why Jeremiah's address (25:3-14), from the hand of the Deuteronomic editor, begins by alluding to sayings against Judah and ends by mentioning a book containing prophecies against foreign nations (25:13). The linkage served the theological purpose of the editor who wished both to explain the disasters that had overtaken Judah and to hold out hope for the future. We have just seen that this is an important theme in the Deuteronomic history (e.g., I Kings 8:46-53), as it is in a later strand of Deuteronomy itself (Deut. 4:25-31). We may find here an important clue to the organization of the book and to the understanding of prophecy that informs the presentation of Jeremiah himself.

While the sayings against the nations (Jer. 46-51) cannot have been compiled before the exilic period, they may well have had their point of departure in Jeremiah's own words. We are informed that Zedekiah went to Babylon in 594 B.C.E. (probably to reaffirm his loyalty after the abortive plotting of that year), that among his retinue was Seraiah brother of Baruch, a royal official, and that this person was commissioned by Jeremiah to take with him a scroll containing predictions of the fall of Babylon and drop it in the Euphrates (51:59-64). While, needless to say, it is no longer possible to reconstruct the contents of this scroll, the anti-Babylonian sayings of chs. 50-51 may well be based on genuine oracles of Jeremiah. If so, they have certainly been expanded and edited in the light of later situations, perhaps at about the same time as the anti-Babylonian poems in Isa. 13.

In its original form, the address of Jeremiah (Jer. 25:3-14) concluded the first collection of sayings against Judah covering the twenty-three years from his commissioning as a prophet (1:2) to the fourth year of Jehoiakim, which was also the year of Nebuchadrezzar's accession and his victory at Carchemish. A fuller account of this turning point in the prophet's career is given in ch. 36.[48] Baruch, we are told, wrote the sayings of the previous twenty-three years at Jeremiah's dictation and was told to read them publicly in the Temple, from which Jeremiah was at that time debarred—not surprisingly, since he had recently predicted its destruction (7:1 to 8:3; ch. 26). Baruch did so on the occasion of a public fast in December of the following year, a fast probably occasioned by Nebuchadrezzar's recent advance into the country. After this public reading the scroll was read again in the presence of a group of officials including members of the family of Shaphan, which supported the prophet. After urging Jeremiah and his scribe to go into hiding, they had it read to the king, who tore it up, threw it on the fire, and ordered the arrest of its author and transcriber. The writing and public reading of words spoken, in some cases, many years earlier had the aim of affirming their present validity; while, conversely, Jehoiakim's destruction of the scroll was designed to render the words inoperative. Baruch, however, rewrote the sayings, again at Jeremiah's dictation, and was rewarded with a personal message promising that he would at least survive the disasters in store for the country (ch. 45).[49]

There is no reason to doubt that at least the nucleus of this second edition of Baruch's scroll is to be found in the first section of the book (1-25) and that it consisted for the most part of sayings directed against Judah and Jerusalem. Several of these have survived in their original poetic form; others have been paraphrased in prose by the Deuteronomic editor; and there are additions and glosses of uncertain provenance and date.[50] One type of prose composition, which occurs frequently in chs. 1-36, is a paraphrase of a prophetic saying provided with a minimum of narrative framework.[51] Comparison with similar prophetic discourses in the history of the monarchy confirms the impression that this corresponds to a typically Deuteronomic procedure.[52]

The first section of the book (1-25) also contains several passages in which the prophet laments and complains to God and which have been known in the modern period, not altogether appropriately, as the "confessions" of Jeremiah.[53] Like several of the monologues in Job, these betray rather close affinity in style and language with the psalms of individual lamentation, a fact that has led many commentators to doubt their biographical relevance. While some of these "confessions" may well be more or less free compositions in liturgical form, there is no good reason to doubt that they accurately reflect Jeremiah's own condition. And there is certainly no good reason for arguing from a liturgical form to a cultic origin, in the sense that Jeremiah actually delivered them during Temple worship as an official or self-appointed representative of the people.[54] Much more in evidence is a more or less continuous biographical account of Jeremiah's activity and suffering, especially but not exclusively during the period immediately preceding and following the fall of Jerusalem.[55] While it is possible that this *historia calamitatum* goes back to Baruch, it too shows signs of Deuteronomic editing, the purpose of which was to present Jeremiah as the model of the unheeded and persecuted prophet who, in spite of everything, remains faithful to his commission in the manner of Moses.[56]

The origin of the so-called "book of consolation" in Jer. 30-31 (with some additions in ch. 33) poses a special problem since, exceptionally, it holds out the promise of a new order for a restored and reunited people under a Davidic dynast. While some recent attempts have been made to read it in the context of the Josian reforms, and therefore to attribute it directly to Jeremiah, it stands in such stark contrast to the preaching of the prophet elsewhere in the book that this conclusion must be considered unlikely. There is also clear evidence of Deuteronomic editing, especially in the passage promising a new covenant (31:31-34), and a general consonance with the exilic Deuteronomic perspective as attested in the history and the book of Deuteronomy itself.[57]

The last part of Jeremiah consists in the sayings against foreign nations (46-51), already mentioned, and a final chapter dealing with the reign of Zedekiah and taking the story down to the paroling of Jehoiachin by the Babylonian king Evil-merodach (Amel-Marduk). With some minor additions and subtractions, this is parallel to the narrative with which the Deuteronomic history ends (II Kings 24:18 to 25:30). It confirms the view that the book as a whole was edited by adherents of the Deuteronomic school not earlier than about 560 B.C.E., the thirty-seventh year of Jehoiachin's exile. Its inclusion made it possible to end the book on the same note of hope as the history.

From what has been said so far it will be apparent that the editors and transmitters of Jeremiah have been at pains to present him as fulfilling the paradigm of the prophetic role in Israel. According to the Deuteronomic perspective this implied, more than anything else, concern with law and covenant after the manner of Moses. Jeremiah was the last of "his servants the prophets," a long line of emissaries sent to warn Israel of the consequences of religious infidelity.[58] Like Moses, prophet *par excellence*, he proclaimed the law, interceded with God for the people in time of distress, accepted rejection as the price of fidelity to his calling, suffered persecution, and faced the challenge of those who did not accept his authority.[59] It is precisely the regularity and consistency with which these Deuteronomic perspectives inform the book that rule out the possibility of explaining the similarities in terms of a style of public discourse or preaching characteristic of that time. There is also the fact that undoubtedly genuine sayings of Jeremiah differ in some significant respects from the Deuteronomic theology. With all due regard for the danger of circular reasoning, it can be affirmed, for example, that while the Deuteronomists regularly offer alternatives, after the early period Jeremiah himself seldom if ever does.[60]

An adequate appreciation of the pervasiveness of the Deuteronomic perspective in this prophetic book would call for detailed rhetorical and thematic analysis of the different kinds of material in it, and especially the longer prose passages. We have space for only two further examples, one rhetorical and the other thematic. At several points we find an explanation of the disasters that are to overtake

Judah—or have already overtaken it—in the form of question and answer (Jer. 5:19; 9:12-14; 16:10-13; 22:8-9). The analogy is not so much with the query of the son answered by the father which we associate with the Passover seder (cf. Ex. 13:14-15; Deut. 6:20-25) but with a rhetorical form employed by the Deuteronomists for explaining the prospect or reality of political disaster (Deut. 29:24-28 [MT 29:23-27]; I Kings 9:8-9); a form that is not found elsewhere.[61]

A more substantive example would be the criteria for distinguishing between true and false prophecy and the characterization of false prophecy in general. In his diatribe against contemporary holders of the office (Jer. 23:9-40) and his dealings with specific representatives—Hananiah, Ahab, Zedekiah, and Shemaiah (chs. 28-29)—Jeremiah reflects the Deuteronomic doctrine on prophecy and follows the Deuteronomic criteria and guidelines. False prophecy is rebellion (Jer. 28:16; 29:32; cf. Deut. 13:5) and punishable by death (Jer. 28:16-17; cf. Deut. 18:20). The false prophet is, in the first place, the one who speaks in the name of another deity and thus tempts to idolatry (Deut. 13:1-3; 18:20); a situation which, for Jeremiah, was attested only in Samaria (Jer. 23:13, though the reference is perhaps to a previous age). Much more to the point was the case of prophets who spoke in the name of Yahweh but who had not been commissioned to do so. In keeping with Deuteronomic doctrine (Deut. 18:20) these are condemned by Jeremiah. They speak their own words (Jer. 23:36), visions of their own heads (23:16), not having received their commission in the divine council (23:18, 22). Prophets whose predictions do not come true are thereby proved to be false (Deut. 18:21-22), a consideration that appears to govern Jeremiah's dealings with the optimistic prophet Hananiah, though he tendentiously limits the application of the criterion to those who predict well-being (Jer. 28:8-9). It is, finally, of interest to observe that in both Deuteronomy (Deut. 13:1-5) and Jeremiah (Jer. 23:25-28, 32; 29:8) prophecy is linked with dreams and their interpretation.[62]

A particularly important aspect of this prophetic portrait is the commissioning (Jer. 1:4-19), which is remarkably similar to that of Moses as described in the earlier of the two versions in the Pentateuch (Ex. 3:1 to 4:17). The two narratives share the same basic structure: divine address, expostulation of the one addressed, confirmation and encouragement designed to overcome his hesitation, an act of installation accompanied by a form of words, specification of the mission entrusted to the prophet designate, and a visionary experience.[63] While the Moses narrative in Exodus does not refer, as does Jer. 1:5, to designation and consecration from the womb, the preceding

account of birth and miraculous escape from death as an infant (Ex.
2:1-10) functions in the same way. Both Moses and Jeremiah are
reluctant to answer the call and come up with the same excuse, an
inability to speak in public (Ex. 4:10; Jer. 1:6). Both are *sent* on a mission
and the word of reassurance is the same, "I am [will be] with you" (Ex.
3:12; Jer. 1:8, 19). The touching of Jeremiah's mouth and the
accompanying declaration, "I have put my words in your mouth" (Jer.
1:9), echo the assurance given to Moses that Yahweh will be "with his
mouth" (Ex. 4:12) and will put his words in the mouth of Aaron his
spokesman (Ex. 4:15). Whereas the vision of the burning bush leads
into the commissioning of Moses, Jeremiah's visions come at the end, at
least in the present state of the text (Jer. 1:11-16).

However one goes about explaining the close affinity between these
two accounts, it confirms the impression that Jeremiah is being
presented from the beginning of his career as a "Mosaic" prophet. We
should also note that the account of his call illustrates very well the
Deuteronomic theory of prophecy as set out in Deut. 18:15-18.
Following the "Mosaic" model, the true prophet is "raised up" by
Yahweh, who puts his words in the prophet's mouth and commissions
him to speak (Deut. 18:18; Jer. 1:7, 9, 17). We can go further and
suggest that for the Deuteronomic redactor Jeremiah is the last of "his
servants the prophets," bringing to an end a long history of prophetic
emissaries that began with the exodus from Egypt (Jer. 7:25).[64] It may
be for this reason that the indications of Deuteronomic editing are so
much more in evidence here than in any other of the prophetic books.

What we see in the book, then, is the Deuteronomic portrait of
Jeremiah and—to pursue the metaphor—the recovery of the prophet's
real likeness would call for a painstaking work of restoration. Our task
begins with the superscription to the book (1:1-3), which informs us
that Jeremiah ben-Hilkiah belonged to a family of priests at Anathoth,
a village about three kilometers north of Jerusalem, and that his
prophetic career began in the thirteenth year of Josiah, i.e., 627 B.C.E. As
noted earlier, the same date is given in ch. 25, which encapsulates
twenty-three years of prophetic activity. Doubts as to whether Jeremiah
actually did function as a prophet during the reign of Josiah, first
raised by Friedrich Horst in 1923, have not been stilled in spite of all the
arguments and counterarguments produced since then. For if he was
commissioned to prophesy in 627 he would have been active during
eighteen years of Josiah's reign and therefore also during that king's
reforms and the last period of Assyrian hegemony. Yet there is only
one saying dated to the reign, a prose saying of doubtful authenticity
(Jer. 3:6-10),[65] and not the slightest allusion to the kind of dealings

between prophet and king that are attested for later reigns. It must also seem strange that the sayings in the first part of the book (chs. 1-6), if dated to Josiah's reign, depict a situation of widespread apostasy involving even the monarchy (2:26; cf. 2:8; 4:9). For according to the Chronicler (II Chron. 34:3) the reforms began in the twelfth year of the reign, and therefore before Jeremiah's call, and the "conversion" of the young king even earlier. It is therefore difficult to see how Jeremiah's comminations against kings and princes would have made sense at any time between his call and the death of Josiah in 640 B.C.E.

A further difficulty is the absence of any anti-Assyrian oracle from these early sayings, especially in view of Jeremiah's commission as "prophet to the nations" (1:5). Where Assyria is mentioned in this first section, it is either an allusion to past history (2:36) or in a context that suggests the short period of Egyptian hegemony during the early years of Jehoiakim's reign (2:14-19). Yet Assyria was to remain at the center of international affairs for about fifteen years after the date assigned to Jeremiah's call in the superscription.[66]

A focal point of this discussion, and one still awaiting a satisfactory solution, is Jeremiah's attitude to Josiah's reforms. Assuming that the date at Jer. 1:2 is correct, the first period of his activity would have coincided with the reforms, and it would be strange indeed if he had nothing to say about them. He commends Josiah by way of contrast with the despised Jehoiakim (22:15-16), but the allusion is quite general and retrospective. An undated prose passage has him publicly endorsing a covenant (11:1-17) which, not unreasonably, has been taken to refer to the Josian reform. But the passage in question is transparently a Deuteronomic composition,[67] so that all we can safely deduce from it is that the editor wished to present him as supporting the reform. For much the same reason the so-called "book of consolation" (chs. 30-31) cannot be read as Jeremiah's own reflections on the Josian covenant, as was indicated earlier. In short, there is no saying of Jeremiah that can with confidence be taken as proof that he supported the reform, and certainly none dating from the reign of Josiah.

On the other hand, we do not have the impression that Jeremiah emerged after the death of Josiah as a completely unknown figure on the Jerusalem political and religious scene. His prediction of the destruction of the Temple in the first year of Jehoiakim (609 B.C.E.) was important enough to be taken up at the highest level. He also enjoyed from the beginning the patronage of the powerful family of Shaphan, which had been active in the reform movement during the reign of Josiah.[68] But in the absence of reliable information it is impossible to say what contribution, if any, he made to public life during the latter part of Josiah's reign.

In the present state of our knowledge, all we can say is that, if Jeremiah did not enter public life as a prophet after the death of Josiah at Megiddo in 609, he embarked on a decisively new phase of his career at that time. The dating of the call to the thirteenth year of Josiah allowed the Deuteronomic editor to represent him as supporting the reform. It also permitted him to credit Jeremiah with a ministry of forty years' duration, a number that has obvious associations with the Mosaic tradition.[69] This would be one more indication that, for those who edited the book, his ministry recapitulated and rounded off the history of prophecy that began with Moses.

Whatever Jeremiah may have thought of Josiah's reforms, it was not long before the promulgation of a written law produced its own bureaucracy, a corps of legal scribes whose claim to authority would eventually come into conflict with the prophetic claim. It is in the light of this development that we are to understand Jeremiah's polemic against "handlers of the law" (Jer. 2:8) and scribes whose false pen had turned it into a lie (8:8-9). And, in any case, the reform movement was dealt a fatal blow by the death of Josiah and the failure of "the people of the land" to establish his younger son Shallum (Jehoahaz) securely on the throne in his place (II Kings 23:30-34).

The priestly clan established at Anathoth in Benjamin, to which Jeremiah belonged, traced its ancestry back to Abiathar, survivor of the Shiloh priesthood who was exiled there during Solomon's reign (I Kings 2:26). A family background of this kind makes it easier to explain the influence of Ephraimite traditions on Jeremiah and his interest in the destiny of the northern tribes. During the earliest phase of his career, represented by the collection of sayings in Jer. 2-6,[70] much is made of the exodus and wilderness traditions and the temptation represented by the fertility cults, to which Israel had succumbed since the occupation of the land. The metaphorical way of speaking of religious infidelity as prostitution suggests that Jeremiah had learned from Hosea, though similar denunciations of the Baal cult occur in more recent Judean prophecy (e.g., Zeph. 1:4-5). We really do not know how effective the reforms under Josiah were outside the capital. What we do know is that the king's death and the brief period of independence were followed by a revival of native cults which the ensuing disasters did nothing to discourage (Jer. 7:9; 44:15-19; Ezek. 8; etc.).

As we read these early sayings we have the impression that Jeremiah has not yet found his own voice, but that in his denunciations and recapitulations of a long history of national infidelity he is in the process of assimilating the prophetic tradition and bringing it to bear on the contemporary situation. It is noteworthy, too, that at this early stage he still holds out the possibility of repentance ("turning") on condition that Israel abandon idolatry (Jer. 3:21-23) and practice truthfulness and justice (4:1-2). Yet there is already the sense that this will not happen, that his people have hardened their hearts too often against the saving word (6:10). And so the collection ends with the sad acknowledgment that his task of assayer and tester of the people has not been successful (6:27-30).

A major focus of discussion in this first part of the book is the repeated threat of invasion from the north (Jer. 4:5-8; 6:1-5, 22-26; cf. 10:22; 13:20).[71] On the basis of a reference of uncertain interpretation in Herodotus (I.103-105) these passages are occasionally taken to refer to the Scythians, who are thought to have invaded Palestine shortly after 630 B.C.E. It has further been proposed that Jeremiah predicted such an invasion, that this prediction was not fulfilled, and that in consequence he retired from public life, emerging only after the death of Josiah to deliver the "Temple sermon" (Jer. 7:1 to 8:3) after the accession of Jehoiakim. All of this is quite uncertain. If, moreover, Jeremiah began his activity as a prophet only after the death of Josiah, the "enemy from the north" would most naturally refer to the Babylonians and their allies (including the Scythians), who constituted a threat to the area after its subjugation to Egypt. This would also be suggested by Jeremiah's peroration, which links the Babylonians with "the tribes of the north" (25:9, 26; cf. 1:15). The same motif is further elaborated in the oracles against the nations, in which Babylon is itself threatened with annihilation at the hands of northern nations (50:3, 9, 41; 51:48).

After the death of Josiah at Megiddo the party that had supported the reforms attempted to perpetuate them by putting his younger son, Shallum, on the throne. The Egyptians, however, deposed him in favor of Eliakim (Jehoiakim), a more pliant representative of their interests. This move marked the end of the reform movement, the revival of syncretist cults (especially the cult of Asherah), and the beginning of a period of domestic strife that lasted to the destruction of Jerusalem. In the same year Jeremiah delivered a memorable diatribe in the Temple precincts which led to his arrest and trial by the ruling party (Jer. 7:1 to 8:3; 26:1-24). In spite of insistence on the death penalty by the Temple staff, he was acquitted following appeal to precedent by provincial elders who were present, and as a result of support in high places. Nevertheless, his prediction that the Temple would be destroyed earned him the lasting opposition of king and Temple personnel (including prophets), who succeeded in having him debarred from the Temple itself, at least for the next few years (36:5).[72]

During those years, down to the decisive Babylonian victory at Carchemish (605), Jeremiah continued in opposition to king, court, and Temple, attacking Jehoiakim mercilessly and predicting that he would come to a bad end (13:18; 22:13-23). More than any other, Jeremiah illustrates, especially during this period, the prophet's fundamental concern with political and social life. His self-appointed task was that of interpreting the changing pattern of political events in the light of the tradition mediated through his own highly personal experience of God. That this interpretation was carried out through actual participation in the events is obvious from the opposition that it engendered, not to mention the attempt on his life by members of his own clan (11:18-23). The resulting isolation and internal conflict seem to have intensified through the remaining years of his life.

After the battle of Carchemish the balance of power shifted decisively in favor of the Babylonians, who took control of Syria and Palestine from the Egyptians. Jehoiakim was soon forced to submit to a new master who invaded the country in order to secure tribute and reduce isolated pockets of resistance.[73] These events may have occasioned the liturgy of fasting during which Jeremiah's scroll was read in the Temple (Jer. 36:9). About the same time, however, a bad situation was made worse by a drought of exceptional severity during which Jeremiah refused to discharge the prophetic function of intercession.[74] In the last year of the century the Babylonian army was once again in the country, this time on its way to Egypt, where, however, it was turned back. It was doubtless this temporary failure which led Jehoiakim to refuse tribute, the predictable outcome of which was a punitive expedition in which levies from neighboring provinces, traditional enemies such as Damascus, Moab, and Ammon, took part.[75] It may have been on this occasion that Jeremiah brought Rechabites into the Temple precincts, offered them wine, which they naturally refused, and proposed them as a model of a community faithful to its traditions (Jer. 35).

The last years of Jehoiakim are left in some obscurity by both the Deuteronomic history and the Babylonian Chronicle. Whatever the sequence of events during the siege of Jerusalem,[76] the new king Jehoiachin lasted only three months, capitulated, and was deported together with several thousand of the aristocracy and artisan classes, among them a priest called Ezekiel.

The next eleven years, from the first to the second deportation, were the most intense and painful of Jeremiah's life. Nebuchadrezzar's appointee, another son of Josiah called Mattaniah, who was given the throne name Zedekiah, was not the person to meet the challenge of that situation. From the beginning he was under pressure to join in concerted action against the new overlord by neighboring states, a policy supported by powerful elements at the court. It seems that he was himself doubtful about the prospects of success and was therefore disposed to listen to Jeremiah even during the critical days of the siege (Jer. 37:3-10, 16-21; 38:14-28). Jeremiah, in his turn, was not without sympathy for him (34:1-5) and certainly did not share the aspirations of those who looked for a speedy return of the exiled Jehoiachin, widely regarded as the legitimate ruler both in Judah and the Diaspora (22:24-30).

The situation in the capital reached a climax four years into the reign when a revolt broke out in the Babylonian army and, a little later, Psammetichus II came to power in Egypt. From then on, the hopes of the war faction in Jerusalem focused on Egypt, which was soon busy fomenting revolt among the smaller western states. Delegates from these states met in Jerusalem where, during their conference, they were confronted by Jeremiah wearing the yoke-bar and thongs used to restrain prisoners of war and predicting the divinely-willed ascendancy of Babylon (27:1-15). This message, which went directly counter to that of numerous nationalistic prophets of the region (27:9), led to a confrontation in the Temple with a Gibeonite prophet, Hananiah ben-Azzur, who predicted that in two years Judah would be independent and Jehoiachin back on the throne (28:1-4). After an initial hesitation, understandable in view of the political situation, Jeremiah reappeared, this time with an iron yoke, and predicted the death of Hananiah (in keeping with the Deuteronomic law concerning false prophets), which is reported to have occurred within the year (28:10-17).

These disturbances also affected the Babylonian diaspora, which appears to have kept in close touch with developments in Judah. We hear of a certain Shemaiah, a prophet in Babylon, who wrote to the Temple authorities in Jerusalem urging them to take action against Jeremiah (Jer. 29:24-28). Other Diaspora prophets are known to have been executed for fomenting sedition (29:21-23). Meanwhile Jeremiah urged the exiles to come to terms with their situation, in the conviction that the future lay with them rather than with those who had been left behind (ch. 24).

There can be no doubt that, in setting himself against what appears to have been the national mood, Jeremiah was putting his life on the line. Opposition came from many quarters—the royal court (where, however, he seems to have had some influential friends), his hometown, and especially the Temple bureaucracy. One incident, undated, led to his arrest by Pashhur, chief of the Temple police, and exposure in the stocks at one of the Temple gates. This came after the smashing of an earthenware jar at the Potsherd Gate (later the Dung Gate) facing the Valley of Hinnom to symbolize publicly the fate of the city (Jer. 19:1 to 20:6). The deepening alienation of the prophet is seen in his refusal to marry, to take part in rites of mourning or celebration (16:1-9), and especially to discharge the crucial prophetic function of intercession (11:14-17; 14:11-12). Social recognition of the role of prophet did not necessarily imply social acceptance or prevent people from thinking of such persons as strange, forbidding, even deranged (e.g., Jer. 29:26). From the account of his trial, it seems that his support group was limited to members of one or two upper-class families (Shaphan, father of Ahikam, 26:24, and Neraiah, father of Baruch and Seraiah, 51:59 and 32:12), together with some of the country elders and nobility, the so-called "people of the land" who had supported Josiah's reforms. Apart from these he must have been quite on his own. Like that of no other prophet, his career illustrates the saying of Bonhoeffer that when God calls a man he calls him to die.

The revolt backed by Egypt which broke out in 589 B.C.E.[77] brought a swift reaction from the Babylonians at the beginning of the following year. A spirit of desperate enthusiasm fired the war party, which even succeeded in having Hebrew slaves released to meet the manpower shortage during the siege (Jer. 34:8-10). While the city continued to be invested for at least a year and a half, other Babylonian units were ranging the country, reducing the few cities that were still in a position to resist. The siege was lifted briefly as a result of Egyptian intervention after the accession of Apries in Egypt (Jer. 37:5), but the relief was short-lived and the Babylonians were soon back in front of the walls. The population of the city, swollen by refugees from the countryside, suffered extremes of starvation until the walls were finally breached and city and Temple put to the torch by the army commander Nebuzaradan. Zedekiah himself was captured while trying to escape and, after seeing his children slaughtered before his eyes, was blinded and led into captivity.

From the record of events in Jer. 32-34 and 37-39 we have the impression of Zedekiah as a pathetic figure, uncertain of what to do, fearful for his life from the pro-Egyptian faction at the court, hoping for a last-minute miracle. He sent a delegation to Jeremiah urging him to intercede, only to learn that he had run out of options and had no choice but to surrender (37:3-10). After the temporary raising of the siege resulting from the approach of the Egyptian army (Jer. 37:3), Jeremiah left the city to visit Anathoth, perhaps to initiate negotiations for the purchase of the field. Arrested on a charge of desertion, he was beaten and thrown into prison.[78] There he was visited by the king, to whom he gave the same message as before (37:11-21). Transferred to better prison quarters, he received a visit from his uncle Shallum, from whom he bought the field and closed the transaction (ch. 32); an act which was, in effect, an affirmation of faith in the future of his people and of their devastated land. As the situation deteriorated, with houses being torn down to expedite defense (33:4), the Babylonians masters of the entire country with the exception of Lachish and Azekah,[79] and the besiegers preparing to breach the walls, Jeremiah's plight became worse. The pro-Egyptian party demanded the death penalty for treason and had him put in a cistern, presumably leaving him to die. Released by a palace eunuch, he had a final meeting with the king, with whom he pleaded in vain to surrender the city (ch. 38).

After the destruction of the city, Jeremiah was protected by a special decree of Nebuchadrezzar[80] and given the choice of staying in Judah or accompanying the exiles to Babylon. Choosing the former alternative, he was entrusted to the new governor Gedaliah, another member of the Shaphan family (ch. 39), after whose assassination he was taken forcibly to Egypt by the insurgents or their sympathizers (chs. 40-43). The last we hear of him is that his preaching to this new Egyptian diaspora went unheeded (ch. 44).[81] We must suppose that he died in one of the Jewish settlements in the Nile delta not long after the fall of Jerusalem.

Looking back over Jeremiah's place in the history of prophecy, we can discern many lines of continuity with a tradition that by his time was firmly established. His Benjaminite origins, the probable descent of his family from the Shiloh priesthood of the pre-state period, and the affinities with the teaching and language of Hosea of the early sayings, have suggested the conclusion that he was firmly rooted in the Ephraimite prophetic tradition.[82] There is clearly an element of truth in this but it should not be exaggerated. To what extent a distinct, identifiable Ephraimite tradition survived after half a millennium in Anathoth, especially in view of its proximity to Jerusalem, is debatable to begin with. Then, as we have seen, Jeremiah drew his support less from Anathoth—which he condemned—than from certain families at the court and from the "elders of the land," who, to judge by their intervention in his trial, aligned him with Micah, a Judean prophet, rather than with Ephraimite intermediaries (Jer. 26:17-19). In the previous chapter we noted the affinities between sayings emanating from the Micah circle and the Deuteronomic program.[83] In view of the Deuteronomic predilection for Jeremiah, this may be another indication that Jeremiah represents more than one segment of prophetic experience and preaching.

While Jeremiah has much in common with earlier prophetic figures like Amos, Hosea, and Micah, even a casual reader will notice some equally striking differences. We can best appreciate what these differences imply by looking more closely at the literary differences. Gerhard von Rad has observed how, beginning with Jeremiah, the traditional forms of prophetic speech are breaking up and dissolving into longer and less clearly structured discourses. There is also a greatly increased emphasis on biographical narrations corresponding to a greater interest in the messenger as against the message.[84] Amos, for example, contains only one short biographical memoir (7:10-17) whereas we have something approaching a biography of Jeremiah from conception to his last days in Egypt. The frequent parallels between the Deuteronomic "biography" of Moses and that of Jeremiah have often been noted; and the book of Deuteronomy itself is a prophetic discourse of Moses presented within a historical and biographical context.

What seems to be happening is that the idea of instrumentality, basic to prophecy, is becoming increasingly a matter not just of speaking but of a service that tends toward a total life investment. The greatly increased emphasis in Jeremiah on prayer, suffering, interiority, identification with the grief and anger of God, points in this direction and indicates a notable broadening in the way the prophetic function is perceived.

A further indication is the frequency of mimetic and symbolic actions recorded in the book.[85] Grounded, as it seems, in homeopathic magic, this type of act has been routinized in various specialized areas of public activity such as warfare, medicine, law, and art. In its prophetic form, the intent was not just to supplement the spoken word with a kind of visual aid but to enhance its force and strengthen its efficacy. In early ecstatic prophecy the performance of such mimetic acts, e.g., butting with iron horns or shooting arrows to simulate victory (I Kings 22:10-12; II Kings 13:14-19), does not appear to have had any further impact on or implications for the performer. In Jeremiah, however, the range of such acts has increased to the point of drawing the consciousness of the actor more deeply into identification with his mission. Here again, then, we are approaching the point where the person, as much as the spoken word, is the message.

At almost any point of contact, a reading of Jeremiah affronts our liberal assumptions about the nature of religion. He was a person whose career took him into the public arena of national policy and who spent his life trying to influence decision-making at the highest level. Yet here, where we would look for nuance, the acknowledgment of political realities and the ability to compromise, we find only absolute, uncompromising assurance: "Is not my word like fire, and like a hammer which breaks up rocks?" (Jer. 23:29). There is also the fact that his own deepening sense of rejection led him to an overwhelming conviction of human sin and bondage; he speaks of the inability to abjure evil and the desperate sickness of the human heart (13:23; 17:9). The nation that believes itself to be the elect of God stands under a divine judgment no less real for being unacknowledged. Its people are clay in the hands of the potter, who makes or breaks as he wills (18:1-11). It is indeed possible to know the divine will—preeminently through the prophetic word—but there are many ways of evading the consequences of that knowledge. There are—fortunately, we may say—other emphases in the Hebrew Bible, including that of the exilic editors who modified and mitigated Jeremiah's preaching in the light of a quite different situation. But there can be no doubt that Jeremiah's own teaching and life were a major factor in the formation of the religious consciousness peculiar to early Judaism and the movements that arose within it, including early Christianity.

Notes

1. See above, p. 122, and Ch. 3, n. 117.

2. Cushi is certainly a proper name (cf. Jer. 36:14) but as an ethnic designation also could have appeared problematic; cf. the problem of Moses' Cushite wife (Num. 12:1), a subject of protracted discussion in the midrash, and Amos 9:7, where *kušiyyîm* are foreigners *par excellence*. It is perhaps worth noting that the short book of Zephaniah mentions the people or the land twice (2:12; 3:10). See further the commentaries and J. Heller, "Zephanjas Ahnenreihe," *VT* 21, 1971, 102-104.

3. This is clear from "the remnant of the house of Judah" (Zeph. 2:7), "the remnant of my people," "the survivors of my nation" (v. 9), the promise of restoration (v. 7; cf. 3:20), and the taunts of surrounding lands (vs. 6, 10).

4. "From this place" (*min-hammāqôm hazzeh*, Zeph. 1:4) looks like a Deuteronomic addition, and in the same verse the phrase "with the priests" (*'im-hakkōhᵃnîm*) has been added by a glossator unaware that Zephaniah was using the term *kᵉmārîm* (pagan priests) deliberately for the Jerusalem priesthood.

5. See K. Elliger, "Das Ende der 'Abendwölfe,' " in W. Baumgartner et al. (eds.), *Festschrift Alfred Bertholet zum 80. Geburtstag,* Tübingen: J. C. B. Mohr (Paul Siebeck), 1950, 158-175; M. Stenzel, "Zum Verständnis von Zeph. iii, 3b," *VT* 1, 1951, 303-305.

6. Especially the Day of Yahweh (Amos 5:18-20; 8:9-14; cf. Zeph. 1:14-18), represented as a day of battle (Zeph. 1:16), the use of a standard form of the curse (Amos 5:11; cf. Zeph. 1:13), and the theme of seeking Yahweh in the hope of salvation (Amos 5:4-7, 14-15; cf. Zeph. 2:3). The juxtaposition of the woe on Jerusalem (3:1-7) with the anti-Assyrian oracle (2:13-15) is also reminiscent of Amos 1:3 to 2:8.

7. It would be hazardous to conclude from these topographical allusions that the inhabitants of the city were anticipating the (alleged) Scythian invasion of ca. 630 B.C.E. Quite apart from the mythological undertones of such references, it would be natural for any real or anticipated invasion to approach the city from the north. On the "Scythian question" in Jeremiah, see below, p. 163.

8. See above, pp. 120-123.

9. The parallelism between the three divine requirements of Micah 6:8 and the three imperatives addressed to the "humble of the land" in Zeph. 2:3 is quite close; and especially interesting is the use of verbal forms from *pā'al* and *'āśāh* with *mišpaṭ.*

10. This, however, may be part of the Deuteronomic editor's interpretative expansion; cf. Isaiah's prophecy addressed to Hezekiah (II Kings 20:16-18) and the "Temple sermon" of Jeremiah (7:1 to 8:3).

11. Especially the abolition of non-Yahwistic cult centers (12:2-3) and proscription of Canaanite cults (12:29-31; 16:21-22; 18:9-14; 20:18).

12. II Kings 18:4, 22; II Chron. 29:3-19; 30:1-14; 31:1-2.

13. Y. Aharoni in M. Avi-Yonah (ed.), *Encyclopedia of Archaeological Excavations in the Holy Land* I, Englewood Cliffs: Prentice-Hall, 1975, 82-89.

14. Among recent restatements see E. W. Nicholson, *Deuteronomy and Tradition,* Philadelphia: Fortress Press, 1967, and A. W. Jenks, *The Elohist and North Israelite Traditions,* Missoula, Mont.: Scholars Press, 1977.

15. Of a quite general nature are Hos. 4:1-3 (reminiscent of the Decalogue) and the allusions to murder, villainy, and robbery at 6:9 and 7:1.

16. A. Bentzen, *Die josianische Reform und ihre Voraussetzungen,* Copenhagen: G. E. C. Gadd, 1926; G. von Rad, *Studies in Deuteronomy,* London: SCM Press, 1953, especially 66-68; "The Levitical Sermon in I and II Chronicles," in *The Problem of the Hexateuch and Other Essays,* Edinburgh: Oliver & Boyd, 1965, 267-280.

17. See also above, pp. 99-100, for the meaning of "Levite," "Levitical priest," "son of Levi" in Deuteronomy.

18. Amos 7:16; Micah 2:6, 11; Ezek. 21:1, 7. NEB "go drivelling on" at Amos 7:16 is therefore unjustified, in spite of the meaning "to drip" of the stem.

19. Removing landmarks (Deut. 19:14; Micah 2:2), usury and abusive debt collection (Deut. 24:6, 10-13, 17; Micah 2:8, 9a), defense of the poor (Deut.

15:4; 14:28-29, etc.; Micah 3:1-2; 6:10), maintenance of process of justice (Deut. 16:18-20; Micah 3:9), condemnation of bribery (Deut. 16:18-20; Micah 3:11), correct weights and measures (Deut. 25:13-16; Micah 6:10-11).

20. The most detailed presentation is that of M. Weinfeld, *Deuteronomy and the Deuteronomic School,* Oxford: Clarendon Press, 1972.

21. Prov. 25:1; Jer. 2:8; 8:8-9. In *b. Baba Batra* 15a, Proverbs, Ecclesiastes, Song of Songs, and Isaiah are attributed to Hezekiah and his men, which at least testifies to the persistence of a tradition of literary activity.

22. Suffice it to mention the rules for the holy war (Deut. 20:1-20) and the covenant formulations and curses, which, as noted earlier (p. 94 and Ch. 3, n. 38), bear comparison with Assyrian vassal treaties.

23. Max Weber, *The Sociology of Religion,* 51.

24. See P. A. H. de Boer, "An Inquiry Into the Meaning of the Term *maśśā',*" *OTS* 5, 1948, 197-214; R. R. Wilson, *Prophecy and Society in Ancient Israel,* 257-259. The term is used generally by Judean prophets and in most cases for oracles against foreign nations. If *śar hammaśśā'* (or *bʰmaśśā'*) at I Chron. 15:22, 27 is a liturgical title meaning "master of the oracle," as suggested by S. Mowinckel, *The Psalms in Israel's Worship* II, 56, we would have confirmation of the cultic setting of this type of saying.

25. Nahum 1:3a, which contradicts the preceding verse, is an explanatory gloss explaining God's anger as the result of his refusal to condone immorality. In 4b a word beginning with *daleth* is required in place of *'umlal,* and in 6a *lʰpānāyw* (for *lipnê*) should come after *yaʿᵃmôd.*

26. In addition to the commentaries, see P. Humbert, "Essai d'analyse de Nahoum i,2–ii,3," *ZAW* 44, 1926, 266-280; J. de Vries, "The Acrostic of Nahum in the Jerusalem Liturgy," *VT* 16, 1966, 476-481; D. L. Christensen, "The Acrostic of Nahum Reconsidered," *ZAW* 87, 1975, 17-30.

27. Since the identity of Elkosh is unknown, arguments for the non-Judean origin of Nahum are bound to be speculative even when as ingenious as that of A. S. van der Woude, "The Book of Nahum: A Letter Written in Exile," *OTS* 20, 1977, 108-126.

28. It so happens, however, that the prophet's name fits his function; cf. the opening words of Second Isaiah: *naḥᵃmû naḥᵃmû 'ammî* (Isa. 40:1).

29. This point is made quite properly by Van der Woude (n. 27). It is not impossible that such material could have circulated quite openly in the provinces during the disturbances following on the death of Ashurbanipal (627 B.C.E.).

30. By emending the last word of Nahum 3:17, *'ayyām,* to *'ôy lāhem* (the Stuttgart Bible has *'ôy mah*) and joining it to the following verse, some commentators identify vs. 18-19 as a separate woe saying, a very brief one by comparison with vs. 1-17.

31. See again R. R. Wilson, *Prophecy and Society in Ancient Israel,* 276-277.

32. P. Humbert, "Le Problème du livre de Nahoum," *RHPR* 12, 1932, 1-15; J. Lindblom, *Prophecy in Ancient Israel,* 253.

33. See II Kings 23:4; II Chron. 34:6-7. For archaeological confirmation,

see J. H. Hayes and J. M. Miller (eds.), *Israelite and Judaean History*, 465. According to Albrecht Alt, "Judas Gaue unter Josia," *PJB* 21, 1925, 100-116, the city lists in Josh. 15 and 19 derive from an administrative document of Josiah's reign.

34. The exact sequence of events is unclear. See Hayes and Miller, 471, and bibliography, 469.

35. For parallels to Habakkuk we should look especially at psalms that open with a complaint addressed to Yahweh, e.g., Ps. 3:1-2; 10:1; 13:1-2; 22:1-2; 74:1; 94:3. In some instances the divine response is assumed to have been received (through a cultic intermediary) and is followed by praise, thanksgiving, paying of vows; e.g., Ps. 20:5; 22:21; 28:5. In other psalms we have direct divine address, e.g., Ps. 50:7-23; 81:5-16; 82:2-4; 91:14-16; 95:8-11, and in one case in answer to a complaint, 60:6-8 (= 108:7-9).

36. B. Duhm, *Das Buch Habakuk. Text, Übersetzung und Erklärung*, Tübingen: J. C. B. Mohr, 1906, 19-23; and, in favor of the text as it stands, P. Humbert, *Problèmes du livre d'Habacuc*, 34.

37. In addition to the works cited in the bibliography, see P. Humbert, "Essai d'analyse de Nahoum i,2–ii,3," *ZAW* 44, 1926, 266-280; M. J. Guenthaner, "Chaldeans or Macedonians?" *Bib* 8, 1927, 129-160, 257-289; W. Staerk, "Zu Habakuk i,5-11. Geschichte oder Mythos?" *ZAW* 51, 1933, 1-28.

38. E. Nielsen, "The Righteous and the Wicked in Habaqquq," *StTh* 6, 1953, 54-78.

39. II Kings 23:35; Jer. 22:13-19; 26:1-23.

40. Here (Hab. 2:1) we should perhaps read *mispeh* for *māṣôr*, parallel with *mišmeret*, as at Isa. 21:8; cf. the designation *ṣōpeh*, watchman, for prophet (e.g., Ezek. 3:17) and the frequent use of this verb in association with prophecy (Isa. 21:6; 52:8; 56:10; Jer. 6:17; Ezek. 3:17; 33:1-9; Hos. 9:8; Micah 7:7).

41. Other aspects of this important text are discussed by M. Stenzel, "Habakuk 2,1-4, 5a," *Bib* 33, 1952, 506-510; S. Schreiner, "Erwägungen zum Text von Hab. 2,4-5," *ZAW* 86, 1974, 538-542; J. A. Emerton, "The Textual and Linguistic Problems of Habakkuk II. 4-5," *JTS* 28, 1977, 1-18; J. G. Janzen, "Hab. 2:2-4 in the Light of Recent Philological Advances," *HTR* 73, 1980, 53-78.

42. See M. Stenzel, "Habakuk II,15-16," *VT* 3, 1953, 97-99; E. Otto, "Die Stellung der Wehe-Worte in der Verkündigung des Propheten Habakuk," *ZAW* 89, 1977, 73-107.

43. R. R. Wilson, *Prophecy and Society in Ancient Israel*, 278-279.

44. Jer. 33:14-26, absent from LXX, looks like a commentary on 23:5-6 and has affinities with Haggai and Zechariah, especially in the use of *ṣemaḥ* (branch) for the Davidic ruler (Zech. 3:8; 6:12). It is also reminiscent of certain sections of Test. Levi (8:1-15) and Test. Judah (21:1-5; 24:1-6) from the Hasmonaean period.

45. On the text in general, see E. Tov, "L'Incidence de la critique textuelle sur la critique littéraire dans le livre de Jérémie," *RB* 79, 1972, 189-199.

46. Among the many studies that have pursued the implications of

Mowinckel's C source should be mentioned J. P. Hyatt, "Jeremiah and Deuteronomy," *JNES* 1, 1942, 156-173; "The Deuteronomic Edition of Jeremiah," in *Vanderbilt Studies in the Humanities*, Nashville: Vanderbilt University Press, 1951, I, 71-95; H. H. Rowley, "The Prophet Jeremiah and the Book of Deuteronomy," in H. H. Rowley (ed.), *Studies in Old Testament Prophecy*, Edinburgh: T. & T. Clark, 1950, 157-174; H. Cazelles, "Jérémie et le Deuteronome," *RSR* 38, 1951, 5-36; E. Nicholson, *Preaching to the Exiles*, especially 20-32; Hyatt (1942), Rowley, and Cazelles deal with the related question of Jeremiah's attitude to the Josian (Deuteronomic) reform.

47. I Kings 8:46-53; II Kings 17:7-23; 21:10-15; 24:2-4.

48. Nicholson, *Preaching to the Exiles*, 39-40; M. Kessler, "Form-Critical Suggestions on Jer. 36," *CBQ* 28, 1966, 389-401.

49. T. H. Robinson, "Baruch's Roll," *ZAW* 42, 1924, 209-221; G. Wanke, *Untersuchungen zur sogenannten Baruchschrift*, Berlin: Walter de Gruyter, 1971 (only Jer. 26-28 and 36 could have been written by Baruch); W. L. Holladay, "A Fresh Look at 'Source B' and 'Source C' in Jeremiah," *VT* 25, 1975, 394-412.

50. While few conclusions of this kind will pass unchallenged, there must be substantial doubt about the Jeremian origins of the following: Jer. 3:6-10, 11-14, 15-18, 24-25; 5:18-19; 9:12-16, 23-26; 10:1-16 (10:11 is an Aramaic gloss within this editorial expansion); 12:7-13, 14-17; 15:5-9; 22:8-9. In addition, most if not all of the following are Deuteronomic reworkings of Jeremian sayings: Jer. 7:1 to 8:3; 11:1-17; 16:1-21; 17:19-27; 18:1-12; 19:1 to 20:6; 21:1-10; 22:1-5; 23:1-8; 25:1-14.

51. Among those who have argued against the Deuteronomic origin of Mowinckel's C source, which includes the prose paraphrases, Helga Weippert, *Die Prosareden des Jeremiabuches*, believes they could have been composed by Jeremiah himself, while W. Thiel, *Die deuteronomistische Redaktion von Jeremia 1-25*, assigns them to disciples of the prophet during the exilic period.

52. E.g., I Kings 11:29-39 (Ahijah) and II Kings 22:14-20 (Huldah).

53. See G. von Rad, "Die Konfessionen Jeremias," *EvTh* 3, 1936, 265-270; S. H. Blank, "The Confessions of Jeremiah and the Meaning of Prayer," *HUCA* 21, 1948, 331-354; J. Bright, "Jeremiah's Complaints: Liturgy or Expressions of Personal Distress?" J. I. Durham and J. R. Porter (eds.), *Proclamation and Presence*, London: SCM Press, 1970, 189-214 (Bright accepts the latter alternative against H. Reventlow); A. H. J. Gunneweg, "Konfession oder Interpretation im Jeremiabuch," *ZTK* 67, 1970, 395-416; R. P. Carroll, *From Chaos to Covenant*, 107-135.

54. H. Reventlow, *Liturgie und prophetisches Ich bei Jeremia*, Gütersloh: Gütersloher Verlagshaus Gerd Mohn, 1963, while failing to establish this hypothesis, has provided a valuable focus for discussion.

55. The Jeremian "passion narrative" is, for the most part, concentrated in chs. 37-44. On the chronology of this section and the sayings in general, see, in addition to the commentaries, H. G. May, "The Chronology of Jeremiah's Oracles," *JNES* 4, 1945, 217-227; and, under the same title, M. B. Rowton, *JNES* 10, 1951, 128-130.

56. The theme of the persecuted prophet, which will serve to structure important early Christian perceptions of the ministry of Jesus, is only hinted at in the traditions about Moses (e.g., Num. 11-12, 16) and the Deuteronomic history (I Kings 19:10, 14). Its later development owes much to Jeremiah and the Isaian Servant.

57. For a different view see J. Bright, *Jeremiah*, 276-287, questioned by R. P. Carroll, *From Chaos to Covenant*, 204-225.

58. Servant ('ebed) is a synonym for prophet in Deuteronomic writings (e.g., Josh. 1:1-2; I Kings 14:18; 15:29; 18:36; II Kings 9:36; 10:10; 14:25), and the term *ʿbādāyw* (*ʿbāday) hann°bî'îm*, "his servants the prophets," is used of the prophetic succession as a whole (II Kings 9:7; 17:13, 23; 21:10; 24:2; cf. Jer. 7:25; 25:4; 26:5; 29:19; 35:15; 44:4; Amos 3:7).

59. See the remarks of E. Nicholson, *Preaching to the Exiles*, 45-58, and W. L. Holladay, "The Background of Jeremiah's Self-Understanding," *JBL* 83, 1964, 153-164.

60. The call to repentance is an important aspect of prophetic preaching according to the Deuteronomic school (e.g., II Kings 17:13; cf. Jer. 25:5-6; 26:3; 35:15). It is heard in Jeremiah's early preaching (3:21-23; 4:1-2) together with invitations to accept the offer of salvation (4:14). The possibility of "turning" and consequent well-being is contingent on, or closely tied in with, prophetic intercession; so that when Jeremiah decided that intercession was no longer possible (7:16; 11:14-17; 14:11-12), the fate of the people was sealed as far as he was concerned.

61. Cf., however, *ANET*, 299-300. On this question-and-answer form, see E. Nicholson, *Preaching to the Exiles*, 59-61. W. Brueggemann, "Jeremiah's Use of Rhetorical Questions," *JBL* 92, 1973, 358-374, has drawn attention to another rhetorical feature of Jeremiah's preaching, especially in evidence in the early chapters (2-6), that does not appear to be particularly characteristic of the Deuteronomists.

62. On Jeremiah and the "false prophets," see T. W. Overholt, *The Threat of Falsehood: A Study in the Theology of the Book of Jeremiah*, London: SCM Press, 1970; J. L. Crenshaw, *Prophetic Conflict*, Berlin: Walter de Gruyter, 1971, especially 49-61; F. L. Hossfeld and I. Meyer, *Prophet gegen Prophet*, Freiburg: Schweitzerisches Katholisches Bibelwerk, 1973; I. Meyer, *Jeremia und die falschen Propheten*, Freiburg: Universitätsverlag, 1977.

63. The structure of these and similar passages has been analyzed by N. Habel, "The Form and Significance of the Call Narratives," *ZAW* 77, 1965, 301-323.

64. See above, n. 58.

65. Doubts have arisen especially on account of the metaphor of the two sisters who were prostitutes (Ezek. 23). On the relation between the two prophetic books, see J. W. Miller, *Das Verhältnis Jeremias und Hezekiels sprachlich und theologisch untersucht*, Assen: Van Gorcum, 1955.

66. Much has been written on the date of Jeremiah's call, so that it is possible to mention only some of the more significant contributions: F. Horst, "Die

Anfänge des Propheten Jeremia," ZAW 41, 1923, 94-153; T. C. Gordon, "A New Date for Jeremiah," ExpT 44, 1932-33, 562-565; H. Bardtke, "Jeremia der Fremdvölkerprophet," ZAW 53, 1935, 218-219 ("thirteenth" is a scribal error for "twenty-third"); J. Milgrom, "The Date of Jeremiah, Chapter 2," JNES 14, 1955, 65-69 (from the period 627-616 B.C.E.); P. E. Broughton, "The Call of Jeremiah," Australian Biblical Review 6, 1958, 41-43; H. H. Rowley, "The Early Prophecies of Jeremiah in Their Setting," BJRL 45, 1962-63, 198-234 (= Men of God: Studies in Old Testament History and Prophecy, London: Thomas Nelson & Sons, 1963, 133-168); C. F. Whitley, "The Date of Jeremiah's Call," VT 14, 1964, 467-483; J. P. Hyatt, "The Beginnings of Jeremiah's Prophecy," ZAW 78, 1966, 204-214 (rejects his own earlier arguments for late years of Josiah's reign, JBL 59, 1940, 509, and supports Whitley's arguments for the year of Jehoiakim's accession).

67. Typically Deuteronomic phrases are: "to command the covenant," "the iron furnace" (referring to slavery in Egypt), "fulfil the oath which I swore to your fathers," "walk in the stubbornness of his [evil] heart," "bring upon them [you] the words of this covenant."

68. Shaphan, "secretary" (sōpēr) during the reign of Josiah, exercised some jurisdiction over the Temple, received the newly discovered book from Hilkiah, and decided what to do with it (II Kings 22:3-10). He and his son Ahikam were members of the delegation sent to consult with the prophetess Huldah (22:11-14). Ahikam protected Jeremiah at the time of his trial (Jer. 26:24), another son of Shaphan bore Jeremiah's letter to the Babylonian Diaspora (Elasah, Jer. 29:3), while yet another, Gemariah, had a room in one of the Temple gatehouses in which Baruch read the scroll (Jer. 36:10). He was one of those who urged the king not to burn it (36:25). His son, Micaiah, was also active at that time (36:11-13) while another grandson of Shaphan, Gedaliah, was made governor of the province after the fall of Jerusalem and was appointed Jeremiah's protector (Jer. 39-41; II Kings 25:22-25).

69. Eighteen years under Josiah, eleven under Jehoiakim and eleven under Zedekiah, the total remaining unaffected by the few months of the reigns of Jehoahaz (II Kings 23:31) and Jehoiachin (II Kings 24:8).

70. See the essay by H. H. Rowley referred to in n. 66, above.

71. In addition to entries in n. 66, see B. S. Childs, "The Enemy from the North and the Chaos Tradition," JBL 78, 1959, 187-198.

72. It is worth noting how much of Jeremiah's activity took place in the Temple. The oracle accompanying the jar-breaking was repeated in the Temple court (Jer. 19:14), where the confrontations with Pashhur and Hananiah also took place (ch. 20; 28:1, 5). The "Temple sermon" also, of course, was delivered there (26:2, 7; cf. 7:2) and the trial followed at the New Gate of the Temple (26:10). There also the Rechabites were offered wine (ch. 35) and the scroll was read by Baruch, again at the New Gate (36:10). In his letter to the authorities Shemaiah simply assumed that Jeremiah, as a prophet, was under Temple jurisdiction (29:24-28).

73. The capture of Ashkelon is recorded in the Babylonian Chronicle (*ANET,* 563) and probably alluded to at Jer. 47:5, 7.

74. Several passages appear to refer to a drought (Jer. 8:14-15, 20; 9:10, 12, 15 [MT 9:9, 11, 14]; 9:20-22 [MT 9:19-21], reinforced by the allusion to Mot, bringer of aridity and death in the Baal cycle from Ugarit). The liturgical character of the language in 14:1 to 15:3 has often been noted.

75. II Kings 24:1-2. Jeremiah's saying against Damascus (49:23-27) may have been based on an older oracle antedating the incorporation of that kingdom into the Assyrian empire in 732 B.C.E. (cf. Amos 1:3-5); but there may be intended an allusion to the Syrian contingents that fought alongside the Babylonians in 601 (cf. Jer. 35:11).

76. See above, n. 34.

77. Jer. 37:5. One of the contemporary Lachish ostraca speaks of a visit by the army commander Coniah to Egypt, which may point in the same direction (*ANET,* 322).

78. A little later the pro-Egyptian party demanded the death penalty on the grounds that he was "weakening the hands of the soldiers" (Jer. 38:4); cf. the same phrase used in Lachish ostracon VI (*ANET,* 322).

79. In Lachish ostracon IV, from the time of the siege, a certain Hosea, commander of an outlying garrison, wrote to Jaosh, governor of Lachish: "Let (my lord) know that we are watching for the signals of Lachish, according to all the indications which my lord has given, for we cannot see Azekah" *(ANET,* 322).

80. Jer. 39:11-12. If historically reliable, a valuable indication that prophetic sayings could be very widely disseminated and could come to the attention of the highest authorities. Nebuchadrezzar probably regarded Jeremiah as a Babylonian agent and may have interpreted his predictions of defeat and destruction as an additional divine authorization for conquest (cf. the claim attributed to Sennacherib that he was acting under mandate from Yahweh, II Kings 18:25).

81. Some implications of this rejection of Jeremiah *after* the fulfillment of his predictions are discussed below, p. 186.

82. R. R. Wilson, *Prophecy and Society in Ancient Israel,* 231-251.

83. See above, p. 122.

84. G. von Rad, *Old Testament Theology* II, 274-277; *The Message of the Prophets,* 162, 167.

85. The filthy loincloth (Jer. 13:1-11), refusal to marry and have children (16:1-9), visit to the potter (18:1-11), public smashing of a pot (19:1-15), the wooden and iron yoke-bar (27:1 to 28:17), purchase of land at Anathoth (32:1-44), offering wine to the Rechabites (35:1-11), hiding stones in the palace courtyard in Egypt (43:8-13).

V
BETWEEN THE OLD ORDER AND THE NEW

1. PROPHECY IN CRISIS

P. R. **Ackroyd,** *Exile and Restoration,* Philadelphia: Westminster Press, 1968, 17-38; "The History of Israel in the Exilic and Post-exilic Periods," in G. W. Anderson (ed.), *Tradition and Interpretation,* Oxford: Clarendon Press, 1979, 320-328; L. C. **Allen,** *The Books of Joel, Obadiah, Jonah and Micah,* Grand Rapids: Wm. B. Eerdmans Publishing Co., 1974, 127-172; M. **Bič,** "Zur Problematik des Buches Obadjah," *SVT* 1, 1953, 11-25; J. **Blenkinsopp,** "Abraham and the Righteous of Sodom," *JJS* 33, 1982, 119-132; E. **Bonnard,** "Abdias," *SDB* VIII, 693-701; B. S. **Childs,** *Introduction to the Old Testament as Scripture,* 411-416; J. L. **Crenshaw,** *Prophetic Conflict,* Berlin: Walter de Gruyter, 1971; S. J. **DeVries,** *Prophet Against Prophet: The Role of the Micaiah Narrative (1 Kings 22) in the Development of Early Prophetic Tradition,* Grand Rapids: Wm. B. Eerdmans Publishing Co., 1978; O. **Eissfeldt,** *The Old Testament: An Introduction,* 401-403; G. **Fohrer,** "Die Sprüche Obadjas," *Studia Biblica et Semitica Theodoro Christiano Vriezen,* Wageningen: H. Veenman, 1966, 81-93; S. **Herrmann,** "Prophetie und Wirklichkeit in der Epoche des Babylonischen Exils," *Arbeiten zur Theologie* 1, 1967, 32; E. **Janssen,** *Juda in der Exilzeit,* Göttingen: Vandenhoeck & Ruprecht, 1956; A. **Lods,** *The Prophets and the Rise of Judaism,* London: Kegan Paul, Trench, Trubner & Co., 1937, 173-183, 205-210; J. **Muilenburg,** "Obadiah, the Book of," *IDB* III, 578-579; J. M. **Myers,** "Edom and Judah in the Sixth-Fifth Centuries B.C.," *Near Eastern Studies in Honor of W. F. Albright,* Baltimore: Johns Hopkins University Press, 1971, 377-392; E. W. **Nicholson,** *Preaching to the Exiles,* New York: Schocken Books, 1970; M. **Noth,** *The History of Israel,* London: A. & C. Black, 1960², 289-299; T. H. **Robinson,** "The Structure of the Book of Obadiah," *JTS* 17, 1916, 402-408; W. **Rudolph,** "Obadja," *ZAW* 49, 1931, 222-231; *Joel—Amos—Obadja—Jona,* Gütersloh: Gütersloher Verlagshaus Gerd Mohn, 1971, 295-322; J. M. P. **Smith,** "The Structure of Obadiah," *AJSL* 22, 1905-06, 131-138; J. D. W. **Watts,** *Obadiah,* Grand Rapids: Wm. B. Eerdmans Publishing Co., 1969; H. W. **Wolff,** *Obadja, Jona,* Neukirchen-Vluyn: Neukirchener Verlag, 1977; "Obadja—ein Kultprophet als Interpret," *EvTh* 37, 1977, 273-284; "Prophecy from the Eighth Through the Fifth Century," *Int* 32, 1978, 17-30.

The sixth century B.C.E., in some respects one of the great turning points of human history,[1] saw the end of more than four centuries of the independent existence of Judah, during almost half of which, however, that nation had been in vassalage to Assyria, Egypt, and Babylon in succession. In the normal course of events, the extinction of dynasty and national cult would have signaled the end of the nation and its religion, especially in view of the Josian reforms, which aimed at concentrating the cult exclusively in the Jerusalem Temple. That it did not do so can be counted one of the more interesting and important circumstances of ancient history, the effects of which are still with us. The most obvious explanation is the Babylonian policy of allowing exiled groups to settle in separate communities, in some cases perhaps on uninhabited sites, thus making it easier for them to maintain their own identity.[2] Then, of course, most of the population stayed in the land, where the problem of continuity was not so severe. We must also suppose that the basic capacity for adaptation had already developed before the successive deportations of those disastrous decades. There is good reason to believe that the policy of cultic centralization was not as thorough and successful as it is represented as being, and that the basic social substructures, e.g., the institution of the elders, remained intact.

In the present chapter we are concerned with the impact of these events on prophecy. It was noted earlier that the tendency to bring the history of prophecy to an end during the exilic period, which could actually have drawn on rabbinic precedent,[3] contributed to a prejudicial theological interpretation of developments during the Second Commonwealth.[4] Classical prophecy has been widely understood in modern biblical scholarship as the apex of religious development in Israel, with the result that after it came to an end, there was thought to follow a gradual falling away from this high plateau as one approached the time of Jesus and early Christianity. In some of the most influential theologies of the Old Testament the Second Commonwealth is not studied with anything like the close and critical attention bestowed on the earlier period. What we too often find instead are generalizations of a prejudicial nature (religious formalism, legalism, chauvinism, etc.) passed on, like the patristic *catenae,* from one generation to the next.[5] The antidote is to let the texts speak for themselves, and one of the things they tell us is that prophecy did not come to an end during the Babylonian exile, though it did undergo rather profound transformations. Before examining these, however, we must take a brief look at the political and social transformations of that time which affected every aspect of religious life.

It is unfortunate that the crucial sixty years from the first deportation to the edict of Cyrus (598-538 B.C.E.) are so poorly documented. We gather, nevertheless, that the cumulative effect of Babylonian campaigns and the successive deportations was widespread destruction and disruption and considerable depopulation. This situation is reflected in prophetic texts that can be dated to this time and in Lamentations,[6] and it seems to be supported by the results of excavations in Judah and the Negeb.[7] Edomite encroachments on Judean territory made a major contribution,[8] with the result that quite a chapter of anti-Edomite polemic can be assembled from prophetic books and other texts; so much so that Edom was still used in the Roman period as a code name for unjust oppression (e.g., in the Tannaitic midrash *Mekilta*).[9]

To this polemical literature the small book attributed to the prophet Obadiah belongs. Presented as a vision (cf. Isa. 1:1; Nahum 1:1), it contains three brief anti-Edomite sayings (Obad. 1b-4, 5-7, 8-14, 15b) rounded off with a typical finale threatening all hostile nations, including Edom, with divine judgment (Obad. 15a, 16-18). A late Second Temple editor has added some supplementary verses promising the return of dispersed Israel to the homeland and the establishment of God's kingdom in Jerusalem (19-21).[10]

The problem of date and authorship, still under discussion, is complicated by parallels to the first two sayings in Jer. 49:9-10, 14-16. Since, however, neither version refers to the fall of Judah, which is clearly alluded to in the third saying (Obad. 11-14), the most likely hypothesis is that both have drawn on a traditional stock of anti-Edomite oracles—of the kind that have been incorporated into the Jacob cycle (Gen. 25:23; 27:39-40)—which was greatly amplified after the Edomite attacks following the fall of Jerusalem. The cultic character and origin of this kind of saying suggests, but cannot prove, that Obadiah was one of the surviving central cult prophets like Nahum. The name, meaning "servant of Yahweh," is common, being attested from the time of the early monarchy to the Second Temple period.

After the fall of Jerusalem the Babylonians appointed a native as governor, Gedaliah of the family of Shaphan, who took up residence at Mizpah (probably Tell en-Naṣbeh, about twelve kilometers north of Jerusalem), no doubt because of the devastation in the capital. The fact of his appointment, taken with what we know of his family background and sympathy for Jeremiah, suggests that he had belonged to the peace party during the reign of Zedekiah.[11] The abortive revolt of Ishmael, member of the royal family, began with the assassination of Gedaliah and ended in further deportations and expatriations, with the result that a great deal of land changed hands during this period. While this hardly amounted to a social revolution, as has been claimed, it helped to exacerbate relations between Palestinian and Babylonian Jews after it became possible for some of the latter to return. Those who remained in Judah, including the class referred to as "the poor of the land" (Jer. 40:7, etc.), were to claim that the deportees had, in effect, been expelled from the cult community and had therefore lost title to their land (cf. Ezek. 11:14-17). We must suppose that this argument did not persuade the original titularies, who could in any case appeal to the ancient law forbidding the alienation of hereditary property (Lev. 25:23).

The ownership of real estate was only one factor contributing to conflict between "natives" and those second- or third-generation Babylonian Jews who chose to return during the early Persian period. There was also the understandably greater incidence of marriage with foreigners and syncretist worship in the homeland, which was to become a divisive factor after the reestablishment of the Temple cult.[12] Almost without exception, prophetic writings which have survived from that time of transition support the Diaspora Jews as the legitimate heirs of the old Israel, from Jeremiah who spoke of them as the "good figs" (Jer. 24:1-10) to Haggai who condemned their opponents as ritually defiled (Hag. 2:10-14). While most of this prophetic activity was going on among the deportees and their descendants in Babylon, some of it may be represented by material originating in Judah which has survived by being incorporated into prophetic books. This may be the case with Isa. 21, Jer. 30-31, and parts of Ezek. 34-37, but the indications do not take us beyond a reasonable possibility.

Little is known of religious life in Judah during the decades following on the final loss of independence. Some cultic activity could have continued on the site of the Temple (as is suggested by Jer. 41:5) but if so, the cult was certainly not confined to Jerusalem. In spite of the Deuteronomic prohibition, temples dedicated to the Yahweh cult continued in use outside the capital.[13] The history of the Diaspora can be traced back to successive deportations by the Assyrians in the eighth and seventh centuries.[14] Most of these deportees were from the Northern Kingdom, and after their relocation on the upper reaches of the Tigris and Euphrates they disappeared from history. Judean deportees, on the contrary, were able to stay together and organize some form of community life, settling in such southern Mesopotamian centers as Tel-Abib, Nippur, and Babylon itself.[15] Skilled craftsmen would presumably have found work, or been put to work, in the cities, others would have engaged in commerce,[16] others again in agriculture.[17] Whatever their conditions in the early years of the exile, they were soon in a position to purchase property and send gifts back to the homeland. Leadership appears to have been exercised by elders (Jer. 29:1; Ezek. 8:1, etc.) who would no doubt have been concerned to maintain links with the past, not least by preserving genealogical records. In spite of the favorable sociological structure provided by separate settlements, resistance to assimilation no doubt called for great vigilance, which will help to explain why circumcision, Sabbath observance, and dietary prescriptions achieved during that time the confessional status that they have preserved ever since.

It is also worth noting that several categories of cult personnel, from priests to Temple servants, maintained their identity and status over several generations.[18] Unfortunately, we do not know how they were employed during the period in question. The substantial amount of literature produced by the Babylonian Diaspora would seem to presuppose a well-developed social, economic, and organizational substructure. One possibility, often suggested, is that it took the form of a network of synagogues that served the purposes of both prayer and education.[19] At this stage such an institution may have involved nothing more than meeting together in a house of adequate size. The elders, we recall, were in the habit of conferring with Ezekiel in his house (Ezek. 8:1; 14:1; 20:1). A second possibility, not incompatible with the first, is that the deportees built a temple at Casiphia, one of the principal centers of the Diaspora, which in Ezra's day was the home of a certain Iddo, with whose help Ezra was able to recruit cultic personnel.[20] Both of these conclusions are tentative since they depend on inference rather than historical data.

We are also reduced to speculation when we go on to ask how these Babylonian Jews were affected by state policy during this long period of time. They may have thrown in their lot with the opposition to Nabonidus (556-539), the last of the Babylonian kings, who neglected the state cult of Marduk for that of the North Mesopotamian moon deity Sin, and they may also have suffered for it. It seems tolerably clear, at any rate, that they supported the Persians, which gave them the decisive advantage of control of the cult after the return to Jerusalem.

We must now go on to ask how this situation, profoundly disorientating as it must have been, affected prophecy in its institutional

forms and socially idiosyncratic manifestations. While it is obvious that
prophecy did not come to an end, the sense that one long phase of its
history now belonged to the past is reflected in the Deuteronomic
editing of Jeremiah[21] and allusions to "the former prophets" which we
begin to hear soon after the return from exile (Zech. 1:1-6; 7:7). Vague
references to the drying up of inspiration will not suffice as an
explanation of this state of affairs, since they do not explain why
inspiration wilted then and not at another time.[22] Those optimistic
prophets who, as seen earlier, functioned primarily but probably not
exclusively in the cult, were proved wrong and discredited. Ezekiel
predicted that they would no longer have a place in the register of the
house of Israel (Ezek. 13:9), and in fact none appear in the carefully
preserved lists of cultic officials from the early Persian period. With all
due allowance for the polemical cast of the literature, the decline in the
quality of official, public prophecy is already apparent between the first
and the second deportation. Both Jeremiah (29:8) and Ezekiel (13:7-9,
23; 22:28) bracket prophecy with divination. Ezekiel also extends his
polemic to women prophets who were practicing the magical arts by
tying bands around the wrists of their clients and covering their heads
with shawls while pronouncing spells (13:17-23). This may suggest that
more traditionally Israelite forms of prophecy were waging a losing
battle against the allure of Babylonian magic, divination by a variety of
techniques, and dream interpretation.[23] It is also noteworthy that
Ezekiel follows up his attack on false prophecy with a condemnation of
syncretism (14:1-11), and that the same connection is made by the exilic
Deuteronomist (Deut. 18:9-14, 15-22; cf. 13:1-5, 6-18). In the absence
of a national cult under royal patronage this kind of situation is hardly
surprising.

Given the close association of all forms of prophecy with the
monarchy, it is strange that the loss of royal patronage has been so
seldom acknowledged as a basic factor in creating a situation fatal to the
exercise of the kinds of prophecy attested during the preexilic period.
A closely related factor is the dominance of the priestly and scribal
classes during the Babylonian and early Persian periods. Contact with
Babylonian scholarship favored the written word over oral delivery
and the wisdom of the past over intermittent inspiration in the present.
The priestly classes who edited and expanded the foundation narrative
(the JE of modern scholarship), and who were also familiar with the
Sumero-Akkadian scribal tradition, elaborated a theology in which the
prophetic functions of revelation and intercession were subsumed in
and reabsorbed by the cult.[24] And, not least important, the Persian
government gave its full support to the Jerusalem cult and its leaders, a

policy that tended to inhibit the kind of public dissent characteristic of some forms of prophecy under the monarchy.

After the extinction of the monarchy, the same close association between prophet and king can be seen in the expressions of hope for a Davidic restoration in prophetic texts from the late Babylonian and early Persian periods. From time to time during those years the political situation must have seemed to justify such hopes. Though Jehoiachin had joined other former rulers in enforced exile in Babylon, he was still widely recognized as the legitimate king and is even referred to as "king of Judah" on a tablet from the time of Nebuchadrezzar.[25] Dates appear to have been calculated from his accession (Ezek. 1:2), and the exilic historian ends his work, certainly by design, with the notice that he was set free at the beginning of the reign of Nebuchadrezzar's successor Amel-Marduk (II Kings 25:27-30). According to the Chronicler, the first governor of Judah after the return was Sheshbazzar (Ezra 5:14). If he is the same person as the Shenazzar son of Jehoiachin of I Chron. 3:18, it would be easier to understand how Zerubbabel, nephew of Sheshbazzar, could become the focus of nationalistic aspirations during the disturbances following on the death of Cambyses (Hag. 1:12-15; 2:21-23; Zech. 4:6-10). Be that as it may, the exiled king and his sons—the latter referred to but unfortunately not named on the Weidner tablets—must have been an important part of the aspirations of many in the homeland and the diaspora between the first deportation and the return in the early Persian period.

Prophetic texts that can be dated to that epoch suggest that there focused on Jehoiachin and his descendants a kind of christology, complete with titulary, based on the assumption that the dynastic promise was still valid and that therefore the dynasty was still the indispensable instrument of well-being and salvation. A passage in Jeremiah (33:14-16—identical with 23:5-6) speaks of a future in which Yahweh will raise up a "righteous Branch" (*ṣemaḥ ṣaddîq*) whose name will be "Yahweh (is) our righteousness" (*YHWH ṣidqēnû*).[26] Like other prose passages in the book, this one is probably based on a word of Jeremiah himself. It may then be suggested that the symbolic title conceals a pun on the name of the reprobate Zedekiah (*ṣidqiyāhû*, meaning "Yahweh is my righteousness") and that the designation *ṣemaḥ ṣaddîq* refers, by contrast, to the deposed Jehoiachin and his family as the "legitimate descendants" of David. The same title, "the Branch," was conferred on Zerubbabel (Zech. 3:8; 6:12) in keeping with similar usage already well established in the prophetic tradition.[27]

Linked with this title is the other one of Servant (*'ebed*) that has achieved such notoriety from the misnamed "Servant Songs" in Second Isaiah. A Deuteronomic addition to the Jeremiah text discussed a moment ago (Jer. 33:14-16) uses this title of the Davidic king and affirms the indefectibility of the dynastic promise (33:17-26). The same title occurs in Ezek. 34-37, which, as suggested earlier, may represent a distinct exilic collection of material (Ezek. 34:23-24; 37:24-25). It is also conferred on Zerubbabel who is therefore designated both Branch and Servant (Zech. 3:8-10). The Deuteronomic use of the term for both king and prophet, with its emphasis on service and instrumentality,[28] marked the furthest point reached to that time in the understanding of the function and purpose of institution and office. Though often lost sight of, its importance for the future can hardly be exaggerated.

So far in this section we have limited ourselves to describing social and political changes as they affected the exercise of prophecy in its different forms. We must now go further and note how these changes precipitated an inner crisis in prophecy, bringing to the surface unresolved conflicts and antinomies that seem to be inseparable from it. Something of this is already apparent in the polemic of Jeremiah and Ezekiel against those whom they took to be false prophets. Their major point was that these prophets were deceiving people with a false message of assurance originating in self-induced visions and dreams.[29] The content of the message, similar to that of prophets in neighboring lands (Jer. 27:9), can be deduced from quotations attributed to these opponents of Jeremiah and Ezekiel: national well-being, freedom from invasion and related evils, successful rebellion against the oppressor.[30] It is important to note that they are not condemned as apostates or devotees of alien deities. They worshiped the same god, used the same traditional forms of prophetic speech (e.g., Jer. 23:38; 28:2) and were probably indistinguishable from prophets like Jeremiah in appearance and demeanor. While some were attached to the Temple, others may have been employed in different capacities, e.g., as messengers and couriers on behalf of the king and court.[31]

The very violence of Jeremiah's attack, especially when taken in conjunction with his own doubts and self-questioning, suggests that the task of refuting these "false prophets" and establishing his own credentials was far from easy. The accusation of venality and immorality (Jer. 14:18; 23:11-15; 29:23), a routine way of discrediting opposition, does not reach the heart of the matter even if true as stated. The allegation that they were not divinely commissioned (Jer. 14:14; 23:18-22) is of its nature unverifiable, and the same applies to the argument that their visions were of human not divine origin (Jer. 23:16; Ezek. 13:2-3). Doubts about the propriety of certain ways of obtaining a revelation, especially by dreams, also seem to be unjustified in the light of prophetic history as a whole. The charge that they stole sayings from one another, practiced plagiarism in other words, may simply reflect the fact that they appealed to a well-established prophetic tradition and exhibited a strong sense of solidarity, neither of which, in itself, is a matter of reproach.

This appeal to tradition, mediated or filtered through an intense personal experience of God and brought to bear on the interpretation of contemporary events, is of course a crucial aspect of the complex phenomenon of prophecy. If we take the trouble to reconstruct what we can of the theology of the optimistic prophets, we shall see that they set great store on the covenant fidelity of Yahweh, his promise to the reigning dynasty (II Sam. 7), and providence for Jerusalem established on the best prophetic precedent (Isa. 37:33-35, etc.). The counterargument that this is a selective reading of the tradition is not in itself entirely persuasive. In response to Hananiah's prediction of freedom within two years (Jer. 28:1-4), Jeremiah appealed to prophetic tradition to make the point that the burden of proof rests with the prophet of well-being rather than with the one who, like himself, predicted disaster (28:5-9). The argument, however, is far from cogent, since it is simply not the case that prophets whom Jeremiah would have accepted as genuine predicted only doom. And, in a more general sense, it is unclear why the criterion of falsification should apply only to optimistic predictions. What it seems to amount to is that, in the last resort, the prophet can count only on his ability to communicate the quality of his own vision, his own sense of absolute certitude, the self-authenticating character of the word like fire, like wheat compared with chaff, like a hammer that breaks up rocks (Jer. 5:14; 23:28-29). The indications are that Jeremiah himself managed to convince only a very small number of people, and it is particularly significant that this was so even after the destruction of Jerusalem, which he had successfully predicted.

Jeremiah's career illustrates, certainly to a greater degree than Jeremiah himself or his editors intended, the destabilizing influence of prophetic dissent and the difficulty of controlling it.[32] The inability of the public to distinguish between conflicting claims and predictions led not only to a breakdown of prophetic authority in general but to widespread questioning of the religious premises on which the society rested and from which it drew its self-understanding. The contribution of optimistic prophets to this crisis is easier to assess since it could be argued, *post factum,* that they had deceived the people into fatally misreading the contemporary political situation.[33] This was especially the case with short-term predictions of the kind made by Hananiah so that, had he lived a year or so longer, his credibility would presumably have been damaged beyond repair. But it would also have been possible to argue that prophets like Jeremiah had actually contributed to bringing about the disasters that they foretold, both by their effect on public morale and by virtue of the belief that such prophecies, especially when accompanied by symbolic acts, had a performative and self-fulfilling character. The failure of his preaching to the small Diaspora in Egypt *after* the disasters had taken place (Jer. 44:1-19) is an important indication that prophets who predicted disaster were not automatically vindicated after the event.

It is clear, at any rate, that the criterion of historical falsification does not do justice to the complex nature of prophecy. As formulated in Deuteronomy (18:21-22), it cannot be applied by the prophet's contemporaries except for short-term predictions, which in fact it seems designed to discourage. It also threatens to reduce the prophetic function to that of predicting by suggesting that a prophet can lose his credentials by getting one such prediction wrong. Such a ruling might well have discredited not only Hananiah but also Huldah, Amos, and perhaps Jeremiah himself. Once again, therefore, we come up against the impossibility of discriminating between true and false prophecy on the basis of objective and verifiable criteria.

The broader implications of the collapse of confidence in prophecy can be seen in the widespread malaise, reflected in the literature of that age of transition, concerning the intentions and even the character of the god in whose name the prophets, whether optimistic or pessimistic, claimed to speak.

The problem may first be illustrated by two well-known incidents recorded by the Deuteronomic historian. The first, concerning the Judean man of God who fell foul of a prophet at Bethel (I Kings 13:1-32), is a classic case of conflicting prophetic revelations. Since it presupposes the extension of Josiah's reforms to the Bethel area and has unmistakable echoes of the mission of Amos under a later Jeroboam, this narrative appears to have been freely elaborated by the historian, and may therefore be read as reflecting the problematic nature of prophetic revelation in the last days of the Kingdom of Judah.[34] It also illustrates the Deuteronomic doctrine of false prophecy as a kind of testing of the prophet's audience (Deut. 13:3). In this instance, however, we would have to say that the line between testing and deception is very thin indeed. There is no hint of disapproval of the mendacious oracle which led to the Judean prophet's death and it was Yahweh, after all, who stationed that uncharacteristic lion in the prophet's path as he journeyed home.

The second incident also deals with conflicting prophetic revelations, this time between the ecstatic prophets of a king of Samaria and Micaiah ben-Imlah (I Kings 22:1-38).[35] Whatever its historical basis, it seems to have been put together as a kind of test case to justify a minority revelation which is unfavorable over against a prophetic consensus which is optimistic and corroborative of official policy. Looking beyond this intention of the writer, however, we can detect a new and disturbing element, namely, that false prophecy is explained as the outcome of a divine purpose to deceive by means of a supernatural agent (called simply the Spirit), functionally similar to the Satan who will emerge at a somewhat later stage.[36] The correspondence with the situation during the last days of Judah is unmistakable. Both Jeremiah (4:10) and Ezekiel (14:9), in effect, accuse Yahweh of deceiving the people and leading them to ruin through the false prophets. No one doubted that the disasters were the work of Yahweh—indeed, the result of a deliberate decision on his part (Lam. 2:8; cf. Amos 3:6). While the all-important question *why* he chose to do it remained in doubt, there was no doubt at all that conflicting prophetic revelations and claims played an important part in bringing it about (Lam. 2:14, etc.).

Anxious questions about the moral character of the god of traditional religion, reflecting the impact of the disasters of that time, may have left more of a mark on the Hebrew Bible than is generally acknowledged. In view of the identification of Jerusalem with Sodom in prophetic diatribe (Isa. 3:9; Jer. 23:14; Ezek. 16:43-58), for example, it may be proposed that the dialogue of Abraham with Yahweh over the fate of Sodom (Gen. 18:22-33) is a late addition to the story reflecting the religious crisis of the sixth century B.C.E.[37] The dialogue deals with two related issues: the fate of the righteous caught in the destructive flow of events directly attributable to divine causality; the possibility that, at a certain critical mass, the righteous can save the wicked from the fate which they deserve. That these were issues of great moment both before and after the fall of Jerusalem is apparent in the writings which have survived from that time. Jeremiah asserted, with rhetorical exaggeration, that the presence of one righteous person would have saved Jerusalem (Jer. 5:1). Ezekiel, on the contrary, argued that if a land (Judah, for example) suffered the disasters of war, even those models of righteousness Noah, Daniel, and Job would, if present, save only themselves (Ezek. 14:12-20). In keeping with this rigorously individualistic approach to culpability and retribution, Ezekiel also rejected the traditional idea of solidarity in the kinship group, and thus sought to answer the charge that his contemporaries were being punished for the sins of their ancestors (Ezek. 18:1-20). The same position is taken by Jeremiah's editor (Jer. 31:29) and finds expression in one of the later strands of Deuteronomy (Deut. 24:16; cf. II Kings 14:6).

Reading Gen. 18:22-33 as a kind of midrash inspired by the fate of Jerusalem and the theological problems to which it gave rise also sets in higher relief some interesting and neglected parallels between this passage and the book of Job. Both protagonists know that they have no right to question God, but they do so notwithstanding (Job 9:12). Both presume to speak, while confessing that they are but dust and ashes (Job 42:6), and both raise the question of how a just God can destroy the righteous with the wicked (Job 9:22). Both narratives, finally, illustrate the limitations of the prophetic function of intercession. Like Jeremiah, Abraham intercedes with God, but once his intercession comes to an end the fate of the city is sealed.

In summary, then, prophecy did not come to an end with the loss of independence and exile but was forced by the pressure of social and political change into different directions which will occupy us in the remainder of this book. For those who, after the destruction, still had the faith and courage to pick up the pieces and build a future it must have appeared that the older forms of prophecy, in spite of their religious and ethical achievements, were no longer adequate to the needs of a new and quite different situation. It is in fact unlikely that the older prophetic writings would have survived the catastrophes of the early sixth century if they had not been made available and serviceable by appropriate reinterpretation and contextualization. We must now go on to see what can be known or reasonably conjectured about this process of transmission and interpretation which bridged the gap between the old order and the new.

2. THE EXILIC-DEUTERONOMIC RESPONSE

P. R. **Ackroyd**, *Exile and Restoration*, 62-83; E. **Auerbach**, "Die grosse Überarbeitung der biblischen Bücher," *SVT* 1, 1953, 1-10; W. **Brueggemann**, "The Kerygma of the Deuteronomistic Historian," *Int* 22, 1968, 387-402; M. **Cogan**, "Israel in Exile—the View of a Josianic Historian," *JBL* 97, 1978, 40-44; F. M. **Cross**, "The Themes of the Book of Kings and the Structure of the Deuteronomistic History," *Canaanite Myth and Hebrew Epic*, Cambridge, Mass.: Harvard University Press, 1973, 274-289; W. **Dietrich**, *Prophetie und Geschichte*,

Göttingen: Vandenhoeck & Ruprecht, 1972; R. D. **Nelson,** *The Double Redaction of the Deuteronomistic History,* Sheffield: JSOT Press, 1981; E. W. **Nicholson,** *Deuteronomy and Tradition,* Oxford: Basil Blackwell, 1967, 107-118; *Preaching to the Exiles,* New York: Schocken Books, 1970; M. **Noth,** *Überlieferungsgeschichtliche Studien,* Tübingen: Max Niemeyer, 1967[3] (= *The Deuteronomistic History,* Sheffield: JSOT Press, 1981); J. A. **Soggin,** "Deuteronomistische Geschichtsauslegung während des babylonischen Exils," in F. Christ (ed.), *Oikonomia: Oscar Cullmann zum 65. Geburtstag gewidmet,* Hamburg-Bergstedt: Reich, 1967, 11-17; H. W. **Wolff,** "Das Kerygma des deuteronomistischen Geschichtswerk," *ZAW* 73, 1961, 171-185 (= "The Kerygma of the Deuteronomic Historical Work," in W. Brueggemann and H. W. Wolff (eds.), *The Vitality of Old Testament Traditions,* Atlanta: John Knox Press, 1975, 83-100.

The history of the kingdoms, written from the Deuteronomic perspective during the last decades of independence, was reissued in an expanded and revised form about the middle of the sixth century either in Babylon or in Palestine. The authors were certainly aware of the erosion of prophetic authority among their contemporaries and the questions being raised about the special relationship between Israel and its God and the conditions necessary for securing his cooperation. Their response is written clearly into the record: both kingdoms were destroyed because of sin (II Kings 21:10-15), and the destruction could have been avoided had king and people heeded the prophets sent to them by God (II Kings 17:13, 23; 20:16-18; 22:15-20; 24:2, 13). They thereby clear God of the charge of injustice, put the blame where it belongs and, at the same time, provide an overall theological rationale for prophecy.

Deuteronomy itself adopts a reflective approach to the phenomenon and contains what might be called a first sketch for a doctrine of prophecy (Deut. 13:1-5; 18:9-22). Major emphasis is on prophecy as a native Israelite phenomenon, contrasted with the different forms of divination and mediation practiced among the nations. The principle of historical falsification applies to all prophets (18:21-22), but the ability to predict correctly is not enough to authenticate a prophet and his message. He must also, on penalty of death, speak in the name of Israel's God (13:1-5). Genuine prophecy originated as God's answer to the people's request for mediation at Sinai-Horeb. It is therefore modeled on the ministry of Moses, which means that it is concerned essentially with covenant and law. When the prophet acts in that capacity—and only then—he does so with full divine authorization and must be obeyed.

The programmatic statement at the end of the book (Deut. 34:10-12), which denies parity between the mode of revelation proper to Moses ("face to face") and prophetic mediation, seems to be designed as a warning against a possible misunderstanding of Deut. 18:15-18, as if prophetic communications throughout the history were on the same level as the Mosaic revelation. It therefore sets aside an epoch in the past, which ended with the death of Moses, as normative for all subsequent expressions of religious life including prophecy. It has no intrinsic connection with Deuteronomy itself but serves as a finale to the Pentateuch as a whole.[38]

The attribution of Deuteronomy to Moses allowed the author to look at prophecy from the perspective of the beginning, while the Deuteronomic historians view it retrospectively from the end of an epoch. While the latter remain faithful to the Deuteronomic "doctrine" on prophecy (e.g., in assigning prophets the role of preaching the law, II Kings 17:13) they are also concerned to justify its historical function of warning against the consequences of religious infidelity. In both Deuteronomy and the history, however, prophecy—or at least this kind of prophecy—seems to be thought of as belonging to an epoch (that of the monarchy) which is reaching or has reached its end. Pointing in this direction is the concern in Deuteronomy to bring prophecy within an institutional grid, and thus to define and limit the scope of prophetic authority.[39] There are also the indications, noted earlier,[40] that the Deuteronomic editor of Jeremiah viewed this prophet as recapitulating and bringing to an end the series of "servants" that began with Moses. The question then must be asked: Did the exilic Deuteronomic school foresee any future for prophecy in the different dispensation which was then being projected for the future?

Since the history ends on an upbeat note, recording the freeing or paroling of the exiled Jehoiachin (II Kings 25:27-30), it might be thought that the historian had in mind the restoration of the monarchy, which might be taken to imply the restoration of the *status quo ante,* including the kind of prophecy attested under the monarchy. If, however, we go on to examine other passages of Deuteronomic origin that refer explicitly to the exilic situation, and more specifically to the appropriate response of the people to this situation, a rather more nuanced conclusion may seem to be in order.[41] For although we hear of the need to listen to Yahweh's voice, which would quite naturally be taken to refer to prophecy (Deut. 4:30; cf. 18:15), the emphasis seems to be on the action of the people as a whole. They are to seek Yahweh, to return to him, to pray, supplicate, and confess their sins, and in no case is mention made of prophetic intercession. If, moreover, the so-called "book of consolation" in Jeremiah (chs. 30-31) is of Deuteronomic origin or inspiration,[42] we would have to add that the law is to be put in their midst and written on their hearts (Jer. 31:31-34), again with no allusion to the mediating role of the prophet. What we are to conclude from this is not entirely clear, and it is quite possible that the Deuteronomists themselves were not entirely clear on the forms of religious life appropriate for the restored community. This uncertainty may well have extended to the most appropriate forms of mediation, especially in view of the ambiguities and antinomies besetting prophecy in the last years of the kingdom and the early years of the exile.

There seems to be general agreement that the same school was responsible for collecting and editing prophetic material during the exilic period. We noted earlier that the Deuteronomic history, while assigning a decisive role to prophets, mentions none of the canonical prophets by name.[43] Since it is unlikely that the historian was unaware of their existence, the most probable explanation is that the prophetic collection was intended as a kind of supplement to the history. The more difficult question which remains to be answered is that of the extent of this hypothetical exilic-Deuteronomic collection. The notorious difficulties involved in reconstructing the editorial history of prophetic books suggests that the most prudent course is to risk error on the side of less rather than more; or, in other words, to assign editorial expansions to this source only when there is clear evidence of Deuteronomic language or a point of view that is unambiguously characteristic of this school.

Superscriptions that contain chronological indications according to reigns, especially where there is the kind of synchrony between the kingdoms which we find in the history, provide one of the more probable indications of Deuteronomic editing. If we attend to this factor alone, we would be led to conclude that the exilic-Deuteronomic corpus contained Amos, Hosea, Isaiah, Micah, possibly Zephaniah, and certainly Jeremiah out of the fifteen books of the Latter Prophets.[44]

An unnoticed pointer to the likelihood of Deuteronomic expansions in prophetic books is the tendency of the historian to expand predictions of individual prophets to take in more distant events. Thus, the unnamed man of God who prophesied the end of the Shiloh priesthood is also made to predict the rise of the Zadokites and the destitution of the provincial priests as a result of Josiah's reforms (I Sam. 2:27-36). The man of God from Judah who condemned the Bethel sanctuary also went on to predict Josiah's activity in the northern territories (I Kings 13:1-2). Ahijah's condemnation of Jeroboam, which originally dealt only with the dynasty founded by that king, was extended to take in the fall of Samaria (I Kings 14:15-16).

And Huldah uttered an oracle of good omen concerning Josiah, but is presented by the historian as the Hebrew Cassandra predicting the fall and destruction of the city (II Kings 22:14-20).

If this suggests that something of the same happened with the prophetic books (and perhaps specifically with reference to the Josian reforms and the exile) the indications are not (leaving aside Jeremiah) exactly overwhelming. At this point we shall have to summarize briefly results already obtained, and it will be unnecessary to add that many of them are tentative. In Amos, references to the fate of Bethel may have been added, or modified, in the light of Josiah's action against that sanctuary in the seventh century (Amos 3:14; 5:6). The oracle against Judah, predicting the destruction of Jerusalem on account of sin (2:4-5), is certainly Deuteronomic. In the poem or riddle about prophecy in the following chapter (3:3-8), there occurs an explanatory gloss (v. 7) the purpose of which is to exonerate Yahweh of responsibility for the fate of Jerusalem, in keeping with the apologia of the Deuteronomic historian.[45] Allusions to the exodus, wilderness period, and occupation of the land (2:9-12) may be from the same source, as also the prose addition to the prophet's condemnation of contemporary worship (5:25-27).

Of the greatest importance for understanding the reformulation of prophecy in the light of the exilic experience are the passages in Amos that enjoin a seeking of Yahweh which can lead through judgment to salvation (Amos 5:4-5, 6, 14-15). We will now be in a better position to compare these with the message of the Deuteronomists addressed to the exiles, which is couched in the same terms (e.g., Deut. 4:27-31; Jer. 29:10-14). The conclusion would suggest itself that the Deuteronomists made prophecy serviceable to their contemporaries by reading a message of judgment as one of salvation through judgment. In embracing this alternative, they may well have followed the lead of an earlier editor who was unable to accept Amos' message of total rejection (see the addition at Amos 9:8b). It may also be recalled in this context that even with respect to the Northern Kingdom the historian's attitude is not uniformly negative (II Kings 13:5, 23; 14:27).

Apart from the titles, there is little in either Hosea or Micah that can be attributed with the same degree of probability to the Deuteronomic editor. Affinities there certainly are, especially where Hosea speaks of the broken covenant (Hos. 6:7; 8:1), but they are more probably due to the influence of these prophets and their disciples on the Deuteronomic school than the reverse. The allusion to the reunification of the kingdoms under a Davidic king in Hosea (3:4-5) is also a well-attested exilic theme and may derive from the same source. Despite some recent attempts to identify large-scale reworkings of Isaian sayings from the time of Josiah,[46] the editorial history of the book seems to have passed through different channels. The Deuteronomic historian had access to biographical traditions about this prophet which convey a rather different impression from the sayings (Isa. 36-39). It would not be surprising, in view of the interest of the school in prophetic biography, if these hagiographical narratives were added to the sayings by a member of the school during the exile. Biographical interest is also much in evidence in the Deuteronomic edition of Jeremiah which, as noted earlier, parallels in some important respects the Deuteronomic portrait of Moses. The point has been made that the Deuteronomic concentration on Jeremiah arose out of the conviction that with him a definite phase in the history of prophecy had drawn to a close. At a time of profound spiritual disorientation survivors of the reform party under Josiah summoned the remnant of Israel to return to its origins in the belief that the God of the exodus, the God of Moses, though hidden, would once more reveal his face: "From there you will seek Yahweh your God, and you will find him, if you search after him . . . for Yahweh your God is a merciful God; he will not fail you or destroy you or forget the covenant with your fathers which he swore to them" (Deut. 4:29, 31).

3. EZEKIEL

P. R. **Ackroyd,** *Exile and Restoration,* 103-117; P. **Auvray,** "Ezéchiel," *SDB* VIII, 1970, 759-791; D. **Baltzer,** *Ezechiel und Deuterojesaja,* Berlin: Walter de Gruyter, 1971; G. R. **Berry,** "The Composition of the Book of Ezekiel," *JBL* 58, 1939, 163-175; K. W. **Carley,** *Ezekiel Among the Prophets,* London: SCM Press, 1975; R. E. **Clements,** "The Ezekiel Tradition: Prophecy in a Time of Crisis"; R. **Coggins** et al., *Israel's Prophetic Tradition,* 119-136; G. A. **Cooke,** *The Book of Ezekiel,* Edinburgh: T. & T. Clark, 1936; W. **Eichrodt,** *Ezekiel, A Commentary,* Philadelphia: Westminster Press, 1970; G. **Fohrer,** "Die Glossen im Buche Ezechiel," *ZAW* 63, 1951, 33-53; *Die Hauptprobleme des Buches Ezechiel,* Berlin: Walter de Gruyter, 1952; F. S. **Freedy,** "The Glosses in Ezekiel i-xxiv," *VT* 20, 1970, 129-132; G. **Hölscher,** *Hesekiel. Der Dichter und das Buch,* Berlin: Walter de Gruyter, 1924; C. G. **Howie,** *The Date and Composition of Ezekiel,* New Haven: Society of Biblical Literature, 1950; "Ezekiel," *IDB* II, 1962, 203-213; W. A. **Irwin,** *The Problem of Ezekiel,* Chicago: University of Chicago Press, 1943; J. W. **Miller,** *Das Verhältnis Jeremias und Hezekiels sprachlich und theologisch untersucht,* Assen: Van Gorcum, 1955; H. **Reventlow,** *Wächter über Israel. Ezechiel und seine Tradition,* Berlin: Walter de Gruyter, 1962; H. H. **Rowley,** "The Book of Ezekiel in Modern Study," *BJRL* 36, 1953-54, 146-190 (= *Men of God: Studies in*

Old Testament History and Prophecy, London: Thomas Nelson & Sons, 1963, 169-210); S. **Talmon** and M. **Fishbane,** "The Structuring of Biblical Books: Studies in the Book of Ezekiel," *ASTI* 10, 1976, 129-153; C. C. **Torrey,** *Pseudo-Ezekiel and the Original Prophecy,* New Haven: Yale University Press, 1930; M. **Tsevat,** "The Neo-Assyrian and Neo-Babylonian Vassal Oaths and the Prophet Ezekiel," *JBL* 78, 1959, 199-204; J. W. **Wevers,** *Ezekiel,* London: Thomas Nelson & Sons, 1969; W. **Zimmerli,** "Das Gotteswort des Ezechiel," *ZTK* 48, 1951, 249-262 (= *Gottes Offenbarung. Gesammelte Aufsätze,* Munich: Chr. Kaiser, 1963, 133-147); "Die Eigenart der prophetischen Rede des Ezechiel," *ZAW* 66, 1954, 1-26 (= *Gottes Offenbarung,* 148-177); " 'Leben' und 'Tod' im Buche des Propheten Ezechiel," *TLZ* 13, 1957, 494-508 (= *Gottes Offenbarung,* 178-191); "Israel im Buche Ezechiel," *VT* 8, 1958, 75-90; "The Special Form- and Traditio-Historical Character of Ezekiel's Prophecy," *VT* 15, 1965, 515-527; "The Message of the Prophet Ezekiel," *Int* 23, 1969, 134-136; *Ezechiel,* Neukirchen-Vluyn: Neukirchener Verlag, 1969 (= *Ezekiel,* Philadelphia: Fortress Press, 1979); "Ezekiel," *IDBS,* 314-317.

The problem of working back from book to author is particularly severe in Ezekiel. The book is ascribed to a certain Ezekiel ben-Buzi, of a priestly family, who had an extraordinary vision in Babylon in the year 593 B.C.E. It is generally assumed that he arrived there with the first batch of deportees in 598. If, however, he was active for a time in Jerusalem before going to Babylon, he may have had this experience shortly after arriving in the Diaspora. According to the dates attached to thirteen sections in the book,[47] he remained active at least until 571. He was married and his wife died during the siege of Jerusalem (24:15-18). That is about all that we learn from the book itself and we have no other sources of biographical information. The often bizarre symbolic mimes and gestures that he is described as performing (see especially chs. 4, 5, and 12), the ecstatic experiences to which he was subject, the loss of speech and perhaps also movement (3:25-27), have suggested to some commentators that he suffered from some physical or psychological disorder—aphasia, catatonia, epilepsy, and schizophrenia have all been suggested, the last in an original way by Karl Jaspers.[48] While quite possible, especially in view of the frequent association between sickness and possession, such suggestions are speculative and are, moreover, often based on ignorance of the editorial history of the book.

The debate on that history has been going on since the beginning of the century and will no doubt continue. While there is no consensus, the following summary statement would find acceptance among many critical scholars today. While not a late Second Temple pseudepigraphal work, as suggested by C. C. Torrey and one or two others,[49] in its final form the book is the product of a school which owed allegiance to Ezekiel, which was closely associated with the cult, and which inherited the ancient traditions of the priesthood as did Ezekiel himself. The difficulty of distinguishing between the contribution of Ezekiel and that of his school, while real enough, is not so great that we cannot detect signs of reworking, especially in those passages which speak of new possibilities and a new order for the future. There is also the important point that the fall of Jerusalem stands between the early career of the prophet (593-586) and the later period of his activity and that of his discipleship. As is the case with the formation of the Gospels, spanning the second destruction in 70 c.e., this catastrophic event has left its mark on the book itself. To take only one example, predictions of exile have been expanded to take in the terrible fate of Zedekiah, last king of Judah (Ezek. 12:12-13). More generally, there is a marked shift from indictment of the nation, one of the most radical in prophetic writings, to emphasis on a new dispensation. Of course Ezekiel may himself have reedited and expanded his earlier preaching, as Jeremiah did. Yet it is impossible to explain the book as we have it without positing a school that continued his work, adapting his teaching to new situations as they arose.[50]

It is no doubt to this school that we owe the striking architectonic unity of the book. It has often been observed that the internal organization of the material follows the triadic pattern: judgment on Israel (1-24), judgment on hostile nations (25-32), salvation for Israel (33-48). This, however, is not peculiar to Ezekiel and may belong to a later process of reediting and restructuring. At a different level a more complex pattern is detectable that may tell us more about the production of this particular work. The book opens with a detailed description of a vision in which Ezekiel saw what, in the final summing up, is identified as "the Glory of YHWH" (Ezek. 1:28). This "glory" (*kābôd* in Hebrew) is a technical term in ancient priestly tradition for the mysterious manifestation of the divine presence in worship. Whatever its origins—perhaps at the pre-state sanctuary of Shiloh—it inevitably came to be associated with the Jerusalem Temple and its inner sanctuary, the Holy of Holies. In a later vision (chs. 8-11) the prophet saw this *kābôd* abandon the Temple five years before the latter was destroyed, moving first to the main entrance of the building (9:3; 10:3-5), then to the east gate (10:18-19), thence finally to the Mount of Olives (11:22-23).[51] Since it was the same manifestation that appeared to Ezekiel in Babylon, this must be the first stage in its relocation among the exiles there. In the final vision (chs. 40-48), dated to the twenty-fifth year of the exile or, in other words, half way to the jubilee year of release, he saw it return by the same way it had left (43:1-5), thus completing the cycle from exile to restoration, from absence to return.

The reversal of order, following which the vision of the *kābôd* vouchsafed to Ezekiel in Babylon now stands at the beginning of the book, occurred when this vision was prefaced to the original account of the prophet's commissioning. The latter, which is of an entirely different kind, features the command to eat a scroll containing an ominous message for the prophet's contemporaries (Ezek. 2:3 to 3:11). No adequate explanation of the resulting chronological confusion, reflected in the dates at the beginning of the book (1:1-3), has been offered to date. One is tempted to refer the thirtieth year of 1:1 to the prophet's age, since thirty is the minimum age for ordination to the priesthood (Num. 4:30). According to priestly tradition, moreover, the *kābôd* was supposed to appear to the ordinands during this ceremony (Num. 9:4-6). But the matter can no longer be decided with certainty.[52]

The affinities of this theological-symbolic schema with priestly tradition in the early books of the Bible are clearly detectable and important for our attempt to locate Ezekiel and his school. According to this tradition, Moses also had a vision of the *kābôd* during which he too was accompanied by a group of elders (Ex. 24:9-11, 15b-18a; Isa. 24:23; cf. Ezek. 8:1). In both cases, moreover, the vision led to a commissioning.[53] The appearance of the *kābôd* in the wilderness often presaged judgment on a faithless people as it does in Ezekiel (e.g., Ex. 16:7, 10-12; Num. 14:10b-12; 16:19, 42). The most distinctive feature of the throne in Ezekiel, however, is its mobility, an aspect that occasioned much learned speculation among the prophet's disciples (e.g., the expansions dealing with the wheels, Ezek. 1:15-21; 10:9-13), not to mention later readers (e.g., the fantastic suggestion that it describes a spaceship). Mobility is also the salient characteristic of the Ark in the wilderness according to priestly tradition (e.g., Ex. 40:34-38), and here too this characteristic is a function of Israel's absence from and eventual return to the land. That this *topos* was based on ancient ideas is suggested by the story of the exile and eventual return of the Ark-sanctuary, the "Glory," during the Philistine wars (I Sam. 4:21-22).

It would not be difficult to show that these affinities with the Priestly strand in the Hexateuch are consonant with the narrative structure of P as a whole. While there is, as is to be expected, a wide range of disagreement on the subject, it is reasonable to assume that P begins with the creation of the world, understood as a kind of cosmic temple, reaches its climax with the establishment of the mobile wilderness sanctuary (Ex. 39-40), and ends with the setting up of that sanctuary at Shiloh in the Promised Land (Josh. 18).[54]

If this is granted, it seems that the teaching of the prophet, as transmitted by his disciples, has been organized in a thematic unity that moves between the poles of exile and return, divine absence and presence. The concentration by the school of Ezekiel on the central issue of cult and divine presence, on which other matters such as land tenure depended (see especially Ezek. 11:14-21), their familiarity with the old sacral law,[55] their polemic in favor of Diaspora Judaism and of the Zadokite priesthood (e.g., Ezek. 40:46; 43:19; 44:15-31; 48:11),[56] suggest strongly that we are dealing with a priestly elite, probably in the Babylonian Diaspora, which was actively preparing for the return to Judah. The further conclusion seems unavoidable that this group overlapped with the authors of the exilic or early postexilic rewriting of the ancient traditions and laws known to modern biblical scholarship as the Priestly strand (P). We may then see in the book taken as a whole the early stages of the process by which prophecy was absorbed, or reabsorbed, into the priesthood and the cult.

It will be useful at this stage to summarize the contents of the book. The first section (Ezek. 1-7) records the vision of the mobile throne in Babylon (ch. 1), followed by the prophetic commission to preach to an obdurate people (2:1 to 3:11). Ezekiel then went to Tel-abib, one of the centers of the Diaspora, where he stayed in a catatonic state for a week (3:12-15). After receiving a further charge to act as watchman for Israel (3:16-22), he had another vision of the *kābôd* in a plain, during which he was told that he must remain secluded in his house and would be temporarily deprived of speech (3:22-27).[57] He was also commanded to perform certain acts presaging the coming disaster (4:1 to 5:4). The section ends with comminations against Jerusalem and Judah and what appears to be a sermon based on Amos' fourth vision (Ezek. 5:5 to 7:27; cf. Amos 8:1-3).

If, as suggested, the original call of the prophet is to be found in the scroll vision, it may have taken place before his departure for Babylon since it concludes with a command to go to the *gôlāh* (Ezek. 3:11). It is in fact difficult to avoid the conclusion that part of Ezekiel's early activity took place in Judah. He records the death of a certain prince Pelatiah in Jerusalem while he was actually prophesying (11:13), and the symbolic carrying of an exile's baggage could not very well have been intended for people already in Babylon (12:1-7).[58] The school of Ezekiel linked the original call with the vision of the Ark-throne by making the commission emanate from the One on the throne (1:28). The event of the prophet's calling may well have been precipitated by the political disturbances caused by Zedekiah's plotting against Nebuchadrezzar in 594 (Jer. 28), the failure of which led to the dispatch of a diplomatic mission to Babylon (Jer. 51:59).

The next section (Ezek. 8-11) records a third vision, dated a year later in 592, in which he was transported in the spirit to Jerusalem and given a supernaturally guided tour of the Temple and its precincts. What he saw there shows the extent of the triumph of the syncretists under Zedekiah, a mere thirty years after the great religious reforms of Josiah. The "lustful image" near a gate of the inner court was probably the nude Canaanite goddess well represented in archaeological finds. The animal and reptile figures were probably of Egyptian origin— understandably, given the pro-Egyptian policy pursued by Zedekiah during the last years of his reign. Further on there were women engaged in the Tammuz cult and a cult group worshiping the rising sun. As he returned to the point where the tour began, he saw supernatural agents of destruction being sent out to annihilate the city with the exception of the faithful few who were marked with the letter *taw* on their foreheads. Ezekiel attempted to intercede, but it was too late. As these things were happening, the *kābôd* left its place and settled on the hill to the east of the city.

Toward the end of this section there has been placed a short sermon which takes issue with the claims of those who remained in Judah and supports the Babylonian *gôlāh* as the true Israel of the future (11:14-21). As was noted in the previous section, the former argued that the deportees had been expelled from the cult community and had therefore forfeited title to their land (11:15; cf. 33:23-29; 36:2).[59] Ezekiel countered this with the argument that Yahweh had himself become a sanctuary for the exiles—proved by the appearance of the *kābôd* in Babylon—and that it was the Palestinians who, by their apostasy, had forfeited a place in the future restoration. We note here how, as in P, the covenant formulation (11:20) is restated as a promise of divine presence (cf. Gen. 17:8; Ex. 6:7-8).

The final and longest section of Ezek. 1-24 consists of about twenty-five discourses, practically all of which begin with the same formula: "the word of Yahweh came to me." After the performance of further acts presaging the coming disasters (12:1-20), we find Ezekiel correcting some current misrepresentations of his prophetic activity with the characteristic device of quoting the words of his contemporaries (12:21-28). This leads to an extended polemic against the professional prophets which draws heavily on Ezekiel's older contemporary Jeremiah (cf. Jer. 23:9-40; chs. 27-29).[60] The line of argument is much the same. While using an identical form of words, these other prophets are not commissioned. They see their task as fulfilling the expectation of their audience and thereby promote an attitude of self-deceptive complacency. Even more than Jeremiah, Ezekiel emphasizes—here and elsewhere (Ezek. 3:16-22; 33:1-9)—the grave responsibility of the prophet to the community which he must serve. He is also more aware of the likelihood of collusion between the prophet and his public which disingenuously solicits his guidance (14:1-11).

Ezekiel is often, and rightly, represented as the exponent of personal responsibility, and it will already be clear that this emphasis stems from the seriousness with which he took his own commission as prophet. The further point was made in a previous section that his teaching on this point was offered as a response to the theological problem posed by the massive disasters visited on Judah in the early decades of the sixth century. The argument that the children were being punished for the sins of their parents and that therefore God's ways were unjust (Ezek. 18:2, 19, 25, 29—all quotations from the opposition) called forth a denial of the old formula according to which God visits the iniquity of the fathers on the children to the third and the fourth generation (Ex. 34:7; Num. 14:18). Typically, Ezekiel expounds his teaching on this point in the form of a case history—similar to the casuistic passages in Deuteronomy—involving three generations in which there is no transmission of guilt from one to the other (Ezek. 18). The practical and pastoral conclusion is that the person remains free to "turn" from one way of life to another. This "turning" (the literal meaning of the Hebrew *tᵉšûbāh*, usually translated "conversion"), meaning a radical redirection of one's life, is one of the most important aspects of Ezekiel's preaching to the *gôlāh* community.

The other side of the problem of divine justice is dealt with in an earlier passage (Ezek. 14:12-23) in the same section. Like the author of Gen. 18:23-32 (Abraham bargaining with God over the fate of Sodom), Ezekiel here raises the question whether the presence of a few righteous people could save a sinful land. Unlike the author of the Genesis midrash, however, Ezekiel denies this possibility. Noah, Daniel, and Job, those traditional paradigms of righteousness, would—were they present—save no one but themselves, not even their sons and daughters. Here too, therefore, Ezekiel is at pains to emphasize the element of personal responsibility and dispel the idea that its place can be taken by prophetic or priestly intercession.

We have taken these two passages (Ezek. 18; 14:12-23) as examples of the ethical teaching of Ezekiel and his school, but it will be clear that elements of this teaching are to be found in all parts of the book. The general impression gained by a reading of the book as a whole is that moral guidelines are related directly to the kind of community Israel was intended to be. Hence the starting point is the special relationship with Israel's God and therefore the primary imperative is the rejection of idolatry (e.g., 5:11; chs. 6-8; 14:1-11; chs. 16; 23). In keeping with the priestly ethic in the Pentateuch and the Holiness Code (Lev. 17-26), there is no distinguishing in principle between ethical and ritual. Idolatry is directly connected with violence, murder, adultery, and other crimes or disorders. One of the most highly specific indictments in Ezekiel (22:6-12) lists incest and coition during the woman's menses alongside murder, adultery, perjury, and the like. In this respect it is true to traditional ethical catechesis as found, for example, in the Ritual Decalogue (Ex. 34:11-26) and the Holiness Code (Lev. 17-26). This does not mean, of course, that all of these were put on the same level, but it does imply that the concern was to outline a way of life consonant with being *this* kind of community. The fact, already noted, that land tenure was directly linked with participation in the cult is also significant in this respect, since participation in the cult was itself contingent on the pursuit of a common ideal of the moral life. The ethical teaching of Ezekiel, and of the prophets in general, presupposes an intrinsic relation between morality and worship.

The long series of discourses or sermons in Ezek. 12-24 also contains a number of striking and, in some cases, remarkably sustained figurative or allegorical narratives: the wood of the vine which is good only for burning (ch. 15), the unfaithful and ungrateful wife (ch. 16), the eagles (ch. 17), the lioness and her whelps (19:1-9), the ravished vineyard (19:10-14), the two sisters who become prostitutes (ch. 23). While the close links between prophecy and poetry are apparent throughout the history, we get the impression that Ezekiel was a poet and literary artist in a more self-conscious way than any of the other prophets. During his lifetime, in fact, he had the reputation of being skillful with words (Ezek. 33:30-33), a "parable monger" and adept at figurative speech (20:49). At least one of his compositions, a lament on the last kings of Judah, passed into common usage (19:14).

With the exception of the first (Ezek. 15), all of the compositions in question are figurative retellings of the history of Israel. While the allegories about eagles and lions (chs. 17 and 19) restrict themselves to the last years of the Kingdom of Judah, the remaining two (chs. 16 and 23) cover the entire history: Israel in Egypt; Jerusalem brought under the covenant relationship; the Divided Monarchy; dealings with Philistines, Assyrians, and Babylonians; the end of nationhood. It will be seen that Ezekiel's verdict on the monarchy is radically negative. It went wrong right from the start and was the principal architect of Israel's ruin. Here too we detect affinity with priestly tradition in the Hexateuch, which brings the history to an end with the occupation of the land and completely ignores the subsequent history. In more general terms, in fact, Ezekiel marks a decisive stage in the establishment of the pre-state period as normative for Judaism and therefore in the emergence of an authoritative Pentateuch. He differs from his prophetic predecessors, however, in one significant aspect, namely, in tracing Israel's infidelity back to the very beginning, in Egypt (23:3). This had important consequences for both him and his school, as we shall see.

The arrangement of sayings in this section does not always follow a logical order, as has often been noted. Thus, the ethical teaching in Ezek. 18 is quite different from the figurative narratives that precede and follow it, yet it has been put here because it begins with a *māšāl* (proverb). Again, the oracle against Ammon (21:28-32) belongs logically to the sayings against hostile nations (chs. 25-32), but it has been drawn into association with the preceding sayings (21:1-27) by the catchword "sword." The most important of the remaining compositions, the review of Israel's history in 20:1-44, has obvious affinities with the figurative narratives already discussed. The latter appear to be related to, and may be derived from, a type of psalm that presents the history of unfaithful Israel as a parable and a riddle (Ps. 78:2; cf. Ezek. 17:2). The historical review itself is structurally similar to the acknowledgment of a sinful history in Ps. 106, which ends with a prayer for the ingathering of the people. The setting of Ezek. 20:1-44 is a consultation of the prophet by elders whose request, whatever it was, was refused. It is possible, especially in view of warnings against syncretism that follow (vs. 32, 39-44), that they were seeking his approval of a separate cult establishment in Babylon; and it is even possible, as was noted earlier, that such a center was actually set up. At any rate, the historical review, which closely parallels the Priestly narrative in the Pentateuch, reveals sin and infidelity right from the beginnings in Egypt. It ends unexpectedly with a reaffirmation of the special relationship, in language reminiscent of the exodus theme, in spite of the unbroken history of infidelity. Some have seen here, not inappropriately, an anticipation of the Reformation doctrine of *sola gratia*.[61]

The diatribes, mock laments, taunt songs, etc., against hostile nations (Ezek. 25-32) form a distinct compilation similar to those found in other prophetic books (especially Isa. 13-23 and Jer. 46-51). It is made up of three blocks of material: sayings directed against Judah's immediate neighbors (Ezek. 25), a collection of material in verse and prose against Tyre (26:1 to 28:19), a longer series of anti-Egyptian sayings (chs. 29-32). As indicated by the dates, the nucleus of the collection goes back to a political commentary by Ezekiel on events associated with Nebuchadrezzar's campaigns in Syria, Palestine, and Egypt. These have been expanded in the light of subsequent history, as is the case with similar sayings in other prophetic books. The oracle against Ammon (25:1-7; cf. 21:28-32), for example, takes in reference to Arab encroachments in the middle of the sixth century which brought that kingdom to an end. Inevitably, the poems announcing the destruction of Tyre look beyond the unsuccessful siege by the Babylonians—which lasted thirteen years according to Josephus (*Ant.* X.228)—to its conquest by Alexander in 332.[62] Similarly, the sayings about Egypt go beyond Hophra's unsuccessful attempt to raise the siege of Jerusalem in 588 (Jer. 37:1-10) to Babylonian campaigns against Egypt in the last years of Nebuchadrezzar's reign.

That sayings against foreign nations, which grew out of the ritual curse pronounced by the seer on the eve of hostilities, continued right to the end as part of the prophet's stock-in-trade, serves to remind us once again that the prophet operated not in a timeless world but in the political sphere.[63] In the final analysis, the impetus for Ezekiel's prophetic activity stemmed from a religious experience through which the tradition in which he stood was mediated and reformed. Since, however, religion and politics were facets of the same reality, this particular appropriation of the tradition came to expression as a decision in the political sphere, one which in this case happened to be at odds with official policy.

This collection of sayings originally formed a quite distinct book. It was put after the book of sermons and visions (Ezek. 1-24) to counterbalance the prophet's indictment of Israel and to prepare for the projection of a new order in the last part of the compilation. This move is apparent from the dramatic ending to the first collection (24:25-27)—which is taken up at 33:21-22—namely, the arrival of a courier with the news that Jerusalem had fallen and the sudden unloosening of the prophet's tongue. It is also suggested by the fact that ch. 33 appears to be little more than a recapitulation, or alternative version, of some of the more important teachings in the first book: the responsibility of the watchman (33:1-9; cf. 3:16-21), the possibility and necessity of conversion (33:10-20; cf. 18:5-32), the conditions for secure possession of the land (33:23-29; cf. 11:14-21). At the same time, this chapter prepares the reader for the last section of the book

(34-48) in which is to be found the answer to the agonizing question put to Ezekiel by his contemporaries: "How then can we live?" (33:10).

It is important, first of all, to dispel the idea that the vision of the Temple (Ezek. 40-48) is a quite distinct block whose relation to the rest of the book is purely extrinsic. We have seen that it records the return of the *kābôd* as the final stage of a structural theme that informs the entire book. Moreover, the last of the sermons in 34-37 prepares explicitly for the vision with its reference to the future sanctuary which will sanctify Israel (37:28). It does not of course follow that 40-48, which in any case has gone through various stages of expansion, can be confidently attributed to Ezekiel himself. Indeed a great deal of the preceding chapters (34-39) provides reasonably clear indications of later authorship. The condemnation of the shepherds of Israel (34)—an indictment of the monarchy—appears to be an elaboration of Jer. 23:1-8 and ends with the promise of a Davidic ruler in terms closer to Jeremiah and Deuteronomy than to the genuine sayings of Ezekiel in 1-24.[64] The address to the mountains of Israel (36:1-15), which has drawn along the saying against Mount Seir (Edom) as a kind of counterweight (35), also has little of Ezekiel in it. The sermon which promises a new heart and spirit (36:16-38) has made generous use of earlier Ezekiel sayings. There are clear echoes of the review of Israel's infidelity in ch. 20 and the promise of repatriation and a new heart and spirit follows the same lines and uses the same language as the saying at 11:14-21. Leaving aside for the moment the vision of dry bones (37:1-14), the last of the sermons in 34-37, which holds out the prospect of the two kingdoms reunified under a Davidic ruler (37:15-28), appears to come from the same source as ch. 34. It seems likely, then, that all of 34-37, with the exception of the two sermons in 36:16 to 37:14, derives from individuals or groups outside the school of Ezekiel who cherished the hope of a new national unity, incorporating all of the tribes, under the rule of a Davidic dynasty.

In this section the vision of the dry bones in the plain (Ezek. 37:1-14) is quite distinct in form and content and must be from Ezekiel himself or a disciple. It begins not with the conventional "The word of Yahweh came to me" (as in 34:1; 35:1; 36:16; 37:15) but with the narrative introduction of the earlier visions. Like the vision of the *kābôd* (3:22; 8:4) it took place in the plain, and it uses the same language of the hand and spirit of Yahweh (cf. 1:3; 3:22, 24; 8:1). While the vision narrative has clearly been suggested by the quotation from the *gôlāh* community—"Our bones are dried up" (37:11)—it seems likely that it harks back to the posthumous miracle of Elisha when the dead man was restored to life after coming in contact with the bones of the prophet

(II Kings 13:20-21). This, at any rate, would be consonant with an important aspect of Ezekiel's prophetic self-understanding. It is a remarkable fact that, while he is clearly familiar with the prophetic tradition as a whole, Ezekiel is, at several points, more in line with the "primitive" prophecy of the archaic period. The extraordinary behavioral effects of possession, including levitation and second sight, bring to mind the careers of Elijah, Elisha, and their colleagues. Both the mobile throne and the chariot of Elijah descend from the whirlwind surrounded by fire (cf. II Kings 2:1, 11). Much of the language of spirit possession and the hand of Yahweh is borrowed from these narratives (e.g., I Kings 18:46; II Kings 3:15). Like Elisha (II Kings 6:32), Ezekiel is consulted by the elders in his house; and even the familiar "You shall know that I am Yahweh" already occurs in these early prophetic legends (I Kings 20:13, 28; cf. II Kings 5:8). While the major prophetic books have little to say about the spirit, for Ezekiel, as for primitive prophecy, it is the decisive agent, being not only the principle of movement and renewal but the dynamic factor in prophetic possession (Ezek. 2:2; 3:24; 11:5; 37:1).[65]

This remarkable narrative (Ezek. 37) perfectly epitomizes the function of prophecy at a crucial moment of history. The *gôlāh* community, which has lost its will to survive, is vivified by the spirit activated through the word of God addressed to the community. This happens in two stages. First, it is the prophetic summons which brings the *disjecta membra* together into a community. Only then can the spirit come into them, bringing the will to live and accept the future. In the explanation of the vision (vs. 11-14)—again, a feature typical of the book—that future is identified as settlement in the land, and the further point is made that they will recognize their god for who he is only when the miracle has taken place.

The long and rather rambling prophecy about Gog and the land of Magog (Ezek. 38-39) has been inserted to complete the immediately preceding prediction of everlasting well-being under a Davidic king; so much is clear from the connection between the end of the prediction (37:28) and the vision of the future Temple (40-48). This apocalyptic fantasy of the final, miraculous defeat of the forces of evil in the land of Israel has given rise to a great deal of labored and even bizarre speculation. On the one hand, it has been read as a coded prophecy about historical events that are taking place or about to take place; after all, the words *rō'š mešek* (ruler of Meshech, 38:2) sound suspiciously like Russia and Moscow. More surprisingly, a great deal of effort has gone into determining the historical identity of the places mentioned in the text. We must begin, however, from the observation that all of them, with the exception of Persia (38:5), occur in the so-called "Table of the Nations" in Gen. 10. In other words the apocalypticist, who probably knew less about their location than we do, has put together his piece as a kind of mosaic of biblical references and motifs—including phrases like "seize spoil, carry off plunder" (cf. Isa. 8:1-4), "I will send fire on Magog" (cf. Amos 1:4), and the like. What we have, then, is an apocalyptic tract from long after the time of Ezekiel inspired by the prophetic Day of Yahweh (Ezek. 39:8) and, more specifically, the prediction in Jeremiah and elsewhere of the coming of a foe from the north (Ezek. 38:17).[66]

The last section of the book (Ezek. 40-48) is presented as a vision of the future Temple, though it will be obvious at several points that this visionary context has been overlooked. The nucleus of the vision, dated to the year 573 B.C.E., is a description of the Temple to be built according to a heavenly model—a common motif in the ancient Near East. This detailed architectural survey leads up to the return of the *kābôd* and the divine address assuring the permanent presence of God to his people (40:1 to 43:11a). So far this is entirely consonant with and indeed integral to the book as a whole. To this nucleus, however, there have been added not only several supplements (43:13-17; 44:1-3; 46:19-24) but a substantial amount of cultic and ritual prescription and instruction dealing with the altar (43:18-27), the duties and prerogatives of cultic personnel (44:4-31), and the role in the Temple cult of the civic ruler (45:9 to 46:18). The present state of the text, especially where the law of the Temple is announced but not followed up (43:11b-12), suggests that some of this legislation has fallen out, possibly because of discrepancies with cultic law in the Pentateuch.[67]

Different again is the quite schematic and utopian account of the allotment of land (45:1-8; 47:13 to 48:35), which brings to mind the assignment of tribal territories after the setting up of the sanctuary at Shiloh (Josh. 18:1 to 19:51, basically a P narrative). Toward the end of the book (Ezek. 47:1-12) the Eden myth emerges once again (cf. 28:12-19)[68] with the powerful image of the stream that issues from the Temple and becomes a great river bringing life and healing to the barren wastes of the Judean wilderness. There seems to be no good reason to doubt that this goes back, directly or indirectly, to Ezekiel himself.

The expansion of Ezekiel's vision to accommodate material unique in the prophetic literature was clearly dictated by polemical factors. Stipulations concerning the civic ruler, who is referred to as the prince *(hannāśî')* but never the king in this section, have much in common with "the law of the king" in Deuteronomy (Deut. 17:14-20). They are not, however, essentially at variance with Ezekiel's own critical attitude to monarchy, and it was Ezekiel himself who suggested the more modest title for the office (Ezek. 12:10; 21:25). The situation is quite different with the priesthood, however. For here it is clear that a Zadokite group, to which we owe the legal expansions, has used the prophetic vision to further its own claims. Only those descendants of Levi who belonged to the Zadokite group could function as priests, while all the others, from now on called simply Levites, must serve as minor cultic personnel, and this as punishment for their religious infidelity (40:46b, a gloss; 43:19; 44:10-16; 45:1-8; 47:10-11). Nothing of this goes back to Ezekiel, who never refers to Zadokites and even criticizes the Jerusalem priesthood for neglect of its responsibilities (7:26; 22:26) and presumably also practicing or at least condoning the practice of alien cults (ch. 8). Tension between Zadokite priests and Levites, and the consequent subordination of the latter, may be traced back to the reforms of Josiah (Deut. 18:6-8; cf. II Kings 23:9), though Deuteronomy itself never speaks of Zadokites and makes no distinction in principle between Levitical priests in Jerusalem and those of the disestablished provincial cult centers.[69] Subsequently, however, there must have taken place a power struggle between different factions of the priesthood, in which control of the substantial revenues involved in Temple service played a significant role, a struggle from which the Zadokite group emerged victorious. It was this group which claimed the prophetic authority of Ezekiel for its own control of the cult and which actually assumed control after the reestablishment of Temple worship in the early Persian period. Here, then, we have an early example of the assimilation of prophecy into the priesthood, which is an important feature of Second Temple religious history.

As we look back over the book, we realize how complex and many-sided a figure was Ezekiel. The historian will view him as one of the leading opponents of the war party in the last years of Zedekiah and a major force for survival and eventual return among the deportees in Babylon, where the urge to rebel was by no means extinguished. (We recall, for example, the two Diaspora prophets who were executed by the Babylonians shortly after the first deportation, Jer. 29:21-22.) As a polemicist, he represented the claims of the Diaspora community, which was to play such a dominant role in shaping the future down to Ezra and beyond. As a prophet, he defies classification, combining the mantic features of the primitives with membership in the central cultic elite. He was not, as Hölscher believed, a visionary who was transformed into a *littérateur* by his editors. He was a visionary who also happened to have an extraordinary breadth of learning seen, for example, in his interest in the archaic period of history, use of mythological themes and command of the form and substance of sanctuary law. Moreover, both aspects were at the service of his contemporaries over a period of at least two decades. He therefore exemplifies prophecy as a form of pastoral ministry and community leadership. While it may be oversimplified to speak of him—with Wellhausen—as the father of Judaism, his capacity to generate a following, demonstrated in the editorial history of the book, and to project a new form of life for communities that doubted their ability to survive, was certainly a major factor in the emergence of Judaism in the early Persian period.

4. SECOND ISAIAH AND THE REVIVAL OF PROPHECY

K. **Baltzer,** "Zur formgeschichtlichen Bestimmung der Texte vom Gottes-knecht im Deutero-Jesaja-Buch," in H. W. Wolff (ed.), *Probleme biblischer Theologie. Gerhard von Rad zum 70. Geburtstag,* Munich: Chr. Kaiser, 1971, 27-43; *Die Biographie der Propheten,* Neukirchen-Vluyn: Neukirchener Verlag, 1975; J. **Begrich,** *Studien zu Deuterojesaja,* Munich: Chr. Kaiser Verlag, 1963; S. H. **Blank,** "Studies in Deutero-Isaiah," *HUCA* 15, 1940, 1-46; P. A. H. **de Boer,** *Second Isaiah's Message (OTS* 11), Leiden: E. J. Brill, 1956; P.-E. **Bonnard,** *Le Second Isaïe, son disciple et leurs éditeurs, Isaïe 40-66,* Paris: J. Gabalda, 1972; D. J. A. **Clines,** *I, He, We, and They: A Literary Approach to Isaiah 53,* Sheffield: *JSOT* Press, 1976; B. **Couroyer,** "Isaïe XL,12," *RB* 73, 1966, 186-196; F. M. **Cross,** "The Council of Yahweh in Second Isaiah," *JNES* 12, 1953, 274-278; G. R. **Driver,** "Isaiah 52:13–53:12: The Servant of the Lord," in M. Black and G. Fohrer (eds.), *In Memoriam Paul Kahle,* Berlin: Walter de Gruyter, 1968, 90-105; O. **Eissfeldt,** *The Old Testament: An Introduction,* 330-341; K. **Elliger,** *Deuterojesaja in seinem Verhältnis zu Tritojesaja,* BWANT IV, Stuttgart: W. Kohlhammer, 1933, 11; I. **Engnell,** "The 'Ebed Yahweh Songs and the Suffering Messiah in 'Deutero-Isaiah,' " *BJRL* 31, 1948, 54-93; G. **Fohrer,** *Das Buch Jesaja* III, Zurich: Zwingli, 1964; H. L. **Ginsberg,** "The Oldest Interpretation of the Suffering Servant," *VT* 3, 1953, 400-404; M. **Haran,** "The Literary Structure and Chronological Framework of the Prophecies in Is XL-XLVIII," *SVT* 9, 1963, 127-155; G. H. **Jones,** "Abraham and Cyrus: Type and Anti-type?" *VT* 22, 1972, 304-319; O. **Kaiser,** *Der Königliche Knecht,* Göttingen: Vandenhoeck & Ruprecht, 1959; K. **Koch,** "Die Stellung des Kyros im Geschichtsbild Deuterojesajas und ihre überlieferungsgeschichtliche Verankerung," *ZAW* 84, 1972, 352-356; J. Lindblom, *The Servant Songs in Deutero-Isaiah,* Lund: Gleerup, 1951; J. L. **McKenzie,** *Second Isaiah,* Garden City: Doubleday & Co., 1968; R. F. **Melugin,** *The Formation of Isaiah 40-55,* Berlin: Walter de Gruyter, 1976; J. W. **Miller,** "Prophetic Conflict in Second Isaiah: The Servant Songs in the Light of Their Context," in J. Stoebe (ed.),

Wort–Gebet–Glaube. Walter Eichrodt zum 80. Geburtstag, Zurich: Zwingli Verlag, 1970, 77-85; S. **Mowinckel,** "Die Komposition des deuterojesajanischen Buches," *ZAW* 49, 1931, 87-112, 242-260; *He That Cometh,* Oxford: Clarendon Press, 1959, 187-260; J. **Muilenburg,** "Isaiah, Chapters 40-66," *IB* IV, 1966, 381-651; C. R. **North,** *The Suffering Servant in Second Isaiah,* Oxford: Oxford University Press, 1956²; *The Second Isaiah,* Oxford: Clarendon Press, 1964; H. M. **Orlinsky,** "The So-Called 'Servant of the Lord' and 'Suffering Servant' in Second Isaiah," *VTS* 14, 1967, 1-133; D. F. **Payne,** "The Servant of the Lord: Language and Identification," *EvQ* 43, 1971, 131-143; G. **von Rad,** *Old Testament Theology* II, 238-262; L. **Rignell,** *A Study of Isaiah Ch. 40-55,* Lund: Gleerup, 1956; B. J. **Roberts,** "The Second Isaiah Scroll from Qumran," *BJRL* 42, 1959, 132-144; H. H. **Rowley,** *The Servant of the Lord and Other Essays on the Old Testament,* Oxford: Basil Blackwell, 1965², 1-93; J. A. **Soggin,** "Tod und Auferstehung des leidendes Gottes-Knechtes: Jesaja 53 8-10," *ZAW* 85, 1975, 346-355; H. E. **von Waldow,** "The Message of Deutero-Isaiah," *Int* 22, 1968, 259-287; C. **Westermann,** *Isaiah 40-66, A Commentary,* Philadelphia: Westminster Press, 1969; R. N. **Whybray,** *The Heavenly Counsellor in Isaiah xl 13–14: A Study of the Sources of the Theology of Deutero-Isaiah,* Cambridge: Cambridge University Press, 1971; *Isaiah 40–66,* London: Oliphants, 1975; *Thanksgiving for a Liberated Prophet,* Sheffield: JSOT Press, 1978; L. E. **Wilshire,** "The Servant-City: A New Interpretation of the 'Servant of the Lord' in the Servant Songs of Deutero-Isaiah," *JBL* 94, 1975, 356-367; W. Zimmerli, *"Pais Theou,"* *TDNT* IV, 654-677.

Ezekiel's vision of the new Temple is dated to the twenty-fifth year of the exile (573 B.C.E.). After the passage of another quarter of a century a new generation of prophets was announcing emancipation to take place in the jubilee year of divine favor.[70] By then Nebuchadrezzar was long dead, Nabonidus had left Babylon for the oasis of Tema in northwest Arabia, and the Iranian Cyrus of Anshan had conquered Ecbatana, capital of the Medes, and was extending his rule into Asia Minor. With the collapse of the Babylonian empire only a matter of time, it was possible to hold out hopes for repatriation and the restoration of political autonomy in the homeland. By far the most important of these seers active during the last decade of Babylonian rule is the anonymous[71] author of sayings and sermons preserved in Isa. 40-55, the so-called Second Isaiah.

Since the end of the eighteenth century, Isa. 40-66 has been widely acknowledged to be a separate collection of later date than Isa. 1-39. Critical scholarship has also, by and large, accepted Bernhard Duhm's arguments for a distinction between chs. 40-55 and 56-66, the former exilic and the latter for the most part postexilic. Duhm was also the first to draw attention to the so-called "Servant Songs" (Isa. 42:1-4; 49:1-6;

50:4-11; 52:13 to 53:12) as distinct compositions.[72] While these conclusions have stood the test of time, it would be an oversimplification to conclude that the Isaiah scroll displays a straightforward sequence of preexilic (1-39), exilic (40-55), and postexilic (56-66) material. We have already noted that significant additions were made to the first part both during and after the Babylonian exile. The anti-Babylonian poems, for example, could not very well have been written before the death of Nebuchadrezzar in 562 B.C.E. and may be from a decade or two later.[73] Other sayings predicting repatriation, the subjugation of the nations including Edom, the reestablishment of the dynasty and the preeminence of Jerusalem, also make best sense if read in the historical context of the late exilic or early postexilic period.[74] While the second part of the scroll has a much more unitary character, it too shows signs of editorial expansion. We shall also go on to observe that the latter section of it (Isa. 49-55) has some distinctive characteristics that set it apart from the earlier section (40-48). It is generally acknowledged, finally, that the so-called Third Isaiah has its own editorial history and may have taken over prophetic sayings from the time of the First Temple.

The join between the first and second parts of the scroll is also not as clean as is sometimes thought. The historical appendix (Isa. 36-39) ends with a prediction of exile in Babylon (39:5-8) and thereby sets up a contrast between the historical judgment foretold by Isaiah and the assurance of emancipation and repatriation conveyed in Isa. 40-55. It also sets the scene for the "proof from prophecy" which is such an important feature of Second Isaiah—in the sense that the god who, through his prophets, foretold these "former things," and then brought them about,[75] thereby demonstrated his ability to bring about the "new thing" (43:19) that was now being announced. The Isaiah scroll, then, shows the same pattern of judgment followed by salvation that we have seen in other prophetic books,[76] with the difference that here the juxtaposition carries a more explicit and sustained theological message.

It is also important to note that the chapter immediately preceding the historical appendix (Isa. 35) belongs thematically and linguistically with the poems of Second Isaiah. Suffice it to note the themes of Zion restored, Israel as blind and deaf, the new miracles in the wilderness, the *via sacra* over which the exiles are to return home (35:8-10; cf. 40:3-5). The connection was broken by the insertion of the historical narrative, which established a different connection, between a prediction made by Isaiah during the reign of Hezekiah and its fulfillment viewed as the essential prerequisite for a new dispensation to follow. Close correspondence with the Deuteronomic understanding of prophecy suggests, but of course cannot prove, that adherents of the Deuteronomic school were responsible for attaching chs. 40-55 to 1-39.

Not much needs to be said in support of the proposition that Second Isaiah comes from a later epoch than that of Isaiah of Jerusalem. The historical context is no longer the Kingdom of Judah during the period of Assyrian supremacy but the Jewish gôlāh in the last years of Babylonian rule. Reference to the Iranian Cyrus, king of Anshan (not confined to those passages where his name occurs, 44:28; 45:1), to Babylonian deities, to the anticipated fall of Babylon, to the repatriation of the exiles, put this conclusion beyond reasonable doubt.[77] There are indeed links with the eighth-century Isaiah—e.g., the frequent use of the title "the Holy One of Israel"—but the differences in form and literary texture are more in evidence than the similarities. We cannot explain the attachment of chs. 40-55 to the first part of the scroll by appealing to an Isaian "school" that remained active over the intervening span of years—a hypothesis for which there is absolutely no evidence. The ardent attachment of the first Isaiah to Zion as political reality and symbol of a beleaguered people would certainly be part of an eventual explanation, but the main point would be the perceived connection between prophecy and fulfillment to which we have just referred.

Prophetic books are not lavish in providing biographical information, and Isa. 40-55 is no exception. One rather obvious reason for anonymity could be the political situation in which the prophet addressed his audience. Predictions of the victory of Cyrus and the fall of Babylon, together with satire directed at the Babylonian imperial cult, even when circulating in the restricted ambient of the Diaspora communities, could not have been free of risk. Earlier prophets who preached sedition had been tortured and executed by the authorities (Jer. 29:21-22). Whether the author of all or part of Isa. 40-55 met a similar fate must remain an open question, depending as it does on the uncertain interpretation of the third and fourth of the Servant Songs—to which we shall return.

The opening verses of Second Isaiah have often been taken to reflect a prophetic commissioning from Yahweh in the heavenly assembly after the manner of the earlier Isaiah (6:1-13).[78] It should, however, be noted that in the opening apostrophe (40:1-2) the verbs are in the plural, which means that the command to proclaim the end of exile, represented as penal servitude, is addressed to a plurality. Likewise in Isa. 35:3-4 (occurring in a passage that belongs with the same exilic material) a plurality is commissioned to comfort the people with the good news of imminent salvation, and in Isa. 52:7-10 an individual herald is linked with a prophetic group that rejoices in anticipation of the same event.[79] The command to prepare the way of Yahweh in preparation for his parousia (40:3-5) is also addressed to a plurality, and only then (vs. 6-8) do we hear the seer himself speaking, in a passage that seems to allude cryptically to the end of Babylonian rule. The interpretation of the fourth apostrophe (vs. 9-11) is complicated by the feminine form *m'baśśeret* (herald), which is often taken to be in apposition to Zion-Jerusalem (as in RSV). But the point of the commission is precisely to bring good news *to* Zion (40:1; cf. 52:7-8). There is, besides, something rather forced in the image of Jerusalem climbing up a high mountain to make the proclamation.[80]

In summary, then, the commission to proclaim the termination of exile following on the end of Babylonian rule and leading to a new era of salvation appears to have been addressed to an individual seer with his prophetic following. It would be natural at least to begin with the assumption that the seer in question, whom we hear from time to time speaking in his own name (Isa. 40:6; 48:16;[81] 49:1-6), is the author of much of the material in Isa. 40-55. It may also be assumed, as a reasonable hypothesis, that much of the material in the last part of the book (56-66) emanates from this seer's disciples, who perpetuated his message after his death. We shall go on to suggest that the identity of the Isaian Servant, in dispute since antiquity (see, for example, Acts 8:34), may best be approached by working back from the disciples to the master.

In order to understand the historical location and career of Second Isaiah it is important to note the distinction, alluded to earlier, between the two sections of this part (Isa. 40-48 and 49-55).[82] The first section, beginning and ending with the theme of return from exile, focuses on the expectation of a new era to be inaugurated by Cyrus. The second section, on the other hand, says nothing about him, is in general much less interested in the contemporary political situation, and is concerned instead with the internal situation of the community. It was to be expected that the campaigns of Cyrus and the growing internal opposition to Nabonidus, last of the Babylonian kings (556-539), should have occasioned an outburst of prophetic activity in the Diaspora. By 550 B.C.E., Cyrus had united the Persian tribes under him and occupied Ecbatana, capital city of the Medes. In the course of the next three years his campaigns in Armenia and Asia Minor had been crowned by the capture of Sardis, capital of the Lydian kingdom, and the annexation of the Greek cities on the Ionian seaboard. These stirring events were the "new thing" proclaimed by the prophet (43:19) and are referred to here and there throughout these chapters.[83] Support for Cyrus must have been strong, though not perhaps unanimous, among the Diaspora communities. From this point of view Isa. 40-48 reads as propaganda for the pro-Cyrus party at a point in time when his conquest of Babylon could be reasonably predicted (see especially 43:14-17; 47:1-15; 48:14).

It is understandable in view of this situation that a long oracle about Cyrus should form the centerpiece of this section (Isa. 44:24 to 45:13). In it he is designated as shepherd and anointed, both well-attested synonyms for king,[84] and the remarkable claim is made that Yahweh was responsible for his success, that his actions were intended to serve the purposes of the dispersed Jewish communities, and that he would see to the repatriation of Jewish exiles and the rebuilding of their destroyed city. For good measure the seer even predicted his future conquest of Egypt, an event which, however, took place only under his son and successor Cambyses (45:14). In other sayings (43:14-17; 47:1-15; 48:14) he prophesied the fall of Babylon and engaged in polemic against Babylonian religion in a manner not unlike that of his contemporary, the Ionian philosopher Xenophanes.[85]

Given the dismal record of optimistic prophets in the last years of the monarchy, it would be surprising if this prophet's proclamation of good news had not been greeted with skepticism. No doubt anticipating such a response, he attempted to disarm criticism by claiming that he spoke in the name of a god who had already demonstrated his ability to inspire predictions of the future and then make it happen. This is a cardinal point in Second Isaiah's apologetic. The proof of divinity is to predict the future and then bring it about. Unlike the Babylonian deities, Yahweh stood behind his prophets (Isa. 44:26). The very disasters through which the people had passed were turned into occasions for faith, in that they had happened in fulfillment of prophecy and therefore provided grounds for confidence now that judgment had given way to salvation (48:3-8). Repeatedly he called his contemporaries, understandably reluctant to put themselves on the line once again, to witness that this reading of contemporary events was the only one that made sense for them.

By its nature prophecy raises the issue of the reality and power of the deity who validates the prophet's message. Many of those exiled must have concluded that the god of Israel had been discredited along with his prophets, and the spectacle of ceremonies and processions in honor of Marduk, city god of Babylon, would have been a constant reminder of his defeat. This situation will help to explain why from that time the god of Israel was increasingly represented as a cosmic deity residing in the circle of the heavens and presiding over the destinies of all nations.[86] The shift in emphasis was clearly intended to counter the allure of Babylonian religion and the Marduk cult in particular. To take only one example, the claim of Isa. 43:10 that

> before me no god was formed,
> nor shall there be any after me

was aimed at the Babylonian theogony according to which Marduk (also known as Bel, Isa. 46:1) was born of the gods Ea and Damkina.[87]

The ultimate act of divine power, the creation of the world, is celebrated in the canonical Babylonian creation myth *Enuma elish*.[88] This sacred text, recited in the course of the New Year *akitu* festival, opens with a theogony according to which the gods, descended from a primordial couple Apsu and Tiamat, caused a disturbance that led Apsu to plan their destruction. On hearing this the god Ea took preemptive action by slaying Apsu, after which he begot Marduk, wisest and strongest of the gods. As a first step toward avenging her dead spouse, Tiamat created a corps of monsters under the command of a certain Kingu, to whom were entrusted the tablets of destiny. Since the high gods, called the Anunnaki, felt unequal to the task of taking on Tiamat, they entrusted it to Marduk. He, however, insisted on supremacy in the pantheon in exchange, and with this went the prerogative of establishing the destinies. After defeating Tiamat in single combat, Marduk took the tablets of destiny from Kingu, created earth and sky out of the dimembered body of Tiamat, fixed the stations of the gods in the zodiacal band and, finally, created mankind out of the blood of Kingu mixed with slime. This last act relieved the lesser gods of the onus of cultic service, and in return for this favor they built the Esagila ziggurat-temple in Babylon for him. After gathering there in solemn procession, they recited his fifty names in a paeon of praise and proclaimed his universal kingship.

It will be obvious that this myth is meant to convey a message about power, one that encapsulates the themes of creation, kingship, and cult. Since Marduk was the city god of Babylon and patron of the empire, its recital also served as a form of political propaganda. As we read Isa. 40-55 it is difficult to avoid the impression that the author set himself the task of countering this ideology of power. All of the elements are present to the extent that we can reconstruct a kind of mirror image of the myth with Yahweh in the place of Marduk. There is the cosmogonic war resulting in the defeat of Tehom (Tiamat), the Great Deep (Isa. 51:9-11). There is the creation of light and darkness

(45:7), the sky, the celestial bodies, and the earth (40:12, 26; 44:24, etc.). The triumphal procession over the *via sacra* (40:3-5; cf. 35:8-10), like the one over which Marduk and Nabu were carried (46:1-2, 5-7), was represented as leading to the sanctuary (44:28) in which the great epiphany of the god was to take place (40:10; 51:7-10). The climax is the proclamation of the kingship of Yahweh bringing the assurance of a favorable destiny (52:7).[89]

This reversal of current assumptions about the location of power is carried over from the act of creation into the historical events of Israel's founding. By creating Israel (Isa. 43:1, 15) Yahweh won the right to be its king (44:6). The first exercise of this right was the rescue from Egypt and the destruction of Israel's enemies at the sea. Now, in these latter days, this act is about to be replicated with the end of captivity and return to the land (43:16-17; 50:2), but without the haste which marked the earlier departure (52:12). The miraculous interventions by which Israel was sustained in the wilderness will also be repeated (35:5-7). The theme of cosmogonic victory is therefore shifted from the time of creation to that of the exodus from Egypt (51:9-10).[90] The implication is that the creative power expressed in the symbolic language of myth is also the redemptive power which now, as in the beginnings of its history, is available to a subjugated and humiliated people; and this in spite of current assumptions about the location of power in the "real world."

The activity of Second Isaiah and his support group (both alluded to, as we have seen, in the introductory verses) was therefore aimed at persuading the Diaspora that, in spite of appearances to the contrary, their god was still in control of the flow of historical events. The frequent use of rhetorical questions, the form of disputation increasingly in evidence from that time,[91] may be taken to reflect preaching that was actually going on in the *gôlāh* assemblies. The thrust of this preaching about the reality of divine power in the political realm was to prepare for the statement that the same god who had guided Israel's destiny from the beginning was behind the meteoric rise to power of Cyrus (Isa. 41:1-4, 25-29; 44:24 to 45:13). As we have seen, this is the central affirmation of the first part of Second Isaiah. The contrast between these theological affirmations and the actual political insignificance of the *gôlāh* community (alluded to at one point as "the servant of rulers," 49:7) has probably suggested the use of the term "servant of Yahweh" for the community. To be more precise, we should observe that where it occurs in the first section (40-48) it refers in practically every case to the Jewish community in exile, whereas in the second section (49-55) this is the exception.[92] Before drawing out the implications of this observation, however, we should first briefly examine the broader context of usage with which the exilic author would in all probability have been familiar.[93]

It seems that the term "servant of Yahweh" (*'ebed YHWH*) was used in Deuteronomic circles for a specially designated intermediary, the model for which was the ministry of Moses himself (Num. 12:7-8; Deut. 34:5; etc.). Since Joshua was the first to replicate this ministry, he too bears the title (Josh. 24:29; Judg. 2:8). Since the prophets also were seen to perpetuate the work of Moses throughout the subsequent history, it was natural that individual holders of the prophetic office and the prophetic succession as a whole should be described in terms of servanthood or mediatorial service.[94] With equal frequency, however, the Davidic ruler is also described as Yahweh's servant,[95] the reason being that the monarchy was also charged with the task of mediation, prophecy and monarchy being viewed as parallel embodiments of the mediatorial function and charismatic office of Moses. The "Mosaic" character of monarchy could, however, be more easily perceived once the imperfect reality had passed from the scene. Hence the frequent allusions in exilic writings to the ideal king of the future as Yahweh's servant.[96] By the time of the exile, then, the parallelism between prophecy and monarchy as executors of the divine will and mediators between God and the people was well established.

Since "servant," understood in this sense, designates a function performed on behalf of Israel, it is understandable that Deuteronomic writings do not refer to the people by this term. Where it occurs elsewhere in exilic writings with reference to the people (Jer. 30:10; 46:27-28; Ezek. 28:25), the latter goes under the name Jacob, a usage that is also found in Second Isaiah.[97] The purpose is clearly to recall the election of the great ancestor who was chosen by God to bring into existence a numerous people and who, like his descendants, was exiled in Mesopotamia, entered into servitude there and, in the course of time, returned to his own land.

In Isa. 40-48, then, it is generally Israel represented by the diasporic "remnant" which is the servant of Yahweh. The one passage which, however, does not fit this pattern is the first of the so-called Servant Songs (42:1-4). Here the speaker is Yahweh, who designates an individual as his servant and chosen one and endows him with the spirit so that he may fulfill his mission of dispensing justice and law to the nations. He will persevere in this task until successful and will discharge it without violence and brutality. This cannot refer to a prophet, since prophets do not dispense justice, least of all to the nations.[98] The strongest indication that the author has a royal figure in mind is the poem about the ideal Davidic ruler of the future (in Isa. 11:1-9), who is also endowed with the spirit, charged with bringing justice to the nations and putting an end to the violence and brutality often characteristic—then as now—of international relations. The same perspective informs other allusions to the ideal king of the future (e.g., Jer. 33:15), and it is especially noteworthy that in the only reference to the Davidic line in Second Isaiah (Isa. 55:3-4) the king is also charged with international responsibilities.

While there can be little doubt that the one who receives this commission is a royal figure, it is much more difficult to determine more precisely who the writer had in mind. The overall context of Isa. 40-48 and the passage immediately preceding (41:25-29) would suggest Cyrus, who is to carry out on behalf of Israel those tasks which would, in normal circumstances, be discharged by its own charismatic leaders. That he is described as Yahweh's servant would not rule out the identification since this title, which is bestowed even on the tyrant Nebuchadrezzar (Jer. 25:9; 27:6; 43-10), is no more remarkable than "shepherd" (Isa. 44:28) or "anointed" (*māšîaḥ* 45:1). But it is difficult to exclude the possibility that the seer had in mind either Jehoiachin or one of his sons, especially in view of the usage as detailed above and the description of the Davidite Zerubbabel as Yahweh's servant (Hag. 2:23; Zech. 3:8). While the Davidic dynasty does not seem to have been central to Second Isaiah and his following, it would be strange if it were not somehow part of the projected future opened up by the momentous events that were taking place on the international scene.

The second section of the book (Isa. 49-55) opens with a speaker addressing the nations. Using the language of prophetic commissioning, he speaks of being called and given a name from the womb, equipped for his task as a weapon in Yahweh's hand, and designated Yahweh's servant through whom he (Yahweh) will be glorified (49:1-6). Practically everything that the speaker says of himself is said elsewhere in Second Isaiah of the community: the sense of failure and rejection (40:27) to which Yahweh responds with the promise of renewed help (41:10), being formed and called from the womb (43:1; 44:1), the provision of necessary equipment (41:15-16), the glorification of Yahweh by means of the one called (44:23). For good measure, this "servant of Yahweh" is actually identified with Israel (49:3), and the following passages are also most readily understood as referring to the *gôlāh* community (49:7-26).[99] The difficulty is, of course, that the mission assigned to the speaker includes the task of bringing Israel back to its god, which task cannot be ascribed to Israel itself. It would therefore be natural to assume that the passage has been expanded to allow for a certain identification between the prophet and Israel, while still describing his own sense of mission to the dispersed communities which bear that name.

At this point we again confront the problem that the powerful appeal of these "Servant Songs" has, paradoxically, rendered them almost immune to interpretation precise enough to allow for straightforward identifications, because of the fact that they have been constantly reinterpreted, and that the earliest stages of this interpretative process have been incorporated in the different versions of the texts. Yet in spite of the many uncertainties some modest progress can be made in delimiting the boundaries within which the relevant texts are to be read. One avenue of approach, which has perhaps not been adequately investigated, would begin from the clear indications in Isa. 56-66 of a prophetic group rejected by the majority that drew its inspiration from the teaching of Second Isaiah and referred to itself as "the servants of Yahweh."[100] The connections of this group with Second Isaiah are suggested not only by the fact that Isa. 56-66 has been appended to the section that includes the "Servant Songs" but also by certain editorial expansions to the last two of these which point to the existence of such a support group.

The first of these (Isa. 50:10-11) follows one of the rare passages in Second Isaiah in which a speaker addresses his public in the first person (50:4-9).[101] While he is identified as "the servant of Yahweh" only in the comment added to his words, the language of "opening" or "wakening" the ear indicates a prophetic teacher. It appears that in carrying out his mission to his fellow exiles he has suffered violence and contumely and has been accused of crimes of which he believes himself innocent. He is therefore certain of his ultimate vindication by Yahweh who will stand by him. The comment added by one of his followers at least makes it clear that the *gôlāh* community is divided between those who adhere to and those who reject the prophet and his teaching. While the precise circumstances can no longer be recovered, the kind of language used (walking in darkness without light) suggests that he has been arrested and imprisoned by the authorities, and for that reason discredited in the eyes of many of his fellow exiles.[102]

It seems reasonable to infer that it is the same individual who, in an earlier first-person passage (Isa. 49:1-6), complains of the failure of his mission while affirming the assurance of vindication by Yahweh. There is even more reason to make a connection with the later and longer passage in which a servant of Yahweh passes from suffering, humiliation, and rejection to ultimate vindication (52:13 to 53:12). Here especially, where the difficulties of interpretation have proved well-nigh insuperable to generations of commentators, all we can hope to do is present a plausible reading consonant with the approach outlined so far.[103] We begin with the observation that the speaker at the beginning and end of the passage is no longer the servant himself but Yahweh (52:13-15; 53:11-12[104]), and that this presentation in the divine first person provides the framework for another speaker who, at one time one of those who rejected the "servant," has now come to understand and accept the significance of his ministry for the exilic community (53:1-11). It seems reasonable to conclude that the intensity of the language in this lament, almost unparalleled in the Hebrew Bible, arises out of the profoundly revealing experience of conversion to discipleship and prepares for the suffering and rejection of the "servants of Yahweh" in Third Isaiah. It is no wonder that it has continued to reverberate throughout Jewish history and that it came to have such a decisive influence on the early Christian understanding of the prophetic ministry of Jesus.

It will suffice to add that the language in which the fate of this anonymous prophet is described is in several respects ambiguous and patient of more than one interpretation. That he is compared to a lamb led to the slaughter (53:7), that he is taken away and cut off from the land of the living (v. 8), that he has his sepulcher with the wicked (v. 9) would, nevertheless, seem most naturally to imply that he was put to death.[105] If this is so, the final promise that he will see his offspring and that his work will bear fruit in the end would imply that he lives on in the prophetic following dedicated to perpetuating his message. It remains to be seen what was made of that message in the new situation opened up by the prospect and reality of return to the homeland.

NOTES

1. The sixth century B.C.E. witnessed the eclipse of Semitic dominance in the Near East after two millennia, the beginnings of Greek philosophy, Zoroastrianism, Buddhism, Confucianism, and, of course, the rise of Judaism. See C. F. Whitley, *The Exilic Age*, London: Longmans, Green & Co., 1957, 1-28.

2. An achievement that, though exceptional, is not unattested; see E. J. Bickerman, "The Historical Foundations of Postbiblical Judaism," in L. Finkelstein (ed.), *The Jews: Their History, Culture, and Religion* I, New York: Harper & Brothers, 1949, 70-71.

3. *b. Baba Batra* 12b.

4. See my *Prophecy and Canon*, 17-23, and "Tanakh and the New Testament," in L. Boadt et al. (eds.), *Biblical Studies: Meeting Ground of Jews and Christians*, New York: Paulist Press, 1980, 96-119.

5. On the treatment of *Spätjudentum* in Old Testament theology, see also James Barr, "Le Judaïsme postbiblique et la théologie de l'Ancien Testament," *RTP* 18, 1968, 209-217.

6. N. K. Gottwald, *Studies in the Book of Lamentations,* London: SCM Press, 1954; D. R. Hillers, *Lamentations,* Garden City: Doubleday & Co., 1972, xv-xxiii.

7. J. H. Hayes and J. M. Miller (eds.), *Israelite and Judaean History,* 475.

8. An inscribed ostracon, found at Arad, about thirty kilometers south of Beersheba, dates from this time and seems to refer to an Edomite attack; see Y. Aharoni, in M. Avi-Yonah (ed.), *Encyclopedia of Archaeological Excavations in the Holy Land* I, Englewood Cliffs: Prentice-Hall, 1975, 87.

9. See especially Amos 1:11-12; Isa. 21:11-12; 34:5-7; 63:1-6; Jer. 49:7-22; Ezek. 25:12-14; 35:1-15; Mal. 1:3-5; Ps. 137; Lam. 4:21-22.

10. The passage (Obad. 19-21) speaks of the return of dispersed Israel from as far away as Mesopotamia and Asia Minor. Sepharad (v. 20), the word for Spain in later Hebrew, could refer to Sardis in Lydia, site of an impressive synagogue, or Saparda, a city in Media. See the commentaries and J. Gray, "The Diaspora of Israel and Judah in Obadiah v. 20," *ZAW* 65, 1965, 53-59; D. Neiman, "Sepharad: The Name of Spain," *JNES* 22, 1963, 128-132.

11. Gedaliah was son of Ahikam, who protected Jeremiah when he was accused of treason (Jer. 26:24; 40:6), and grandson of Shaphan (see above, pp. 166-167). A seal impression found at Lachish (Tell ed-Duweir) inscribed "to Gedaliah who is over the house" probably refers to the same person in his capacity as majordomo of the palace; see Hayes and Miller, 476.

12. See Morton Smith, *Palestinian Parties and Politics That Shaped the Old Testament,* New York: Columbia University Press, 1971, 82-98.

13. E.g., Lachish and Beth-shean, for which there is archaeological evidence, and—at a later time—'Araq el-Emir, Sa'idiyeh, and perhaps Deir 'Alla; for references see M. Smith, 90-93.

14. Tiglath-pileser III (II Kings 15:29; I Chron. 5:6-26; *ANET,* 283), Sargon II (II Kings 17:6, 18), Sennacherib (*ANET,* 288), Esarhaddon (Isa. 7:8; Ezra 4:2).

15. Ezek. 1:3; 3:15; Ezra 2:59 = Neh. 7:61.

16. The fifth-century records of the trading house of Murashu (*ANET,* 221-222) contain good Jewish names like Tobiah (cf. Ezra 2:60).

17. Perhaps indicated by the location of several communities on the canal system fed by the Euphrates; see Ezek. 1:3; 3:15; Ps. 137:1; Jer. 29:5-7.

18. Ezra 2:36-58 = Neh. 7:39-60; Ezra 8:15-20.

19. Cf. the targum on Ezek. 11:16 (*lᵉmiqdāš mᵉʿat*).

20. Frequent allusion to "the place Casiphia" in Ezra 8:15-20 has attracted attention since "place" (*māqôm*) can serve as a synonym for "temple." Moreover Iddo is often attested as a priestly name (e.g., Ezra 5:1; 6:14; Neh. 12:16). In this respect it is worth mentioning the vision of Zechariah (5:5-11) in which the woman whose name is Wickedness is transported to Babylon, where a house is to be built for her. It has been suggested that this refers to a Canaanite goddess worshiped at a syncretist shrine which may have been built by a group that

opposed the resumption of the Jerusalem cult; see M. Smith, *Parties and Politics*, 90-91.

21. See above, pp. 158, 160.

22. See below, p. 226.

23. For examples of Babylonian magic see *ANET*, 309-310; also H. Ringgren, *Religions of the Ancient Near East*, London: S.P.C.K., 1973, 89-99; H. W. F. Saggs, *The Encounter with the Divine in Mesopotamia and Israel*, London: Athlone Press, 1978, 125-152.

24. See my *Prophecy and Canon*, 73-79.

25. See *ANET*, 308, and E. F. Weidner, "Jojachin, König von Juda, in babylonischen Keilinschriften," *Mélanges syriens offerts à M. René Dussaud* II, Paris: Paul Geuthner, 1939, 923-935; W. F. Albright, "King Jehoiachin in Exile," *BA* 5, 1942, 49-55.

26. For the further meaning "victory," i.e., "righteousness vindicated by victory," see *BDB*, 842, where the texts in question are listed with this meaning.

27. E.g., Isa. 11:1-9, where similar terms are used of the descendants of Jesse.

28. Deut. 17:14-20 lays out the Deuteronomic ideal of monarchy; for *'ebed* meaning "prophetic servant" see below, p. 215.

29. Jer. 6:13; 8:10; 14:13-16; 20:6; 23:5-6, 16, 32; 27:9-10, 14-16; 28:15; 29:8-9, 31; Ezek. 13:2-8; 22:28.

30. Jer. 14:13, 15; 37:19; *šālôm:* 4:10; 5:12; 6:14; 8:11; cf. Ezek. 13:10, 16.

31. This task is assigned to a prophet in one of the Lachish ostraca: Letter III, 19-21 (*ANET*, 322); cf. Jer. 23:21.

32. There seems to be a correlation between the growing threat posed by the great powers and the increasing inability of the state to control dissent. The confrontation between Amos and Amaziah (Amos 7:10-17) and the letter of complaint about Jeremiah addressed to the Jerusalem priests (Jer. 29:24-28) show that prophets were under the jurisdiction of the Temple authorities. From the time of Amos we hear of frequent attempts to silence the prophets or bring them into line with official policies (Amos 2:12; Isa. 30:9-10; Micah 2:6-11; Jer. 11:21; 20:1-6, 26). See T. Overholt, "Commanding the Prophets: Amos and the Problem of Prophetic Authority," *CBQ* 41, 1979, 517-532.

33. This is a major point in Josephus' explanation of the fall of Jerusalem in 70 C.E. Josephus liked to think of himself as in the same situation as Jeremiah (*War* V.391, 393; VI.103). Both warned their contemporaries against the danger of the false prophets (*Ant.* X.103-107) but they chose not to listen (*War* VI.285-287).

34. On the tradition history of the passage and the Deuteronomic additions to it see J. Gray, *I & II Kings, A Commentary*, Philadelphia: Westminster Press, 1970², 318-323; also J. L. Crenshaw, *Prophetic Conflict*, 41-42, and R. R. Wilson, *Prophecy and Society in Ancient Israel*, 187-191.

35. See above, p. 75.

36. Job 1-2; Zech. 3:1; I Chron. 21:1.

37. J. Blenkinsopp, "Abraham and the Righteous of Sodom," *JJS* 33, 1982, 119-132.

38. See my *Prophecy and Canon*, 85-95.

39. The passage dealing with prophecy (Deut. 18:9-22) occurs in a section dedicated to public office: monarchy, priesthood, prophecy, judiciary (17:14 to 19:21).

40. See above, pp. 158, 160.

41. I.e., Deut. 4:27-31; 30:1-3; I Kings 8:33-34, 46-53, to which we may add certain passages in Jeremiah that are probably of Deuteronomic origin, especially Jer. 24:7; 29:10-14.

42. This hypothesis would not rule out an authentic core (see, e.g., O. Eissfeldt, *The Old Testament: An Introduction*, 361-362), but indications of a later exilic redaction and, specifically, of Deuteronomic ideas and language (e.g., conditional promise of salvation, the verb *yrš* with reference to possession of the land, 30:2-3), are not lacking; see, e.g., J. P. Hyatt, "Jeremiah," *IB* V, 1956, 1022-1023; E. W. Nicholson, *Preaching to the Exiles*, 85.

43. With the exception of the Isaiah material in II Kings 19-20 and the allusion to Jonah ben Amittai at II Kings 14:25. See above, p. 23.

44. For the pattern, see, e.g., II Kings 14:23, 25. Synchronized reigns occur only in the titles to Hosea and Amos.

45. See above, p. 89.

46. See especially H. Barth and J. Vermeylen, above, pp. 106-107.

47. Ezek. 1:1-2; 8:1; 20:1; 24:1; 26:1; 29:1; 29:17; 30:20; 31:1; 32:1, 17; 33:21; 40:1.

48. K. Jaspers, "Der Prophet Ezechiel. Eine pathographische Studie," in *Arbeiten zur Psychiatrie, Neurologie, und ihren Grenzgebieten. Festschrift K. Schneider*, Heidelberg, 1947, 77-85; see also E. C. Broome, Jr., "Ezekiel's Abnormal Personality," *JBL* 65, 1946, 277-292.

49. On the work of Torrey, Herntrich, Berry, and others, see H. H. Rowley, *Men of God*, 175-184.

50. On the school of Ezekiel, see Zimmerli, *Ezekiel*, 68-74.

51. Cf. H. G. May, "The Departure of the Glory of Yahweh," *JBL* 56, 1937, 309-321.

52. On the date of Ezekiel's call, see Rowley, *Men of God*, 198-203, and Zimmerli, *Ezekiel*, 112-115.

53. The curious passage in which the *kābôd* revealed to Moses is explained as the back of Yahweh (Ex. 33:18-23) reads like a haggadic midrash on the dictum that one cannot see God's face and live. Ezekiel is equally reticent in describing the actual appearance of the one on the throne, using the same indirect kind of language as P (Ezek. 1:26-28).

54. Argued more fully in my paper "The Structure of P," *CBQ* 38, 1976, 275-292, and my *Prophecy and Canon*, 59-69.

55. See especially Zimmerli, *ZAW* 66, 1954, 1-26, and *VT* 15, 1965, 522-524.

56. J. Bowman, "Ezekiel and the Zadokite Priesthood," *TGUOS* 16, 1955-56,

1-14; M. Haran, "Ezekiel's Code (Ezek. 40-48) and Its Relation to the Priestly School," *Tarbiz* 44, 1974-75, 30-53 (Hebrew); J. D. Levenson, *Theology of the Program of Restoration of Ezekiel 40-48,* Missoula, Mont.: Scholars Press, 1976.

57. In addition to the commentaries, see M. Greenberg, "On Ezekiel's Dumbness," *JBL* 77, 1958, 101-105; R. R. Wilson, "An Interpretation of Ezekiel's Dumbness," *VT* 22, 1972, 91-104.

58. For the alternative view that he was active only in Babylon, see Rowley, 194-195.

59. See above, p. 180.

60. For other examples, see J. W. Miller, *Das Verhältnis Jeremias und Hezekiels sprachlich und theologisch untersucht,* 1955.

61. W. Zimmerli, "The Word of God in the Book of Ezekiel," in R. W. Funk (ed.), *History and Hermeneutic,* New York: Harper & Row, 1967, 13.

62. H. J. van Dijk, *Ezekiel's Prophecy on Tyre,* Rome: Biblical Institute Press, 1968.

63. See D. L. Petersen, "The Oracles Against the Nations: A Form-Critical Analysis," SBL Seminar Papers 1, 1975, 39-61.

64. See above, p. 183.

65. Zimmerli, *VT* 15, 1965, 516-521.

66. C. G. Howie, "Gog and Magog," *IDB* II, 1962, 436-437.

67. The Babylonian Talmud (*b. Shabb.* 13b; cf. *b. Hag.* 13a; *b. Menaḥ.* 45a) has preserved an artless story about a certain Hananiah ben-Hezekiah who burned the midnight oil with a vengeance—three hundred jars of it—in the course of harmonizing Ezek. 40-48 with the legislation in the Pentateuch.

68. In addition to the commentaries, see H. G. May, "The King in the Garden of Eden: A Study of Ezekiel 28:12-19," in B. W. Anderson and W. Harrelson (eds.), *Israel's Prophetic Heritage,* 166-176.

69. See above, pp. 99-100.

70. At Isa. 40:2 a prophet is commanded to announce the completion of the fixed time of service *(ṣābā'),* and at Isa. 61:2 the year of Yahweh's favor *(šᵉnat-rāṣôn lᵉYHWH)* is proclaimed. The Jubilee features the proclamation of liberty and return to ancestral land (Lev. 25:8-24, especially vs. 10, 13) and is connected with the idea of the sabbatical rest of the land in the exilic conclusion to the Holiness Code (Lev. 26:34-45). See M. Noth, *Leviticus, A Commentary,* Philadelphia: Westminster Press, 1977², 183-193, 199-201; A. J. Wenham, *The Book of Leviticus,* London: Hodder & Stoughton, 1979, 317-324; A. van Selms, "Jubilee, Year of" *IDBS,* 496-498.

71. At Isa. 42:19 MT has *mᵉšullām* in apposition to "the servant of Yahweh"; and since Meshullam is elsewhere attested as a personal name (e.g., II Kings 22:3) it has been suggested that it may be the prophet's name, perhaps the elder son of Zerubbabel (I Chron. 3:19). See C. R. North, *The Suffering Servant,* 89-90.

72. O. Eissfeldt, *The Old Testament: An Introduction,* 304, 333-334, 341-343.

73. Isa. 13:1-22; 14:3-11, 12-21; 21:1-10.

74. E.g., Isa. 2:1-4; 4:2-6; 11:1-9, 11-16; 14:1-2; 29:22-24; 32:1-8; 34.

75. Isa. 41:22; 43:9, 18-19; 46:9; 48:3-5; cf. 65:16-17.

76. Amos 9:11-15; Micah 4-5; Zeph. 3:8-20; Jer. 30-33; Ezek. 34; 36-37.

77. The broad consensus that Second Isaiah was active in Babylon is challenged from time to time; see, e.g., J. D. Smart, *History and Theology in Second Isaiah,* Philadelphia: Westminster Press, 1965, 20-23. While it is true that there is nothing in Isa. 40-55 that obliges us to opt for Babylon rather than Judah, the frequent polemic against Babylonian deities, cults, and practices (e.g., astrology, 46:1; 47:13) as well as the theme of repatriation specifically from Babylon (e.g., 48:20) render a Babylonian location extremely probable.

78. See, *inter alios,* F. M. Cross, "The Council of Yahweh," and C. Westermann, *Isaiah 40-66,* 32-46 (who deemphasizes the call).

79. On "watchman" *(ṣōpeh)* as a synonym for prophet, see above, p. 130.

80. *mᵉbaśśeret* may therefore be taken as *nomen officii;* cf. *sōperet* (Ezra 2:55) and *qōhelet;* on which see Gesenius-Kautzsch, *Hebrew Grammar,* §122r.

81. The last part of 48:16 appears to be a fragment with no relationship to its context: "And now the Lord Yahweh has sent me, and his spirit . . ."; see Westermann, *Isaiah 40-66,* 203.

82. The difference is not one of authorship but of theme. Isa. 40-48 begins and ends with the theme of exodus from Babylon (40:1-5; 48:20-22), there is a perceptible shift in the understanding of servanthood from 40-48 to 49-55, anti-idolatry polemic (see below, n. 91) occurs only in Isa. 40-48 and, in general, 49-55 is transitional between 40-48 and 56-66.

83. Isa. 41:2-4, 25-29; 45:1-7.

84. *māśîaḥ* does not, of course, have the same connotations as in apocalyptic writings of a later date. While this is the only occurrence of the word with reference to a non-Israelite, it is no more surprising than the allusion to Nebuchadrezzar as "my servant" (Jer. 25:9; 27:6; 43:10).

85. G. S. Kirk and J. E. Raven, *The Presocratic Philosophers: A Critical History with a Selection of Texts,* Cambridge: Cambridge University Press, 1962, 163-181.

86. Cf. Gen. 1:1 to 2:4 (P); Amos 4:13; 5:8-9; 9:5-6; Job 38, etc. The theme is dealt with by C. Stuhlmueller, *Creative Redemption in Deutero-Isaiah,* Rome: Biblical Institute Press, 1970.

87. Cf. also Isa. 45:5-7, 21-22.

88. *ANET,* 60-72.

89. The working out of this theme is dealt with at greater length in my "The Unknown Prophet of the Exile," *Scripture* 14, 1962, 81-90, 109-118.

90. One of the adversaries mentioned here is Yamm (Sea) who, in the Bronze Age Baal cycle from Ugarit, is defeated by Baal. Here Yamm is brought into association with the Reed Sea, over which Yahweh exercised dominion in the exodus.

91. Cf. the use of rhetorical questions (e.g., in Isa. 40:12-31), forensic terminology (e.g., Isa. 41:21), and a wide range of rhetorical figures, especially in the polemic against idolatry (Isa. 40:18-20; 41:6-7; 44:9-20; 45:20-21; 46:1-7); cf. Hag. 1:4-11; 2:3, 11-19; Zech. 1:3-6; 7:5-7; Mal. 1:2-14; 2:10-17; 3:6-8, 13-15.

92. In Isa. 40-48: 41:8, 9; 43:10; 44:1, 2, 21 (twice); 45:4; 48:20; parallelism with "messenger(s)" in 42:19 and 44:26 render the collective meaning less certain while 42:1 almost certainly alludes to an individual. Apart from "servants of rulers" (49:7, and 54:17 in the plural), all occurrences in 49-55 refer to an individual (49:3, 5, 6; 50:10; 52:13; 53:11).

93. See W. Zimmerli, *TDNT* IV, 654-677, and *The Servant of God,* Naperville, Ill.: Alec R. Allenson, 1965².

94. Individual prophetic servants: I Kings 15:29; II Kings 9:36; 10:10; 14:25; the prophets as a whole: II Kings 9:7; 17:13, 23; 21:10; 24:2, etc.

95. E.g., II Sam. 3:18; I Kings 8:24-26; 11:13.

96. Jer. 23:5-6; 30:8-9; 33:14-26; Ezek. 34:23-24; 37:24-25; cf. Hag. 2:23; Zech. 3:8 (Zerubbabel).

97. Isa. 41:8; 44:1-2, 21; 45:4; 48:20.

98. See the discussion of C. Westermann, *Isaiah 40-66,* 92-97.

99. In 49:7 the phrase "the servant of rulers" *('ebed mōš⁽lîm)* would most naturally refer to Israel in exile. In the following salvation oracle (49:8-26) the community goes under the name "Zion"; cf. Zech. 2:7 (MT 2:11), *ṣiyyôn yôšebet bābel* (emended), "Zion dwelling in Babylon."

100. Isa. 65:8-9, 13-16; 66:14, on which see below, pp. 245-251.

101. Isa. 40:6a; 48:16b (see above, n. 81); 49:1-6.

102. We may raise the question whether Isa. 30:20-21, which alludes to a teacher now hidden who will be seen once again and his message heard, does not refer to the prophetic leader and teacher of Second Isaiah. O. Kaiser, *Isaiah 13-39,* 301, believes it may come from as late as the Seleucid period and, specifically, from the scribal and apocalyptic milieu of Daniel.

103. On the prophetic interpretation of Isa. 52:13 to 53:12, see C. R. North, *The Suffering Servant,* Chs. IV-VI *passim.*

104. The textual condition of Isa. 53:11 does not allow a precise distinction between speakers.

105. R. N. Whybray, *Thanksgiving for a Liberated Prophet,* 92-106, presents the most up-to-date arguments for the view that the Servant was not put to death.

VI
PROPHETS AND PROPHECY IN THE SECOND COMMONWEALTH

1. PALESTINIAN JUDAISM IN THE EARLY PERSIAN PERIOD

P. R. **Ackroyd,** "Studies in the Book of Haggai," *JJS* 2, 1951, 163-176; 3, 1952, 1-13; "The Book of Haggai and Zechariah I-VIII," *JJS* 3, 1952, 151-156; "Some Interpretative Glosses in the Book of Haggai," *JJS* 7, 1956, 163-167; *Exile and Restoration,* 138-217; "The History of Israel in the Exilic and Post-exilic Periods," in G. W. Anderson (ed.), *Tradition and Interpretation,* Oxford: Clarendon Press, 1979, 320-350; S. **Amsler,** "Zacharie et l'origine d'apocalyptique," *SVT* 22, 1972, 227-231; W. A. M. **Beuken,** *Haggai-Sacharja 1-8,* Assen: Van Gorcum, 1967; K.-M. **Beyse,** *Serubbabel und die Königserwartungen der Propheten Haggai und Sacharja,* Stuttgart: Calwer Verlag, 1972; M. **Bič,** *Die Nachtgesichte des Sacharja,* Neukirchen-Vluyn: Neukirchener Verlag, 1964; E. J. **Bickerman,** "The Historical Foundations of Postbiblical Judaism," in L. Finkelstein (ed.), *The Jews: Their History, Culture, and Religion,* 70-114; R. P. **Carroll,** "Twilight of Prophecy or Dawn of Apocalyptic?" *JSOT* 14, 1949, 3-35; T. **Chary,** *Les Prophètes et le culte à partir de l'exil,* Paris: Desclée, 1955, 119-159; A. **Deissler,** "Aggée," *SDB* VIII, 701-706; J. A. **Fischer,** "Notes on the Literary Form and Message of Malachi," *CBQ* 34, 1972, 315-320; K. **Galling,** "Die Exilwende in der Sicht des Propheten Sacharja," *VT* 2, 1952, 19-36; *Studien zur Geschichte Israels im persischen Zeitalter,* Tübingen: J. C. B. Mohr (Paul Siebeck), 1964; "Serubbabel und die Wiederaufnahme des Tempels in Jerusalem," in A. Kuschke (ed.), *Verbannung und Heimkehr. Festschrift W. Rudolph,* Tübingen: J. C. B. Mohr (Paul Siebeck), 1961, 67-96; E. **Hammershaimb,** *Some Aspects of Old Testament Prophecy from Isaiah to Malachi,* Copenhagen: Rosenkilde & Bagger, 1966; P. D. **Hanson,** *The Dawn of Apocalyptic,* Philadelphia: Fortress Press, 1975; S. **Herrmann,** *A History of Israel in Old Testament Times,* Philadelphia: Fortress Press, 1975, 298-338; F. **Hesse,** "Haggai," *Verbannung und Heimkehr,* 109-134; J. **Jeremias,** *Die Nachtgesichte des Sacharja,* Göttingen: Vandenhoeck & Ruprecht, 1977; A. **Lods,** *The Prophets and the Rise of Judaism,* London: Kegan Paul, Trench, Trubner & Co., 1937, 184-199, 265-280; R. **Mason,** *The Books of Haggai, Zechariah, and Malachi,* Cambridge: Cambridge University Press, 1977;

H. G. **Mitchell**, J. M. P. **Smith**, J. A. **Bewer**, *A Critical and Exegetical Commentary on Haggai, Zechariah, Malachi, and Jonah*, Edinburgh: T. & T. Clark, 1912; F. S. **North**, "Critical Analysis of the Book of Haggai," *ZAW* 68, 1956, 25-46; A. T. E. **Olmstead**, *History of the Persian Empire*, Chicago: University of Chicago Press, 1948; R. **Pautriel**, "Malachie, Le Livre de," *SDB* V, 739-746; A. **Petitjean**, *Les Oracles du Proto-Zacharie*, Paris: J. Gabalda, 1969; L. G. **Rignell**, *Die Nachtgesichte des Sacharja*, Lund: Gleerup, 1950; W. **Rudolph**, *Haggai—Sacharja 1-8—Sacharja 9-14—Maleachi*, Gütersloh: Gütersloher Verlagshaus Gerd Mohn, 1976; K. **Seybold**, *Bilder zum Tempelbau*, Stuttgart: Katholisches Bibelwerk, 1974; M. **Smith**, *Palestinian Parties and Politics That Shaped the Old Testament*, 82-98; E. **Stern**, *The Material Culture of the Land of the Bible in the Persian Period 538-332 B.C.*, Warminster: Aris & Phillips; Jerusalem: Israel Exploration Society, 1982; G. **Wallis**, "Wesen und Struktur der Botschaft Maleachis," in F. Maass (ed.), *Das ferne und nahe Wort. Festschrift Leonhard Rost*, Berlin: A. Töpelmann, 1967, 229-237; A. **Weiser**, *Das Buch der zwölf Kleinen Propheten*, Göttingen: Vandenhoeck & Ruprecht, 1963; G. **Widengren**, "The Persians," in D. J. Wiseman (ed.), *Peoples of Old Testament Times*, Oxford: Clarendon Press, 1973, 312-357; "The Persian Period," in J. H. Hayes and J. M. Miller, *Israelite and Judaean History*, 489-538; H. W. **Wolff**, "Prophecy from the Eighth Through the Fifth Century," *Int* 32, 1978, 17-30.

A great deal of misunderstanding has arisen from the common assumption that for all practical purposes prophecy came to an end with the Babylonian exile. At the risk of laboring the obvious, therefore, we should begin by noting that five of the fifteen books in Latter Prophets are entirely postexilic compositions,[1] and that numerous additions to the remaining books, including substantial sections such as Isa. 24-27 and 56-66, come from this period. Despite laments that prophetic guidance was no longer available (Lam. 2:9), prophetic activity was in evidence from the earliest years of the return (Zech. 7:2-7; 8:9). In order to understand how prophecy functioned and in what ways it was different from earlier forms we must first take stock of the quite different political situation in which the province of Judah found itself after the transition from Babylonian to Persian rule.

The change did not at first make that much difference. Palestinian Jews[2] came within the satrapal system of the Persian empire, which was based on Assyrian and Babylonian imperial administration. Since Syria and Palestine had most recently been ruled from Babylon, they first formed part of the satrapy named after that city. Only after the revolt of Babylon in 482 B.C.E., suppressed with exceptional brutality by Xerxes, did these regions come to form a separate administrative entity known as the "Beyond the River" satrapy (Ezra 5:6, etc.). The center of imperial administration was the old Median capital of Ecbatana

(Hamadan) until Darius moved it to Susa and Persepolis. Jerusalem and the surrounding area of Judah (Yehud) formed one of several provinces, together with Syria, Samaria, Megiddo, and others, under the jurisdiction of the local satrap, probably resident in Damascus.[3]

Under Persian rule these provinces enjoyed a fair degree of autonomy, issuing their own coinage, policing their own territory, and collecting tribute and taxes. In keeping with the policy of the Persian rulers, in this respect much more enlightened than that of their predecessors, the juridical status of local political entities was generally respected. Judah's was one of several provinces the status of which was determined by its Temple and the cult carried on there. It was the policy of the central government to sponsor, subsidize and, where necessary, restore such local cults. So, for example, the founder of the Achaemenid empire claimed to have restored the Marduk cult in Babylon after the neglect that it had suffered under the last Babylonian king, Nabonidus.[4] He also restored the cult of the moon god Sin at Ur and his successor Cambyses, though not always faithful to this policy, claimed to have purified the great sanctuary of Sais in Egypt. Later still we find Darius reproving the satrap Gadatas for imposing tribute on the shrine of Apollo in Magnesia. It is therefore by no means implausible that the same king should have subsidized the rebuilding of the Yahweh Temple in Jerusalem (Ezra 6:8).

In keeping with this policy, local law codes remained in force and were backed by the coercive power of the central government. Darius mandated a codification of ancient Egyptian laws and enjoined their observance, and in the same spirit a later king commissioned Ezra to enforce "the law of the God of heaven" among Jews in the Trans-Euphrates satrapy (Ezra 7:14, 25-26). Included were laws governing the upkeep and correct performance of the cult. Complaints of royal commissioners under Cyrus about the laxity of temple officials in Babylon have come down to us, and among the Elephantine papyri there is a letter from the satrap in Egypt ordering the Jewish settlers to observe Passover according to the traditional order.[5] This suggests the conclusion that much of the legislation in the Pentateuch formed the civil constitution of the Jerusalemite temple-community backed by the authority of the imperial government.[6] It is also by no means improbable that Darius' interest in codifying laws extended to the Jewish community and marked an important stage in the consolidation of Israel's legal traditions.

The province of Judah, therefore, can be described as a temple-community not unlike others in the Persian empire (for example, in some of the Greek cities along the Ionian seaboard). These temples were not just places of sacrifice and prayer; they served as administrative centers with their own bureaucracies, issued loans, controlled and collected revenues from real estate, supported colleges of scholars and scribes, not to mention hordes of temple servants including butchers, bakers, keepers of sacrificial herds, and the like. Supreme authority over this organization was, of course, vested in the monarch. It was in his capacity as legal successor to the Babylonian kings that Cyrus restored the Esagila shrine in Babylon, and it was the same kind of juridical claim that underpinned imperial control of the Jerusalem Temple, formerly a dynastic shrine. An important reminder of this status was the requirement that prayers for the well-being of the imperial family be incorporated into the daily liturgy (Ezra 6:10).

Royal authority was normally exercised through officials and commissioners appointed by the central government whose principal concern was to oversee the financial management of this complex operation and ensure political stability. Expediency and good sense would occasionally dictate the appointment of local people to discharge these functions. Cyrus, for example, appointed a Lydian to oversee the Sardis treasury, while under Darius a Davidite, Zerubbabel, was sent out as governor of Yehud. Under normal circumstances, however, the day-to-day task of administration devolved on the priesthood.

This last point is particularly important for understanding the situation in Jerusalem and Judah after the return. The authority of the Temple clergy was not confined to control of the sacrificial cult, as important as that was. Since the legal standing of residents was contingent on participation in and support of the cult, in a real sense their civic existence depended on the priesthood. It was noted earlier that title to real estate was also contingent on good standing in the cultic community, and that this juridical situation inevitably sowed the seeds of conflict once the descendants of former residents began to trickle back from the Diaspora.[7] The priesthood, therefore, wielded enormous power not only in the religious sphere (the cult being the primary and indispensable means of salvation) but also economically and politically.

The different status of Jerusalem in the early Persian period was bound to encourage intragroup conflict, and it is important for understanding prophetic texts from that time to see how it developed. Our principal source, the Chronicler, is committed to the view that the *gôlāh* Jews alone were in direct line of succession to the old Israel and, as such, were responsible for the reestablishment of the sacrificial cult. While this information must be accepted with reserve, it is plausible that they would tend to keep to themselves and that disputes over property, genealogical claims, and other matters would tend to develop. The situation would also have been exacerbated by accusations of religious infidelity—meaning syncretic practices— which were bandied back and forth at that time. Once again, the Chronicler's view of the *gôlāh* as alone remaining faithful is certainly oversimplified. Yet it seems plausible in view of the circumstances of the exile and the high motivation required for repatriation that the *gôlāh* group was distinctive in this sense also.

Right from the beginning of the period the basic issue was that of qualification for membership in the Jerusalem temple-community. Since the passing of the nation-state, albeit long in vassalage to foreign powers, the matter could not be decided purely on grounds of national identity. Other factors entered into play including, for the first time, laws governing ritual purity (e.g., Hag. 2:10-14). It is therefore no surprise to find disagreement on the status of specific categories of people, including those who had defiled themselves with idolatry, resident aliens *(gērîm)*, and eunuchs. With respect to this last category, for example, Isa. 56:3-5 expresses an inclusive attitude quite at variance with the Deuteronomic law (Deut. 23:1). For the same reason, marriage with women outside the group became increasingly problematic and emerged as a major issue at the time of Ezra and Nehemiah.

In a later section it will be shown in some detail how conflict was not confined to repatriates versus natives but was going on in the *gôlāh* group itself. One of the major issues here was control of the cult and the status of Temple personnel. Some of those who claimed priestly lineage but who could not substantiate their claim were excluded "until there should be a priest to consult Urim and Thummim" (Ezra 2:59-63). These were members of priestly groups that had settled in Babylon. The ruling was obviously handed down by other priests, already in place, and it is interesting to observe that the revival of even the idea of this ancient form of divination marks a stage in the assimilation of prophetic-divinatory functions by the priesthood.[8] More significant, however, are the indications of conflict within the ranks of the priesthood that led to the emergence of a second order of clergy. Such a distinction was unknown during the time of the monarchy and is attested only in the very latest editorial stratum of Deuteronomy (27:14).[9] By the time the Priestly source (P) came to be written, however, Levites formed a distinct corps of minor clergy excluded from performance of the central cult acts. It seems likely that the disestablishment of provincial sanctuaries by Josiah contributed to this situation by creating a large body of unemployed priests who could not be absorbed into the ranks of the Jerusalem Temple clergy (II Kings 23:9; cf. Deut. 18:6-8). Since it was for the most part the latter who were deported, the gap would necessarily have been widened. In fact only 74 Levites are listed in the *gôlāh* census in Ezra 2 as against 973 priests, and Ezra himself had difficulty recruiting Levites for his mission as he prepared to leave Babylon (Ezra 8:15-20).

In the Zadokite additions to Ezek. 40-48, anti-Levitical polemic explains their subordinate status as the result of lapse into apostasy (Ezek. 44:10-14). More obliquely the Priestly source testifies to the infighting that resulted in the triumph of the Aaronites over other branches of the priesthood (e.g., Lev. 10; Num. 16). Since the only reference to Aaron in Deuteronomy is not particularly flattering (Deut. 9:16-21), it seems that these narratives reflect events and developments close to the time of the composition of P.[10] According to the Chronicler (I Chron. 6:8), Aaron was the ancestor of the Zadokite line, which controlled the Jerusalem cult after Abiathar, descendant of the Shiloh priesthood, was banished during the reign of Solomon (I Kings 2:26-27, 35; cf. I Sam. 2:27-36; 3:10-14). By the time of the reestablishment of the cult, the Zadokites had survived more than one challenge to their monopoly, obliging the challengers to accept a subordinate cult status or be excluded entirely from the clerical ranks.

The Chronicler has it that Cyrus issued a rescript informing all and sundry that Yahweh, having put him in power, commanded him to see to the rebuilding of the Temple in Jerusalem (II Chron. 36:22-23; Ezra 1:1-4). While the authenticity of this text is not entirely above suspicion,[11] the permission granted to the deportees to return and the subsidizing of the cult (Ezra 6:4) were quite in keeping with Persian policy, as we have seen. The Chronicler goes on to describe the enthusiastic response to the rescript among Babylonian Jews who left en masse for the homeland under the leadership of a certain Sheshbazzar, described as prince *(nāśî')* and governor *(pehāh)* of Judah (Ezra 1:5-11; 2:63; 5:14). The same Sheshbazzar, bearer of a good Babylonian name, is also credited with having laid the foundations of the Temple (Ezra 5:16), though elsewhere the Chronicler tells us that this happened only several years later (Ezra 3:1-13). It is possible that this Sheshbazzar is identical with Shenazzar, one of Jehoiachin's sons (I Chron. 3:17-18), in which case he would have been the uncle of Zerubbabel, governor during the reign of Darius. But for the whole of this period the Chronicler's information is confused and self-contradictory, and it is especially doubtful whether there was such a large-scale *aliyah* at that time as is suggested by the register at Ezra 2:1-70 (= Neh. 7:6-73), which gives a number around 50,000.[12] It seems more likely that initially only a small number trickled back, and that these early repatriates were joined by others who accompanied Cambyses' campaign against Egypt in 525 B.C.E. If the response had been as enthusiastic as the Chronicler would have us believe, it is difficult to understand why it took almost a quarter of a century to complete work on the Temple.

After Cambyses died in Palestine on his way back from Egypt, his place was taken by another son of Cyrus, Bardiya, who had himself proclaimed king and won acceptance throughout most of the empire. After reigning only a few months he was captured and executed by Darius, descendant of a cadet line of the Achaemenids, who for the next two years was engaged in a desperate struggle to secure his claim, put down rebellions, and restore law and order. The official version put out by Darius—in the famous rock inscription of Behistun—was that Bardiya was killed by Cambyses and that the person killed by Darius was a look-alike of Bardiya, a pretender whose name was Gaumata. It would, however, be prudent to suspect that this version was a piece of propaganda designed to legitimize Darius' shaky claim to the throne.[13] His usurpation resulted in rebellions in many parts of the empire, particularly in Egypt and the satrapy of Babylon, to which Judah belonged. The last of the revolts in Babylon was instigated by a royal scion who called himself Nebuchadrezzar IV and who held out until the winter of 521 B.C.E.

It is unlikely that these nationalist uprisings at both ends of the satrapy would have left the intervening provinces unaffected. The Chronicler's version of events in Judah during this period (Ezra 3-6) raises a host of problems, but he at least testifies to the fact that the rebuilding of the Temple was carried out in response to prophetic preaching and was even mandated by a prophetic oracle (Ezra 5:1-2; 6:14). Among these prophets involved in the work from the beginning two are known by name: Haggai and Zechariah.

The oracles of Haggai have been provided with dates, put into a narrative framework (Haggai 1:1, 12-14), and interspersed with traditional prophetic formulae, perhaps by the circle or school that goes under the name of the Chronicler.[14] The numerous occurrences of "oracle of Yahweh" *(n'um YHWH)* are meant to give the impression of a prophet in the classical tradition, but both in form and content Haggai is quite different. Much of the material belongs rather to the category of disputation: admonitions to pay attention (Hag. 1:5, 7; 2:15, 18); the use of rhetorical questions (1:4; 2:3, 16, 19); anticipating objections and answering them (1:2-6)—all of which will appear in a more developed form in Malachi. The use of ritual law to make a point

(Hag. 2:10-14) is also quite unique in this respect. Granted that a hard-and-fast distinction between judgment and salvation cannot be applied to different categories of prophet under the monarchy, the frequency of words of assurance—"Fear not" (Hag. 2:5), "I am with you" (1:13; 2:4), "Take courage" (2:4)—suggests that Haggai stands rather in the tradition of optimistic prophecy associated with the state cult. The prediction addressed to the Davidite Zerubbabel of an imminent end to the contemporary political order (Hag. 2:6-9, 20-23) is not essentially different from Hananiah's prophecy of emancipation from the Babylonian empire—a prophecy delivered in the Temple (Jer. 28:1-4).

The close association between priests and prophets in the Temple is illustrated by the account of a delegation sent by a certain Bethel-sarezer to inquire about the proper time for fasting to commemorate the destruction of Solomon's Temple (Zech. 7:1-7). The question was put to priests and prophets by the head of the delegation, Regem-melech, but the answer came from Zechariah upon divine inspiration. Since the tradition to which the Chronicler had access associates Haggai with Zechariah (Ezra 5:1; 6:14), and since both were fervent advocates of the rebuilding, Haggai was himself in all probability a cult prophet. The same conclusion is suggested by the *halakah* on a point of ritual purity recorded by Haggai (Hag. 2:10-14; cf. Lev. 22:4-7). The point, which concerned the entire community addressed rather than a section of it or a different group such as the Samaritans (Hag. 2:14; cf. 1:2),[15] seems to be that whatever cult had been carried out since the destruction of the Temple had not rendered them acceptable to God but that, on the contrary, their polluted state had rendered their cult unacceptable. In view of the denunciations in Jeremiah, Ezekiel and, at a somewhat later time, Third Isaiah, the reference is most likely to syncretic practices. It therefore seems tolerably clear that both Haggai and Zechariah (the author of chs. 1-8), whatever their origin, were central cult prophets, in the line of those who functioned during the time of the First Temple (e.g., II Kings 23:2).

The editorial framework to Haggai's preaching, especially the dates, turn this little book into a kind of diary covering several stages in the work of rebuilding the Temple. To this extent, it is comparable to the Chronicler's somewhat garbled account of the same event in Ezra 3-6. The latter is also punctuated by dates from the seventh month of the first year of a presumed return under Zerubbabel to the sixth year of Darius, when the work was finished (Ezra 3:1, 6, 8, 10; 6:15, 19). Any attempt to synchronize the dates in Ezra with those in Haggai—probably from the same source—would, however, be too speculative to be useful. In Haggai the dates cover the short period from the sixth to the ninth month—autumn and early winter—of the second year of Darius. In the first of five sections (Hag. 1:1-14) the prophet addressed a reproach to the governor Zerubbabel, the high priest Joshua ben-Jehozadak, and the community in general. People were saying that the time was not ripe for the rebuilding, perhaps with reference to the seventy years of Jeremiah (Jer. 25:11-14; 29:10-14), to which Zechariah also alludes (Zech. 1:12).[16] The miserable economic and social condition of the community (cf. Zech. 8:10, which adds social unrest and political strife) are directly attributed to lack of enthusiasm for rebuilding the Temple. The Temple must be built so that Yahweh may manifest his glory. In other words, the rebuilding is the necessary precondition for the great parousia that will usher in the new age proclaimed by the prophets. We see already that in this respect the message of Haggai is not essentially different from the eschatological teaching of Third Isaiah, which will be discussed in the next section. Haggai, therefore, proclaimed the eschatological hope at the center of the cultic establishment. The editor notes the positive response to this preaching (Hag. 1:12-14; cf. Ezra 5:1-2; 6:14).

The second sermon is dated to the twenty-fourth day of the same month, but has either fallen out or been displaced, with a resulting confusion in chronology (Hag. 1:15; 2:15-19). In Hag. 2:15-19, at any rate, the *peripateia,* the turning point from curse to blessing, is the laying of the foundation stone. The next sermon, about a month later (Hag. 2:1-9), has to take issue with discouragement in prosecuting the work which finds expression in unfavorable comparisons with the First Temple (cf. Ezra 3:12-13). The guarantee of success is the presence of the divine Spirit manifested in eschatological prophecy. In a short while a great political upheaval will result in the restoration of the Temple to its former splendor. The same announcement is made more clearly and specifically in the last of the prophet's recorded oracles about two months later (Hag. 2:20-23). There are to be world-shaking events that will bring the present political order to an end, at which time Zerubbabel, servant and chosen of Yahweh, will reign as messiah. The point is made with the help of the symbolic icon of Yahweh's signet ring, used by Jeremiah with reference to the exiled Jehoiachin, Zerubbabel's grandfather (Jer. 22:24).[17]

There can be little doubt that we are dealing with a messianic movement in Judah triggered by the political turmoil in the empire between the death of Cambyses in July 522 and the final restoration of order by Darius two years later. As we have seen, the Chronicler's account is vitiated by a tendency to telescope events that happened in the reigns of Cyrus and Darius and consequently to confuse the roles of Sheshbazzar and Zerubbabel. He does, however, provide one interesting piece of information, namely, the intervention of Tattenai, satrap of the Trans-Euphrates area, who put a stop to the work pending confirmation of Zerubbabel's work permit (Ezra 5:3-17). The dates in Haggai run from about August to December of the second year of Darius. Since the latter seized power in the autumn of 522, the second year of his reign would be 520. As early as the Greek historians, however, there has been some uncertainty as to the calculation of *regnal* years of several of the Persian kings including Darius I. Since the revolt of Nebuchadrezzar IV, referred to earlier, covers exactly the same time of year as in Haggai (i.e., August to November, allowing some time for news to travel) it is plausible to suggest that the messianic movement in Judah, which focused on the person of the Davidite Zerubbabel (clearly not his original name), was part of the larger disturbance in the satrapy.[18] What happened to this Jewish messiah we do not know. Zechariah 6:9-14 has been taken to imply that he was recalled and his place taken by the high priest. The night visions of Zechariah, at any rate, provide an interesting test case of the disconfirmation of eschatological hopes and the process of adjustment that it entailed.

Zechariah's account of the delegation about fasting (Zech. 7:1-7), mentioned earlier, strongly suggests that he was one of the central cult prophets associated with the Temple priesthood. He is also identified as a *nābî'* in the superscription, which, however, appears to have inexplicably confused him with the Zechariah ben-Jeberechiah mentioned at Isa. 8:2. He should probably not be identified with the priest Zechariah son of Iddo in the census list at Neh. 12:16 since this Zechariah was a contemporary of the high priest Joiakim, successor to Joshua. Besides, Iddo and Zechariah are extremely common names. The book consists of eight vision reports sandwiched between a sermon-like introduction (Zech. 1:1-6) and a concluding section dealing with fasting and prospects for the future (chs. 7-8). The dates affixed to the introduction and conclusion (Zech. 1:1; 7:1) span the period from the second to the fourth year of Darius, while the night visions—or at least the first of them—date to the eleventh month of Darius' second year; in other words, exactly two months after the last dated oracle of Haggai (Zech. 1:7; cf. Hag. 2:10, 20).

While they have clearly undergone editorial deletions and additions, the vision reports in Zechariah exhibit a certain structural unity and doubtless go back to the time indicated and the person to whom they are attributed. The same is not the case with the framework to the visions, which shows fairly clear signs of being a later compilation. The preface (Zech. 1:1-6) is in effect a short sermon on repentance or "turning" *(t̆šûbāh),* apparently related to Mal. 3:7:

> From the days of your fathers you have turned aside from my statutes and have not kept them. Return to me, and I will return to you, says Yahweh of hosts.

This is the message and the language of the Deuteronomists, and there are indications that both Malachi and the author of Zech. 1:1-6 have modeled themselves on this source. Zechariah 1:1-6 reminds the hearers that "the former prophets" (1:4; cf. 7:7, 12) or "my servants the prophets" (1:6, a Deuteronomic expression) preached repentance to the Israel of an earlier day, that their message fell on deaf ears, and that the result was disaster. Their predictions were verified, and it was left to the forefathers to acknowledge the justice of God and lament their mistakes during the exile. It will be obvious that this is nothing else but a summary of Deuteronomic teaching.

The concluding section of Zechariah, on the other hand, looks forward to a new future when the former curse will be turned to blessing. Here there are two distinct but related themes. The first is introduced by the delegation on fasting, which provided the occasion to distinguish between authentic and inauthentic penitential exercises. The same theme is pursued, and in the same way, in Isa. 58:1-9, the conclusion to which provides the resolution to the situation in Zechariah:

> You shall call, and Yahweh will answer;
> You shall cry, and he will say, "Here I am."

Compare Zech. 7:13:

> As I called, and they would not hear,
> So they called, and I would not hear.

The point is that fasting is worse than useless if unaccompanied by active concern for others, especially disadvantaged classes such as widows, the fatherless, resident aliens, and the poor (Zech. 7:8-10; cf. Isa. 58:6-7). The forefathers neglected this message and the result was exile. In the age to come, however, the fasts that commemorate the destruction of city and Temple will be turned into festivals of rejoicing (Zech. 8:18-19).

This outlook on the future broadens into the theme of eschatological reversal, projecting an age when Yahweh, having returned to Zion, will confer a new name on the city and Temple. Here too the perspective is identical with that of Third Isaiah (Isa. 60:14; 62:1-5, 12), which also speaks of the Temple as "my holy mountain" (*har qodšî*, 56:7; 57:13; 65:11, 25; 66:20). The population of Jerusalem will overflow, it will be augmented by a faithful people returned from the Diaspora, the land will be fertile, foreigners will come to worship Yahweh in the Temple, and the religious prestige of the Jew will be such as to attract a host of proselytes. As in Haggai, the turning point is the laying of the foundation stone of the Temple. Henceforth, whatever the uncertainties of the present time, it only remains for the people to grasp the opportunity, responding to the divine initiative by a life of religious fidelity (Zech. 8:14-17).

As stated earlier, the vision sequence in Zechariah is dated two months after Haggai's proclamation of the imminent messianic reign of Zerubbabel. There is no indication of place; while the Chronicler's narrative suggests Judah shortly after the return of Zerubbabel, it could also be Babylon shortly after the collapse of the last revolt in that city. In the first of the night visions (Zech. 7:7-17) the prophets saw a supernatural courier on horseback to whom a cavalry patrol reported that all was quiet in the land. This was bad news, since messianic hopes depended for their fulfillment on the collapse of Persian rule when faced with movements of nationalist revival. On hearing the news, the angel interpreter, who appears to be identical with the courier, interceded with Yahweh to take pity on Jerusalem now that the seventy years foretold by Jeremiah were coming to an end. The result was positive, and the seer was commissioned to proclaim that Yahweh had indeed returned from Babylon, that in spite of everything the Temple must be rebuilt, after which the promised reversal of fortune would take place.

Like other examples of the disconfirmation of eschatological predictions, in the Bible as elsewhere, the outcome was not complete collapse of the hopes entertained but rather a reassertion of goals, a rescheduling of the expected millennium.[19] Initially the establishment of the kingdom was connected with the laying of the foundation stone, thereafter with the completion of the building. The Temple was in fact completed and dedicated in the sixth year of Darius (Ezra 6:15), but it did not stop there. We hear of messianic movements supported by prophets in the reign of Artaxerxes I (445/4 B.C.E.) that focused on the person of Nehemiah. Though they come in the form of allegations directed at the commissioner by his enemies (Neh. 6:6-7), they provide a plausible indication that the hopes aroused by the building of the Temple were rekindled seventy years later—the same interval of time as that of the exile—with the prospect of rebuilding the city. Thus the messianic movement in the early Persian period, initially focused on the Davidite Jehoiachin and his family, had an essential point of reference in the rebuilding of Temple and city; a fact not unimportant for understanding later developments, including Christian messianism.

The second vision, of four horns cast down by four smiths (Zech. 1:18-21 [MT 2:1-4]) alludes, in all probability, to the suppression of the Babylonian revolts led by native princes calling themselves Nebuchadrezzar III and IV respectively. Uncertain as it is, this interpretation is to be preferred to the more common practice of referring to Assyria, Babylon, Media, and Persia as the four horns, since only the first two could be said to have scattered Israel while the Persians, far from scattering them, allowed them to come together. Whatever hopes may have focused on the Babylonian revolts while they were in progress, the memory of the hated conqueror of Jerusalem, whose name the rebels bore, would have facilitated a reinterpretation after resistance collapsed. In the third vision (Zech. 2:1-5 [MT 2:5-9]) the prophet saw a man with a measuring line who explained that he was going to measure Jerusalem, presumably with a view to the rebuilding of the walls. Through another heavenly intermediary, the angel interpreter repeated the message of the first vision about the future state of Jerusalem. Reuse of the Isaian *topos* of Yahweh as a wall of fire around the city (Isa. 4:5) may have served as a warning against building the walls at that time—an act that could have been interpreted as the first stage of a plan to rebel. The vision has been expanded by an address to Jews still in Babylon to leave quickly for 'ereṣ yiśrā'ēl in order to escape the retribution about to fall on the rebellious city.

The fourth in the series of visions is introduced in a different way (Zech. 3:1) and is the only one in which the angel interpreter does not speak with the seer. It is also out of chronological order since it looks forward to the coming of the messiah, known as the Branch (3:8; cf. 6:12). In fact, it seems that we should take chs. 3 and 4 as a continuous symbolic narrative that has been put in place as the centerpiece of seven rather than eight visions, with a marked correspondence between the first and the seventh (6:1-8). The logical order in this centerpiece is difficult to determine, the more so because it has been expanded by oracles addressed to Zerubbabel (4:6-10a) which affirm that he is the one to complete the rebuilding of the Temple, while urging the renunciation of force. The golden lampstand supporting a bowl with seven lamps and flanked by two olive trees may be taken to represent the Temple and the dual leadership of civic ruler and high priest (4:1-3, 11-14).[20] This leads naturally to the scene in which the case brought against Joshua the high priest by the Satan[21] is dismissed by

Yahweh presiding over a judicial session in heaven. Though soiled and barely saved from destruction—a veiled reference to lapse into apostasy—he and his colleagues are to be given control of the Temple and thus serve as harbingers of the coming messianic age (3:1-8, 9b-10). The stone with seven eyes, later explained as the eyes of Yahweh which survey the whole earth (3:9a; 4:10b), doubtless refers to the zodiacal band and the seven planets and indicates that, despite appearances to the contrary, nothing that happens on earth escapes Yahweh's surveillance and control.

The problematic nature of dual leadership in the Jerusalem community and the disappointment of hopes placed in Zerubbabel can also be read between the lines of the oracle with which the visions are rounded off (6:9-15). The prophet is commissioned to take silver and gold from certain wealthy Jews newly returned from Babylon, make a crown (the Hebrew has "crowns"), and put it on the head of Joshua the high priest. However, the portentous saying (Zech. 6:12-13) with which this act is to be accompanied:

> Behold the man whose name is Branch;
> He shall "branch" from where he is,
> He shall build the temple of Yahweh . . .
> He shall assume royal honor,
> He shall ascend the throne and reign!

makes it quite clear that the crown was intended not for Josiah but Zerubbabel. The substitution of the former for the latter, and the insistence on the high status of the priest that follows, are understandable in view of the enhanced role of the Temple clergy after Zerubbabel had disappeared from the scene.

The fifth vision (Zech. 5:1-4) featured a flying scroll which the angel interpreter explained as containing a curse on theft and perjury. Since its dimensions were exactly those of the vestibule of Solomon's Temple (I Kings 6:3), the audience was meant to understand that this document of improbable size emanated from the Temple. In view of the connection between the Temple and ownership of land, discussed earlier, it may be conjectured that the condemnation of theft and perjury had to do with illegal expropriation of real estate that had been going on in Judah during the captivity. Equally fantastic appears to be the imagery of the next vision (Zech. 5:5-11), in which the prophet saw a large barrel with a woman in it being transported out of Judah by two female figures with stork's wings. Since the woman represents the people's iniquity, the action may be taken to symbolize the purging of idolatry with special reference to the addictive cult of the Canaanite fertility goddess (cf. Ezek. 8:3; Jer. 44:15-19). It also seems to imply that a temple to this goddess was either planned or actually built in Babylon, recalling the cult of Anath-bethel among Jewish colonists who settled on the island of Jeb in Upper Egypt, perhaps about this time.[22] The seventh and last vision (Zech. 6:1-8), reminiscent of the first, has four chariots setting off to the four corners of the earth on patrol. The reference to the chariot drawn by black horses that brought the spirit of Yahweh to the north country (i.e., Babylon, as at 2:6) is obscure. In view of the passage immediately following, it may refer to a prophetically inspired movement in the *gôlāh* that led a group of Jews to return. On this uncertain note the visions come to an end.

While in general faithful to a well-established prophetic genre, the vision reports of Zechariah introduced a new element that is symptomatic of what was happening to prophecy at that time. While previous visions, e.g., those of Micaiah and Isaiah, had supernatural beings speaking to each other and to the seer, Zechariah for the first time introduced a supernatural agent who explained what was going on. The significance of this move will appear more clearly if we recall that *mal'āk* (angel, messenger) had come to be used as a synonym for prophet (Isa. 42:19; 44:26; Hag. 1:13; Mal. 3:1; II Chron. 36:15-16). And in fact the *angelus interpres* of the visions assumes the prophetic role of intercession (Zech. 1:12) and the giving of oracles (1:14-17; 2:4-5). That he also interprets suggests a shift from direct inspiration to the interpretation of previous prophetic sayings. While much of the symbolism of the night visions remains obscure, there is enough evidence of the reuse and reinterpretation of prophetic *topoi* to put this conclusion beyond reasonable doubt: the seventy years of Jeremiah (Zech. 1:12; Jer. 25:11; 29:10), the smiths (Isa. 54:16-17), the measuring line (Ezek. 42:20), the north country (Jer. 1:13-16), the Branch (Jer. 23:5; 33:15), the wall of fire (Isa. 4:5), perhaps also the horsemen who brought news of the fall of Babylon (Isa. 21:9). From this point on, the eschatological reinterpretation of the "former prophets" (Zech. 1:4; 7:7, 12) will be an important factor in the religious history of the Second Temple period.

The same term has been used to provide a title to the last book in the prophetic corpus (Malachi = my messenger). In reality, this short collection of prophetic sayings is the last of three anonymous booklets of roughly equal length, all of which are introduced under the rubric "oracle" *(maśśā')* and begin "The word of Yahweh . . ." (Zech. 9:1; 12:1; Mal. 1:1). The name, however, has clearly been borrowed from the reference to the eschatological precursor within the book ("Behold, I send my messenger," 3:1)—incongruously, since the anonymous seer did not think of himself in that role. The reason, one would suppose, was the need to arrive at the number twelve and thus permit the entire prophetic corpus to symbolize the three patriarchs and the twelve sons—in other words, the ideal Israel of the past. We shall see that this suggestion is congruous with the last verses of Malachi (4:4-6 [MT 3:22-24]), which serve as the finale to the prophetic corpus as a whole, perhaps even to Torah and Prophets together.

We will not be surprised to hear that the book of Malachi provides no biographical information on the author. The content suggests that it dates from sometime between the reestablishment of the Jerusalem cult (515) and the mission of Nehemiah (445), therefore probably during the reign of Xerxes (486-464) or early in the reign of Artaxerxes I Longimanus (464-425), a period about which we know practically nothing as far as Judah is concerned. The author's intense concern with the cult, together with his ferocious attack on the priesthood, suggests, but of course cannot prove, that he was either a Temple prophet or a Levite. Of even greater interest, however, is the evidence provided by the book for a quite remarkable collapse of religious enthusiasm in the community, including the Temple priesthood, within the half-century or so following the dedication of the Temple.

As in Haggai and Zechariah, the prose of Malachi has been worked over to bring it into line with preexilic prophecy. Here too, however, the frequent and tedious insertion of "oracle of Yahweh (of hosts)" fails to disguise the quite distinctive category of disputation and polemic, featuring question and answer, objection and refutation.[23] We have the impression of a much-compressed account of real disputes going on in the Temple precincts during the period prior to and perhaps during the reforms of Nehemiah. Thus, skepticism about the reality of God's love and providence—occasioned by a miserable economic situation aggravated by natural disasters (Mal. 2:13-16; 3:10-11)—is answered by referring to the fate of Edom, the traditional enemy, at that time being occupied by the Nabatean Arabs (1:2-5). The main point of contention, however, was neglect of the cult—offering sick and useless animals—and of tithing. While both of these could be explained by the economic hardships that seem to have been endemic during the first half of the fifth century, the prevalent sense of boredom (1:13) and religious skepticism (1:2; 2:17; 3:14-15) was probably due to the disconfirmation of the hopes aroused by the completion of the Temple and the official restoration of the cult. In view of the high expectations with which the *bᵉnê-haggôlāh* returned to the homeland, it is ironic that Malachi should contrast the miserable state of affairs in Jerusalem with the cult of Yahweh in the Diaspora, which was even then attracting proselytes from among the nations (1:11; cf. Zeph. 3:9-10; Isa. 56:3-8).[24]

Another issue, potentially just as fatal to the life of the community, was the increasing tendency of Jewish men to marry non-Jewish women and, as a natural concomitant, to take over the cults of their gods. This tendency, which finds some confirmation in archaeological remains from the period,[25] was a major concern of the reform party during the missions of Ezra and Nehemiah (Ezra 9:1-2; 10:2-5; Neh. 10:30 [MT 10:31]; 13:23-27). Malachi, in fact, ends with a passage in which those who feared Yahweh covenanted together and had their names written in a "book of remembrance" in a way strikingly reminiscent of the covenanting that took place during Nehemiah's administration (Mal. 3:16-18; Neh. 9:38 to 10:1 [MT 10:1-2]).[26] As the context makes clear, those whose names appeared in the record constituted the true eschatological community as distinct from the reprobates destined for destruction at the final judgment.[27]

In answer to the question "Where is the God of justice?" (Mal. 2:17) the seer announced the imminent advent of a messenger, called the messenger of the covenant, who would prepare for the final theophany in the Temple by purifying the Levites and thus preparing the community for the final judgment (3:1-4). The final paragraph of the book, which is also the conclusion to the prophetic corpus as a whole, identifies this eschatological precursor as Elijah who is to return from heaven before the end to reunite divided Israel.[28] While this interpretation of Mal. 3:1 comes from a later time, it is consonant with the kind of language used in the text, which connotes a prophetic figure. The closest parallel occurs at Ex. 23:20:

> Behold, I send my messenger[29] before you to guard you on the way
> and to bring you to the place which I have prepared.

Given the possibility of reading "place" *(māqôm)* as "temple," in keeping with well-established usage, the adaptability of the text to the situation would have needed no justification. Moreover, the identity of this mysterious emissary of Yahweh was patient of more than one interpretation. According to an earlier prophetic tradition (Hos. 12:13) it was Moses himself in the guise of prophet. The author of Mal. 3:1 seems to have taken up this tradition, associating it with the promise of a prophet like Moses at Deut. 18:15-18, interpreted in an eschatological sense. In this form the expectation of an eschatological prophet persisted down to the end of the Second Temple and is attested in the Qumran texts and early Christian writings.[30]

The dependence of Malachi on Deuteronomic language and thought is not restricted to this instance; it is pervasive throughout the book. Important Deuteronomic themes such as the love of Yahweh for Israel (Deut. 7:7-8, etc.; cf. Mal. 1:2), the father-son relationship (Deut. 1:21; 32:5-6; cf. Mal. 1:6; 2:10; 3:17), the name of Yahweh (Deut. 12:5, etc.; cf. Mal. 1:6, 11, 14; 2:2, 5; 3:16; 4:2 [MT 3:20]), the acknowledgment of him as the one God (Deut. 6:4; cf. Mal. 2:15), appear throughout. The same goes for stipulations of law to which the book refers which draw not on the Priestly legislation but the Deuteronomic lawbook: sacrificial offerings (Mal. 1:8, 13-14, based on Deut. 15:21; 17:1) and tithing in particular (Mal. 3:10; cf. Deut. 18:1-8). The falling away of Judah is referred to comprehensively as "abomination" (*tôʿēbāh,* Mal. 2:11), an important legal term for the Deuteronomists (e.g., Deut. 14:3; 17:1, 4; 23:17-18). In general, the distinctive Deuteronomic style is much in evidence (e.g., Mal. 2:2-3; 3:7).

Dependence on Deuteronomy could also give substance to a suggestion made earlier, that the author may himself have been a Levite. Over against the current corruption of the priesthood he sets an ideal portrait of Levi that draws on features emphasized in Deuteronomy (Deut. 21:5; 33:10). It will be recalled that, unlike P, Deuteronomy makes no distinction between priest and Levite but assigns the same status to all Levitical priests, sons of Levi. The covenant with Levi to which Mal. 2:4-7 appeals does not go back to the incident of the apostasy at Baal-peor (Num. 25:10-13), as is generally alleged, but to the oracle of Moses on Levi in which the latter is praised for having kept the covenant, as a result of which the sons of Levi "shall teach Jacob thy ordinances and Israel thy law" (Deut. 33:10). There is also more than one indication that the prophet has in mind the apostasy of Aaron at Sinai in which Levites took an active role in punishing the transgressors, as a result of which they were ordained for divine service (Ex. 32:25-29; cf. Deut. 33:9). This would be consonant with the criticism of the priesthood in the book, and it is also noteworthy that the account of the Levitical *revanche* ends with a reference to the angel-messenger and the day of judgment (Ex. 32:34).

2. MESSIANIC MOVEMENTS IN THE EARLY PERSIAN PERIOD: THIRD ISAIAH

R. P. **Carroll,** *When Prophecy Failed,* 150-156; K. **Elliger,** *Die Einheit Tritojesajas,* Stuttgart: W. Kohlhammer, 1928; "Der Prophet Tritojesaja," *ZAW* 49, 1931,

112-140; G. **Fohrer,** *Das Buch Jesaja* III, Zurich: Zwingli, 1964; P. D. **Hanson,** *The Dawn of Apocalyptic,* 32-208; A. S. **Herbert,** *The Book of the Prophet Isaiah: Chapters 40-66,* Cambridge: Cambridge University Press, 1975; W. **Kessler,** "Zur Auslegung von Jes. 56-66," *TLZ* 81, 1956, 335-338; *Gott geht es um das Ganze. Jesaja 56-66 und Jesaja 24-27 übersetzt und ausgelegt,* Stuttgart: Calwer Verlag, 1960; H.-J. **Kraus,** "Die ausgebliebene Endtheophanie. Eine Studie zu Jes. 56-66," *ZAW* 78, 1966, 317-332; J. **Lindblom,** *Prophecy in Ancient Israel,* 403-422; F. **Maass,** "Tritojesaja," in F. Maass (ed.), *Das ferne und nahe Wort. Festschrift Leonhard Rost,* Berlin: A. Töpelmann, 1967, 151-163; W. S. **McCullough,** "A Re-Examination of Isaiah lvi-lxvi," *JBL* 67, 1948, 27-36; J. L. **McKenzie,** *Second Isaiah,* Garden City: Doubleday & Co., 1968; J. **Muilenburg,** *IB* V, 1956, 381-419, 652-773; H. **Odeberg,** *Trito-Isaiah,* Uppsala: Lundequist, 1931; O. **Plöger,** *Theocracy and Eschatology,* Richmond: John Knox Press, 1968; J. **Schreiner,** *Sion-Jerusalem, Jahwes Königssitz. Theologie der heiligen Stadt im Alten Testament,* Munich: Kösel, 1963; E. **Sehmsdorf,** "Studien zur Redaktionsgeschichte von Jesaja 56-66," *ZAW* 84, 1972, 517-576; C. **Westermann,** *Isaiah 40-66, A Commentary,* Philadelphia: Westminster Press, 1969; R. N. **Whybray,** *Isaiah 40-66,* London: Oliphants, 1975; W. **Zimmerli,** "Zur Sprache Tritojesajas," *Gottes Offenbarung,* Munich: Chr. Kaiser Verlag, 1963, 217-233.

One of the most difficult tasks of the historian of the Second Commonwealth is to assess the impact of international events on developments within the Jewish communities as these are reflected in the surviving texts. The difficulties are especially in evidence with respect to millenarian and messianic movements, which are attested from the early days of the restoration, come to the surface sporadically thereafter, and reach a climax during the last two centuries under Roman rule. One approach, represented by Otto Plöger's *Theocracy and Eschatology* and Paul D. Hanson's *The Dawn of Apocalyptic,* is to postulate a gradual movement within prophetic circles in the direction of apocalyptic as it comes to expression in the Enoch literature and Daniel. While such a reading of the history can be illuminating in some respects, it can also be misleading. It will generally tend to neglect the broader historical and cultural context of Palestinian Judaism and the impact upon it of political events in the great centers of power. It will tend to give the impression that eschatological faith can flourish only at the periphery of a religious organization or that it is somehow innately hostile to the idea of a community based on law and cult, whereas such prophetic groups as are known to us demand legal observance as a necessary condition for the coming of the millennium. The major problem, however, is that the history of Judaism during this long period is for the most part so poorly known, there are so many gaps in our knowledge, especially for the century before and the century after

Alexander, that trajectories of this kind risk being too speculative to be useful.

We took note in the previous section of a messianic (i.e., nationalist and royalist) movement in the early Persian period that gathered strength under the impact of political and social crisis. Focusing—even before the ascendancy of Cyrus—on the exiled Jehoiachin, it was transferred in time to his grandson, whose Babylonian name was Zerubbabel.[31] An obvious but important point is that this movement was closely associated with plans for rebuilding both the Temple and the city. Successive stages, marked by alternating hope and disillusionment, can be observed: the expectation of returning to the homeland, the laying of the foundations of the Temple, the resumption of work during the revolts against Darius, and the completion of the work a few years later. That it did not end there is suggested by the complaint made against the Jerusalemites at the beginning of Xerxes' reign (486-484 B.C.E.). The mission of Ezra, which probably took place in the seventh year of Artaxerxes I (therefore 458 B.C.E.),[32] was almost certainly motivated by an even more serious uprising in Egypt, this time with the backing of Athens (460-454). While we have no evidence that Palestinian Jews took part in the uprising, another letter from the satrapal authorities to the central government, complaining that the city walls were being rebuilt as a prelude to revolt, resulted in a decree forbidding the work to continue (Ezra 4:7-23).

When Nehemiah arrived on his first mission in 445 B.C.E., perhaps significantly seventy years after the completion of work on the Temple,[33] he found the walls torn down and the gates gutted by fire. We do not know whether this resulted from an overenthusiastic implementation of the rescript of Artaxerxes or as a result of Jewish participation in the revolt of the satrap Megabyzus which took place about this time. When Nehemiah in his turn set about rebuilding, the action was again interpreted as a preparation for rebellion (Neh. 2:19; 6:6), and it was even alleged that he himself harbored messianic pretensions. While these allegations were almost certainly fabricated by the opposition,[34] they serve to show that messianism was still very much a live issue. As in the days of Haggai and Zechariah, prophets played an important role in these events and two of them, Shemaiah and Noadiah, are known by name (Neh. 6:6-14). Nothing that we are told about Nehemiah or, for that matter. Ezra, obliges us to believe that they were antieschatological; and we must bear in mind that the Chronicler, who transmitted and edited this material, had absolutely no interest in highlighting messianic disturbances.

Since messianic movements find a more sympathetic hearing among the economically oppressed, it should be added that social conditions in Judah during the early Persian period appear to have been generally bad and occasionally disastrous. Heavy tribute was levied by the central government, little if any of it benefiting the provinces, which were systematically drained of bullion. The resulting inflation and large-scale insolvency drove farmers off their land and benefited no one except the moneylenders. Bad as it was from the beginning, this situation got much worse after the accession of Xerxes (486), who levied taxes of a confiscatory magnitude to finance his crusade in Europe.[35]

Like the messianic movements that sprang up under Roman rule, those which we know of during the Persian period were not all of one kind. There were those who opted for armed rebellion with a view to regaining independence under a Davidic ruler. Others disavowed such direct action (e.g., Zech. 4:6; 9:9-10) in the belief that God would himself intervene, and that this intervention could be brought forward by fidelity to the laws, purified worship, and penitential practices. While this issue of engaging in or abstaining from military action has been much discussed apropos of the Asidaeans of the Seleucid epoch,[36] it is equally relevant for the Persian period. There were also forms of millenarian prophecy for which the Davidic ruler played either a minor role or none at all. Third Isaiah, for example, manifests a throughgoing eschatological perspective and yet never laments the passing of the monarchy or alludes to its future restoration.

We must now look at this important (and, in English-language scholarship, neglected) collection of prophetic material to see, if possible, how it fits into the religious history of the period and within which group it originated. It was argued earlier that Isa. 56-66 comprises a separate corpus with close ties to Isa. 40-55, especially the latter part of it (Isa. 49-55); that in all probability it derives from the discipleship of Second Isaiah; and that these disciples formed a prophetic and eschatological group within the postexilic community under a leader whose voice is heard proclaiming his mission in the Spirit (Isa. 59:21; 61:1-4). It was also suggested that the editorial expansions to the third and fourth of the "Servant Songs" (Isa. 50:10-11; 53:1-11) provide an important link between Second and Third Isaiah or, in other words, between the anonymous exilic prophet and his following.[37]

Third Isaiah opens with a remarkably liberal statement on membership in the community, conferring secure status on non-Jewish adherents of the Yahweh cult and on eunuchs, permitting them to participate in the cult on condition of observing the community's covenant requirements, especially regarding the Sabbath (Isa. 56:1-8). The same broad perspective is apparent in the final section (66:18-23) dealing with proselytism, missionary preaching, the ingathering of the nations and dispersed Jews to participate in the parousia in Jerusalem. The open admissions policy stated or implied in these two passages is at variance with the Deuteronomic law of the community (Deut. 23:2-9), and with some aspects of the program of Ezekiel in chs. 40-48 (especially 44:7-8) and that of Ezra and Nehemiah (Ezra 9:1-4; Neh. 9:2). They may therefore have been added as "book ends" at a later date according to an editorial technique detectable in other biblical compositions.[38] Comparison with Zech. 14:16-21, which speaks of the nations coming to Jerusalem to celebrate the Feast of Tabernacles, and with Jonah, which pioneers a new understanding of prophecy,[39] would suggest the century between the administrations of Nehemiah and the conquests of Alexander. These passages presage later developments, including the early Christian belief that the mission to the Gentiles must be completed before the parousia. The final verse (Isa. 66:24) foresees the defeat and destruction of rebellious elements in the community in a way that is meant to recall the opening verses of the Isaiah scroll and thus affirm its essential unity.[40]

Immediately after the opening verses there occurs a section (Isa. 56:9 to 57:13), possibly based on preexilic prophetic diatribe, that launches an attack on prophets (watchmen[41]) and rulers (shepherds) who have abandoned their tasks for the pleasures of the moment. One is reminded of the gloss on Isa. 9:14 ("So Yahweh cut off from Israel both head and tail") which identifies rulers as the head and lying prophets as the tail. The seer's polemic is also directed against the syncretists who take part in fertility cults and sexual rites and who are contrasted with the devout (*'anšê-ḥesed*) who are suffering persecution. The allusion to the righteous one (*ṣaddîq*) who has perished and whose death has gone unlamented (57:1) is generally given a collective meaning by the commentators but may in fact refer back to the righteous Servant (53:11) whose disciples perpetuated his message after the return from captivity.[42]

That message is restated in terms reminiscent of Second Isaiah in the following section (Isa. 57:14-21). The way is to be prepared for the parousia when God, who dwells in the heavenly temple, will take up his residence with the lowly and humble, those who mourn among his people. Preparing for the parousia was doubtless understood by these "mourners" to consist in faithful observance of the covenant requirements. The theme of eschatological reversal, taken up in the

Gospels, foresees that those who now mourn will rejoice when the great day dawns.[43] The section ends with a quotation from Second Isaiah ("There is no peace for the wicked," 48:22) which, though often quoted facetiously since, was intended as a verdict of eschatological judgment on the reprobates, those who rejected the prophetic message.

The nucleus of the collection, containing a compendium of the eschatological teachings of the group, is found in Isa. 60-62. Like 57:14-21, they come from either the last years of the exile or the early years after the return[44] and betray no sign of the opposition and conflict to which these teachings were to give rise with the passing of time. They begin with an apostrophe to Jerusalem: the glory of God will appear in Zion bringing salvation to an oppressed people, those scattered abroad will return, the nations will be subject to Israel, will bring tribute and help rebuild the city, the Temple will once again be glorious and shine at the center of the earth. The prospect of a renewal of the heavens and the earth, a cosmic *apokatastasis* that comes to expression here and elsewhere in Third Isaiah, is often represented to be a later and more explicitly apocalyptic development.[45] We may concede that this is possible, though there is no overwhelming argument to support it and there are sufficient grounds to distrust theories of development based solely on thematic arguments.

It is important to note that throughout Third Isaiah prophetic-eschatological faith is focused on Temple and altar (e.g., Isa. 60:7, 13; 61:6; 62:9). There is therefore no opposition *in principle* between the bearers of this faith and the Temple authorities and no evidence that the former were anticultic. The seer who speaks for them in fact goes on to expound a teaching not unlike the priesthood of all the faithful. The entire people will in the last days be relieved of servile labor, as are the priests, and will receive tithes from the nations. In this way the covenant to the house of Levi will be extended to all (cf. Num. 25:10-13).

At one point in this extended apostrophe, admittedly an obscure one, we catch a glimpse of the prophetic group in whose name the anonymous seer is speaking (Isa. 62:6-7). Addressing Jerusalem, he speaks of watchmen stationed on the walls whose task is to remind Yahweh continually of his promise to liberate the city. These *mazkîrîm* (literally, "those who bring to remembrance") are therefore charged with the task of intercession and prayer on behalf of the entire community, functions that since the beginning have been associated with the prophetic office.

Commentators have often noted the strongly liturgical flavor of much of the material in Second and Third Isaiah, though they have not always drawn the correct conclusions from this observation. It does not follow that a passage like Isa. 58:1-14 originated in a cultic setting since the author may simply have adopted a traditional cultic form for his own purposes. The passage in question is a prophetic answer to the community, which could not understand how its communal fasts were failing to influence Yahweh to do something about the disastrous economic conditions that then prevailed. The problem and the solution are much the same as in Zech. 7, which actually presents an oracle delivered in the Temple. The same conditions are presupposed in Isa. 59:1-20, where the change of tone and the alternation between speakers (second, third, and first person) suggest that the saying has been modeled on a communal lament in which cult prophets played a part. The same appears to be the case with the long passage 63:1 to 65:7, which reflects a kind of drama celebrating proleptically the event of salvation in response to the community's plea. Like several of the psalms,[46] this one opens with praise, continues with confession of sin, and ends with petition. The strangely worded appeal at 63:16 seems to be saying that, though the ancestors who enjoyed God's favor are dead and gone, he is still their father and must look on the miserable condition of his children.[47] According to the traditional model there would be a divine response giving assurance of salvation. Here, however, the divine readiness to act is thwarted by the false worship in which the prophet's contemporaries were indulging (65:1-7). This response is addressed to the people as a whole and not just to the priesthood who controlled the Temple.[48] This is not to deny that the latter also indulged in such practices, but Third Isaiah, unlike Malachi, does not make a special point of polemicizing against the priesthood.

In the last two chapters we come upon clear indications of internal conflict in the province of Judah involving the prophetic-eschatological group within which Third Isaiah originated. We may begin with the oracle of assurance in 66:5 addressed to those who "tremble at his word." From it we learn that these "quakers" (*ḥᵃrēdîm*) are hated and cast out by their fellow Jews: in effect, excommunicated.[49] Why? The reason given is "for my name's sake" (*lᵉmaʿan šᵉmî*), i.e., by virtue of their association with the seer who is addressing them, whom we must presume to be their leader.[50] A further reason is implied in the taunt that their "brethren" direct at them: "Let Yahweh be glorified that we may see your joy." This is not directed at their eschatological beliefs as such, but at the typically sectarian conviction that they, and they alone, will share in the rejoicing accompanying the parousia. In an earlier passage (65:8-12) Yahweh's servants and chosen ones are contrasted with the apostates (i.e., syncretists) who worship Gad and Meni, gods of good luck, following which judgment is pronounced on the reprobates (65:13-14). The language is that of eschatological reversal familiar to readers of the Gospels. It suggests that the taunt of the "brethren" is their answer to the claim, put forward here, that the "servants" will rejoice at the parousia while their opponents will be put to shame.[51] This impression is confirmed as we go on to read that the name of these opponents will serve as a curse for Yahweh's servants, while the latter will be called by a new name, one appropriate to the new age about to dawn.[52]

The first two sayings in the last chapter (Isa. 66:1-4) seem to deal with quite different matters. The first (vs. 1-2) has generally been interpreted as a rejection of the proposal to rebuild the Temple, and therefore as a position directly opposed to Haggai and Zechariah, and the second (vs. 3-4) as a brutally explicit condemnation of animal sacrifice.[53] If, however, the one who "trembles at my word" in the first saying belongs to the same category as the "quakers" of v. 5 who look with eager anticipation to the parousia, an event which, if it is not to take place in the Temple, is at least inseparable from it,[54] this interpretation can hardly be correct. It would be pertinent to refer to Solomon's prayer at the dedication of the First Temple (I Kings 8:27-30), since it shows that support of the Temple is compatible with disavowal of popular misunderstandings of its place in the religious life of the community. In Third Isaiah the idea of heaven as God's dwelling is linked with his being present to the faithful in the community: "I dwell in a high and holy place, and with the one who is broken and lowly of spirit" (57:15; cf. also 63:15 and 40:20). As for the saying about the sacrificial cult, it should be noted that the juxtaposition of legitimate with illegitimate cult acts (e.g., the slaughtering of an ox with human sacrifice) refers to acts performed by those who have chosen their own ways and delight in their idols (66:3), that is, those addicted to syncretic cults whose basic attitude vitiates even the legitimate cultic acts that they perform.[55]

Isaiah 66:1-5, then, testifies to a serious rift within Palestinian Judaism of the early Persian period involving a prophetic-eschatological minority led by a seer who understood his mission, and that of his followers, after the manner of the exilic Second Isaiah. The group described themselves as "those who tremble at his word" (66:1-5), implying a reverential and fearful attention to eschatological prophecy as passed on in the exilic and postexilic "Isaian school." Other self-descriptions occurring in Third Isaiah are "servants of Yahweh" (65:8-9, 13-16), "mourners" (57:18; 61:2; 66:10), "devout" (57:1), and perhaps "Amen people" (65:15-16a).[56] They were excluded at some point from participation in the Temple cult, which would help to explain their miserable social and economic status. Their opponents, while not necessarily opposed to their eschatological teaching in itself, rejected their exclusivist claims, were addicted to syncretic cults, and included at least some of the Temple authorities. With respect to the Temple, therefore, we have a situation in some respects similar to that of the Qumran sectarians. In more general terms, the group marks an important point of transition from prophetic discipleship to sect.

A curious fact, little noted in the commentaries, is that Ezra was supported in his mission by a group described as "those who tremble at the word (commandment) of the God of Israel" (Ezra 9:4; 10:3), essentially the same self-description that we have encountered in Third Isaiah.[57] Shortly after his arrival in Jerusalem, Ezra was confronted with the need to do something about the regrettable tendency of the Diaspora Jews (bᵉnê-haggôlāh, Ezra 8:35) to marry foreign women. After his initial and somewhat intemperate reaction, the initiative was taken by these "quakers" (9:4), who from then on were closely associated with Ezra in fasting, penitential prayer, and keeping vigil in preparation for the covenant, which was carried out according to their counsel (10:3).

At first sight there would appear to be nothing in common between the group so described in Third Isaiah, which was ostracized and disowned by the majority, and Ezra's support group, which appears to form an elite within the gôlāh community. It might also be argued that what caused the latter to tremble was solicitude for the law rather than prophetic revelations (Ezra 10:3). On the other hand it is important not to set a prophetic-eschatological orientation over against concern, even intense concern, for law observance. There are also certain features of these ḥᵃrēdîm that suggest a connection. In Third Isaiah mourning is associated with fasting as eschatological joy is with feasting (65:13-14, etc.), and the same association occurs where the Ezra narrative speaks of those who supported the reform program. Parallelism between "all who trembled at the words of the God of Israel because of the faithlessness of the returned exiles" (Ezra 9:4) and Ezra "mourning over the faithlessness of the exiles" (10:6) suggests that trembling and mourning are being predicated of a penitential group within the community among whose members Ezra found his main support. In this respect we have an anticipation of the milieu in which Daniel circulated during the Seleucid persecution: mourning, fasting, penitential prayer, intense concern with the law and with prophecy.[58]

There is also the fact that marriage with foreign women, the main problem confronting Ezra, brought with it involvement in non-Yahwistic and syncretic cults (Ezra 9:1) and affected not only the community leaders but priests and Levites (9:1-2; cf. 10:18-24). This is precisely the situation against which the "quakers" and "servants" of Third Isaiah protested, obviously with very limited success. Confirmation is at hand in Malachi, the anonymous author of which is clearly concerned with the same issues. It was noted earlier that in Mal. 3:16-18 it is those who fear and serve God who enter into covenant, presumably to remove the abuses castigated by the prophet.[59] After our discussion of Third Isaiah, we are now in a stronger position to suggest that the covenant alluded to in this passage is in all probability the same as the one initiated by the *ḥ°rēdîm* of Ezra 9-10.

Our conclusion, that Ezra's program was accepted and enforced not only by a minority group but by one which derived its inspiration from prophetic-eschatological teaching, and which *on that basis* supported his work, will appear paradoxical in view of conventional scholarly representations of Ezra and his mission. It would imply that that mission resulted in a temporary setback for the civic and religious leadership of the community which had compromised itself by syncretism and a no-less-temporary enhancement of status for his prophetic support group. It would also help to explain the apparently limited success of his mission, to judge by the situation that confronted Nehemiah on his arrival in Jerusalem.

Whatever the later fortunes or misfortunes of this prophetic group which owed allegiance to the person and teaching of the anonymous prophet of the exile, it presages in important ways the emergence of sects in the Roman period, not excluding early Palestinian Christianity. It also illustrates the social dynamics involved in the formation of prophetic subgroups and their consolidation around the teaching and memory of a charismatic figure. In these respects its significance for the future can hardly be exaggerated.

3. TEMPLE PROPHECY

J. W. **Ahlström,** "Some Remarks on Prophets and Cult," in J. C. Rylaarsdam (ed.), *Transitions in Biblical Scholarship*, Chicago: University of Chicago Press, 1968, 113-129; *Joel and the Temple Cult of Jerusalem*, Leiden: E. J. Brill, 1971; L. C. **Allen,** *The Books of Joel, Obadiah, Jonah, and Micah*, Grand Rapids: Wm. B. Eerdmans Publishing Co., 1976; T. **Chary,** *Les Prophètes et le culte à partir de l'exil*, Paris: Desclée, 1955; H. **Gese,** "Zur Geschichte der Kultsänger am zweiten Tempel," in *Abraham unser Vater. Juden und Christen im Gespräch über die Bibel*, Leiden: E. J. Brill, 1963, 222-234; E. **Hammershaimb,** *Some Aspects of Old*

Testament Prophecy from Isaiah to Malachi, Copenhagen: Rosenkilde & Bagger, 1966; M. **Haran,** *Temples and Temple-Service in Ancient Israel,* Oxford: Clarendon Press, 1978; A. B. **Johnson,** *The Cultic Prophet and Israel's Psalmody,* Cardiff: University of Wales Press, 1979; A. S. **Kapelrud,** *Joel Studies,* Uppsala: Lundequist, 1948; H.-J. **Kraus,** *Worship in Israel,* Richmond: John Knox Press, 1966, 101-112, 229-236; R. **Mosis,** *Untersuchungen zur Theologie des chronistischen Geschichtswerkes,* Freiburg: Herder, 1972; S. **Mowinckel,** *The Psalms in Israel's Worship,* Nashville: Abingdon Press, 1967, II, 53-73; J. M. **Myers,** *I Chronicles,* Garden City: Doubleday & Co., 1965, xv-xciv; J. **Newsome,** "Toward a New Understanding of the Chronicler and His Purposes," *JBL* 94, 1975, 210-212; D. L. **Petersen,** *Late Israelite Prophecy,* Missoula, Mont.: Scholars Press, 1977; H. H. **Rowley,** *Worship in Ancient Israel,* London: S.P.C.K., 1967, 144-175, 176-212; W. **Rudolph,** *Joel—Amos—Obadja—Jona,* Gütersloh: Gütersloher Verlagshaus Gerd Mohn, 1971; A. **Welch,** *The Work of the Chronicler,* London: Oxford University Press, 1939, 42-54; C. **Westermann,** *Basic Forms of Prophetic Speech,* 163-168; T. **Willi,** *Die Chronik als Auslegung. Untersuchungen zur literarischen Gestaltung der historischen Überlieferung Israels,* Göttingen: Vandenhoeck & Ruprecht, 1972; H. G. M. **Williamson,** *Israel in the Book of Chronicles,* Cambridge: Cambridge University Press, 1977; *1 and 2 Chronicles,* Grand Rapids: Wm. B. Eerdmans Publishing Co., 1982; H. W. **Wolff,** *Joel and Amos,* Philadelphia: Fortress Press, 1977.

In Israel, as everywhere else in the Near East, ecstatic prophets were attached to temples and carried out specific functions there including intercessory prayer and the giving of oracles, especially in critical situations.[60] Apart from explicit attestations,[61] some aspects of their activity can be cautiously deduced from prophetic oracles in the hymns and the attribution of psalms to prophets.[62] We have seen that one or another of the canonical prophets may have belonged to the ranks of these temple ecstatics, while others may have begun their career, but not ended it, in that capacity. Temples were in any case appropriate places for prophetic preaching (e.g., Jer. 7:1 to 8:3; 36:4-8), though it does not follow that prophets who chose to address their public in a temple belonged to the temple staff.

One of the most important aspects of the transformation that prophecy underwent after the loss of national independence was its reabsorption into the cult. The Priestly source (P), which comes from this period of transition and reflects a concern for the reestablishment of genuine worship, provides some interesting clues to this process. During the wilderness period, which for P served as a model for the life of the cultic community, divine communications were received in the mobile sanctuary where Moses heard the voice of God addressing him from above the "mercy seat" (Ex. 25:22; Num. 7:89). While this representation still preserves something of the ancient oracle tent, it also anticipates the *bath qol* (heavenly voice) which was later to serve as a kind of surrogate prophecy.[63] Charismatic succession, especially in the case of Joshua, was effected by an act, comparable to the ordination of priests, by means of which the charisma was transferred from Moses to his successor.[64] Guidance in the wilderness was effected not through the prophetic word but by the fire and cloud that hovered over the sanctuary (Num. 9:15-23, etc.). According to the Priestly version of Moses' call, Aaron acted as his *nābî'*, and did so in such a way as to suggest that the prophetic task of confronting the king had passed by default to the eponym of the priesthood (Ex. 7:1).

The change in the location and consequent understanding of prophecy is apparent in the early Persian period with the predominance of liturgical forms and cultic concerns in Haggai, Zechariah, Third Isaiah, and Malachi. It is also much in evidence in the address of a certain Joel ben-Pethuel to the congregation, which included farmers and vintners, on the occasion of a disastrous plague of locusts that had ruined the crops. There is no doubt that this really happened, though at what point in time during the Persian period it is impossible to determine.[65] The problem of dating is compounded by the fact that the plague was reinterpreted at a later time as a harbinger of the last days and the consummation of history.[66] Leaving this eschatological rereading aside for the moment, we have, if not the outline, at least the main elements of a penitential liturgy in which the cult prophet played an important role.

The opening address to the congregation (Joel 1:2-12) concludes with a call to the priests to convoke a solemn service of fasting and repentance (1:13-18) to which the people were summoned by the blowing of the shofar (2:1, 15). There follow the prayer of petition (1:19-20) and the call to fast and repent (2:1-17), and the liturgical action ends with an oracle of assurance delivered by the prophet (2:18-27). In view of the many verbal and thematic contacts of Joel with Amos (which may help to explain the place of Joel in the *Dodekapropheton*), it is worth noting that the first two visions of Amos (7:1-6) also deal with locusts and drought, and that these disasters are averted by prophetic intercession. We are not told, and we certainly cannot assume, that this function was discharged in the cult. But by the time of Joel there can be no doubt that the averting of disaster could be achieved, if at all, only by the cultic act of the entire community. For Joel, whose criticism of his contemporaries is mild in comparison with that of Amos (Joel 1:5; 2:12), the current threat to the economic existence of the community can be turned aside only by means of cultic acts performed in the Temple, in which the prophet played a leading role.

By far the most important source of information on the organization and personnel of the Second Temple is the work of the Chronicler, which represents the final stage of a rewriting of the history from the perspective of the Jerusalem cult community. The dating of this work is one of the many issues in Second Temple studies on which there is no consensus and no likelihood of reaching one in the foreseeable future. On the assumption that the work took in the missions of Ezra and Nehemiah, it could not very well have appeared in its final form earlier than the first decades of the fourth century B.C.E., and could be later.[67] Using the technique of genealogical linkage, much in use in P, the author traced the history of the postexilic cult community to the beginnings of history (I Chron. 1-9), though the actual narrative only begins with the death of Saul and the accession of David (I Chron. 10). For the Chronicler it was David rather than Moses who founded the cultic establishment and the different orders of Levites, though this act had to be repeated more than once throughout a long history marked by frequent apostasy.[68] The author gives prominence to the guilds of Temple musicians who are described as discharging their functions by virtue of prophetic inspiration. They were also founded by David in his capacity as divinely inspired charismatic (I Chron. 25:1-8). It was probably among these Temple musicians that the tradition of David as prophet originated, a tradition that could be taken for granted by the Roman period.[69]

For the Chronicler, then, the composition and rendition of liturgical music was a form of prophecy. In the act of worship prophetic and poetic inspiration came together. These Levitical singers cannot be represented as in direct line of descent from the Temple prophets, whose existence, if not their activity, is well attested during the time of the First Temple. There are indications that these musicians or poets[70] achieved a progressively more important place in the hierarchy of the Second Temple, in which process the attribution of prophetic gifts no doubt played a legitimating role. They also usurped the oracular function of earlier cult prophecy, discharging this function not only in the Temple but on the battlefield (II Chron. 20:13-23).[71] One of the Levitical leaders, Chenaniah by name, has a title that, obscure as it is, seems to connote both a musical and oracular function (I Chron. 15:22, 27).[72] The usurpation can be detected with particular clarity at one point of the history, the account of Josiah's reforms, where the Chronicler has simply substituted "Levites" for "prophets," leaving the rest of his source intact (II Chron. 34:30; cf. II Kings 23:2).

This extension of prophecy to cover liturgical music in which God was acknowledged, thanked, and praised[73] continued into the Roman period and beyond. Not only is it well represented in early Christianity and the Qumran community, but its traces can be detected in Jewish liturgical practice long after the destruction of the Second Temple.[74]

Another aspect of the Chronicler's reinterpretation of prophecy is the surprising transformation of preexilic prophets into historians, as seen in his allusion to chronicles authored by Samuel, Nathan, Isaiah, and other prophetic figures, some of them otherwise unattested.[75] This aspect also survived into the Roman period, was exploited by Josephus,[76] and no doubt serves to explain the inclusion of historiography under prophecy in the Hebrew Bible.

4. THE ESCHATOLOGICAL REINTERPRETATION OF PROPHECY

G. W. **Anderson,** "Isaiah XXIV-XXVII Reconsidered," *SVT* 9, 1963, 118-126; R. E. **Clements,** *Isaiah 1-39,* Grand Rapids: Wm. B. Eerdmans Publishing Co., 1981, 196-224; R. J. **Coggins,** "The Problem of Isaiah 24-27," *ExpT* 90, 1979, 328-333; F. M. **Cross,** "New Directions in the Study of Apocalyptic," in R. W. Funk (ed.), *Journal for Theology and the Church; 6: Apocalypticism,* New York: Herder & Herder, 1969, 157-165; *Canaanite Myth and the Hebrew Epic,* Cambridge, Mass: Harvard University Press, 1973, 343-346; M. **Delcor,** "Les Sources du Deutero-Zacharie et ses procédés d'emprunt," *RB* 59, 1952, 385-411; H. **Gese,** "Anfang und Ende der Apokalyptik dargestellt am Sacharjabuch," *ZTK* 70, 1973, 20-49; P. D. **Hanson,** "Jewish Apocalyptic Against Its Near-Eastern Environment," *RB* 78, 1971, 31-58; "Old Testament Apocalyptic Reexamined," *Int* 25, 1971, 454-479; "Zechariah 9 and the Recapitulation of an Ancient Ritual Pattern," *JBL* 92, 1973, 37-59; O. **Kaiser,** *Isaiah 13-39, A Commentary,* Philadelphia: Westminster Press, 1974, 173-233; M. A. **Knibb,** "Prophecy and the Emergence of the Jewish Apocalypses," in R. Coggins et al., *Israel's Prophetic Tradition,* 155-180; W. R. **Millar,** *Isaiah 24-27 and the Origin of Apocalyptic,* Missoula, Mont.: Scholars Press, 1976; R. **North,** "Prophecy to Apocalyptic via Zechariah," *SVT* 22, 1972, 47-72; B. **Otzen,** "Traditions and Structures of Isaiah XXIV-XXVII," *VT* 24, 1974, 196-206; D. L. **Petersen,** *Late Israelite Prophecy,* 1-54; O. **Plöger,** *Theocracy and Eschatology,* Richmond: John Knox Press, 1968; "Prophetisches Erbe in den Sekten des frühen Judentums," *TLZ* 79, 1954, 291-296; C. **Rowland,** *The Open Heaven,* London: S.P.C.K., 1982, 193-213; W. **Rudolph,** *Haggai—Sacharja 1-8—Sacharja 9-14—Maleachi,* Gütersloh: Gütersloher Verlagshaus Gerd Mohn, 1976, 159-246. M. **Saebo,** *Sacharja 9-14,* Neukirchen-Vluyn: Neukirchener Verlag, 1969; O. **Steck,** "Das Problem theologischer Strömungen in nachexilischer Zeit," *EvTh* 28, 1968, 447-448; J. **Vermeylen,** "La Composition littéraire de l' 'apocalypse d' Isaïe,' "

ETL 50, 1974, 5-38; H. **Wildberger,** *Jesaja* II, Neukirchen-Vluyn: Neukirchener Verlag, 1978, 885-1026; H.-W. **Wolff,** *Joel and Amos*, 57-86.

Thus far in this chapter we have noted several aspects of a profound and widespread transformation that prophecy underwent after the loss of national independence and royal patronage. This transformation affected not only the institution itself, seen most clearly in the Chronicler's history, but also the way prophecy was seen to function within the group. Increasing reference to former prophets, occasional laments for the absence of prophetic guidance and, not least, the well-attested practice of adapting earlier prophetic sayings to new situations—e.g., in Zech. 1-8—are symptomatic of this new situation. With the availability of prophetic material in writing, the emphasis was less on direct inspired utterance and more on the inspired interpretation of past prophecy. Correspondingly, there was an increasing sense that, in the normal course of events, God does not communicate directly but has revealed his will and purpose in past communications whose bearing on the present situation remains to be elucidated.

With this extremely important shift in emphasis the role of biblical interpretation, as understood in Judaism and Christianity, began to be decisive for the self-understanding of the community that preserved the writings. And since any text can be interpreted in more than one way, control of this function was also a political factor in the disposal of power within the community. Thus, on the one hand, we can detect a tendency toward the institutionalization of exegesis which, in the case that concerns us here, reached classical formulation in the view of the prophets as tradents of the Law. On the other hand, though, there were those who, while not necessarily denying them this function, chose to emphasize the projection of a future reality quite different from the present.

It is important to add that this transformation should not be viewed—as it has been routinely in Christian scholarship—as symptomatic of religious decline, the "drying up of inspiration" (whatever that means), or the triumph of the letter over the spirit. One could illustrate this *locus communis* from any number of commentators from Wellhausen down to the present. Alfred Lods, for example, in a work bearing the significant title *The Prophets and the Rise of Judaism*, comments that

> the fate of prophecy was sealed when, side by side with the living word of the messenger of Yahweh, there appeared a new authority, that of the written word.

This was with reference to developments in late-seventh-century Judah. As we move into the Second Temple period we are invited to note how

> the inward flame which had inspired the movement until now is growing dim, and may soon be extinguished.[77]

More helpful would be a careful analysis of the quite different sociopolitical situation which obtained at that time and which made it impossible for prophecy to function as previously. Less obviously, it should not simply be assumed that the preexilic canonical prophets represent the apogee of religious development so that whatever followed would inevitably be construed as a declension from that high ideal. In one sense, the change in the forms and understanding of prophecy in the Second Commonwealth derived from an appreciation of the failure of earlier prophecy to solve certain crucial problems (especially that of criteria for discernment) and to provide a firm basis for the ongoing life of the community. And finally, it is not self-evident that the consolidation of scribalism in the Second Temple period, with the emergence of an intellectual and theological tradition into which prophecy was inevitably drawn, must be viewed as a symptom of decline.

Simply put, the problem for those who preserved these texts and took them seriously was: How can the word of God addressed to our ancestors who lived in a different age and faced different problems become a word of God for us today? Since, as far as we know, the prophetic books did not generate commentaries before the Roman period, we have to reconstruct the solutions to this problem from the editorial history of the texts themselves. We have noted already, at more than one point, the difficulties attending this task; for the process of editing began long before the time of which we are speaking. Doctrinaire theories (e.g., a prosodic typology rigidly applied) and general thematic treatments (e.g., the degree of mythological over against historical reference) are perhaps least likely to succeed. While certainty is rarely to be had, the best strategy seems to be that of working at a certain level of concreteness and specificity from the clearer instances of glosses and larger expansions generally recognized as such; where, for example, the intent of commenting on a previous passage is fairly explicit or where certain regularly recurring formal and literary features strongly suggest such an intent. By prudent use of such a method it may be possible to recover fragments of a chapter in the history of prophecy during a period about which we know very little: the centuries that precede and follow the conquests of Alexander (ca. 433-198 B.C.E.). To this end we will examine briefly Joel 2:28 to 3:21 (MT 3-4), Zech. 9-14, and certain parts of the Isaiah scroll, especially Isa. 24-27, the so-called "Isaian apocalypse."

In dealing earlier in this chapter with the address of Joel ben-Pethuel to the congregation, we noted that a later hand had transformed the plague lamented by the prophet into a proleptic symbol of final judgment to take place on the Day of Yahweh. Many commentators therefore assume that even in the first part of this booklet all references to the Day (Joel 1:15; 2:1b-2a, 11b) are editorial. While this is certainly possible it is by no means inevitable, since, whatever its origin, the idea of the Day of Yahweh was familiar to preexilic prophets (e.g., Amos 5:18-20; 8:9-14; Zeph. 1:14-18).[78] The second part of the book begins with a prediction that in the latter days the Spirit will be poured out on the entire community (this is the sense of the phrase "all flesh"), resulting in a great eruption of prophetic activity (Joel 2:28-29 [MT 3:1-2]). The closest parallels to this word about the re-creative powers of the divine Spirit are to be found in the address of Ezekiel, or one of his disciples, to a defeated and dispirited people in exile (Ezek. 39:29; 36:26; 37:1-14). Only here in Joel, however, is the Spirit spoken of as the source of prophetic activity, though there is perhaps more than an echo of the words of Moses of Joshua in the episode, discussed earlier, of the ordination of elders at the wilderness sanctuary: "Would that all Yahweh's people were prophets, that Yahweh would put his spirit upon them!" (Num. 11:29). The distinguishing factor is that an age is anticipated in which the Spirit will endow not just designated individuals but the entire community, or at least those in the community whose profession of faith matched that of the anonymous seer. In the course of time both Judaism and early Christianity (Acts 2:16-21) would find in this passage an essential aspect of eschatological and messianic faith.

The following passage (Joel 2:30-32 [MT 3:3-5]), which goes on to speak of a cosmic upheaval, seems to be related to an earlier saying (2:10) about the effect of divine judgment on the earth and the heavenly bodies. Here, however, these cosmic events are reinterpreted as *signs* of the final judgment, a familiar representation in Jewish and early Christian apocalyptic. The effect of the final judgment will be to reveal the true Israel, those who call on the name of Yahweh or, in other words, those who share the writer's eschatological faith. It is important to note that in support of this belief the seer appeals to the authority of a prophetic word spoken in the past:

> On Mount Zion and in Jerusalem there will be a remnant which escapes, *as Yahweh has said.* (Joel 2:32)

The reference may be to Obad. 17, where the same assertion occurs in practically identical form. Much the same idea is expressed at Isa. 4:2-6, where the term "escaped remnant" (*p'lêṭāh*) is also used, as it is elsewhere in the Isaiah scroll (10:20; 37:31-32). The fuller description which follows of the judgment of the nations in the valley of Jehoshaphat (Joel 3:1-3 [MT 4:1-3]), to be preceded by the final showdown in Jerusalem (3:9-21 [MT 4:9-21]), also draws its inspiration from prophetic sources, especially the prophecy of Obadiah and the apocalyptic battle against the legendary Gog as described in Ezek. 38-39. The oracle against Phoenician and Philistine cities, which refers to the slave trade, in Jewish prisoners of war, with the Greeks (Joel 3:4-8 [MT 4:4-8]), is often identified as a still later insertion from the time of the Diadochoi, suggested by the general allusion to the slave trade at 3:3. This is probably correct, since it is only here that we have a specific political reference of any kind in the book.[79]

The difficulty of dating editorial expansions of prophetic books is well illustrated by the material we have just briefly considered. Apart from the reference to the Greeks, which is not all that helpful and in any case applies only to the passage in which it occurs (Joel 3:4-8 [MT 4:4-8]), there are no datable historical allusions, despite the intensely political character of this kind of writing and the general probability that it was precipitated by real historical crises. All we can say is that the nucleus of the book has been expanded by a commentator closely familiar with the prophetic heritage, whose intent was to bring out more clearly its eschatological meaning. We would probably not be far wrong in dating the bulk of this material to the last century of Persian rule and the saying directed at the Philistine and Phoenician cities to the century that followed.[80]

The same problem confronts the reader of Zech. 9-14 and is even more frustrating, since many of the sayings in this collection do refer to quite specific historical events which, however, we are for the most part unable to elucidate. We noted earlier that Zech. 9-11, 12-14, and Malachi comprise three anonymous additions to the prophetic corpus, all introduced in the same way and of roughly equal length; and that the expedient of attaching the first two to Zechariah and giving the last a fictitious title had the purpose of rounding off this second collection at twelve. This in itself would indicate an important stage in the formation of the prophetic corpus to be dated no earlier than the reign of Darius. The first of the three "appendices" opens with an oracle of a Jewish seer, perhaps living in Syria,[81] against the cities of Phoenicia and Philistia (Zech. 9:1-8). While the language is not specific enough to enable us to pin down the historical reference with certainty—especially since the Phoenician and Philistine cities are linked elsewhere in prophetic texts (Amos 1:3-10; Joel 3:4 [MT 4:4])—the best fit would be with the campaigns of Alexander between the battle of Issus (333) and the conquest of Egypt, the highlights of which were the subjugation of Tyre and Gaza after lengthy sieges. If this is so, we would have an indication of the initial response of Jewish communities to the Macedonian conqueror: satisfaction at the discomfiting of traditional enemies mixed with apprehension for the fate of Jerusalem. In the event, Alexander continued on down the coastal plain delayed only by the five-month siege of Gaza, whose king actually did perish (Zech. 9:5). Stories about Alexander's stopover in Jerusalem and encounter with Jaddua the high priest, picked up or invented by Josephus and reported in the Talmud, are evidently legendary.[82]

The apostrophe to Zion, which follows on quite naturally (Zech. 9:9-10), is of a type familiar to the prophetic tradition (e.g., Zeph. 3:14-20). It proclaims the advent of the Davidic messiah who will bring war to an end, and it does so by recalling the ancient oracle of Judah (Gen. 49:8-12). While it is often taken to be a later insertion, it fits in equally well by way of contrast with the Macedonian world conqueror and may therefore be seen as preparing for the much starker contrast in Daniel's vision of the beasts and the one in human form. The allusion to the setting free of Jewish prisoners and the promise of double recompense, modeled on the language of Second Isaiah (Isa. 40:1-2), leads to a prediction of victory over the Greeks (Zech. 9:13) which is probably a gloss, perhaps from as late as the struggle with the Seleucid rulers. The fiercely confident tone of the poem following (Zech. 10:3-12), which predicts ruin on foreign rulers, military victory for a reunited Jewish people, and the repatriation of their dispersed compatriots, provides no sure clue to its origin unless "Egypt" and "Assyria" are understood as code names for the Ptolemaic and Seleucid empires respectively. The following short poem (11:1-3), which is a mock lament on the defeat or death of foreign rulers, also defies any attempt to place it historically.

Nowhere is the problem more in evidence than in the extended and detailed narrative of the good but unsuccessful shepherd, a narrative that appears to be an allegorization of a prophetic-symbolic action (Zech. 11:4-16).[83] The literary model is clearly Ezek. 37:15-28, the account of a symbolic mime involving sticks marked with the names Judah and Ephraim in which the prophet acts out the role of the Davidic king who is to unite them. In the Zechariah passage the seer is invited to rule over the people in place of their own corrupt leaders who buy and sell them—presumably as the result of failure to pay tribute. In that capacity he took two staffs called Noam (favor) and Ḥoblim (union) and disposed of three of their rulers, presumably the ones who were oppressing them. As a result of worsening relations with the people, however, he annulled the agreements into which he had entered with the foreign rulers who had put him in power and with the Samaritans. The contemptible sum he received in recompense for his trouble ended up in the Temple treasury, and the last act of the mimetic drama presaged a successor who would resume the previous pattern of oppressive and predatory rule.

It can hardly be doubted that this strange narrative mirrors an episode in the history of Second Temple Judaism, but again its details, sharply etched as they are, escape us. The one sure point is the reference to Judean-Samaritan relations.[84] While the long history of estrangement between the two goes back to the early days of the return from exile, indeed to the settlement of foreign elements in the territory of the northern tribes by Assyria, it entered a new phase with the establishment of a Macedonian colony in Samaria following on the unsuccessful rebellion of 332 B.C.E.[85] The political and religious differences between Jerusalem and these others who owed allegiance to the sanctuary at Gerizim continued to be an important factor in the history of the country down into Hasmonaean times, and the present narrative no doubt reflects an episode in that history about which we are entirely in the dark.

The second section (Zech. 12-14) is rather different in some important respects. For one thing it is, with the exception of 13:7-9, entirely in prose, whereas the previous section is mostly in verse. It no longer deals with Judean-Samaritan relations but with matters that concern the Jerusalem community, and it draws largely for inspiration on Ezekiel (e.g., the fountain and the river in Jerusalem, Zech. 13:1 and 14:8). Formally, it is composed for the most part of some sixteen short eschatological logia beginning with the formula "on that day" *(bayyôm hahû)*, which appears only once (9:16) in the previous section. With this formula we come upon a distinct possibility of tracing a line of development in the editorial history of prophetic books.[86] The phrase is, of course, used in all kinds of contexts, sometimes with reference to a past event (e.g., Jer. 39:16; Ezek. 20:6). But it also occurs throughout the prophetic books with reference to a particular event of judgment or salvation in the future. Among these instances, which are of different kinds, there is a type consisting in a short prose paragraph with the phrase at the beginning (in other types it can be in the middle or at the end) that serves as a commentary or *pesher* on an earlier, generally immediately preceding passage, and that extends the horizon of this text into the future. It seems to have been especially favored by commentators on the Isaiah scroll, whether the perspective is merely futuristic (e.g., the series appended to an oracle on Tyre [Isa. 23:1-12] and one on Egypt [Isa. 19:1-15]) or eschatological in the commonly accepted sense of that term (e.g., Isa. 10:20-23; 11:10-11; 27:12-13). In some few instances (Isa. 4:2-6; 17:7-9; 27:1) there is no apparent link with the immediate context, at least not in the sense of text followed by commentary, and with this we are close to the kind of series we have identified in Zech. 12-14. After the final redaction of the prophetic corpus around the beginning of the second century B.C.E. this process could no longer be incorporated into the text but was carried on in commentaries, of which the earliest examples known to us are the Qumran prophetic *p'shārîm*.

From all of these *bayyôm hahû* passages one could put together quite a compendium of eschatological teaching emanating from sages and seers of the Second Temple period, teaching that is backed by the authority of the prophetic word spoken in the past. The collection in Zech. 12-14 foresees the destruction of foreign powers hostile to Israel with the exception of a remnant that will join the Yahweh cult and take part in the great pilgrim feast of Succoth; the preeminence of Jerusalem, where holiness will extend even to the harness bells on the horses; purification from sin and the end of idolatry; the restoration of the Davidic dynasty; theophany on the Mount of Olives ushering in an age of prosperity and fertility, etc. The only negative elements disturbing this eschatological fantasy are, first, the prospect of a terrible final battle that only a remnant, variously estimated at a third (Zech 13:7-9) or a half (14:2), will survive; and second, a subdued note of tension between the city itself and the people of Judah (12:7; 14:14). The longer passage describing mourning rites for a public figure in whose death the people had somehow been implicated (12:10-14) has given rise to a range of guesses from King Josiah (609 B.C.E.) to Simon Maccabee (134 B.C.E.).[87] It would be tempting to opt for the former since the text mentions the plain of Megiddo where Josiah met his death, and we know from II Chron. 35:25 that he was still being lamented at least as late as the fourth century. Since, however, we have no evidence that his own people were implicated in his death, the temptation should probably be set aside. Simon is almost certainly too late, as is also a more popular candidate, Onias the high priest slain in 170 B.C.E. We have to bear in mind that names from the second century have been proposed only because we know this period quite well, whereas we know practically nothing of the internal history of the community during the fourth and third centuries. It seems most likely then that this passage refers to an unknown figure of that unknown period; either a martyred prophet or, more probably, given the allusions to the house of David, a casualty of the messianic movement, which we have no reason to believe did not remain alive after the time of Nehemiah. It is little wonder that early Christian preaching, especially touching the death of Jesus, has drawn so often on these chapters.

As we look back over this work of commentary in the additions to Joel and Zechariah we cannot help asking who these people were who produced it. They drew their inspiration from written prophecy and themselves claimed an inspiration comparable to that of the prophets. That is to say, they believed that God continued to speak through them by virtue of their understanding of the real meaning of these texts. At the same time they dissociated themselves from contemporary prophetic practitioners whom they dismissed together with such suspect forms of mediation as teraphim, divination, and dream interpretation (Zech. 10:2). In one extraordinary passage (13:2-6) prophecy is even bracketed with the defilement of male prostitution. Prophecy has sunk so low that it is, almost by definition, falsity and therefore subject to the death penalty (Deut. 13:1-5; 18:20). The ecstatic prophet will not advertise his profession by donning the characteristic mantle or exhibiting his self-inflicted lacerations (cf. I Kings 18:28; 20:35-43). On the contrary, he will go to any lengths to avoid being identified as a prophet.[88] So these people would hardly have thought or spoken of themselves as *n^ebî'îm* and probably thought of genuine prophecy as a phenomenon that belonged either to the past or to the new age that God was even then preparing to usher in. It is possible, but no more, that they were in some way associated with the Temple and its personnel; at least there is no evidence of alienation from the Temple establishment. It is also possible, even probable, that this kind of work emanated from associations or conventicles similar to the disciples of Second Isaiah, discussed earlier, and the associations and sects explicitly attested at a somewhat later time. In the absence of information we can say no more than this.

The Isaiah scroll itself testifies to prophecy written down for later generations (Isa. 30:8), a perspective that no doubt helps to explain the vast expansion of the original core of Isaian sayings. It was always understood that it was not written just for the contemporaries of the prophet:

> In that day the deaf shall hear
>   the words of a book,
> and out of their gloom and darkness
>   the eyes of the blind shall see.
> (Isa. 29:18)

It was equally clear, however, that it required interpretation, but to interpret it one had to have the key:

> And the vision of all this has become to you like the words of a book that is sealed. When they give it to one who can read, saying, "Read this," he says, "I cannot, for it is sealed." And when they give the book to one who cannot read, saying, "Read this," he says, "I cannot read." (Isa. 29:11-12)

One suspects that this cryptic saying has to do with the kind of insight required to read prophecy and the eschatological hermeneutic that provides the key to its understanding according to the schools that edited the scroll in the latter part of the Second Temple period. It is at least relevant to note that it follows a passage in verse in which the prophets are denounced as blind, drunk, and asleep; in other words, incapable of understanding. Once again, therefore, we have the contrast between those who called themselves prophets and those who believed that they had been designated to mediate the word of God through their interpretation of what he had spoken in the past.

There are cases in the scroll where the intent to expand an earlier saying, or to add a new saying to meet the different circumstances of the present, is explicitly stated. Such is the long oracle against Moab (Isa. 15:1 to 16:12), to which a later hand has added:

> This is the word which Yahweh spoke concerning Moab in the past.
> But now Yahweh says . . . (Isa. 16:13-14a)

Almost certainly the same hand has brought up to date the oracle dealing with Arab tribes (Isa. 21:13-15) with a brief prediction beginning, "For thus Yahweh said to me" (vs. 16-17). Elsewhere it is fairly clear, even if not explicitly announced, that an earlier saying is being reinterpreted. The poem about the pleasant vineyard in the "Isaian apocalypse" (27:2-5), for example, is clearly related to the song of the vineyard in the first part of the book (5:1-7), and is related as commentary to text. The regular pattern, discussed earlier, of prose commentary introduced with the formulaic "on that day" points in the same direction. A good example of adapting and bringing up to date by successive commentary is the oracle against Shebna, a high official of Hezekiah (22:15-19). A first extension (vs. 20-24) reflects his replacement by a certain Eliakim, and when the latter also failed to live up to expectations, a further installment was called for (v. 25). Other examples of serial commentary would be Isaiah's prediction to King Ahaz about a young woman bearing a son to be called Immanuel (Isa. 7:10-17 + 18-25) and the series of five additions to the oracle about

Egypt (Isa. 19:1-15 + 16-25) which take us down into the Hellenistic period. Such adjustments were especially in order with the oracles against foreign nations to meet changing historical situations. An oracle against Sidon (23:1-14), for example, has been expanded to take in the sister city of Tyre after the latter's punishment at the hands of Artaxerxes III (343) and Alexander (332). The rehabilitation of Tyre about seventy years later by Ptolemy II called for a further extension, this time in the light of the eschatological teaching about the subjection of the nations to Israel (23:15-18).

To the extent that it is possible, the reconstruction of the editorial history must start out from concrete and specific features in the text illustrated by the examples given. Advantage should also be taken of parallels where they occur (e.g., Isa. 2:2-5 and its parallel at Micah 4:1-4), similarity in language and theme with passages known to be of later date than the eighth century (e.g., Isa. 14:1-2; cf. Zech. 8:20-22), and standard ways of introducing glosses (e.g., Isa. 6:13; 9:15). One of the firmest conclusions to emerge from this kind of analysis is that the original nucleus has been interpreted and expanded so as to transform the scroll into a manual of eschatological teaching. Nowhere is this more in evidence than in chs. 24-27, the so-called "Isaian apocalypse."

In a previous chapter we noted that the standard divisions of the Isaiah scroll (chs. 1-39; 40-55; 56-66) are deceptive if they give the impression of a simple sequence of preexilic, exilic, and postexilic.[89] If we exclude the biographical supplement (chs. 36-39), much of the first part is editorial, and a significant proportion of that must be dated quite late in the editorial history of the text. The editorial supplements, moreover, include some rather long sections; e.g., a good part of the oracles against foreign nations (chs. 13-23) and the eschatological finale (chs. 33-35). While forming an independent booklet, chs. 24-27 have been positioned as a supplement to the oracles against the nations. Indeed, since the only concrete historical allusion in the section is to Moab (25:10-12), it has been suggested that the point of departure for the section as a whole was this supplement to the long oracle against Moab in the previous collection (chs. 15-16). While this possibility cannot be excluded, the section has undergone a development of its own and not all the references to a doomed city (24:10, 12; 25:2; 26:5; 27:10)—the anonymity of which has caused exegetes such frustration—can easily be explained in this way.[90]

Isaiah 24-27 can be described as a compendium of mostly eschatological logia, addresses, and psalms with no very obvious internal arrangement or logical sequence. It opens with a divine announcement of a catastrophe that will affect all classes of society equally (24:1-3). The address that follows (24:4-20) has something of the flavor of a liturgical lament for the condition of the earth, which is suffering the consequences of sin. There is a perceptible shift of focus in the middle with what appears to be a reference to rejoicing throughout the Jewish Diaspora and a speaker who does not join in the general euphoria, presumably at the destruction of the city referred to cryptically at 24:10. The refusal to rejoice is best explained as the result of the eschatological position of a minority represented by the speaker.[91] There follows the first of several short passages introduced with the familiar "on that day" formula (24:21-23), which foresees the destruction of heavenly and earthly powers and the establishment of God's kingdom in Zion as adumbrated in the Sinai covenant (cf. Ex. 24:9-10).

An interesting feature of the section is the alternation of sayings with hymns, two of which celebrate the destruction of a hostile city (Isa. 25:1-5; 26:1-6). Even a rapid glance at the history of interpretation will suggest that the problem of the city's identity is insoluble in the present state of our knowledge. Apart from our crippling ignorance of what was happening in the fourth and third centuries, we have to allow for readaptation of a theme that in any case is highly stylized, following an ancient pattern.[92] The first of the hymns is followed by sayings in prose (25:6-12) that speak of the eschatological banquet on Mt. Zion, the abolition of suffering and death, and the advent of salvation. The second is linked with a prayer of petition and longing, similar to the so-called wisdom psalms, which looks forward to liberation from foreign rule and the final resurrection (26:7-19). It is followed by an injunction from an apocalyptic seer to his associates to hide from the coming judgment, which means, in effect, to dissociate themselves from those who did not share their beliefs (26:20-21; cf. 2:10-11, 19, 21-22). Other eschatological sayings follow, based on earlier prophetic and mythological themes. While the historical context remains obscure, the reference to Leviathan and Tannin at the beginning (27:1) and to Assyria and Egypt at the end (27:12-13) may contain a veiled allusion to the Seleucid and Ptolemaic empires, while the city of foolish people (27:10-11; cf. Sir. 50:26) may at this point allude to the fate of Samaria after the Macedonian conquest.

The heading of this section would be misleading if it gave the impression that eschatology, understood as a teaching or conviction about the end of history in an absolute or relative sense, was unknown to prophets and others during the period of the First Temple. What Amos, Zephaniah, and others say about the Day of Yahweh *(yôm*

YHWH) implies that it was a familiar idea to their contemporaries. It was to mark a great turning point, a time of salvation and victory for Israel (Zeph. 1:14-16), the banishing of darkness and insecurity (Amos 5:18-20; 8:9; Zeph. 1:15), the end of want and sorrow (Amos 8:10), etc. Structurally, it fitted into a larger mythic scenario which can be partially reconstructed from psalms and hymns and according to which the end corresponds to the beginning; cosmogony provides the clue to eschatology. Thus the so-called primeval history in Gen. 1-11, which draws heavily on the Sumero-Akkadian scribal tradition, presents a model of history beginning with creation and ending with uncreation and the emergence of a new order. True to this model, Jeremiah draws a picture of divine judgment as a progressive undoing of creation into chaos:

> I looked on the earth, and lo, it was waste and void; and to the heavens, and they had no light.
> I looked on the mountains, and lo, they were quaking, and all the hills moved to and fro.
> I looked, and lo, there was no man, and all the birds of the air had fled.
> I looked, and lo, the fruitful land was a desert, and all its cities were laid in ruins before Yahweh, before his fierce anger.
>
> (Jer. 4:23-26)

Hence many of the elements in the teaching of those who edited and expanded the prophetic books in the late Persian and early Hellenistic periods were developments of thought patterns attested in the earliest stages of the prophetic movement.

If, notwithstanding, we look for new departures, we shall find them at the points where this mythic construct was brought to bear on the ongoing theological problem created by Israel's subjection to foreign rule, as the hope for emancipation flowed or ebbed with the changing international situation. While the limitations of our historical knowledge rule out firm trajectories, it is possible to detect the gradual consolidation of what might be called an eschatological doctrine dealing with the destiny of Israel, the nations, and the entire created order. Increasingly in evidence is also schism within Jewish communities precipitated by the acceptance and interpretation of prophetic texts as validating this teaching.[93] This is a crucial issue since it leads into the emergence of sects, including early Palestinian Christianity: a subject which, however, belongs to a later chapter of the history.

5. JONAH

S. **Abramsky,** "Jonah's Alienation and Return," *Beth Mikra* 24, 1979, 370-395 (Hebrew); I. A. **Ben-Yosef,** "Jonas and the Fish as a Folk Motif," *Semitics* 7, 1980, 102-117; J. A. **Bewer,** *A Critical and Exegetical Commentary on Jonah,* Edinburgh: T. & T. Clark, 1912, 3-65; A. **Brenner,** "The Language of Jonah as an Index of Its Date," *Beth Mikra* 24, 1979, 396-405 (Hebrew); R. E. **Clements,** "The Purpose of the Book of Jonah," *SVT* 28, 1975, 16-28; T. E. **Fretheim,** *The Message of Jonah,* Minneapolis: Augsburg Publishing House, 1977; "Jonah and Theodicy," *ZAW* 90, 1978, 227-237; H. **Gevaryahu,** "The Universalism of the Book of Jonah," *Dor leDor* 10, 1981, 20-27; J. C. **Holbert,** " 'Deliverance Belongs to Yahweh!' Satire in the Book of Jonah," *JSOT* 21, 1981, 57-81; C. A. **Keller,** "Jonas, le portrait d'un prophète," *TZ* 21, 1965, 329-340; D. P. **Payne,** "Jonah from the Perspective of Its Audience," *JSOT* 13, 1979, 3-12; E. **Qimron,** "The Language of Jonah and the Date of Its Composition," *Beth Mikra* 25, 1980, 181-182; A. **Soleh,** "The Story of Jonah's Reflective Adventures," *Beth Mikra* 24, 1979, 406-420 (Hebrew).

Jonah is fifth in the *Dodekapropheton,* between Obadiah and Micah. This position is one of several indications of editorial concern for chronological sequence, since a prophet named Jonah ben-Amittai was active during the reign of Jeroboam II (786-746 B.C.E.). The context (II Kings 14:25) informs us that he predicted the successful outcome of Jeroboam's campaigns to restore the borders of Israel. He was therefore an optimistic and nationalist prophet and, despite the generally negative verdict of the historian on the Northern Kingdom, his intervention is not condemned. Unlike the other prophetic books, however, it bears no title, does not consist of prophetic sayings, and begins at once with narrative. In some respects it resembles other legendary narratives about prophets (e.g., Elijah, Elisha, Isaiah), but its peculiar tone and style mark it as, as most, an imitation of this genre. For this reason alone it is highly unlikely that, as Duhm argued, it stood originally after the allusion to the Northern prophet Jonah in the Deuteronomic history (II Kings 14:25). Nor can it be described as a midrash on that text. Though it does have some of the characteristics of haggadic midrash, its artfulness and complexity put it in a different category; and in any case, if it were to be regarded as narrative commentary, its text would not be II Kings 14:25. Early Christian writers read it typologically, with reference to the descent into death and resurrection of Jesus (e.g., Matt. 12:39-41), and some modern authors have taken it to be an allegory referring to the exilic experience of Israel and taking in also the prophet's name (= dove, son of fidelity?). If allegorical elements can be detected at all, however, it would be in the psalm (Jonah 2:2-9 [MT 2:3-10]), which there are good reasons for thinking is a later and not entirely appropriate insertion into the narrative.

While the story makes use of well-attested folktale motifs (cf. Perseus, Sinbad), it achieves a level of sophistication in its use of ironic contrast, deliberate exaggeration and distortion, and deployment of key words that puts it well beyond the reach of folktale pure and simple. Its author was clearly a trained hand at writing, one who was well versed in the historical, scribal, and prophetic heritage of Israel, and whose intent was to make some specific points for the benefit of a specific audience. It will be our task to try to identify these, regretfully leaving aside any further discussion of the literary quality of this delightful narrative.

The story begins with Yahweh's call to Jonah to preach in Nineveh and Jonah's refusal of the call as he takes a ship at Joppa (Yafo) bound for Tarshish, that is, in the opposite direction (Jonah 1:1-3). The scene then moves to shipboard, where it becomes obvious at once that it is not so easy to flee from the presence of Yahweh; since it is he who hurled a great wind at the sea (1:4) and thereafter stilled it (1:15). The point is obvious: that Yahweh's action is not confined to the land of Israel, but is also experienced, and should be acknowledged, both at sea and in foreign lands (2:10 [MT 2:11]; 3:10; 4:6; etc.); and this in ironic contrast to Jonah's own profession of faith (1:9). In the second episode (1:4-16) it is important to observe the behavior of the pagan sailors during the storm. They pray to their own gods and one of them, the captain or the first mate, constrains an unwilling Jonah to do the same. After casting lots, they hear his story and reluctantly follow his advice and pitch him overboard. Before doing so they address a prayer to Yahweh and, after the storm is miraculously stilled, embrace Jonah's own profession of faith and carry out appropriate cultic acts, including sacrifice, there and then on shipboard.

The large fish that was *appointed* by Yahweh (Jonah 1:17 [MT 2:1]—the same verb is used at 4:6, 7, 8) to serve as a novel form of transportation presumably got him back to his point of departure. There the commission was repeated, and this time Jonah performed, reluctantly, the prophetic role of divine messenger. Here, once again, we are invited to concentrate on the conduct of the pagans, inhabitants of a city that was a byword for oppression and godlessness. They listened to the message, contemptuously brief as it was, and on hearing it they believed God, proclaimed a ritual of fasting that even involved the animal world, prayed, and turned from evil (3:5-9). In other words, they underwent a thorough conversion that, given the identity of the god in whose name the prophet spoke, involved the acceptance by the entire city of the Jewish religion. The reaction of God was equally swift: he also "repented" of the evil which he thought to do to them, and did not do it.

The reaction of Jonah was of a quite different nature. He had, of course, observed how the king of Nineveh *(sic)* and his subjects had responded to the message of doom, but it appears from the subsequent course of events that he at least was not quite sure how Yahweh would react to their repentance. The analogy of Abraham faced with the annihilation of Sodom (Gen. 18:16-33) would suggest that in this situation the prophetic role called for intercession. Instead, he in effect accused Yahweh of discrediting him by not fulfilling the prediction of doom precisely because of his mercy and compassion! To make it worse, he quoted at God the words of the theophany at Sinai (Ex. 34:6) ending with Elijah's despairing cry on his way to the same place (I Kings 19:4).

The final scene (Jonah 4:6-11)[94] leads rapidly to the concluding statement of Yahweh by way of three successive dispositions affecting Jonah as he sat outside the city waiting to see what would happen: a plant that grew overnight with preternatural rapidity to provide him shelter; a worm uncharacteristic of its kind in size and habits that gnawed the plant; a scorching east wind that, combined with the burning sun, made him—once again—want to die. There is something distinctly sapiential about this appeal to the world of nature to make a point about divine causality and divine freedom and then apply it to God's action in history. Jonah's concern for the plant (he was really concerned about himself, but this would not have served the purpose) leads *a fortiori* to the divine concern for the city with its many people and cattle, and at the same time illustrates the freedom of God to create and destroy, to threaten destruction and then be moved by compassion.

What we seem to have in this book is a kind of sapiential critique of prophecy and an attempt to deal with some of the theological problems to which it gave rise.[95] For his protagonist the author chose a nationalist prophet who predicted success during Jeroboam's II's border wars in the eighth century. There also appears to have existed a tradition that he predicted the fall of Nineveh (Tob. 14:4, 8). If he did he was wrong, since Nineveh was destroyed only a century and a half after the lifetime of the prophet; which would have made it easier for the writer to take up the problem of unfulfilled prophecy. His critique is quite radical, since it implies that prophecy of this kind can easily conceal a basically inadequate understanding of God and his purposes.

The most important implication of the story is that the freedom of God is not constrained even by the prophetic word. The fact that God can "repent," that is, in ordinary terms, change his mind, means that he is free even after the prophetic word has been spoken. More specifically and unexpectedly, he is free to respond graciously to true repentance and prayer on the part of Gentiles, even of traditional and archetypal enemies of Israel like the Assyrians. The irony is that *they* understand this but the prophet does not:

> *Perhaps* God will give a thought to us, that we do not perish. (Jonah 1:6)

> *Who knows,* God may yet repent and turn from his fierce anger, so that we perish not. (Jonah 3:9)

From this point of view the book is theologically crucial since it breaks once and for all the bond of what might be called prophetic causality by its emphasis on the divine freedom.

There is another thing the prophet does not understand, and that is the divine will to save. Ironically again, this is the theme of the psalm that he sings in the fish's innards: "salvation belongs to Yahweh!" (Jonah 2:9 [MT 2:10]). In this respect the author aligns himself with a current of thought that finds its best expression in Second Isaiah and his discipleship. We may add that it is quite misguided to represent the book as a protest against the reforming measures taken by Ezra and Nehemiah, and therefore against "Jewish particularism"; for the latter were concerned with matters internal to the *gôlāh* community in Judah and not at all with the fate of the Gentiles.[96] On the other hand, we must be careful in predicating universalism of the author's message and that of his mentors. In Second Isaiah salvation is offered to the Gentiles (Isa. 45:22; 49:6; 52:10), but this implies that they acknowledge the Lordship of Israel's God when it is made known to them (Isa. 45:23; 51:5) and embrace the religion of Israel (Isa. 44:4-5; 55:5; 66:23) which is therefore to be proclaimed among them (Isa. 42:4, 6; 66:19). This is in fact what happens to the pagans in the book (Jonah 1:16; 3:5). If we must find a target for the writer's criticism, it would not be Ezra and Nehemiah but the kind of prophetic threat represented by the author of the "Isaian apocalypse," a threat directed, as we have seen, against an unnamed city. Of its inhabitants the author says:

> This is a people without discernment;
> therefore he who made them will not have compassion on them,
> he that formed them will show them no favor.
>
> (Isa. 27:11)

Nineveh, on the contrary, will be saved *even though* its people do not know their right hand from their left.

Both the freedom of God and his will to save had already been clearly affirmed in the ethical teaching of Ezekiel:

> If a wicked man turns away from all his sins which he has committed, . . . none of the transgressions which he has committed shall be remembered against him; for the righteousness which he has done he shall live. Have I any pleasure in the death of the wicked, . . . and not rather that he should turn from his way and live? (Ezek. 18:21-22)

In what appears to be a Deuteronomic expansion of the incident of Jeremiah's visit to the potter (Jer. 18:5-12), this teaching is applied on the political level:

> If at any time I declare concerning a nation or a kingdom, that I will pluck up and break down and destroy it, and if that nation, concerning which I have spoken, turns from its evil, I will repent of the evil that I intended to do to it. (Jer. 18:7-8)

The declaration in question refers, of course, to judgment oracles addressed by prophets to foreign nations. That it is this teaching which the story purports to illustrate is as explicit as could be expected:

> When God saw what they did, how they turned from their evil way,
> God repented of the evil which he had said he would do to them;
> and he did not do it. (Jonah 3:10)

There is perhaps a further aspect to the author's critique that concerns the matter of worship. As it opens, the story three times emphasizes that the prophet is fleeing from the presence of Yahweh (*millipnê YHWH,* Jonah 1:3, 19), a phrase with well-known cultic connotations. It may be no accident that the psalm put into his mouth speaks of its author having been cast out from the divine presence (2:4 [MT 2:5]), which would most naturally mean that, like the author of Isa. 66:5, he had been expelled from the cultic community. Yet the story goes on to show that God is present elsewhere than in the sanctuary or in the land of Israel. His activity, and therefore his presence, is attested on the high seas and in the pagan land of Assyria. And just as the author of the psalm knows that his prayer reaches the Temple even though he is far distant from it (Jonah 2:7 [MT 2:8]), the pagans themselves offer cultic worship to Yahweh where they are. Indeed the sailors even offer sacrifice on board ship in defiance of the Deuteronomic law. Here too the author of the book aligns himself with a view, certainly not uncontested, according to which God accepts and indeed enables worship directed to him by the Gentiles (Zeph. 3:9-10; Mal. 1:11, 14).

We have seen that the author chooses as his protagonist a prophet who balks at his call for fear of being discredited by Yahweh's regrettable tendency to be moved by the repentant sinner (Jonah 4:1-2; cf. Zech. 13:4-6). Consequently, he also refuses to discharge the prophetic function of intercession both during the storm and at Nineveh. In the first episode he sleeps instead of praying. And since the author speaks not of ordinary sleep but the preternatural kind put on the Man in the garden and on Abraham during the covenant-making (Gen. 2:21; 15:12, *tardēmāh*), there is perhaps more to this sleep than meets the eye. A clue may be found in Isaiah's critique of contemporary prophets:

> Yahweh has poured out upon you a spirit of deep sleep *(tardēmāh)*;
> he has closed your eyes, O prophets, and covered your heads, O seers. (Isa. 29:10)

This is the sleep of imperception and spiritual dullness. Jonah does not even appreciate the irony of confessing faith in the God of heaven, maker of the sea and dry land (Jonah 1:9), while fleeing from his presence. Worse, he has closed his eyes and his mind to what is the will of God in this particular situation, misled as he is by his own rigid and unyielding view of the prophetic office.

The book, then, addresses itself to the problem of unfulfilled prophecy and the anger and frustration that it occasioned. By implication, it also offers a solution to the problem of theodicy, to which, as we saw earlier, prophecy whether fulfilled or not gave rise. By emphasizing the supreme freedom of God, it interposes the possibility of salvation between the prophetic word and its assumed effect. At the same time, it intends to pioneer a new understanding of the office based on the profound and simple conviction that God's ultimate will is to save. This new form, which might be called apostolic prophecy, has implications that we have not yet worked out or perhaps even fully grasped.

Notes

1. Joel, Jonah, Haggai, Zechariah, Malachi.

2. *yᵉhûdîm*, meaning "Jews" rather than "Judeans" (as, for example, in II Kings 16:6, when the Northern Kingdom was still in existence), is first attested in Jeremiah (32:12; 34:9; 40:11-12; 41:3; cf. 38:19) and II Kings (25:25; 43:9;

44:1; 52:28, 30). Following Josephus (*Ant.* XI.173), however, we should trace the origins of Judaism to that community formed of the descendants of the preexilic Judeans which took shape in and around Jerusalem in the early Persian period. Neh. 4:1-2 (MT 3:33-34) suggests that at the time of Nehemiah's mission Samaritans did not think of themselves as Jews.

3. Morton Smith, *Parties and Politics,* 193-201, argues strongly against Alt's thesis that Judah was under the jurisdiction of Samaria. For a balanced appraisal see G. Widengren in Hayes and Miller, *Israelite and Judaean History,* 509-511.

4. For the Cyrus cylinder, see *ANET,* 315-316.

5. For the "Passover Papyrus," see *ANET,* 491, and W. Beyerlin, *Near Eastern Religious Texts Relating to the Old Testament,* Philadelphia: Westminster Press, 1978, 254-255, with bibliography.

6. This does not imply that the Pentateuch was in final form by the early Persian period or even by the time of Ezra, whose "law of the God of heaven" (Ezra 7:12) cannot simply be equated with the Pentateuch.

7. See above, pp. 180, 198.

8. Originally, perhaps, a kind of dice for giving simple Yes or No answers, they were incorporated into the high priest's vestments (Ex. 28:30; Lev. 8:8); see I. Mendelsohn, "Urim and Thummim," *IDB* IV, 739-740; E. Lipinski, "Urim and Thummim," *VT* 20, 1970, 495-496.

9. See above, pp. 99-100. The different editorial strata in Deut. 27 can be discerned by the quite distinct allusions to Levi as a tribe (v. 12), the Levitical priests (v. 9), and Levites as distinct from priests (v. 14). In Deuteronomy all "Levitical priests," whether engaged in cult at the central sanctuary or not, have in principle the same status (Deut. 18:6-8). The Deuteronomic history does not attest to the existence of Levites as distinct from priests either. I Kings 8:4 ("the priests and the Levites brought them up") is absent from some of the best manuscripts of LXX and is almost certainly a gloss, the purpose of which is to correct the previous statement; elsewhere in this record we hear only of priests (I Kings 8:3, 6, 10-11). II Kings 23:4 appears to speak of the high priests and the priests of the second order, but we should read the singular, *kōhēn mišneh,* with II Kings 25:18. No preexilic prophet mentions Levites, and even the term "Levitical priests" occurs only in the Deuteronomic stratum of Jeremiah (33:17-22).

10. Significantly, Deut. 11:6 refers to the fate of Dathan and Abiram but is silent on Korah's rebellion (cf. Num. 16:3-11 [P]).

11. It is defended by E. J. Bickermann, "The Edict of Cyrus in Ezra 1," *JBL* 65, 1946, 249-275; G. Widengren, in Hayes and Miller, *Israelite and Judaean History,* 498-499, and R. de Vaux, "The Decrees of Cyrus and Darius on the Rebuilding of the Temple," *The Bible and the Ancient Near East,* London: Darton, Longman & Todd, 1972, 61-96. We must at least admit significant editing by the Chronicler, as De Vaux and others attest.

12. This census list is more probably an updated version from the late fifth

century of an earlier register, as suggested by W. F. Albright, *The Biblical Period,* 62-63, n. 122.

13. A. T. E. Olmstead, *History of the Persian Empire,* 107-118; cf. G. B. Gray, *CAH* IV, 1926, 173-177, 662-663. Unfortunately, J. M. Cook, *The Persian Empire,* London: J. M. Dent & Sons, 1983, appeared too late to be used in this chapter.

14. See the commentaries and R. A. Mason, "The Purpose of the 'Editorial Framework' of the Book of Haggai," *VT* 27, 1977, 415-421.

15. K. Koch, "Haggais unreines Volk," *ZAW* 79, 1967, 52-66; H. G. May, " 'This People' and 'This Nation' in Haggai," *VT* 18, 1968, 190-197.

16. In that case, however, it is difficult to see how they reached such a conclusion. Calculated from 586, the seventy years would then have been only four years short of completion, while seventy-eight years would have passed since the first deportation. The probability that the Jeremian prophecy nevertheless lies behind the urgent preaching of Haggai is increased by the fact that (according to Ezra 6:15) the Temple actually was rebuilt four years later. We recall that Jeremiah promised that in seventy years Yahweh would bring them back "to this place," at which time they would seek him and their prayers would be heard (Jer. 29:10, 12-13).

17. K. M. Beyse, *Serubbabel und die Königserwartungen der Propheten Haggai und Sacharja,* Stuttgart: Calwer Verlag, 1972.

18. On the basis of this synchrony and the current understanding of Jeremiah's prophecy (n. 16) we may therefore tentatively suggest that Haggai preached during 521 and the rebuilding was completed by the end of 517 B.C.E.

19. R. P. Carroll, *When Prophecy Failed: Cognitive Dissonance in the Prophetic Traditions of the Old Testament,* 157-183.

20. M. Barker, "The Two Figures in Zechariah," *HeyJ* 18, 1977, 38-46, suggests ingeniously but unconvincingly that the two "sons of oil" in Zech. 4:14 represent two branches of the priesthood that had reached, or were being urged to reach, a negotiated settlement.

21. The Satan (Adversary) appears elsewhere as fulfilling a specific function only at I Chron. 21:1 and Job 1-2. Functionally similar is "the Spirit" who volunteers to deceive Ahab in Micaiah's vision, I Kings 22:21-22.

22. Morton Smith, *Palestinian Parties and Politics,* 90-91. For a different interpretation, emphasizing the economic ills of the time, see Margaret Barker, "The Evil in Zechariah," *HeyJ* 19, 1978, 20-26.

23. E. Pfeiffer, "Die Disputationsworte im buche Maleachi," *EvTh* 19, 1959, 546-568; H.-J. Boecker, "Bemerkungen zur formgeschichtlichen Terminologie des Buches Maleachi," *ZAW* 78, 1966, 78-80; J. A. Fischer, "Notes on the Literary Form and Message of Malachi," *CBQ* 34, 1972, 315-320.

24. In addition to the commentaries see J. Swetman, "Malachi 1.11: An Interpretation," *CBQ* 31, 1969, 200-209.

25. Morton Smith, *Palestinian Parties and Politics,* 90; E. Stern, *The Material Culture of the Land of the Bible,* 158-195.

26. While there is no explicit mention of a covenant in Mal. 3:16-18, the

conferring together *(nidb°rû)* which resulted in winning the divine favor points in that direction, and it is they who write (presumably their names) in the *sēper zikkārôn*. The abuses against which Malachi preaches—neglect of the cult, lack of support for clergy, marriage with foreign women—are those to remove which Nehemiah insisted on a written and signed covenant. Mal. 3:16-18 therefore either anticipates or is identical with the covenanting during Nehemiah's mission.

27. They are known as Yahweh-fearers *(yir'ê YHWH)*, servants of God *('ōbēd °lōhîm)*, righteous *(ṣaddîq)* as distinct from the wicked, and they give special attention to the divine Name *(ḥōšbê š°mô)*. The language is therefore strongly reminiscent of the different ways in which the prophetic group attested in Third Isaiah is described. They too are servants of Yahweh (Isa. 65:8-9, 13-16; 66:14) who venerate his Name (59:19; cf. 65;15-16) and await the final judgment which will vindicate the righteous (65:13-14; 66:5, 24). See further below, pp. 248-251.

28. Cf. the interpretation in Sir. 48:10 with its allusion to the Isaian Servant (Isa. 49:5-6).

29. Reading *mal'ākî* for MT *mal'āk* with Old Greek, Samaritan, and Vulgate.

30. 1QS 9:11; 4QTest; John 1:21, 25; 6:14; 7:40; Acts 3:22.

31. Also to his son if Sheshbazzar is identified with the Shenazzar of I Chron. 3:18. This, however, is quite uncertain.

32. We are assuming that the chronological order presupposed by the Chronicler, though not without its difficulties, is defensible and should be maintained. The interminable debate on this issue is summarized in his customary thorough fashion by H. H. Rowley, *The Servant of the Lord*, Oxford: Basil Blackwell, 1965[2], 135-168. P. R. Ackroyd, *Israel Under Babylon and Persia*, 191-196, and again in G. W. Anderson (ed.), *Tradition and Interpretation*, 333-334, makes out a cautious case for 398, the seventh year of Artaxerxes II Mnemon, while Morton Smith, *Palestinian Parties and Politics*, 120-123, vigorously defends the earlier date.

33. Or a little less, depending on the interpretation of chronological data in Haggai and Ezra 1-6; see above, p. 234.

34. There is no indication that Nehemiah was of the royal family and there is, in addition, a distinct possibility that as cupbearer to the king (Neh. 6:11) he was a eunuch.

35. The miserable social and economic conditions in Judah are reflected in Hag. 1:6, 8-11; 2:16-17; Zech. 8:10; Isa. 58:3-4; 59:6, 9-15; Joel 1-2; Neh. 5:1-5.

36. I Macc. 2:42-48; 7:13. These *asidaioi (ḥ°sîdîm)* are described as "mighty warriors of Israel" (2:42) and therefore presumably were not "pacifist." The "many who were seeking righteousness and justice," who went down into the wilderness, refused to fight on Sabbath and were slaughtered (2:29-38) are not identified with the Asidaeans. There is nothing to suggest that they would not have fought on the other six days of the week.

37. See above, pp. 217-218.

38. See Westermann, *Isaiah 40-66,* 295-308.

39. See below, pp. 270-273.

40. *pōšᵉ'îm bî;* cf. *pašᵉ'û bî,* Isa. 1:2.

41. *ṣōpîm,* synonymous with *nᵉbî'îm;* cf. Ezek. 3:17; 33:7; Jer. 6:17; Isa. 52:8. In Isa. 62:6 the similar *šōmᵉrîm,* "watchmen" or "guardians," is used.

42. B. Renaud, "La Mort du juste, entrée dans la paix (Isa. 57, 1-2)," *RSR* 51, 1977, 3-21, understands the "removal" of the just as a reward, and therefore as implying survival of death.

43. "Mourners" is almost a title for the community; see Isa. 57:18-19; 61:2-3; 66:10; cf. Ezra 10:6; Neh. 1:4; Dan. 10:2-3.

44. Isa. 60:13 suggests that the Temple has not yet been rebuilt, cf. 63:18; 64:10-11. The allusion to "ancient ruins" at 61:4 (cf. 58:12) also points to an early date.

45. Westermann, *Isaiah 40-66,* 298-299, 363-364, 408, 410, 427-428.

46. Ps. 44; 74; 77; 79.

47. P. D. Hanson, *The Dawn of Apocalyptic,* 92-93, takes this verse to indicate a rift between what he calls "the central Israelite community," i.e., the Zadokite priests and their allies, and the group represented by the speaker. The context, however, makes it quite clear that the latter is praying in the name of the community as a whole, the "holy people" that once possessed and now has lost its sanctuary (v. 18). This is not the language of a group ostracized by the Temple authorities.

48. Hanson, *The Dawn of Apocalyptic,* 146-150, argues at length that the seer is denouncing the Zadokite priesthood, but in order to do so he must interpret the abuses symbolically, which is quite unnecessary. The reproach is explicitly addressed to a nation *(gôy)* and people *('am).* Use of cultic terminology does not imply that priests are being addressed, and *kî qᵉdaštîkā* cannot be translated "or I will communicate holiness to you."

49. The verbs used are strong. "Hate" involves active dissociation as in the divorce formula; *niddāh* (pi'el), "cast out," occurs only here and at Amos 6:3 *(hammᵉnaddîm lᵉyôm rā')* with the sense of "conjure," "set aside," probably by magical means. At Isa. 66:5 we are approaching the meaning "excommunicate" which the verb has in Mishnaic Hebrew.

50. They are therefore not being persecuted on account of the *divine* name, as is often assumed. Matt. 10:18, 22 is based on this passage.

51. *yikkābēd YHWH wᵉnir'eh bᵉśimḥatkem, wᵉhēm yēbōšû* (66:5); cf. *hinnēh ᵃbāday yiśmāḥû wᵉ' attem tēbōšû* (65:13).

52. Isa. 65:15-16 is difficult. "The Lord YHWH will put you to death" is probably a later insertion. Verse 16a reads: "he who blesses himself in the land will bless himself by the God Amen, and he who takes an oath in the land will swear by the God Amen." Since this sounds strange, most commentators take it on themselves to emend MT *'āmēn* to *'emet, 'ōmen,* or *'ēmûn.* MT is, however, textually unassailable and makes sense. If we retain it, it follows from the logical connection of v. 15 with v. 16 that this is to be the new name of the faithful community, a community which, in other words, says Yes to God. This seems to

be the way the text is understood by Paul (II Cor. 1:17-20) and the author of Revelation (3:14). Isa. 62:1-5 provides another example of eschatological name-giving.

53. Very common in the older commentators, e.g., Wellhausen, Budde, Gressmann, Torrey; for a survey of opinions see Muilenburg, *IB* V, 758-760. Muilenburg's own view, that the seer is opposing the view that limits salvation to the cult, is shared by Westermann, *Isaiah 40-66*, 412-414, and Whybray, *Isaiah 40-66*, 279-280.

54. See, eg., Isa. 60:7, 13; 62:9; 66:6, 20-21, 23.

55. Cf. Isa. 57:5-13; 65:1-7, 11; 66:17.

56. On *ḥᵃrēdîm* see n. 57; on the use of *'ebed ('ōbēd)* in Mal. 3:17-18 see n. 27, and on its use in Second Isaiah see above, pp. 215-216; on "Amen people" see n. 52.

57. The verb *ḥrd* is attested frequently with the sense of fearing, shaking, trembling; less frequently with the more specific connotation of numinous fear and trembling (Ex. 19:16; I Sam. 14:15). In the participial form the only occurrences are I Sam. 4:13 *(hāyāh libbô ḥārēd 'al ᵃrôn hāᵉlōhîm);* Isa. 66:2, 5; and Ezra 9:4; 10:3. The close similarity between the last four suggests not a title but a designation that has attained a certain fixity.

58. Ezra 9:5 to 10:1; 10:6; cf. Dan. 10:2-3.

59. See above, p. 241.

60. S. Mowinckel, *The Psalms in Israel's Worship* II, 53-73; H.-J. Kraus, *Worship in Israel*, 101-112; A. B. Johnson, *The Cultic Prophet and Israel's Psalmody*, 109-209.

61. Jer. 23:11; 26:7-8; Lam. 2:20. Note also the frequent linking of prophets with priests in prophetic diatribe.

62. Ps. 20:8; 28:6; 60:6; 81:5; 108:7; 110:1; Jonah 2:2-9 (MT 2:3-8); Hab. 3.

63. In a famous rabbinic story, concerning the oven of Akhnai *(b. Baba Meṣia* 59b), a *bath qol* was disregarded in favor of appeal to Scripture. On the *bath qol* in general see A. Rothkoff, "Bat Kol," *Encyclopaedia Judaica* IV, Jerusalem: Keter Publishing House, 1971, 324-325.

64. In Num. 27:15-23 (P) Joshua possesses the spirit before the hands are laid on him, whereas in the revised version at Deut. 34:9, from the same tradition, he is full of the spirit by virtue of the laying on of hands; an interesting case of the institutionalizing of charisma. See the classic treatment of charismatic authority in Max Weber, *The Theory of Social and Economic Organization*, New York: Free Press, 1964, 324-423.

65. Ahlström, *Joel and the Temple Cult of Jerusalem*, 129, decides for 515-500 B.C.E. but it is doubtful whether we can be so precise.

66. It is widely accepted that Joel 2:28 to 3:21 (MT 3:1 to 4:21) belongs to the later stratum; probably also 1:15; 2:1b-2a, 11b.

67. This is more or less identical with the conclusion reached by H. G. M. Williamson, *Israel in the Book of Chronicles*, 83-86, and *1 and 2 Chronicles*, 15-17, even though he detaches Ezra-Nehemiah from the Chronicler. D. L. Petersen,

Late Israelite Prophecy, 57-60, follows F. M. Cross in dating the nucleus of the work to the early sixth century, with later expansions.

68. I Chron. 23:2-32; II Chron. 29:25-30; 31:2; Ezra 6:18.

69. See I Chron. 17:17; 29:10-19; II Chron. 8:14; Neh. 12:24, 36 (in the last two David is described as "man of God," *'îš-hā'ĕlōhîm).* The "last words of David" (II Sam. 23:1-7), added to the narrative at a late date, are presented as oracular *(nᵉ'um dāwid,* v. 1) and as the product of divine inspiration (v. 2). In early Christianity the psalms of David were read as predictive of Christ and the church (Acts 1:16; 2:25-31, 34), and the Qumran Psalms Scroll (11QPsᵃ) attributes to him 4,050 hymns composed by virtue of his prophetic gift *(nᵉbû'āh).* See J. A. Sanders, *Discoveries in the Judaean Desert of Jordan* IV, *The Psalms Scroll of Qumrân Cave 11 (11QPsᵃ),* Oxford: Oxford University Press, 1965, 137-139.

70. *mᵉšōrᵉrîm,* I Chron. 15:16, 27; II Chron. 5:12-13; 35:15.

71. Cf. the role of Levites in the Qumran War Scroll (1QM).

72. Mowinckel, *The Psalms in Israel's Worship* II, 56, read *śar hammaśśā'* as a title meaning "master of the oracle." While the meaning "precentor" or "director of music" seems more likely, the use of *maśśā'* in this context is nonetheless interesting.

73. E.g., I Chron. 7:41; 16:4; 23:5, 30; II Chron. 5:13; 7:6; 8:14.

74. See, for example, the Qumran *Hodayoth* (1QH); Luke 1: 67-69; I Cor. 14; and the remarks of W. H. Brownlee, *The Meaning of the Qumran Scrolls for the Bible,* New York: Oxford University Press, 1964, 271-273, on liturgical prophecy at Qumran. M. Gertner, "The Masorah and the Levites: An Essay in the History of a Concept," *VT* 10, 1960, 241-284, argues for a connection between Second Temple Levites and the Masoretes.

75. I Chron. 29:29; II Chron. 9:29; 12:15; 13:22; 20:34; 26:22; 32:32; 33:19.

76. See my "Prophecy and Priesthood in Josephus," *JJS* 25, 1974, 239-262.

77. A. Lods, *The Prophets and the Rise of Judaism,* 153, 205.

78. See above, p. 94.

79. J. A. Bewer in J. M. P. Smith et al., *A Critical and Exegetical Commentary on Micah, Zephaniah, Nahum, Habakkuk, Obadiah and Joel,* Edinburgh: T. & T. Clark, 1912, 61 (between 352 and 348 B.C.E.); H. W. Wolff, *Joel and Amos,* 77-78.

80. The problem is different for those who regard Joel as a unity; e.g., J. A. Thompson, *IB* VI, 732-734; A. S. Kapelrud, *Joel Studies,* 193-195, who records without criticism Engnell's view of the book as a liturgical, preexilic unity. For the problem of dating in general, see Wolff, *Joel and Amos,* 4-6, 60-61.

81. Zech. 9:1 begins: "The word of Yahweh is in the land of Hadrach and Damascus is its resting place." The rest is obscure.

82. Josephus, *Ant.* 11.317-347; *Meg. Ta'an.* 339-340; *b. Yoma* 69a.

83. R. C. Dentan, *IB* VI, 1102-1105; M. Delcor, "Deux passages difficiles: Zacharie 12:11 et 11:13," *VT* 3, 1953, 67-77; D. R. Jones, "A Fresh Interpretation of Zechariah IX-XI," *VT* 12, 1962, 241-259; M. Treves, "Conjectures Concerning the Date and Authorship of Zech. IX-XIV," *VT* 13, 1963, 196-207; R. Mason, *The Books of Haggai, Zechariah and Malachi,* 103-110.

84. Explicit in Zech. 11:14 and implied in the adoption of Ezek. 37:15-28 as a model. *haššōm'rîm 'ōtî* (Zech. 11:11, "who were observing me") may also provide a clue by assonance with *šōm'rôn*, Samaria; the Samaritans of a later day referred to themselves as *šōm'rîm*, the observant ones.

85. The importance of this event for later developments is stressed by E. Bickerman, *From Ezra to the Last of the Maccabees*, 41-46.

86. Cf. below, pp. 264-265.

87. See n. 83 and Mason, *The Books of Haggai, Zechariah and Malachi*, 117-120.

88. Cf. above, pp. 181-182.

89. See above, pp. 209-210.

90. On the identity of the city, see H. Wildberger, *Jesaja*, 893-896, 905-906; O. Kaiser, *Isaiah 13-39*, 173-179; W. R. Millar, *Isaiah 24-27*, 15-21.

91. Note the first-person plural and singular, Isa. 24:16; the speaker's lament about treacherous behavior would most naturally be alluding to those who were rejoicing. The preceding exclamation, "I have my secret! I have my secret!" *(rāzî-lî, rāzî-lî)*, should not be emended; *rāz* occurs at Sir. 8:18 and in the Aramaic section of Daniel (2:18, *rāzāh*, etc.). It can have the meaning of a divine plan for the future communicated in cryptic, symbolic fashion and requiring divine illumination for its decipherment. See J. Niehaus, "rāz-p'šar in Isaiah xxiv," *VT* 31, 1981, 376-378.

92. Cf. the lament over the destruction of Ur, *ANET*, 455-463.

93. See the further discussion in my paper "Interpretation and the Tendency to Sectarianism: An Aspect of Second Temple History," in E. P. Sanders et al. (eds.), *Jewish and Christian Self-Definition*, Philadelphia: Fortress Press, 1981, 1-26.

94. It is possible that Jonah 4:5 originally stood before 3:4.

95. This aspect of the book is emphasized by T. E. Fretheim, "Jonah and Theodicy," *ZAW* 90, 1978, 227-237.

96. Typical of this prejudicial approach is the article of W. Neil, "Jonah, Book of," *IDB* II, 1962, 964-967.

INDEX OF SELECTED
BIBLICAL REFERENCES